Progress Report on China-ASEAN Expo
中国—东盟博览会发展报告

2011 第八卷
Volume Ⅷ

丛书编委会主任 李金早 沈北海
Chairs of the Editing Committee Li Jinzao Shen Beihai
陈 武 蓝天立
Chen Wu Lan Tianli

本卷编委会主任 蓝天立
Chair of Editing Committee (Volume Ⅷ) Lan Tianli

主编 郑军健
Editor-in-Chief Zheng Junjian

GUANGXI NORMAL UNIVERSITY PRESS
广西师范大学出版社

Progress Report on China-ASEAN Expo

《中国—东盟博览会发展报告》编辑委员会

中国—东盟博览会作为国家层面的一个国际性展会，已经成为我国和东盟经贸合作的重要平台，中央将大力支持广西办好这个博览会。中国—东盟博览会要长期举办下去，要办出特色，办出实效。

——中华人民共和国主席 胡锦涛（2007年3月9日）

As a state-level international exposition, the CAEXPO has become an important platform for the economic and trade cooperation between China and ASEAN. Chinese central government will continue to grand full support to Guangxi to well organize the event. The CAEXPO should be a long-term program with distinctive features and sound economic outcomes.

—H.E. Hu Jintao, president of China

(March 9, 2007)

中国与东盟国家领导人寄语
中国—东盟博览会

Compliments of Heads of State/Government on the CAEXPO

我们创建了中国—东盟博览会、商务与投资峰会等经贸交流平台，设立了中国—东盟合作基金、中国—东盟公共卫生合作基金和中国—东盟投资合作基金，为东盟国家进行了数万人的能力建设培训。中国—东盟经贸合作正处于历史上最活跃、最富有成效的时期。

——中华人民共和国国务院总理　温家宝（2011年10月21日）

We have co-built such business and trade platforms as the CAEXPO and the CABIS, and established the China-ASEAN Cooperation Fund, China-ASEAN Public Health Cooperation Fund as well as China-ASEAN Investment Cooperation Fund. China has provided training programs on capacity building for tens of thousands of people from ASEAN countries. All these show that China-ASEAN economic cooperation has never been more dynamic and more fruitful.

—H.E. Wen Jiabao, premier of the State Council of China (October 21, 2011)

中国—东盟博览会、中国—东盟商务与投资峰会已成为中国同东盟国家对话、交流、合作的有效平台。

——中国人民政治协商会议第十一届全国委员会主席 贾庆林（2010年10月19日）

The CAEXPO and the CABIS have become the effective platforms for the dialogues, exchanges and cooperation between China and the ASEAN countries.

—H.E. Jia Qinglin, chairman of the 11th National Committee of the Chinese People's Political Consultative Conference (October 19, 2010)

中国—东盟博览会、中国—东盟商务与投资峰会已连续举办六次。东盟国家领导人多次出席，各国工商界踊跃参加。会议办出了实效，得到了肯定。

——中华人民共和国国务院副总理 李克强（2009年10月20日）

The CAEXPO and the CABIS, which have been held for 6 straight years, attract the repeat participation of ASEAN state leaders and business elites, reaping fruitful outcomes and gaining positive comments from all parties concerned.

—H.E. Li Keqiang, vice-premier of the State Council of China (October 20, 2009)

中国—东盟博览会和中国—东盟商务与投资峰会是展示我国改革开放30年辉煌成就的重要窗口，已成为中国和东盟发展战略伙伴关系、促进互利合作共赢的重要平台，服务了国家周边外交战略，推动了中国—东盟自由贸易区建设。

——中华人民共和国国务院副总理 王岐山（2008年10月21日）

The CAEXPO and the CABIS are important showcases of China's tremendous achievements in the reform and opening-up in the previous 30 years. And as important platforms for China and ASEAN to develop their strategic partnership and to promote reciprocal cooperation for win-win results, the CAEXPO and the CABIS comply with China's diplomatic strategies and promote the CAFTA construction.

—H.E. Wang Qishan,vice- premier of the State Council of China (October 21, 2008)

中国—东盟博览会要常办常新，越办越好。

——时任中华人民共和国副主席 曾庆红（2005年10月18日）

The CAEXPO shall be a grand event held on regular basis with new features and sound outcomes.

—H.E. Zeng Qinghong,
the then vice -president of China (October 18, 2005)

中国—东盟博览会要一年比一年办得好，一年上一个台阶。

——时任中华人民共和国国务院副总理 吴仪（2004年11月2日）

The CAEXPO shall be a better and better event with richer outcomes year on year.

—H.E. Madam Wu Yi, the then vice -premier of the State Council
of China (November 2, 2004)

中国—东盟博览会的成功举办，为促进中国—东盟自由贸易区建设，进一步深化中国与东盟战略伙伴关系搭建了一个重要平台。

——时任中华人民共和国国务院副总理 曾培炎（2007年10月27日）

The successful CAEXPO has built up a vital platform to accelerate the CAFTA construction and to further enrich the China-ASEAN strategic partnership.

—H.E. Zeng Peiyan, the then vice- premier of the State Council
of China (October 27, 2007)

中国—东盟博览会很成功，办得很好。

——文莱达鲁萨兰国苏丹　哈桑纳尔·博尔基亚（2006年10月31日）

The CAEXPO is well organized and very successful.

—His Majesty Sultan Haji Hassanal Bolkiah Mu'izzaddin Waddaulah, the Sultan and Yang Di-Pertuan of Brunei Darussalam (October 31, 2006)

中国—东盟博览会在促进中国与东盟合作交流中发挥了积极的作用，为促进中柬之间的传统友谊作出了新的贡献。

——柬埔寨王国首相　洪　森（2011年10月20日）

The CAEXPO has played a positive role in advancing cooperation and exchanges between China and ASEAN, and made new contribution to cementing the time-honored friendship between China and Cambodia.

—H.E. Samdech Hun Sen, prime minister of Cambodia (October 20, 2011)

十分高兴在中国—东盟博览会看到印尼的企业家和印尼商品，希望印尼工商界通过博览会继续加强与中国的经贸往来。

——印度尼西亚共和国总统　苏西洛·班邦·尤多约诺（2006年10月31日）

It is my pleasure to see enterprises and commodities from Indonesia at the CAEXPO and I hope that Indonesian business circle could further enhance trade ties with their Chinese counterparts via the CAEXPO.

—H.E. Dr. H. Susilo Bambang Yudhoyono, president of Indonesia (October 31, 2006)

中国—东盟博览会对中国和东盟经贸关系起到了非常大的促进作用，许多东盟国家都非常积极参与，会使中国与东盟的关系进一步发展。

——时任老挝人民民主共和国副主席 朱马里·赛雅颂（2005年10月19日）

The CAEXPO greatly promotes the economic and trade relations between ASEAN and China. Many ASEAN countries participate in it actively. With it, the ASEAN-China relationship will gain further development.

—H.E. Choummaly SAYGNASONE, the then vice-president of the Lao People's Democratic Republic (October 19, 2005)

中国—东盟博览会已日益壮大，汇聚来自中国、东盟和世界其他地区的商家，促进区域合作及全球融合。

——马来西亚总理　纳吉布·敦·拉扎克（2011年10月21日）

The CAEXPO has been growing stronger year on year, attracting businesses from China, ASEAN and other countries and regions in the world, boosting the regional cooperation and global integration.

—Right Honourable Dato' Sri Mohd Najib Tun Abdul Razak, prime minister of Malaysia (October 21 ,2011)

中国—东盟博览会是中国与东盟各国最好的交流合作平台，让参展商得到了实实在在的利益。

——时任缅甸联邦总理　吴登盛（2008年10月21日）

The CAEXPO is the best platform for the exchanges and cooperation between China and ASEAN, which brings pragmatic profits for exhibitors.

—H.E. Lt-Gen Thein Sein, the then prime minister of Myanmar (October 21, 2008)

菲律宾全力支持每年在这里举办的中国—东盟博览会，并愿共同搭建好这一加强合作、共同发展的平台。

——时任菲律宾众议长 普罗斯培·诺格拉雷斯（2008年10月22日）

The Philippines will provide full support to the CAEXPO and is willing to jointly build the event as a platform to enhance cooperation for common development.

—H.E. Prospero Nograles, the then speaker of the House of Representatives of the Philippines (October 22, 2008)

中国—东盟博览会的举办为新加坡企业进入广西和中国市场搭建了良好的平台，新加坡完全支持博览会的举办。

——新加坡共和国总理 李显龙（2006年10月31日）

The CAEXPO shapes a sound platform for Singapore-based enterprises to access to the market of Guangxi and China as a whole, to which, Singapore offers full support.

—H.E. Lee Hsien Loong, prime minister of Singapore (October 31, 2006)

中国—东盟博览会给中国和东盟各国企业搭建了一个相互交流与合作的平台，促进了中国—东盟自由贸易区建设。

——时任泰王国总理　素拉育·朱拉暖（2006年10月31日）

The CAEXPO forms a platform for bilateral communication and cooperation among enterprises of China and ASEAN, and propels the CAFTA construction.

—H.E. Surayud Chulanont, the then prime minister of Thailand (October 31, 2006)

中国—东盟博览会将大力促进中国—东盟自由贸易区的形成，而这对中国与东盟则是共赢的。

——越南社会主义共和国总理　阮晋勇（2006年10月31日）

The CAEXPO will effectively accelerate the forming of the CAFTA, which will bring about win-win results for China and ASEAN.

—H.E. Nguyen Tan Dung, prime minister of Viet Nam (October 31, 2006)

深化合作 共同繁荣

——在第八届中国—东盟商务与投资峰会开幕式上的讲话

中华人民共和国国务院总理 温家宝

（2011年10月21日）

尊敬的纳吉布总理，

尊敬的洪森首相，

女士们，先生们：

今年是中国—东盟友好交流年，也是中国—东盟建立对话关系20周年。这次峰会以“深化区域合作，实现共同繁荣”为主题，很有意义。我代表中国政府，对会议的召开表示热烈祝贺，对各位嘉宾的莅临表示诚挚欢迎。

中国与东盟国家或山水相连，或隔海相望。自古以来，我们的祖先就共同生息、繁衍在亚洲这片热土上。“远亲不如近邻”。地缘这根纽带把我们紧密联系在一起，无论在中国，还是在东盟国家，随处都可以看到双方文化交流、影响、融合的印记，至今传诵着郑和下西洋、文莱渤泥王来华、万隆会议这样脍炙人口的历史佳话。中国和东盟各国人民之间的传统友谊源远流长、历久弥新。

上世纪八、九十年代以来，随着中国改革开放的深入推进，中国和东盟关系进入一个新的历史时期。我们本着加强沟通、增进互信、密切合作、互利共赢的宗旨，建立了中国—东盟对话关系，开启了双方关系的新篇章。20年来，双方关系经历了从全面对话伙伴、睦邻互信伙伴到战略伙伴的历史性跨越，中国—东盟全方位、宽领域、多层面的合作格局逐步形成。

中国真心诚意地发展同东盟的关系。作为区域外大国，中国第一个加入《东南亚友好合作条约》，第一个同东盟建立战略伙伴关系，第一个与东盟建设自由贸易区，率先承诺签署《东南亚无核武器区条约》议定书，坚定支持东盟在东亚合作中发挥主导作用。

中国致力于深化与东盟双方务实合作。在双方政府和工商界的共同努力下，20年来双边贸易额年均增长20%以上，目前已接近3000亿美元。中国成为东盟第一大贸易伙伴，东盟也成为中国的第三大贸易伙伴。我们创建了中国—东盟博览会、商务与投资峰会等经贸交流平台，设立了中国—东盟合作基金、中国—东盟公共卫生合作基金和中国—东盟投资合作基金，为东盟国家进行了数万人的能力建设培训。中国—东盟经贸合作正处于历史上最活跃、最富有成效的时期。

中国始终与东盟国家同舟共济。越是在困难和挑战面前，我们越是坚定地站在一起。1997年亚洲金融危机席卷东南亚时，中国坚持人民币不贬值。2008年国际金融危机最严峻的时期，中国出台了一系列应对金融危机的有力措施，促进了中国与东盟国家贸易与投资稳定增长。我们还共同抗击非典、禽流感、甲型H1N1流感等跨境传染病，共同应对历史罕见的印度洋海啸、缅甸风灾等自然灾害。中国—东盟的友好关系经受住了时间和困难的考验。

实践证明，中国和东盟既是唇齿相依、患难与共的好邻居，又是平等互利、合作共赢的好伙伴。正如一句中国谚语讲的那样："邻居好，赛黄金"。我相信，只要我们始终秉持平等互信、求同存异的原则，就能超越政治、经济、宗教、文化等方面差异，排除一切艰难险阻，推动双方合作不断向前发展，实现共同繁荣。

女士们、先生们：

全球经济格局正在发生深刻变化，亚洲的地位和作用日益重要。中国和东盟都是最具活力的经济体，都处在发展转型的关键时期。要抓住难得的历史机遇，推动经济持续平稳较快发展，就要进一步加强区域经贸合作。中国—东盟国家人口众多，市场空间巨大，经济互补性强，合作前景广阔。这些为我们深化贸易投资合作提供了广泛可能。为了推动双方经贸合作再上水平，我们要重点办好几件大事：

第一，共同建设好自贸区。2010年1月1日，中国—东盟自贸区全面建成。这是中国和东盟关系史上又一个重要里程碑，标志着双方经贸关系站在一个新的起点。自贸区的建成，不仅直接扩大区域内市场规模，极大地促进双边贸易快速发展，而且有利于促进农业、交通、旅游、投资等各个领域的合作，使中国和东盟经济在更大范围、更高层次上实现优势互补。中国—东盟自贸区是平等互利、合作共赢的典范。自贸区建成第一年，双方贸易额就达到2928亿美元，同比增长37.5%，创历史新高。2011年前三季度，双方贸易额进一步增长26.4%，东盟对中国出口增速快于进口增速。这些表明，自贸区启动后，东盟的国际竞争力不是削弱而是增强了，东盟对中国的出口能力不是降低而是提高了。自贸区是中国与东盟国家经过多年努力精心培育的利益共同体，来之不易，需要倍加呵护和珍惜。中方愿意继续扩大东盟国家优势产品的进口，妥善解决自贸区建设中出现的各种问题，把工作做实，把好事办好。我们将在南宁建设中国—东盟商品交易中心，作为双方产品的展示交易平台和商贸物流基地，希望东盟企业利用好这个平台，在中国赢得更大的市场份额。

第二，大力推进互联互通。实现东盟内部以及中国—东盟的互联互通，是深化经贸合作和人员往来的重要基础，将为缩小地区发展差距、提升地区竞争力、加快东亚一体化进程发挥重要作用。双方无论在基础设施硬件建设，还是在规制安排、人员交往等软件建设方面，都有巨大的合作空间。我们将与东盟方面密切合作，加强对中国与东盟有关国家互联互通的投入，为促进本地区商品、资本、信息的自由流通、人员往来和经济社会发展创造更好条件。中方愿意继续利用好中国—东盟投资合作基金、中国—东盟银联体及对东盟国家建立的信贷渠道，支持中国—东盟互联互通合作项目的落实。实现互联互通是一项长期而艰巨的任务，对已经形成规划的项目要抓好落实；对尚未确定的领域和项目要抓紧研究，早日推出实施方案。

第三，扩大双方投资合作。东盟国家来华直接投资累计达673亿美元，中国企业对东盟的投资也呈现快速增长态势，累计已达135亿美元。中国政府一如既往地欢迎东盟各国企业来中国投资兴业，特别是到中西部投资。中方也鼓励本国优秀企业扩大对东盟的投资。中方已经承诺在东盟国家各建一个经贸合作区，通过集群式投资提高双方经贸合作水平。中马钦州产业园是双方在中国西部地区合作建设的第一个工业园，具有示范意义，欢迎马方有实力的企业积极参与园区的规划和开发建设。我们也欢迎更多东盟国家企业来中国共建工业园区。

第四，深化区域经济合作。推动东亚区域和次区域合作，是中国和东盟共同的历史使命。东盟在实践中形成的区域合作理念和做法，符合东亚地区的实际，是行之有效的、成熟的，应该坚持下去。中方始终是东亚合作的积极参与者和支持者。中方将鼓励企业参与东盟东部增长区、大湄公河、泛北部湾等次区域合作，给予金融、技术、市场等方面的有力支持，推动形成若干经济增长极。中方愿与东盟密切合作，进一步深化现有各项区域财金合作，扩大货币互换规模和参与范围，完善“清迈倡议”多边化危机救助机制，加强区域经济监测能力建设，推进亚洲债券市场发展，逐步建立稳定、成熟的地区资本市场，进一步增强本地区应对国际金融风险的能力。

第五，拓展人文领域的交流。这是双方人民加深了解、增进友谊的重要方式，是中国—东盟关系可持续发展的重要基础。目前，东盟国家是中国游客的旅游首选地，去年首站前往东盟国家的中国游客超过500万人次。双方留学生和青少年交往也非常活跃，目前超过6000名汉语志愿者在40所孔子学院和课堂里工作，双方互派留学生超过13万人。我们要以办好“中国—东盟友好交流年”为契机，继续加强文化、教育、旅游、青年等领域的交流与合作，努力实现2015年双方人员往来达到1500万人次的目标。

当前国际金融危机依然阴霾重重，世界经济复苏艰难而曲折，不稳定和不确定性上升。一些国家主权债务风险增大，国际金融市场急剧动荡，主要发达国家失业率居高不下，新兴经济体面临通胀压力，世界经济增速出现回落，对亚洲地区已产生明显影响。在这种情况下，中国和东盟国家更需要精诚团结，做好在较长时期内应对挑战的各种准备，以更加务实开放的态度深化区域合作，推动中国与东盟各国经济持续健康平稳发展。

女士们、先生们：

中国—东盟建立对话关系已有20年了。20年在历史长河中只是一瞬，但是对于一个时代来说，时间并不算短。我真诚地希望中国和东盟的合作能有大的进展，不断取得富有意义的成果，造福中国与东盟国家的人民。这里我愿重申，巩固同东盟面向和平与繁荣的战略伙伴关系，推进互利互惠的全方位合作，是中国政府坚定不移的外交政策。我们将长期奉行“与邻为善、以邻为伴”的方针，永远做东盟的好邻居、好伙伴、好朋友。中国的发展将给东盟带来机遇，东盟的繁荣也符合中国的利益。我们愿同东盟各国一道，以中国—东盟自贸区全面建成为新的起点，拓宽合作领域，充实合作内容，提高合作层次，努力开创中国—东盟互利合作、共同繁荣的美好明天。

预祝本届商务与投资峰会取得圆满成功！

谢谢大家！

Strive to Deepen Cooperation for Common Prosperity

Address by H.E.Wen Jiabao Premier of the State Council of the People's Republic of China at the 8th China-ASEAN Business & Investment Summit

(October 21, 2011)

The Honorable Prime Minister Dato' Sri Najib,
The Honorable Prime Minister Hun Sen,
Ladies and gentlemen,

This year is the China-ASEAN Friendship and Exchange Year and the 20th anniversary of China-ASEAN dialogue relations. It is therefore highly relevant for the summit to take "Deepen Regional Cooperation for Common Prosperity" as its theme. On behalf of the Chinese government, I wish to extend warm congratulations on the opening of the summit and sincere welcome to all the distinguished guests present.

China and ASEAN countries are linked by the same mountains and rivers or face each other across the sea. Our forefathers have, since ancient times, lived and multiplied in Asia, the homeland for us all. As the Chinese saying goes, "It's better to have a neighbor close by than a relative far away." Geographic proximity has brought us close to each other. One can easily find vestiges of interaction and integration of our cultures whether in China or ASEAN countries. Stories of Admiral Zheng He's many voyages to the Western Seas, travel to China by Boni King of Brunei, and the Bandung Conference have been told from generation to generation. Indeed, the traditional friendship between the Chinese people and the people of ASEAN countries has run a long course and is poised to become even stronger.

Since the 1980s and 90s, China-ASEAN relations have entered a new historical period with the deepening of China's reform and opening–up. Firmly committed to closer communication, stronger mutual trust, enhanced cooperation and mutual benefit, we launched China–ASEAN dialogue relations and turned a new chapter in the annals of bilateral relationship. Over the past two decades, our relations have witnessed historic progress from all–round dialogue partners to partners of good–neighborliness and mutual trust, to strategic partners. A framework of all–dimensional, wide–ranging and multi–tiered China–ASEAN cooperation has gradually taken shape.

China has every sincerity in advancing its relations with ASEAN. Among big countries outside the region, China is the first to accede to the ***Treaty of Amity and Cooperation in Southeast Asia,*** the first to establish strategic partnership with ASEAN, the first to build free trade area with ASEAN, and the first to commit to signing the ***Protocol to the Treaty on the Southeast Asian Nuclear Weapon–Free Zone***. What is more, China firmly supports ASEAN in playing the leading role in East Asian cooperation.

China is committed to deepening practical cooperation with ASEAN. Thanks to joint efforts of governments and business communities from both sides, our two–way trade has registered an average annual growth rate of more than 20% in the past two decades, reaching nearly US$300 billion a year. China has become the largest trading partner of ASEAN, and ASEAN the third largest trading partner of China. We have launched such business and trade platforms as the China–ASEAN Expo and China–ASEAN Business and Investment Summit, established the China–ASEAN Cooperation Fund, China–ASEAN Public Health Cooperation Fund and China–ASEAN Investment Cooperation Fund. China has provided training programs on capacity building for tens of thousands of people from ASEAN countries. China–ASEAN economic cooperation has never been more dynamic and more fruitful.

China has always stood by ASEAN countries rain or shine. The more difficult and challenging the times are, the more resolutely we have stood together. When a financial crisis swept across Southeast Asia in 1997, China refused to depreciate the RMB. At the height of the international financial crisis in 2008, China introduced a series of strong measures against the crisis and worked for steady growth of trade and investment cooperation with ASEAN countries. We have also worked together against such cross–border diseases as SARS, avian flu, and Influenza A H1N1 and such severe natural disasters as the Indian Ocean tsunami, and cyclone in Myanmar. China–ASEAN friendly relations have withstood the test of time and tribulations.

Facts have shown that China and ASEAN are both good neighbors sharing weal and woe and good partners for win–win cooperation based on equality and mutual benefit. As a popular Chinese saying goes, "Having a good neighbor is better than possessing gold". I believe that as long as we act in the spirit of equality, mutual trust and seeking common ground while shelving differences, we will rise above our political, economic, religious, cultural and other differences, overcome the difficulties and obstacles on the road to progress, and move our cooperation forward towards common prosperity.

Ladies and gentlemen,

The global economic landscape is undergoing profound changes, and the status and role of Asia is becoming increasingly important. As the most dynamic part of

Asia economically, China and ASEAN are both at a critical juncture of transition in development. To seize this rare opportunity for sustained, steady and fairly fast economic development, we need to step up economic cooperation and trade in the region. China and ASEAN, given our huge population, vast market and strong complementarity, stand to gain enormously from our cooperation. I see great possibilities lying ahead in deepening trade and investment cooperation between us. To bring our cooperation to a new high, we need to take the following actions on a priority basis.

First, make our Free Trade Area a success. The China-ASEAN Free Trade Area was launched on 1 January last year. It is another milestone in China-ASEAN relationship, and shows that our economic and trade ties now stand at a new starting line. The FTA has not only increased the market scale in the region and given our trade a powerful boost, but also helped enhance our cooperation in agriculture, communications, tourism, investment and other areas, making our economic complementarity a greater advantage in both scope and depth. China-ASEAN FTA is a good example of equality, mutual benefit and win-win cooperation. In its first year, bilateral trade reached a record high of US$292.8 billion, up by 37.5%. In the first three quarters this year, our trade grew by 26.4%, with ASEAN export to China growing faster than its import from China. All this shows the FTA has increased rather than decreased the international competitiveness of ASEAN, and that ASEAN's capacity to export to China has become stronger rather than weaker. We all have a stake in the China-ASEAN FTA, as we have worked so hard over the years to make it a reality and the FTA deserves our extra care. China is ready to continue expanding imports of competitive products from ASEAN countries, find proper solutions to the problems in the development of the FTA, and work for solid results from all our efforts. We will build the China-ASEAN Plaza in Nanning which will serve as an exhibition and marketing platform and logistic base for products from both sides. We hope that ASEAN businesses will take advantage of this and work to gain greater share in the Chinese market.

Second, work hard to promote connectivity. Connectivity within ASEAN and between China and ASEAN is important groundwork for deepening economic cooperation and people-to-people exchanges. It will play an important role in narrowing development gap within the region, raising regional competitiveness and accelerating the East Asian integration process. There exists vast potential for our cooperation in infrastructure and such "software" development as institution building and personnel exchanges. We will work closely with ASEAN to increase input in connectivity with relevant ASEAN countries so as to create better conditions for free flow of goods, capital and information, personnel exchanges and economic and social development in the region. China is ready to make good use of the China-ASEAN Investment Cooperation Fund, China-ASEAN Inter-Bank Association and line of credit for ASEAN countries to support the China-ASEAN connectivity cooperation projects. To achieve connectivity is a long and arduous task. We should work for sound implementation of the projects where we have already had a plan; and lose no time in looking into the areas and projects yet to be identified and introduce implementation plans at an early date.

Third, step up bilateral cooperation on investment. Direct investment by ASEAN countries in China has reached US$67.3 billion, while investment by Chinese companies in ASEAN, now totaling US$13.5 billion, displays a trend of rapid growth. The Chinese government will, as always, welcome investment by ASEAN enterprises in China, particularly in its central and western regions. China also encourages its top enterprises to increase investment in ASEAN. China has pledged to establish in each ASEAN member country an economic cooperation zone to raise the level of economic cooperation through cluster investment. The China–Malaysia Qinzhou Industrial Park in Guangxi, the first of such joint efforts in China's western region, serves as a good example. We welcome the capable Malaysian companies to get actively involved in the planning and development of the Park. We also hope to see more ASEAN firms coming to China for the development of similar industrial parks.

Fourth, deepen economic cooperation in the region. Greater regional and sub–regional cooperation in East Asia is the common mission for China and ASEAN. The ideas and approaches of regional cooperation developed by ASEAN over the years suit the reality of East Asia. They are well–considered, effective and should be carried forward. China has always been an active participant in and supporter for East Asian cooperation. We will encourage Chinese enterprises to participate in sub–regional cooperation schemes such as BIMP–EAGA, the Greater Mekong Subregion and the Pan–Beibu Gulf, and we will provide strong financial, technology and market access support in hope of creating a number of economic growth poles. China is ready to work closely with ASEAN to deepen existing financial and monetary cooperation in the region, increase the scale and scope of currency swaps, improve crisis response mechanisms under the Chiang Mai Initiative Multilateralization, step up capacity building in regional economic monitoring, advance the development of the Asian bond market, gradually put in place a stable and mature regional capital market and enhance the region's ability to resist international financial risks.

Fifth, expand people–to–people and cultural exchanges. This is an important way to deepen understanding and friendship among peoples and the key foundation for the sustainable development of China–ASEAN relations. ASEAN countries are now top choices of tourism destination for Chinese travelers. More than five million Chinese tourists chose ASEAN countries as their first stop of overseas trips last year. Interactions between young people on both sides, including students, are vibrant. More than 6,000 language volunteers are working in more than 40 Confucius institutes and classrooms in ASEAN countries. China and ASEAN have exchanged over 130,000 students. We should take the China–ASEAN Friendship and Exchange Year as an opportunity to step up exchanges and cooperation in culture, education, tourism, youth affairs and other areas in an effort to achieve the targeted 15 million mutual visits by 2015.

At present, the international financial crisis remains ominous, and world economic recovery is a hard and tortuous course amid growing instability and uncertainty. Sovereign debt risks in some countries are rising. International financial markets are suffering drastic fluctuations and unemployment in major developed countries remains high. Emerging economies are faced with inflationary pressures. World economic growth has shown signs of slowdown, and this has made a visible impact on Asia. Under such circumstances, it is vitally important for China and ASEAN to close ranks, get prepared to meet challenges over a rather long period of time, deepen regional cooperation with a more pragmatic and open attitude and promote sustained, steady and healthy economic development in China and ASEAN countries.

Ladies and gentlemen,

Twenty years have passed since the establishment of our dialogue relations. Twenty years is a blink in the long course of history, but not short for a historical period. I sincerely hope that major progress can be made in our dialogue relations and meaningful fruits can be harvested to the benefit of the people of China and ASEAN countries. I wish to reiterate here that cementing the strategic partnership for peace and prosperity and promoting all-dimensional and mutually beneficial cooperation with ASEAN remains the unswerving policy of the Chinese government. We will continue to follow the long-term policy of pursuing good neighborly relations and partnership with our neighbors, and be a good neighbor, good partner and good friend of ASEAN forever. China's development will bring opportunities to ASEAN, while ASEAN's prosperity serves the interests of China. We will work with ASEAN countries to take the launch of China-ASEAN Free Trade Area as a new starting point to expand, enrich and elevate our cooperation in pursuit of a better future of win-win cooperation and common prosperity.

In conclusion, I wish the Business and Investment Summit a complete success.

Thank you.

(Source: Ministry of Foreign Affairs of China)

在第八届中国—东盟商务与投资峰会开幕式上的主持词

广西壮族自治区党委书记
广西壮族自治区人大常委会主任 郭声琨

（2011年10月21日）

尊敬的温家宝总理，

尊敬的马来西亚总理纳吉布阁下，

尊敬的柬埔寨首相洪森阁下，

尊敬的缅甸副总统吴丁昂敏乌阁下，

尊敬的老挝副总理宋沙瓦阁下，

尊敬的泰国副总理吉滴叻阁下，

尊敬的越南副总理阮春福阁下，

尊敬的文莱工业与初级资源部叶海亚部长，

尊敬的新加坡贸工部林勋强部长，

尊敬的菲律宾贸工部珍艾达·马拉雅副部长，

尊敬的印度尼西亚贸易部穆赫达塔尔部长助理，

尊敬的东盟秘书处素林秘书长，
各位嘉宾，
女士们、先生们、朋友们：

金秋十月，丹桂飘香。今天我们又迎来了第八届中国—东盟商务与投资峰会的隆重举行。

出席今天开幕式的还有，东盟各国代表团主要成员、外交使节、中国政府有关部门和各省、自治区、直辖市的领导，中国和东盟各国商协组织的负责人，中国和东盟企业界代表、专家学者和新闻界人士，以及区域外的贵宾。让我们以热烈的掌声，对中国和东盟国家领导人及各位嘉宾的光临，表示热烈的欢迎和衷心的感谢！

由中国和东盟各国领导人共同确定的中国—东盟商务与投资峰会，自2004年在广西南宁举办以来，在中国和东盟各国的共同努力下，在东盟秘书处的大力支持下，峰会紧扣中国—东盟自贸区建设主题，突出区域经贸合作特色，秉持互利共赢理念，不断创新内容与形式，取得了互惠共利的显著成效，收获了务实合作的丰硕果实，已成为中国与东盟开展高层对话、深化区域经贸合作、实现共同发展繁荣的重要平台，在推动中国—东盟自由贸易区建设中发挥了重要作用。广西作为峰会的举办地，我们将继续努力为各方深化友好交流合作做好服务、提供便利。

下面，请中国国际贸易促进委员会会长万季飞先生致辞，大家欢迎。

谢谢万季飞会长的致辞。下面，让我们以热烈的掌声欢迎温家宝总理作主旨演讲。

感谢温家宝总理的精彩演讲。下面，让我们以热烈的掌声欢迎柬埔寨首相洪森阁下演讲。

感谢洪森首相的精彩演讲。

刚才，洪森首相和温家宝总理分别发表了精彩演讲，共同回顾了中国—东盟商务与投资峰会举办八年来，以及中国—东盟自由贸易区建成运营以来所取得的显著成就，共同展望了中国与东盟深化合作、互利共赢的广阔前景，对务实推进中国与东盟经贸合作提出了富有远见的建议和设想。这充分反映了中国—东盟经贸关系的发展趋势，体现了中国—东盟工商界加强全面合作的共同要求，必将对中国—东盟拓展合作范围、提升合作水平起到重要推动作用。

让我们再次以热烈的掌声对各位领导和各位嘉宾的光临，表示衷心的感谢！

第八届中国—东盟商务与投资峰会开幕式到此结束。谢谢大家！

Address at the Opening Ceremony of the 8th China-ASEAN Business and Investment Summit

by

H.E. Guo Shengkun

Secretary of the CPC Guangxi Committee

Chairman of the Standing Committee of the Guangxi People's Congress

(October 21, 2011)

Your Excellency Premier Wen Jiabao,
Your Excellency Prime Minister Dato'Sri Mohd Najib bin Tun Haji Abdul Razak of Malaysia,
Your Excellency Prime Minister Samdech Hun Sen of Cambodia,
Your Excellency Vice-President Thiha Thura Tin Aung Myint Oo of Myanmar,
Your Excellency Deputy Prime Minister Somsavat Lengsavad of Lao PDR,
Your Excellency Deputy Prime Minister Kittiratt Na-Ranong of Thailand,
Your Excellency Deputy Prime Minister Nguyen Xuan Phuc of Viet Nam,
Honorable Minister Pehin Dato Seri Paduka Awang Haji Yahya of Ministry of Industry and Primary Resources of Brunei Darussalam,
Honorable Minister Lim Hng Kiang of Ministry of Trade and Industry of Singapore,
Honorable Deputy Minister Zenaida Cuison-Maglaya of Ministry of Trade and Industry of the Philippines,
Honorable Assistant Minister Muchtar of Ministry of Trade of Indonesia,

Honorable Secretary–General Surin Pitsuwan of ASEAN ,
Distinguished guests,
Ladies and gentlemen,

Today we are happy to observe again the grand opening of the 8th China–ASEAN Business and Investment Summit in the osmanthus blossom season in October.

Present at the opening ceremony today are also VIPs of the delegations from the ASEAN countries, diplomatic envoys, leaders of the Chinese ministries, provinces, autonomous regions and municipalities, leaders from the Chinese and ASEAN industrial and commercial organizations, the representatives from the Chinese and ASEAN business communities, the experts, scholars and journalists as well as the distinguished guests from outside our region. Let us give our tremendous applause to the attendance of the state leaders from China and ASEAN and all our honored guests, extending our warm welcome and sincere thanks.

Since its inception in Nanning, China in 2004, China–ASEAN Business & Investment Summit (CABIS), with joint efforts of China and the 10 ASEAN member states and great support of the ASEAN Secretariat, has obtained remarkable achievements and gained fruitful results of pragmatic cooperation by seizing the theme of China–ASEAN Free Trade Area (CAFTA), focusing on features of the regional economic cooperation, persisting in the concept of mutual benefits and win–win results and keeping on creating new contents and forms, thus become an important platform to drive China–ASEAN high–level dialogue, deepen regional economic cooperation and progress toward common prosperity and development and played a significant role in the progress of CAFTA construction. As the venue of CABIS, Guangxi will strive further to offer good services and conveniences for bilateral friendly exchanges and cooperation.

I would like to invite Mr. Wan Jifei, chairman of China Council for the Promotion of International Trade, to give a speech.

Thank Chairman Wan for his speech. Now let us warmly welcome His Excellency Premier Wen Jiabao to deliver his keynote speech with loud applause.

Thank Premier Wen Jiabao for his excellent speech. Now let us welcome His Excellency Prime Minister Samdech Hun Sen of Cambodia to make an address with warm applause.

Thank Prime Minister Hun Sen for his excellent speech.

Just now, Prime Minister Hun Sen and Premier Wen Jiabao have respectively delivered their excellent speeches, looking back the prominent achievement since the operation of CABIS for consecutive eight years and the establishment of CAFTA and looking ahead to the broad prospects in terms of deepening cooperation and obtaining win–win results between China and ASEAN. Far–sighted proposals and ideas to drive trade and economic cooperation between China and ASEAN are put forward, which fully reflect the development trend of China–ASEAN economic and trade ties and the common demand of boosting comprehensive cooperation between China–ASEAN business communities. These will greatly enrich the content of China–ASEAN cooperation and improve its level.

Let us express our heartfelt gratitude once again to all the leaders and honorable guests for your presence with a round of applause.

Now the opening ceremony of the 8th China–ASEAN Business and Investment Summit comes to a successful close. Thank you all!

(Soure: China Council for the Promotion of Internationl Trade Guangxi Sub–council)

在第八届中国—东盟博览会开幕式上的致辞

广西壮族自治区主席
中国—东盟博览会组委会副主任

（2011年10月21日）

尊敬的温家宝总理，

尊敬的马来西亚总理纳吉布、柬埔寨首相洪森、缅甸副总统吴丁昂敏乌、老挝副总理宋沙瓦、泰国副总理吉滴叻、越南副总理阮春福、文莱工业与初级资源部部长叶海亚、新加坡贸工部部长林勋强、菲律宾贸工部副部长马拉雅、印度尼西亚贸易部部长助理穆赫达塔尔、东盟秘书长素林，

各位嘉宾，

女士们、先生们：

今天，美丽的绿城南宁花团锦簇，喜迎盛会。我谨代表广西壮族自治区人民政府，向出席第八届中国—东盟博览会的各国领

导人和各位嘉宾表示热烈的欢迎！

8年来，由中国和东盟10国共办的中国—东盟博览会常办常新，硕果累累，搭建了中国和东盟友好交流、经贸合作和深化友谊的重要平台，造福了各国企业和人民，形成了中国—东盟“南宁渠道”，已经成为具有强大吸引力和影响力的国际性经贸盛会，成为中国—东盟自由贸易区建设发展的“助推器”，成为中国与东盟友好合作的象征。

5年前，中国—东盟建立对话关系15周年纪念峰会在广西南宁与博览会同期举办。今天，第八届中国—东盟博览会作为中国—东盟建立对话关系20周年系列纪念活动的重要内容，将集中展现中国—东盟不断扩大交流合作的丰硕成果，完善贸易、工业、农业、投资、金融、旅游、文化、教育等多领域交流合作平台，创造更多商机，必将进一步提升友好合作水平，加深传统友谊，谱写共赢发展的新篇章。

携手办盛会，共创新辉煌。我们愿与各方加强合作，加快建设广西北部湾经济区，共同推进泛北部湾经济合作，共同建设南宁—新加坡经济走廊和跨境经济合作区，共同开创中国—东盟友好合作的美好未来！

预祝第八届中国—东盟博览会圆满成功！

Speech at the Opening Ceremony of the 8th China-ASEAN Expo

by

H.E. Ma Biao

Governor of Guangxi Zhuang Autonomous Region

Co-chair of the CAEXPO Organizing Committee

(October 21, 2011)

H.E. Wen Jiabao, premier of the State Council of the People's Republic of China,
H.E. Dato' Sri Mohd Najib Tun Abdul Razak, prime minister of Malaysia,
H.E. Samdech Hun Sen, prime minister of the Kingdom of Cambodia,
H.E. Thiha Thura U Tin Aung Myint Oo, vice-president of the Republic of the Union of Myanmar,
H.E. Somsavat LENGSAVAD, deputy prime minister of the Lao People's Democratic Republic,
H.E. Kittiratt Na-Ranong, deputy prime minister of the Kingdom of Thailand,
H.E. Nguyen Xuan Phuc, deputy prime minister of the Socialist Republic of Vietnam,
H.E. Pehin Dato Haji Yahya, minister of industry and primary resources, Brunei Darussalam,
H.E. Lim Hng Kiang, minister of trade and industry, the Republic of Singapore,
H.E. Zenaida Cuison-Maglaya, under-secretary of trade and industry, the Republic of the Philippines,
H.E. Dr. Muchtar, chairman of the Indonesian Anti-dumping Committee and the assistant minister of trade sector policy, the Republic of Indonesia,

H.E. Dr. Surin Pitsuwan, secretary–general of ASEAN,

Distinguished guests, ladies and gentlemen, dear friends:

Today, Nanning, the beautiful Green City is celebrating the opening of the great event with beautiful flowers. On behalf of the People's Government of Guangxi Zhuang Autonomous Region, I would like to extend my big welcome to state leaders and distinguished guests attending the 8th China–ASEAN Expo.

The China–ASEAN Expo, co–sponsored by China and 10 ASEAN countries has been held in a sustained way with highlights and great achievements in these eight years. The Expo has served as an important platform for China and ASEAN countries to carry out friendly exchanges, economic and trade cooperation and intensify their friendship. Enterprises and people in the concerned countries have benefited from the Expo and Nanning Channel for the exchanges and cooperation between China and ASEAN has been formed because of the Expo. It has evolved into an international economic and trade event with strong attractiveness and extensive influence, an accelerator for the progress of China–ASEAN Free Trade Area and a symbol of friendly cooperation between China and ASEAN.

The Commemorative Summit Marking the 15th Anniversary of ASEAN–China Dialogue Relations was held concurrently with China–ASEAN Expo five years ago. This year, as an integral part of commemorative activities marking the 20th anniversary of ASEAN–China dialogue relations, the 8th China–ASEAN Expo will showcase achievements of expanded exchanges and cooperation between China and ASEAN, improve the platform of bilateral exchanges and cooperation in multiple areas such as trade, industry, agriculture, investment, finance, tourism, culture and education and create more business opportunities. The Expo will surely upgrade our friendly cooperation, strengthen our traditional friendship and write a new chapter of common development and win–win scenario.

Let's work together to hold a successful Expo and create greater brilliance. We stand ready to strengthen cooperation with all concerned parties to accelerate the construction of Guangxi Beibu Gulf Economic Zone, Nanning–Singapore Economic Corridor and cross–border economic cooperation zones, promote Pan–Beibu Gulf Economic Cooperation and build a bright future for the friendly cooperation between China and ASEAN.

I wish the 8th China–ASEAN Expo a complete success.

(Source: Guangxi Foreign Affairs Office)

在第八届中国—东盟博览会开幕式上的致辞

中国商务部国际贸易谈判代表兼副部长 高虎城

（2011年10月21日）

尊敬的温家宝总理，
尊敬的纳吉布总理，
尊敬的洪森首相，
尊敬的吴丁昂敏乌副总统，
尊敬的宋沙瓦副总理，
尊敬的吉滴叻副总理，
尊敬的阮春福副总理，
女士们，先生们：

今年是中国与东盟建立对话关系20周年。今天，第八届中国—东盟博览会隆重开幕。我谨代表中国商务部，向参加博览会的各国嘉宾和朋友表示热烈的欢迎，向长期以来支持中国和东盟的各界人士表示衷心的感谢！

中国和东盟建立对话关系20年来，各领域友好互利合作不断推进，经贸合作成效尤其显著。我们携手合作，实现了全面建成中国—东盟自由贸易区的目标。我们共同搭建了中国—东盟博览会平台，增进企业间的交流与合作，促进了双边贸易和投资，为双方企业和人民带来了实实在在的利益。

本届博览会将充分反映20年来双方合作的辉煌成就，展示中国—东盟自贸区广阔商机和美好前景，为双方企业创造更多的合作机会。让我们抓住机遇，不断深化互利合作，为促进本地区共同发展、共同繁荣作出新的贡献！

预祝第八届中国—东盟博览会圆满成功！

谢谢大家！

Speech at the Opening Ceremony of the 8th China–ASEAN Expo

by

H.E. Gao Hucheng

China International Trade Representative and Vice Minister of Commerce of China

(October 21, 2011)

H.E. Wen Jiabao, premier of the State Council of the People's Republic of China,
H.E. Dato' Sri Mohd Najib Tun Abdul Razak, prime minister of Malaysia,
H.E. Samdech Hun Sen, prime minister of the Kingdom of Cambodia,
H.E. Thiha Thura U Tin Aung Myint Oo, vice–president of the Republic of the Union of Myanmar,
H.E. Somsavat LENGSAVAD, deputy prime minister of the Lao People's Democratic Republic,
H.E. Kittiratt Na–Ranong, deputy prime minister of the Kingdom of Thailand,
H.E. Nguyen Xuan Phuc, deputy prime minister of the Socialist Republic of Vietnam,
Ladies and gentlemen:

This year marks the 20th anniversary of the ASEAN–China dialogue relations. And today, the 8th China–ASEAN Expo grandly opens. On behalf of the Ministry of Commerce of China, I'd like to extend warm welcome to all the guests and friends attending the Expo and sincere thanks to people from various quarters for your lasting support to China and ASEAN.

Since the establishment of dialogue relations 20 years ago, China and ASEAN have advanced friendly and mutually-beneficial cooperation in a wide range of areas, especially in the economic and trade arena. We have worked together in achieving the goal of fully implementing the China-ASEAN Free Trade Area. We have jointly built the CAEXPO platform, increased the exchanges and collaboration among enterprises, promoted bilateral trade and investment and brought tangible benefits to our businesses and people.

This Expo will fully showcase the remarkable achievements in our cooperation in the past 20 years, highlight broad business opportunities and a bright prospect of CAFTA and foster a partnership among our businesses. Let's seize the opportunities, continuously deepen the cooperation of mutual-benefit and make fresh contribution to the common development and prosperity of the region.

I'd like to wish the 8th CAEXPO a complete success.

Thank you !

(Source: transcript of the recording of the 8th CAEXPO opening ceremony)

目录

附　录

CONTENTS

前　言

中国—东盟博览会组委会副主任兼秘书长
广西壮族自治区副主席　蓝天立

中国—东盟博览会由中国总理温家宝倡议、东盟10国领导人一致赞同、中国和东盟10国政府经贸主管部门共同主办、广西壮族自治区人民政府承办，至今已成功举办八届，成效显著，搭建了中国—东盟友好交流、经贸促进和多领域合作的重要平台。经过八年的成长，博览会在推动全方位与东盟开展合作方面不断创新，成为中国—东盟自由贸易区具有广泛影响力的国际盛会。

一、中国—东盟博览会搭建了全方位合作的平台，成效显著

中国—东盟博览会把友好交流和经贸及社会人文等多领域合作结合为一体，全面开展与东盟合作。八届博览会共有42位中国和东盟国家领导人、1500多位部长级贵宾出席，参展参会客商31.6万人，贸易成交额116.9亿美元，签约国际合作项目投资额491.72亿美元，签约国内合作项目投资额4759.02亿元，围绕贸易、投资、海关、质检、金融、港口、电信、环保及社会人文等多领域举办了200多个高层次会议、论坛和活动，成效显著，服务了中国—东盟合作，服务了中国—东盟自贸区建设和发展，服务了广西发展。

——搭建了友好交流的平台，以政治外交影响力带动经贸等多领域合作。中国和东盟国家领导人亲自推动博览会，每年率团

出席。会期举行多场双方领导人、部长、地方负责人之间的会谈，增进政治互信。每届博览会还举行政要与商界的对话，带动经贸等多领域合作，推动了商家的务实合作，带动了文化、教育等多领域的交流。

——搭建了经贸促进的平台，以经贸合作成果促进政治互信和友好交流。博览会围绕中国—东盟自贸区建设进程以及中国和东盟国家的经济发展水平、资源禀赋、产业结构、行业特点而设置展览内容，高度集中了11国的企业、商品、项目、资金等方面的信息，将自贸区的投资贸易便利化从政府层面推进到了企业层面，成为自贸区建设的“助推器”。

博览会推动了双方企业和行业的对接，促进了双方经贸合作。2004年，首届中国—东盟博览会举办。中国和东盟双边贸易额提前一年实现了1000亿美元的目标。2007年，双边贸易额提前三年实现2000亿美元的目标。2011年，双边贸易额达3628.5亿美元，创历史新高。博览会在其中发挥了重要的作用，体现了自贸区的双赢效果，推动中国—东盟战略伙伴关系提升到一个更高的水平。

——搭建了多领域合作的平台，为中国和东盟在经贸、人文等领域的合作提供机制保障。随着中国—东盟经贸合作不断扩大和深化，对双方在相关领域的合作提出了更多更高的要求。因此，在每届博览会期间，国家有关部委举办海关、检验检疫、金融、港口、物流、教育、文化、体育等一系列会议、论坛和交流活动，开展部长级磋商对话，邀请各国各领域企业家、专家学者参会交流，解决了双边经贸合作快速发展对相关领域服务配套提出的新需求，使经贸合作与社会人文领域交流更紧密结合，为各领域交流合作提供了机制保障，促进了中国与东盟友好关系全面持久稳定发展。此外，博览会还设立“魅力之城”专题，每届每个国家选派一个城市担任“魅力之城”，展示城市形象和发展商机，促进城市合作。每届博览会期间还举办南宁国际民歌艺术节等一系列文化体育交流活动，增进中国与东盟各国友好往来。

二、中国—东盟博览会适应中国和东盟10国共同发展的需要，体现了合作共赢的共同目标

进入新世纪，随着经济全球化和区域经济一体化迅猛发展，中国和东盟各国领导人作出了建设中国—东盟自由贸易区的重要举措。作为推动中国—东盟自由贸易区建设的具体行动，中国—东盟博览会应运而生。近年来，随着中国—东盟自由贸易区建设不断加快并如期建成，以及中国—东盟经贸合作快速发展，双方更加需要中国—东盟博览会这一

务实的交流合作平台来加快促进互利合作。因此，中国和东盟国家领导人对博览会高度重视。中国国家主席胡锦涛对办好博览会作出重要指示，中国国务院总理温家宝两次出席博览会。贾庆林、李克强、曾庆红以及王岐山、吴仪、曾培炎等中国国家领导人分别出席了历届博览会。东盟国家共有32位领导人出席历届博览会。其中，柬埔寨首相洪森出席了六届，越南总理阮晋勇、老挝前总理波松、缅甸前总理梭温均连续出席了三届。自2003年第七次中国—东盟“10+1”领导人会议以来，博览会几乎每年都被写入中国—东盟“10+1”领导人会议的《主席声明》，得到各国领导人的高度评价。

八年来，在中国和东盟各国政府部门、商界、媒体等社会各界的共同努力下，中国—东盟博览会建立了跨国家、跨部门、跨省区的日常工作机制。

（一）建立了组委会机制，组织架构不断完善

为了在组织架构上给博览会成功举办提供有力的保障，中国和越南、老挝、泰国、印尼等东盟国家相继建立了跨部门的博览会组委会。中方组委会由商务部、外交部、中国贸促会等15个部委及广西壮族自治区人民政府组成。首任中方组委会名誉主任是国务院前副总理吴仪。2008年中方组委会顺利换届。新一届组委会名誉主任为国务院副总理王岐山，组委会主任为商务部部长陈德铭。组委会每年召开会议，部署博览会筹备工作，形成了行之有效的工作机制，为博览会的发展提供了强有力的组织保障。

（二）建立11国共办机制，深化共办共赢

共同主办是博览会的特色和基础。几年来，在11国共办方的共同努力下，博览会互利共赢的共办机制不断深化，建立了由各国经贸部长担任组委会共同主任、司局长担任副秘书长、处长为联络官的三级共办工作构架，形成了博览会高官会议、联络官会议等磋商机制、抽签决定国家专题展位排序的惯例，以及每届由一个东盟国家担任主题国，主题国领导人率团出席的机制。

通过以上措施，建立起平等尊重、共同主办、广泛参与的共办工作机制，使东盟国家能将其本国优势领域在博览会上加以充分展示，共同促进博览会的持续发展，为博览会的成功举办提供了保障。

（三）建立与中国国内各省（区、市）的合作机制，服务各省（区、市）与东盟的合作

几年来，博览会与国内各省（区、市）建立了合作机制。同东盟国

家经贸较为密切的上海、浙江、江苏、厦门、重庆等省区人民政府成为博览会的特别合作单位。北京、上海、天津、苏州、深圳、钦州、海南分别成为历届博览会的“魅力之城”。通过与各省（区、市）的合作，博览会服务于国内各省（区、市）与东盟合作的平台作用得到了更有效的发挥。

（四）博览会举办地广西不断加大力度，建立和完善举全区之力办会机制

八年来，广西作为中国—东盟博览会的承办方，不断加强组织领导，加大工作力度，举全区之力，做好每届博览会的筹备工作。广西成立了由自治区主席任组长的中国—东盟博览会、中国—东盟商务与投资峰会（简称“两会”）广西领导小组，还成立了由自治区有关厅局和相关单位组成的“两会”指挥中心，为博览会的成功举办提供了组织保障。

（五）建立与11国主要商协会的长期合作机制，吸引全球企业参与

中国和东盟各国商协会、企业是博览会的重要参与者，也是博览会发展的重要推动者。博览会已成为企业深化务实合作的平台。博览会已有40家中国和东盟商协会成为支持商协会。11国商协会和企业广泛参与，丰富了博览会的舞台，推进了中国—东盟自由贸易区建设和全面经济合作。

中国—东盟博览会不仅有中国和东盟各国的企业参与，而且还吸引了美国、日本、韩国、法国、德国、澳大利亚、加拿大等多个区域外国家和地区的企业参与，有效促进了区域外经济体与中国和东盟国家的交流，进一步加深了相互了解，提升了中国和东盟作为一个整体在全球的影响力。

（六）建立与中外媒体的合作机制，不断扩大博览会的影响力

几年来，博览会秘书处与中国和东盟国家主流媒体、专业媒体、商协会媒体等建立了合作机制，宣传网络覆盖东南亚10国。这些媒体既有主流媒体，也有财经类及相关行业的媒体；既有东盟国家主流的本土语种和英文媒体，又有东南亚华侨华人关注的华文媒体。既有平面媒体，也有网络和电视广播媒体，实现了媒体读者受众群的全方位覆盖，每年到南宁采访博览会的记者不断增多，博览会的影响力不断扩大。

三、广西将继续举全区之力办好中国—东盟博览会，更好地服务中国—东盟友好合作

中国—东盟友好合作迈入新的20年，中国—东盟自由贸易区发展不断推进，中国与东盟的合作进入了全面深入发展的新阶段。广西作为中国—

东盟博览会举办地，以及中国面向东盟的重要门户和前沿地带，将在中国—东盟合作中发挥更加重要的作用。我们要按照《国家“十二五”规划纲要》关于“把广西建成与东盟合作的新高地”的要求，认真贯彻《国务院关于进一步促进广西经济社会发展的若干意见》、《广西北部湾经济区发展规划》，进一步承办好中国—东盟博览会，发挥广西的区位优势，为中国和东盟合作搭好平台。今后，要做好三个方面的工作：

一是加强统筹，进一步完善承办中国—东盟博览会的长效机制。要积极实施更加主动的开放带动战略，努力做到主动地适应广西区情的新变化和广西经济社会发展“跨万亿元”新台阶之后的新趋势和新要求，通过广西与东盟开放合作领导小组及其统筹协调办公室，加强统筹力度，进一步完善博览会筹办工作长效机制，充分发挥博览会平台作用，提高外向型经济发展水平。

二是继续举全区之力承办好中国—东盟博览会。广西将紧紧围绕中国—东盟自由贸易区建设和发展的要求，继续把博览会办得更有特色、更有实效，使之在推动中国与东盟友好合作、服务中国—东盟自由贸易区等方面发挥更加重要的作用。我们将不断完善高规格办会机制，促进政商高端对接，推动友好合作；不断创新展会内容和措施，突出展示双方互补性强的商品，加强投资合作，推动企业“走出去”投资东盟，让双方企业更好地享受中国—东盟自由贸易区商机；不断完善中国—东盟博览会官方网站、中国—东盟中心服务平台等，打造永不落幕的中国—东盟博览会；积极扩大文化、教育、体育等社会人文领域合作，把博览会推动的合作由以经贸、投资领域为主的合作进一步扩展到多领域、多层次的合作，拓宽中国与东盟合作的“南宁渠道”，服务中国与东盟全面合作。

三是进一步发挥中国—东盟博览会作用，继续为中国—东盟友好合作搭建平台。广西将进一步发挥博览会平台作用，进一步完善以交通为重点的基础设施建设，大力推动互联互通，大力推进泛北部湾经济合作、大湄公河次区域合作、中越“两廊一圈”合作、南宁—新加坡经济走廊建设；大力实施广西北部湾经济区发展规划；加快建设中国—马来西亚钦州产业园区、中越跨境经济合作区、边境经济合作区等重大项目；加快建设中国·印尼经贸合作区，推动更多企业“走出去”，为推动中国—东盟友好合作贡献力量！

Foreword

H.E. Lan Tianli

Vice Co-chair and Secretary-General of the CAEXPO Organizing Committee
Vice-Governor of Guangxi Zhuang Autonomous Region

The China-ASEAN Expo (CAEXPO), advocated by the Chinese Premier Wen Jiabao and applauded by the heads of state/government of the 10 ASEAN member states, is jointly sponsored by the ministries of commerce or trade & industry of China and the 10 ASEAN countries and is organized by the People's Government of Guangxi Zhuang Autonomous Region. Having been successfully concluded for 8 straight sessions, it has forged an important platform for the friendly exchanges, business promotion and all-dimensional cooperation between China and ASEAN. With 8 years of development, it has grown to be a widely influential international event in the China-ASEAN Free Trade Area, and makes continuous new contribution to China's cooperation with ASEAN.

I. The CAEXPO builds a sound platform for bilateral cooperation across all dimensions.

The CAEXPO integrates friendly exchanges and economic and trading cooperation with bilateral collaboration in other fields, expanding and deepening the China-ASEAN cooperation. The previous 8 sessions have attracted 42 heads of state/government, over 1500 ministerial dignitaries and 316,000 exhibitors and trade visitors from China and the ASEAN member states, concluded a total trading volume worth US$11.69 billion and contracted international and Chinese domestic cooperation projects with total investment volumes hitting US$49.172 billion and RMB475.902 billion respectively. Meanwhile, over 200 high-end conferences, forums and programs have been arranged concurrently on trade, investment, Customs, quality supervision, harbors and ports, telecommunications, environment, society and culture. The CAEXPO has scored notable outcomes in promoting the China-ASEAN cooperation, in accelerating the construction of the China-ASEAN FTA.

Building a platform for friendly exchanges and driving economic and trading cooperation with political and diplomatic influence: Both Chinese and ASEAN leaders grant full support to the event and personally visit each of the sessions. During the fair period, bilateral meetings and talks between state leaders, ministers and local leaders are arranged to further promote political mutual understanding and trust. Each of the previous sessions has arranged meetings and talks between political leaders and business community, in a bid to drive the bilateral economic and trading cooperation, deepen the practical cooperation among businesses and thus bring more impetus to bilateral collaboration in culture, education and more of other domains.

Forging a platform for business promotion, enabling the fruits made in economic and trading cooperation to, in turn, cement political mutual trust and friendly exchanges: The CAEXPO works to arrange exhibitions that fit the construction progress of the China-ASEAN FTA and the economic development levels, endowments for natural resources and industrial mixes and features of China and the 10 ASEAN countries, and to gather enterprises, commodities, projects and capitals of the 11 countries. Therefore, it has translated the government-to-government paperwork agreement on the investment and trade facilitations of the China-ASEAN FTA into practical benefits for the businesses of both sides, accelerating the construction of this FTA.

The CAEXPO facilitates the exchanges between enterprises and industrial sectors of China and ASEAN and promotes the bilateral economic and trade cooperation. In 2004 when the 1st CAEXPO was held, the bilateral trading volume between China and ASEAN reached the goal of US$100 billion one year ahead of schedule, followed by the year 2007 that saw the goal of US$200 billion reached 3 years in advance. And the figure hit an all-time high of US$362.85 billion in 2011. The CAEXPO has played an important role in the process, for it has evidenced the China-ASEAN FTA as a win-win mechanism and has elevated the China-ASEAN Strategic Partnership to a higher level.

Building a platform for bilateral cooperation in various fields and providing institutional guarantee for the China-ASEAN cooperation in economy, trade, culture and multiple fields: With the China-ASEAN economic and trade cooperation being expanded and deepened, it has raised more and higher demands on relevant cooperation. To this end, the Chinese ministries or commissions will arrange a host of ministerial forums, conferences and programs targeting Customs, inspection and quarantine, finance, ports and harbors, logistics, education, culture and sports, etc., inviting relevant businesses, experts and scholars to talk and accommodate the new needs raised by fast economic and trade cooperation on relevant supporting services, making the economic and trade cooperation more relevant with social and cultural exchanges and providing institutional guarantee for the cooperation in the fields concerned, thus to promote the enduring and stable growth of the China-ASEAN friendly and cooperative relations. Additionally, the CAEXPO sets up the pavilion of Cities of Charm, aiming to showcase images and opportunities of the cities that are selected by China and the 10 ASEAN countries as their Cities of Charm for each session, and to promote the cooperation among those cities. And also a series of cultural and sport exchanges activities will be held concurrently to bolt the friendly exchanges between China and the ASEAN countries.

II. The CAEXPO accommodates the common needs of China and the 10 ASEAN countries for development and upholds the mighty goal they share of promoting win-win collaboration.

With the upswing of economic globalization and regional economic integration in the new century, leaders of China and the ASEAN countries made a joint decision to establish the China-ASEAN FTA, which gave birth to the CAEXPO, a timely event to accelerate the construction process of this FTA. Propelled by the CAEXPO, the China-ASEAN FTA has been established on schedule in recent years. And as the bilateral economic and trade cooperation growths rapidly, both China and ASEAN need the CAEXPO, a practical platform for exchanges and cooperation, to play a better role in promoting the bilateral reciprocal cooperation. The CAEXPO receives keen attention of the Chinese and ASEAN leaders. Chinese President Hu Jintao has given instructions on efforts to organize the event, and Chinese Premier Wen Jiabao has attended the event for two times. Other major leaders including H.E. Jia Qinglin, chairman of the National Committee of the Chinese People's Political Consultative Conference, Vice Premier Li Keqiang, former Vice President Zeng Qinghong, Vice Premier Wang Qishan, former Vice Premiers Wu Yi and Zeng Peiyan have visited the previous sessions. Cumulatively 32 ASEAN leaders have attended the previous 8 CAEXPOs. Among them, Cambodian Prime Minister Samdech Hun Sen has showed presence for 6 sessions, and Vietnamese Prime Minister Nguyen Tan Dung, former Lao Prime Minister Bouasone BOUPHAVANH and former Myanmar Prime Minister Soe Win have made attendance for 3 consecutive times. Starting from the 10th ASEAN-China Summit held in 2003, the CAEXPO has been mentioned in the Chairman's Statements for each year, receiving high acclaims of all Chinese and ASEAN leaders.

Over the past 8 years, with the joint efforts made by Chinese and ASEAN governments, businesses and media, the CAEXPO has established regular working mechanisms involving countries, departments and provinces.

(I) Effective organizing committees and perfect organizing structure

Perfect organizing structure is an important guarantee for the success of the CAEXPO. China and certain ASEAN member states including Vietnam, Lao PDR, Thailand and Indonesia have established the CAEXPO organizing committees of their own which are composed of different departments. The Chinese CAEXPO Organizing Committee consists of 15 ministries and commissions such as the Ministry of Commerce, the Ministry of Foreign Affairs and the China Council for the Promotion of International Trade and the People's Government of Guangxi Zhuang Autonomous Region. The first honorary chair of the Organizing Committee was former Vice Premier Wu Yi, and Vice Premier Wang Qishan becomes her successor after the new Chinese central government was formed in 2008, and Mr. Chen Deming, minister of commerce acts as the chair. The Organizing Committee arranges working meetings every year to coordinate the efforts in organizing the CAEXPO. It has built effective working mechanisms that provide strong back-up for the development of the event.

(II) A co-sponsoring mechanism of 11 countries that shores up bilateral win-win collaboration

The co-sponsoring mechanism involving 11 countries is a unique feature and foundation of the CAEXPO. And thanks to the close cooperation among the CAEXPO Co-organizers of the 11 countries, the CAEXPO's win-win co-sponsoring mechanism has been cemented year on year, which is enriched with a 3-layer working structure, namely, with ministers of commerce or trade & industry as the Co-chairs, official at DG level as the Vice Secretaries General and division directors as the Liaison Officials, and such negotiation mechanisms as the CAEXPO Senior Officials Meeting and Liaison Officials Meeting, coupled with practices like deciding the allocation of national pavilions through lots drawing, and inviting one ASEAN country as the Country of Honor for each CAEXPO, whose state leader will head a delegation to attend the event.

With the above measures, we have built and perfected a co-sponsoring mechanism that features equality, mutual respect, close collaboration and extensive and active participation, enabling the ASEAN member states to showcase their strength and potential more effectively and to contribute to the success and sustained development of the CAEXPO.

(III) Cooperation mechanism among Chinese domestic provinces and cities to promote their cooperation with ASEAN

The CAEXPO has established cooperation mechanisms with Chinese domestic provinces and cities over the past few years. Those provinces and municipalities that maintain close economic and trade relations with the ASEAN countries have become the CAEXPO's Special Partners, and major cities like Beijing, Shanghai, Tianjin, Suzhou, Shenzhen, Qinzhou and Hainan have been Cities of Charm of China for the previous sessions. Close cooperation between the CAEXPO and Chinese provinces and cities gives full play to the platform in promoting their cooperation with ASEAN.

(IV) Guangxi, the host province of the CAEXPO, has established a good mechanism of pooling all available resources in the province to organize such an event

Over the past 8 years, as the CAEXPO's host province, Guangxi maintains immense efforts to pool all existing resources for the preparation for each session. Guangxi has established the Guangxi Leadership Group of the CAEXPO and the CABIS, for which the governor acts as the Head, as well as the Command Center that is composed of all relevant government departments and institutions, in a bid to integrate their resources and coordinate their efforts in organizing the CAEXPO.

(V) Long-term cooperation mechanism among major chambers of commerce and trade associations of China and the 10 ASEAN countries to help mobilize the participation of businesses

Chambers of commerce, trade associations and enterprises of China and ASEAN remain important players in the CAEXPO, who also constitute a strong drive for the development of this event. The CAEXPO have emerged as a platform for deepening practical cooperation among enterprises. 40 Chinese and ASEAN chambers of commerce and trade associations have become its Supporting Chambers of Commerce. Active participation of those chambers of commerce, trade associations and enterprises enriches the CAEXPO and facilitates the construction of the China-ASEAN FTA and the comprehensive economic cooperation between China and ASEAN.

Apart from active Chinese and ASEAN businesses, the CAEXPO also captures keen interests of those of non-CAFTA countries and regions such as the United States, Japan, South Korea, France, Germany, Australia and Canada, which has enhanced and deepened the mutual understanding between China and ASEAN and those economies and expanded the influence of the China-ASEAN region as a whole on the global arena.

(VI) Cooperation mechanism among Chinese and international media that helps grow the CAEXPO's influence and recognition

The CAEXPO has forged partnerships with Chinese and ASEAN mainstream media, trade media and partner media of chambers of commerce, building a media network across the 10 ASEAN countries. Those media include mainstream media, financial media and media targeting specific industrial sectors in local, English and Chinese languages. They are either print media, online ones or TV and radio stations. With them, the CAEXPO builds a full-fledged promotion network and can reach different readers and audient of China and ASEAN. As the number of participating media grows year on year, the CAEXPO's popularity and influence are expanded and strengthened significantly.

III. Guangxi will maintain its successful practice and invest greater endeavor to well organize the CAEXPO to further promote the China-ASEAN friendly cooperation.

As the friendly cooperation between China and ASEAN enters a new round of two decades and the China-ASEAN FTA is striding forward, the China-ASEAN cooperation will soon see a new stage of in-depth development. Guangxi, the permanent host place of the CAEXPO, which is considered an important gateway and frontier of China's cooperation with the ASEAN, will play an increasingly significant role in the cooperation between the two sides. We will uphold the goal set by China's 12th Five-year Plan of building Guangxi a new base for China's cooperation with ASEAN, and will implement the State Council's Opinions on Further Promoting the Social and Economic Development of Guangxi and the Development Scheme of the Guangxi Beibu Gulf Economic Zone, to achieve more successful CAEXPO, leverage the geographical advantages of Guangxi and foster better platforms for the bilateral cooperation between China and ASEAN. The focus of efforts will be put on the 3 aspects as follows:

To strengthen coordination and perfect the CAEXPO's long-term mechanisms: We will press ahead with more aggressive opening-up strategy to promote development, work to fit the new changes happening in Guangxi and to accommodate the new demands raised by the dramatic economic and social development, as a results of the campaign to grow its GDP to one trillion yuan. We will give full play to the Leadership Group for Guangxi's Opening-up and Cooperation with ASEAN and its Coordination Office, strengthen integration and allocation of resources for organizing the CAEXPO and improve the CAEXPO's long-term working mechanisms, in a bid to maximize the role of the event as a platform for cooperation and upgrade Guangxi's outward economic cooperation.

To continue such a practice of pooling all strength and resources of the province to organize the CAEXPO: Guangxi will keep pace with the development of the China-ASEAN FTA and will work on more successful and fruitful CAEXPOs in the years to come, making it a more vital player in promoting the China-ASEAN friendly cooperation and expanding the accessibility and coverage of the CAFTA's facilitations. We will make greater efforts to maintain the CAEXPO a high–end event as always, and work to promote the friendly exchanges and collaboration between political and business communities; We will continue to renew the CAEXPO's exhibitions and programs, give more prominence to the distinctive products of both sides and promote investment cooperation by mobilizing more Chinese enterprises to invest in ASEAN, helping the Chinese and ASEAN enterprises to enjoy the facilitations and business opportunities of the China–ASEAN FTA; We will further optimize the CAEXPO's official website and the China–ASEAN Center's service platform, making the CAEXPO an ever–holding one; We will vigorously expand cultural, educational and sports cooperation, leveraging the significant role of the CAEXPO in driving bilateral cooperation in those fields expect for economy, trade and investment. We will perfect the Nanning Channel for China–ASEAN cooperation and upgrade the comprehensive bilateral cooperation.

To make good use of CAEXPO and build new platforms for the friendly cooperation between China and ASEAN: Guangxi will maximize the role of the CAEXPO and work to perfect infrastructures, particularly the transportation facilities, and strengthen connectivity. We will aggressively press ahead with the Pan Beibu Gulf Economic Cooperation, the Greater Mekong Sub–regional Cooperation, the China–Vietnam Two Corridors & One Rim Cooperation program and the construction of the Nanning–Singapore Economic Corridor; We will actively implement the Development Scheme of Guangxi Beibu Gulf Economic Zone; We will accelerate the building of the China–Malaysia Qinzhou Industrial Park, the China–Vietnam Cross Border Economic Cooperation Zone and other major border economic cooperation zones projects; We will fuel the construction progress of the China–Indonesia Economic Cooperation Zone and encourage more Chinese enterprises to embark on outward investment and economic cooperation, making our new contribution to the friendly cooperation between China and ASEAN.

本届概述

历史的长河奔腾不息，走到了不平凡的2011年。

2011年是中国—东盟建立对话关系20周年、中国—东盟友好交流年和中国—东盟自贸区建成1周年。在此背景下举办第八届中国—东盟博览会具有特殊而深远的意义。20年来，中国—东盟合作领域不断拓展深化，双方关系从对话关系上升为战略伙伴关系；中国—东盟博览会走过8年，常办常新，推动中国—东盟自贸区加速发展，成果显著。中国与东盟友好交流，合作共赢，给双方人民带来巨大福祉，为本地区的和平稳定与繁荣发展作出了重要贡献。

2011年10月21日至10月26日，第八届中国—东盟博览会在中国广西南宁成功举办。同期举办第八届中国—东盟商务与投资峰会。中国和东盟国家领导人、部长级贵宾、国际组织代表、各国商协会会长、世界知名企业家共同出席本次盛会。在中国和东盟共办方共同努力下，第八届中国—东盟博览会作为中国—东盟建立对话关系20周年系列纪念活动的重要内容，凸显“20年合作拓展，自贸区成果显著，博览会常办常新”

2011年10月21日，第八届中国—东盟博览会在中国广西南宁隆重开幕

Opening Ceremony of the 8th CAEXPO in Nanning, Guangxi, China on October 21, 2011

的特点。本届博览会创造了更多商机，进一步提升了中国—东盟友好合作水平，加深了传统友谊，谱写了中国—东盟共赢发展的新篇章。

一　政治外交影响力大，政商互动成效好

作为中国—东盟建立对话关系20周年纪念活动的重要组成部分，第八届中国—东盟博览会受到中国和东盟各国的高度重视，规格高，政治外交影响力大，推动中国—东盟战略伙伴关系迈上了新台阶。

中国国务院总理温家宝、马来西亚总理纳吉布、柬埔寨首相洪森、缅甸副总统吴丁昂敏乌、老挝副总理宋沙瓦、泰国副总理吉滴叻、越南副总理阮春福出席了本届博览会。东盟秘书长素林以及中国和东盟各国商务、环保、质检、金融、电信等多个领域的部长出席本届盛会。出席本次博览会的部长级贵宾有240人，其中中方141人，东盟和其他国家部长级贵宾99人。中国和东盟10国商协会会长、知名企业家、社会各界知名人士出席盛会。

本届博览会会期举行了6场国家领导人会见、12场广西壮族自治区领导与东盟国家领导人和代表团团长、友好城市代表团的会见，举行了巡馆、博览会开幕式、商务与投资峰会开幕式、欢迎宴会、中马钦州产业园区签约及揭牌仪式、主题国"魅力之城"开馆仪式、主题国商品馆开馆仪式、马来西亚领导人与中国企业家CEO圆桌对话会、泰国领导人与中泰企业家见面会等一系列活动。

本届博览会政商互动更多，更有实效。除了马来西亚、泰国领导人与企业家见面会外，还举行了中国—缅甸企业家座谈会、海南省领导与老挝计划投资部副部长会谈等对接活动。会期政商高端对接活动共22场，促进了中国国内各省与东盟及区域外国家的务实合作。

2011年是中国—东盟建立对话关系20周年

2011: The 20th anniversary of ASEAN-China dialogue relations

中国和东盟各国领导人在会期分别发表了讲话，充分肯定了双方20年合作成果，深入分析了当前形势，指明了下一步合作的方向。这对于充分发挥博览会平台作用，进一步深化双方友好合作，具有指导意义。其中，中国国务院总理温家宝在中国—东盟商务与投资峰会开幕式主旨演讲中提出了共同建设好自贸区、大力推进互联互通、扩大双方投资合作、深化区域经济合作、拓展人文领域交流等五条建议。马来西亚总理纳吉布在第八届中国—东盟博览会开幕式致辞时提出，中国—东盟应进一步加强双方的沟通和相互理解。他认为，本届博览会将环保和可持续发展作为重点主题，意义也在于改变我们自己的行为方式，发展更清洁环保的技术，降低排放，确保我们的子孙能从我们手里继承一个清洁、安全和健康的星球。柬埔寨首相洪森也提出了加强绿色农业合作等建议。

二　开幕式和闭幕式隆重热烈，凸显国际性及创新和组织能力

2011年10月21日上午9时，第八届中国—东盟博览会在南宁国际会展中心开幕。南宁国际会展中心朱槿花厅装扮得隆重、热烈。大红的地毯、灯笼，透出喜庆的气氛；绿意盎然的背景装饰，烘托出绿色环保的主题。

第八届中国—东盟博览会开幕式盛况

Opening Ceremony of the 8th CAEXPO

第八届中国—东盟博览会主题国马来西亚的国际贸易和工业部部长穆斯塔法和东盟秘书长素林共同主持开幕式。广西壮族自治区主席马飚、中国商务部国际贸易谈判代表兼副部长高虎城、马来西亚总理纳吉布先后致辞。期间，播放了精彩短片，回顾中国与东盟友好交往的历史，展示中国与东盟友好合作的丰硕成果。

第八届中国—东盟博览会开幕式形象地表达出博览会11国共办、领导人亲自推动的特点，反映中国—东盟建立对话关系20周年的辉煌成

就，展示博览会促进中国—东盟友好交流、推动自贸区建设取得的成果和作出的贡献。开幕式上举行了有11国青少年参加的中国—东盟青少年交流活动中心揭牌仪式，展示了中国与东盟友谊代代相传的深刻寓意，博览会取得的成果得到更具体的展现。

开幕式创意新、构思巧，传递新寓意。开幕式主舞台和背景布置都与2011年博览会特殊背景、重点主题相结合。剪彩方式进行了创新，第三届博览会开幕式上为领导人献上剪彩道具“珍珠”的少女再一次来到开幕式现场，将剪彩道具“花朵”交给了中国与东盟10国青少年，各国青少年用本国语言介绍自己并给领导人献上象征友谊与希望的绣球和表达庆贺与祝福的花朵，体现了中国与东盟友好合作代代传承以及博览会常办常新。博览会开幕式受到了中国和东盟国家领导人、政府官员、商协会会长、企业家的普遍赞誉。

闭幕式和闭幕新闻发布会联合举办，形式新颖，意义深刻，体现了本届博览会在共办机制、展会组织等方面取得了新的成效。

三　展览内容和形式创新，经贸成效取得新突破

本届博览会根据中国—东盟经贸合作快速发展的新形势，新增南宁华南城展区，形成“一会三馆”（南宁国际会展中心、广西展览馆、南宁华南城展览中心三个展馆）的格局，吸引了各国企业踊跃参与。本届博览会总展位数4700个，参展企业2300家，参展参会客商5.06万人，创历届新高。

中国国内参展企业质量保持较高，参展商品更契合东盟国家需求。中国国内各省区市和港、澳、台地区共申请主会场展位2865个，超过主会场国内规划总展位数的30.2%。国际经济合作展区和工程机械、运输车辆展区重复参展率高达90%。参展的名牌企业比往年多，许多企业推出更加契合东盟国家市场的产品。

第八届中国—东盟博览会东盟商品展区

ASEAN Commodities Section of the 8th CAEXPO

东盟和区域外企业参展规模和专业化进一步提高。本届博览会东盟及区域外国家使用展位数均为历届最好水平，6个东盟国家包馆。设立东盟品牌展区，41家东盟品牌企业参展。首次设立大宗商品展区，吸引棕油、木材、矿产品、大米等大宗商品企业参展。博览会上东盟国家优势商品按行业布展，特装率超过90%，专业化水平进一步提高。区域外企业参展更加积极，区域外国家展位数同比增长26%。

采购商数量和质量进一步提高，会期贸易配对针对性强。东盟采购团组有70多个，其中东盟采购商团组数比上届增加20%。会期举办了联合国采购说明会、参展商讲坛等配对活动，还为10个东盟采购团组和1个加拿大采购团组的214家企业和机构举行了4场专场配对会。专门为越南、马来西亚等国组织了国家专场贸易配对会，创新举办中泰橡胶研讨会，组织泰国橡胶企业与青岛、上海的企业进行了配对。举办中马大宗商品配对会，组织60多家马来西亚和中国的棕油、橡胶企业进行了对接。2011年还首次举办了行业协会联谊会，邀请东盟国家的食品农产品、林木等商协会与中方对接。

投资合作进一步机制化，突出“走出去”特色。会期举办博览会投资合作圆桌会议，使博览会成为各国投资促进机构相互交流、发布政策和项目信息、政府与企业间沟通的重要渠道。本届博览会安排了中国“走出去”企业与金融机构对接活动，包括：中国—东盟基础设施投融资合作论坛、金融支持企业“走出去”洽谈会、企业股权（债券）投融资交易会等，为企业投资东盟提供务实的金融支持。会期东盟各国举行了推介会，专业观众踊跃参会，现场座位供不应求。

本届博览会经贸成效取得新突破。商品贸易成交额18.07亿美元，同比增长5.6 %。签约国际合作项目投资额74.2亿美元，同比增长10.86%；签订国内经济合作项目投资额731.1亿元，同比增长8.39%。

四　系列会议和交流活动富有成效，进一步促进多领域合作

与本届博览会同期举办的第八届中国—东盟商务与投资峰会以“深化区域合作，实现共同繁荣”为主题，与会的中国、东盟以及世界10多个国家和地区的政府高官、商界领袖、企业精英、区域组织代表、知名专家学者和媒体记者就进一步深化区域行业之间的务实合作、实现共同发展和繁荣进行讨论和展望。

本届博览会以“环保合作”为重点主题，举办了2011中国—东盟环保合作论坛，并围绕质检、金融、太阳能、药品安全、森林、文化产业、出版、人口与发展、大众体育等领域，举办14个高层国际会议和交流活动，开展了部长级磋商和对话，研究解决这些领域合作中出现的问题，形成更多领域的合作机制，取得了新的成果。

第八届中国—东盟博览会上举办的2011中国—东盟环保合作论坛

The China-ASEAN Forum on Environmental Protection Cooperation 2011 held during the 8th CAEXPO

环保合作首次作为中国—东盟博览会主题，本届博览会期间举行了2011中国—东盟环保合作论坛。中国与东盟多数国家属于发展中国家和新兴工业化国家，且山水相连，在环境保护与发展领域面临许多共同挑战，实现区域、经济、社会、环境的可持续发展一直都是中国与东盟对话合作的主旋律。随着中国—东盟环保合作不断深化，环保合作已经成为双方11大重点合作领域之一。论坛上，中国国家环境保护部官员与东盟国家环保机构官员及相关机构代表共同启动了中国—东盟绿色使者计划。该计划是响应中国总理温家宝在2010年10月第十三次中国—东盟（10+1）领导人会议上的倡议，为中国和东盟国家提高公众环境意识和能力建设提供支持。

博览会不仅促成了绿色商品交易，还为跨国企业搭建了环保技术交流的平台。来自中国和东盟各国的100多位政府官员、专家学者和企业代表参加了中国—东盟太阳能政策对话与技术洽谈会，与会者积极挖掘中国与东盟各国在太阳能领域的无限商机。太阳能产品也成为本届博览会先进技术展节能环保类别的主角，深受现场观众的欢迎，吸引众多客商前来洽谈订购。

会期举办的第一届中国—东盟TBT合作部长会议成果务实。会议围绕“产品质量与安全”这一主题，深入讨论了中国和东盟在产品质量安全领域所面临的问题和挑战，并特别就加强中国—东盟在该领域合作的重要性和应该共同采取的措施进行了深入讨论，会议审议通过了《中国—东盟关于加强产品质量安全合作的联合声明》（《南宁联合声明》），会议发表了有关消除技术性贸易壁垒的《南宁联合宣言》。

中国—东盟出版博览会达成了关于出版合作的《南宁共识》。首次在广西亮相的2011中国—东盟出版博览会分外吸引众人眼球，为中国—东盟博览会注入了新的文化元素。1万多种东盟原版图书和国内精品图书汇聚南宁，来自东盟10国的出版界官员、出版发行协会和出版公司的代表，与中国11家中央和地方出版集团、5家数字出版企业共聚一堂，就加强出版交流合作事宜进行了深入的交流和探讨，并达成有关中国与东盟图书出版界交流合作的《南宁共识》。

第三届中国—东盟金融论坛围绕“务实与创新，中国—东盟区域经济发展的金融合作及财政合作”主题进行了深入研讨，达成广泛共识，促进了中国—东盟金融合作。这是中国—东盟金融合作与发展领袖论坛第三次成功举办，在往届论坛基础上，本届论坛内容设置更加注重务实性和服务性。论坛紧密围绕区域内货币结算、区域经济发展的金融调控、金融财政合作与发展等问题，分设多个议题进行研讨，其中包括“中国—东盟经济技术合作的金融与财政支持”、“区域内货币结算与中国—东盟自由贸易区的金融合作及财务合作”、“金融合作与区域经济发展”、“企业融资上市与区域多元化资本市场发展”、“中国—东盟自由贸易区经济金融发展的相关政策与服务支撑”等。通过金融高层沟通，推进双方达成深入共识。会期还举办一系列投资促进活动，为中国企业“走出去”搭建支撑平台，如金融机构支持企业“走出去”交流洽谈会、企业股权（债券）投融资交易会、投融资项目对接会等，强化金融对区域经济发展的服务。通过举办中国—东盟经济金融合作智库对话、发表中国—东盟金融合作发展机制研究成果等形式，为区域金融合作谋划长远机制，为中国—东盟的商界和金融界开展务实交流和合作提供理论依据和参考指导。

中国—东盟人口与家庭发展论坛作为第八届中国—东盟博览会的首个论坛于10月11日在南宁开幕。论坛旨在进一步推动中国与东盟国家在人口与家庭发展领域的合作与交流，共同提升家庭发展能力，促进人口均衡型、资源节约型、环境友好型的和谐可持续发展社会的建设。

第四届中国—东盟智库论坛围绕“新形势下的中国—东盟合作”主题，围绕自贸区建成1周年，扩大中国—东盟政治、经济、文化合作领域，深化区域行业之间的务实合作，实现共同发展和繁荣进行讨论和展望。与会专家认为，中国—东盟建立对话关系20年来，双方始终以和平友好，发展共赢为主题、以友好合作为主线，见证了从全面对话伙伴、睦邻互信伙伴到战略伙伴的发展历程。双方建立了包括领导人、部长、高官和工作组在内的一整套合作机制，在经贸、投资、农业、金融、信息通讯、基础设施建设等20多个领域开展务实合作，建成了全球覆盖人口最多、区域最广的自贸区。与会专家建议，中国—东盟自由贸易区建成之后，应着重充分利用原产地规则，扩大双边的投资贸易合作，重视产品质量和可持续发展，加强互联互通建设，朝着建立中国—东盟经济共同体，朝着更高的目标迈进。

2011中国—东盟文化产业论坛旨在推动文化产业合作纳入中国—东盟正式合作机制之中，有效促进文化产业在各相关国家中的成长与发展，推动中国—东盟自由贸易区的建设。论坛主题是“博物馆运营管理与文化产品创意开发”。200多位来自中国与东盟各国的文化官员、博物馆馆长、专家，围绕“经济全球化、文化产业发展背景下的博物馆运营管理”、“博物馆文化产品创意开发”和“关于国际间博物馆合作交流的建议”等议题展开讨论。

中国—东盟药品安全论坛暨药品监督管理局局长会议以“加强交流，保障安全，共谋发展，中国—东盟自贸区发展形势下的药品安全合作”为主题，来自东盟10国和中国的食品药品监管官员和专家针对各国药品法律体系和药品监管体制、体系等议题进行了交流。

中国—东盟旅游促进减贫研讨会各方达成共识，中国和东盟可以通过旅游合作，探索中国—东盟各国之间的民间资本进入旅游业，开发区域内旅游资源，促进中国和区域内减贫。

会期举办的其他会议论坛和交流活动都取得了良好成效，为中国与东盟开展经贸和人文领域合作提供了机制保障。

五 宣传报道形式有创新，报道持续时间长，提升了博览会品牌影响力

第八届中国—东盟博览会作为中国—东盟建立对话关系20周年系列纪念活动的重要组成部分，受到中外媒体的广泛关注。同时，博览会宣传推介也与中国—东盟建立对话关系20周年系列纪念活动有机结合，扩大了博览会的品牌影响力。

第十三届“大地飞歌”南宁国际民歌艺术节盛况

The 13th Nanning International Arts Festival of Folk Songs & Gala Show for the Inauguration of the 8th CAEXPO

中外媒体对第八届中国—东盟博览会的报道

Chinese and foreign media zoom at the 8th CAEXPO

博览会举办前，广西参与主办或承办了中国—东盟建立对话关系20周年系列纪念活动，包括：中国—东盟建立对话关系纪念招待会、中国—东盟友谊知识竞赛、中国—东盟互联互通战略研讨会、中国—东盟媒体汽车拉力赛、东盟经贸记者培训班、外语比赛等，进一步发挥了广西和博览会在中国—东盟合作中的作用。其中，中国—东盟建立对话关系纪念招待会文艺演出取得圆满成功。中国国务委员戴秉国，广西壮族自治区领导郭声琨、马飚、陈武、余远辉以及中国—东盟协会负责人、中方有关部委负责人、东盟国家驻华使节等观看了文艺演出并给予高度评价。中国—东盟互联互通战略研讨会深入探讨了中国—东盟互联互通合作和未来发展方向，宣传了广西在互联互通中的作用，得到各方面的好评。中国—东盟友谊知识竞赛增进了中国与东盟各国青年的相互了解，巩固了睦邻友好基础，宣传了广西和博览会在中国—东盟合作中的作用。

第八届中国—东盟博览会继续受到中国国内外主流媒体和专业媒体的高度关注。博览会到会采访媒体和记者比上届更多。本届到会采访的媒体共275家1738名记者，分别比上届增加38.19%和19.2%。其中，东盟媒体69家，而且东盟媒体比上届增长20%，在中国境内举行的同类活动中，参会东盟媒体和记者是最多的。据不完全统计，共刊发有关新闻稿件8300多篇，相关网络记录380多万条，影响力进一步扩大。

会期，中国中央电视台、香港凤凰卫视、香港亚洲电视、广西电视台与东盟及区域外的媒体采取连线互动、专访等多种形式报道本届博览会。其中，马来西亚总理纳吉布、东盟秘书长素林等政要接受了多家媒体的专访。据不完全统计，中外媒体累计发稿8300多篇；网络播发相关新闻（含转载）16万篇，图片3.178万幅，视频415个，网页记录达380多万条；还通过微博和手机报等新的传播方式，扩大宣传面，提升了影响力。中外媒体对会期重要活动进行了大范围、深层次、聚焦式的宣传报道，给人留下深刻印象，营造了隆重热烈的氛围，引起强烈反响。

重大活动的现场直播场次多、规模大。中央电视台、新华网、人民网、中国新闻网等众多媒体对博览会开幕式、商务与投资峰会开幕式等重大活动进行了现场直播。对马来西亚总理纳吉布与中国企业CEO圆桌对话会、泰国副总理吉滴叻与中泰企业家见面会进行了网络直播。

东盟媒体及区域外媒体高度关注，重点报道。泰国、文莱、印尼、菲律宾、越南等东盟国家以及美国、日本等国家的主流媒体，均在头版头条或重要版面刊登、发表博览会相关新闻报道。

本届博览会采取多种举措，为媒体提供更加快捷、周到的新闻宣传服务。开幕式、巡馆等重要活动结束后30分钟在新闻中心提供图文共享资料，其他各场活动均于2小时内在博览会官方网站提供图文和视频资料。

本届博览会围绕中国—东盟合作的新特点，宣传报道声势大，持续时间长，亮点多。广西参与主办或承办一系列国家层面的中国—东盟建立对话关系20周年系列纪念活动，为博览会的举办营造了良好氛围。会前还制作了博览会歌曲集光碟，设计制作更多吉祥物等各种纪念品，提高了博览会的品牌影响力。

六　各项服务更加机制化、规范化，服务质量进一步提高

第八届中国—东盟博览会的布展、现场管理、客户服务等各项服务工作都有了新的提高。

形象搭建突出主题，特装展位数量明显攀升。展馆形象设计融入了本年度的特殊背景以及“环保合作”等多种元素，形象布置主题鲜明，色彩和谐。会展中心特装面积占64%，较往届相比，特装展位数量明显增多。

现场管理得到突破，管理体系更加科学。配合本届博览会重点主题，绿色管理理念首次明确应用到博览会现场管理中。现场节能办公、现场无烟化控制等成为博览会现场管理的新内容。采用“全球眼”对现场绿色管理全程监督。联合执法的内容也进一步拓宽。通关运输、现场物流、保洁工作等服务质量进一步提高。继续开通了南宁往返东盟国家主要城市的10条航线。志愿者管理更加规范，顺利完成了服务博览会的工作。

七　发挥平台作用，带动广西经济社会发展

第八届中国—东盟博览会进一步密切了广西与东盟的友好往来。会

期，广西壮族自治区领导与东盟国家领导人、各国代表团、友好城市代表团等举行了12场会见，就共建广西北部湾经济区，共同推进泛北部湾经济合作、大湄公河次区域合作、南宁—新加坡经济走廊、跨境经济合作区，促进中国—东盟自贸区发展等问题，达成了广泛共识。缅甸副总统吴丁昂敏乌顺访了广西玉林市，并出席了中国（玉林）中小企业商机博览会。

本届博览会服务了广西各地市和各部门。会期展示了中国—马来西亚钦州产业园的形象和钦州对外合作成果，举办了中马钦州产业园项目签约仪式，推进钦州重点项目签订实施。组织南宁市高新区企业参加博览会投资促进活动，组织马来西亚代表团参观考察南宁高新区企业。博览会秘书处还分别与广西相关地市合作举办中国—东盟（柳州）汽车、工程机械及零部件博览会、中国—东盟（百色）现代农业展示交易会、中国(玉林)中小企业商机博览会、梧州宝石节等活动，带动广西会展业发展。广西商务、投资促进、科技、农业、旅游、新闻出版局等多个部门在博览会举办了一系列面向东盟的合作交流活动，成效显著。

本届博览会促进了南宁市服务业的发展。据广西统计局统计，10月20—26日，南宁市酒店平均入住率达51.03%，累计接待宾客8.62万人，其中境外宾客1.19万人，比上届增长6.47%。南宁市12家大型商场共实现商品销售总额1.54亿元，日平均销售额2205万元。南宁市五大公路客运站累计出发和到站车次50632次；铁路旅客到达17.15万人次，发送16.81万人次；南宁吴圩国际机场累计起、降航班1286次，经由航空抵达和发送的旅客人数分别达到6.8万人次和7.1万人次。以上数据均比日常大幅增加。2011年底，南宁机场旅客吞吐量超过600万人次，创历史新高。

第八届中国—东盟博览会结束后，广西统计局对南宁市民进行了第八届博览会的满意度调查，83.84%的被访者感到满意。其中认为非常满意的占33.22%。

中马钦州产业园区签字仪式
China-Malaysia Qinzhou Industrial Park Signing Ceremony

The 8th CHINA-ASEAN EXPO

Overview

The year 2011 was destined to be remarkable in history.

It was the year marking the 20th anniversary of ASEAN–China dialogue relations, the Year of China–ASEAN Friendly Exchanges, and the first year upon the establishment of China–ASEAN Free Trade Area. Therefore, it was of special significance to hold the 8th China–ASEAN Expo in this context. Over the past 20 years, the cooperation between China and ASEAN has been continuously expanded and deepened, while the bilateral relationship has been upgraded from dialogue to strategic partnership. The China–ASEAN Expo has been held for 8 straight years with each session showing new features and outcomes. It has scored remarkable achievements in accelerating the growth of China–ASEAN Free Trade Area (CAFTA). The friendly exchange and win–win cooperation between China and ASEAN have brought enormous benefits to people from both sides, and have made important contributions to the regional peace, stability and prosperity.

From October 21st to 26th, 2011, the 8th China–ASEAN Expo (CAEXPO), as well as the 8th China–ASEAN Business & Investment Summit (CABIS), were successfully held in Nanning, Guangxi, China. Heads of state/government, ministers and other VIPs from China and ASEAN countries, representatives of international organizations, chairmen of business associations from different countries and the world–famous entrepreneurs attended these grand events. As one of the important programs to celebrate the 20th anniversary of the ASEAN–China dialogue relations, the 8th CAEXPO highlighted the concept of 20 Years of Cooperation, Fruitful CAFTA, Ever–improving CAEXPO. The 8th CAEXPO has created more business opportunities, further improved the friendly cooperation and traditional friendship, and wrote a new chapter of the win–win development of China and ASEAN.

I. Strong Political and Diplomatic Influence, Effective Government–to–Business Interactions

As an important event celebrating the 20th anniversary of ASEAN–China dialogue relations, the 8th CAEXPO has become a focus of China and the ASEAN countries. This grand trade event, with high–profiled participants and strong political & diplomatic influence, has lifted China – ASEAN strategic partnership to a new level.

H.E. Wen Jiabao, premier of the State Council of China, H.E. Dato' Sri Mohd Najib Tun Abdul Razak, prime minister of Malaysia, H.E. Samdech Hun Sen, prime minister of Cambodia, H.E. Thiha Thura U Tin Aung Myint Oo, vice–president of Myanmar, H.E. Somsavat LENGSAVAD, deputy prime minister of the Lao PDR and H.E. Kittiratt Na–Ranong, deputy prime minister of Thailand, H.E. Nguyen Xuan Phuc, deputy prime minister of Vietnam showed their presence at the CAEXPO. H.E. Dr. Surin Pitsuwan, secretary–general of ASEAN and the ministers in charge of commerce, environmental protection, quality inspection, financial, telecommunications and other fields from China and the ASEAN countries also attended the event. There were altogether 240 ministerial–level VIPs at this year's CAEXPO, including 141 ones from China and 99 from ASEAN member states and other countries. Chairmen of chambers of commerce and trade associations of China and 10 ASEAN countries, world–renowned entrepreneurs and other celebrities from different fields attended the grand events as well.

During the CAEXPO, various meetings were arranged for participants at different level, including 6 bilateral ones among state leaders, 12 meetings of Guangxi leaders with ASEAN leaders, heads of government delegation, and heads of delegations of Guangxi's sister cities. A series of programs, including pavilion tours of VIPs, opening ceremony of the CAEXPO and that of the CABIS, welcome banquet, signing and launching ceremony of China–Malaysia Qinzhou Industrial Park, inaugural ceremony of both the Pavilion of City of Charm and the Commodity Pavilion of Malaysia, the 8th CAEXPO Country of Honor, the Roundtable Dialogue between Malaysian state leader and Chinese CEOs, and Thai state leader's meeting with entrepreneurs from both China and Thailand etc.

This CAEXPO has promoted more active interactions between political leaders and entrepreneurs, thus achieving more substantial results. Other than the meetings of Malaysia and Thailand leaders and the entrepreneurs, there were also many business–matching activities, such as China–Myanmar Business Seminar, talks between Hainan provincial leader and Lao vice–minister of planning and investment. All 22 high–end government–to–business interaction activities were held during the CAEXPO, which have promoted the pragmatic cooperation between Chinese domestic provinces/cities with ASEAN countries and those outside the region.

Heads of state/government of China and the ASEAN countries delivered speeches, in which they fully recognized the outcomes of 20–year bilateral cooperation, profoundly analyzed the current situation, and pointed out the direction of future cooperation. These speeches would serve as the guidance for better using the CAEXPO as a good platform and further deepening the bilateral friendly cooperation. For instance, in the keynote speech of Chinese Premier Wen Jiabao at the opening ceremony of the CABIS, Premier Wen put forth five proposals, including co–building the CAFTA, forcefully promoting connectivity, expanding bilateral investment cooperation, deepening regional economic cooperation, and broadening people–to–people exchanges. As said by H.E. Dato'Sri Mohd Najib Tun Abdul Razak, prime minister of Malaysia at the 8th CAEXPO opening ceremony, China and the ASEAN countries should strengthen bilateral communication and mutual understanding. As for the Prime Minister Najib, this year's CAEXPO highlighted environmental protection and sustainable development as its theme, indicating that what we can do is to change our ways of life and, by promoting cleaner technologies and reducing fossil fuel emissions, to ensure that our children could have a clean, safe and healthy planet. H.E. Samdech Hun Sen, prime minister of Cambodia also proposed the strengthening of cooperation in green agriculture and other fields.

II. Grand and Ingenious Opening and Closing Ceremonies Featuring the CAEXPO as a Professional-operated International Event with Innovative Ideas

At 9am, October 21st, the 8th CAEXPO was grandly opened in Nanning International Convention and Exhibition Center, whose Chinese Hibiscus Hall was decorated with a giant green backdrop for emphasizing the theme of environmental protection cooperation. Red carpets on the floor and lanterns hung above have all created a festive atmosphere.

The Honorable Dato' Sri Mustapha Mohamed, minister of international trade and industry of Malaysia, the 8th CAEXPO Country of Honor, and H.E. Dr. Surin Pitsuwan, secretary-general of ASEAN jointly presided at the opening ceremony. H.E. Ma Biao, governor of Guangxi Zhuang autonomous region, H.E. Gao Hucheng, China international trade representative and vice-minister of commerce and H.E. Dato' Sri Mohd Najib Tun Abdul Razak, prime minister of Malaysia all addressed the ceremony. During the ceremony, short videos were played, reviewing the history of the amicable exchanges and fruitful results of the friendly cooperation between China and ASEAN.

The 8th CAEXPO opening ceremony has vividly portrayed the fact that the event is co-sponsored by China and the 10 ASEAN countries and joint promoted by their leaders. It also reflected the brilliant achievements of China-ASEAN dialogue relations in the past two decades, and manifested the results and contributions of the CAEXPO in promoting China-ASEAN friendly communication and the development of CAFTA. The opening ceremony also included a launching ceremony of China-ASEAN Youth Exchange & Activity Center, which was attended by teenagers from China and the ASEAN countries, showing that the traditional friendship of both sides would be passed down from generation to generation. It was also a specific achievement scored by the CAEXPO.

The opening ceremony was full of innovative ideas and smart designs that carried new connotations. Both the main stage and backdrop decoration well fit with the 2011 CAEXPO's special significance and its Theme of the Year. The ribbon-cutting moment was also innovated, with young ladies, who served the pearls as the inauguration tool to the leaders at the 3rd CAEXPO opening ceremony, coming back to the stage again. This time, they passed the flowers as tool to the teenagers from China and 10 ASEAN countries. These adolescents introduced themselves in their native languages and then offered the embroidery balls representing friendship and hope, and flowers expressing congratulations and blessings to the leaders, which symbolized that the time-honored bilateral friendship would passed down from generation to generation, and the CAEXPO will make continuous efforts in innovation. The opening ceremony has received wide appreciation from Chinese and ASEAN state leaders, government officials, chairmen of business associations and entrepreneurs.

The closing ceremony and press conference were combined with novel form and profound meaning, which demonstrated the new achievements of this CAEXPO in terms of the co-sponsorship mechanism and exhibition management, etc.

III. Innovative Content and Forms & New Breakthrough in the Trade and Economic Outcomes

Given the rapid development of China-ASEAN business cooperation, the CAEXPO opened a new venue, besides the existing two exhibitions centers, to meet the needs of the swarmed-in exhibitors. It has now three venues, i.e., Nanning International Convention and Exhibition Center, Guangxi Exhibition Hall, and Nanning South China City, which all open arms to entrepreneurs from different countries. The 8th CAEXPO set up 4700 booths in total, and 2300 exhibitors and 50,600 visitors participated in the event, reaching a new historical high.

Quality Chinese domestic exhibitors brought with them quality products well fit for the needs of ASEAN countries. Chinese domestic provinces/cities and its Hong Kong SAR, Macao SAR and Taiwan altogether applied for 2865 booths in the main exhibition venue, which exceeded by 30.2% the originally-planned booth number there. The repeated participation rate in the exhibitions of International Economic Cooperation, Engineering Machinery and Vehicles was up to 90%. There were more brand enterprises attending the event than the past years. Many enterprises also launched products more catering to the ASEAN markets.

Larger exhibition scale and better quality of exhibitors are seen from the ASEAN countries and beyond. The booth number used by the ASEAN exhibitors and those from other countries and regions also reached the highest level ever, with 6 ASEAN countries chartering independent exhibition halls to set up their own commodity hall. The ASEAN Brand Gallery was established and showcased 41 famous-brand enterprises. The Bulky-trade Commodities Exhibition (mainly raw materials) was set up for the first time to display suppliers of palm oil, timber, mineral products and rice. The advantageous commodities of ASEAN countries were sorted by industries, with 90% of the booths being customized, showing the further improvement in specialization. The enterprises from countries and regions beyond the ASEAN proved to be more active in attending the exhibition, as their booth number increased by 26% compared to the same period of last year.

More quality buyers visited the event, thus assured the effectiveness of the CAEXPO trade-matching programs. There were more than 70 buying missions coming from the ASEAN member nations, 20% more than the previous year. The matching activities such as the UN Procurement Presentation and the exhibitors' rostrum were held, as well as 4 matching programs specifically held for 214 enterprises and organizations from 10 ASEAN sourcing groups and a Canadian sourcing group. The CAEXPO also held theme trade-matching programs for Vietnam and Malaysia.

China–Thailand Rubber Seminar was organized for matching the Thai rubber suppliers with Chinese enterprises from Qingdao and Shanghai. It also arranged a Commodity Matching Fair for enterprises of China and Malaysia, which had attracted more than 60 palm oil and rubber companies from Malaysia and China to meet for business talks. The 8th CAEXPO also ran an Industrial Associations Networking Program for the first time, inviting business associations of food, agricultural products and forestry from the ASEAN countries to meet with Chinese businesses.

Investment cooperation mechanism was further perfected, highlighting the "Going Global" of Chinese enterprises. CAEXPO Roundtable Meeting on Investment Cooperation was held to make the event an important channel for investment promotion agencies of different countries to enhance exchanges and release relevant policies and project information, which had also become a platform for government–to–business communication. The CAEXPO arranged matching programs for the Chinese "Going–Global" companies and financial institutions, including the China–ASEAN Infrastructure Investment and Financing Cooperation Forum, Symposium on Financial Institutions Supporting Enterprises to Go Global and Enterprise Equities (Bonds) Investment and Financing Trade Fair etc., in order to provide practical financial support for companies investing in ASEAN. Each of the 10 ASEAN countries has held a promotion conference, at which so many trade visitors actively participated in that shortage of seats happened at the scene.

New breakthrough was made in trade and economic outcomes. The volume of commodity trade deals this year has reached USD1.807 billion, up by 5.6% compared to the same period of last year. The signed international cooperation projects were valued at USD 7.42 billion, up by 10.86% over that of last year, while the signed domestic economic cooperation projects valued at RMB 73.11 billion, up by 8.39% year on year.

IV. Fruitful Conferences and Exchange Activities Furthered the Multi–sectoral Cooperation

The 8th China–ASEAN Business & Investment Summit (CABIS), concurrently held with the 8th CAEXPO, took "Deepening Regional Cooperation for Common Prosperity" as its theme, gathering senior officials, business leaders, entrepreneurs and representatives of regional organizations, well–known experts and journalists from China–ASEAN region and beyond. Participants had in–depth discussions, and shared ideas on further deepening regional pragmatic cooperation for common development and prosperity.

Taking Environmental Protection Cooperation as its Theme of the Year, the 8th CAEXPO held China–ASEAN Environmental Cooperation Forum 2011 as well as other 14 high–end international conferences and exchange activities in the field of quality inspection, finance, solar energy, drug safety, forests, culture industry, publication, population and development, mass sports etc. Ministers and other participants met and tried to find solutions to the problems in bilateral cooperation in those areas and to form workable mechanisms regarding multi–sectoral collaboration, scoring new achievements.

China–ASEAN Environmental Cooperation Forum 2011 was held to fit with the 8th CAEXPO's Theme of the Year "Environmental Protection Cooperation. As China and most of the ASEAN countries are the developing and newly–industrialized countries linked by same rivers and mountains, they are facing many shared challenges in environmental protection and development. To achieve regional sustainable development in socio–economy and environment has remained top priority in the bilateral dialogues and exchanges. After years of continuous development and expansion, the environmental protection cooperation has listed as one of the 11 priority cooperation areas between the two sides. At this forum, the officials from the Ministry of Environmental Protection of China and their counterparts from ASEAN countries as well as representatives from other relevant organizations jointly launched the China–ASEAN Green Envoy Program, in response to the proposal put forward by the Chinese Premier Wen Jiabao at the 13th China–ASEAN (10+1) Summit in October 2010, to support the efforts to raise the public environmental awareness and improve the capacity–building in China and ASEAN.

The CAEXPO not only provided a good place for the transaction of green products but also set up a platform for the transnational companies to have exchanges in the environmental technologies. More than 100 government officials, specialists, scholars and business professionals from China and the ASEAN countries took part in the China–ASEAN Solar Energy Cooperation Semiar. All the participants have actively explored the limitless commercial opportunities in solar industry in China and ASEAN countries. The solar energy products became the leading product of energy conservation and environmental protection in the advanced technology exhibition during this CAEXPO, which had attracted many merchants to negotiate and place orders.

During the fair period, the 1st China–ASEAN Ministers Conference on TBT Cooperation was concluded with concrete outcomes. On the theme of product quality and safety, this conference held in–depth discussion on the problems and challenges that China and ASEAN were confronted with in this field, especially on the importance of bilateral cooperation in this field and the measures they should take. It adopted the ***China–ASEAN Joint Declaration on Strengthening the Cooperation in Product Quality and Safety (Nanning Joint Declaration*** for short) and it also issued the Nanning Joint Statement on eliminating the technical barriers to trade.

The Nanning Consensus on Publication Cooperation was reached at the China–ASEAN Publishing Expo. Making its first appearance in Guangxi in 2011, the Publication Expo has attracted lots of people and introduced new cultural elements to the CAEXPO. More than 10,000 kinds of ASEAN books and the hot–sold books in China were brought to Nanning. The officials of competent government authorities, representatives of the publication associations and those of the publishing companies from 10 ASEAN countries had an in–depth discussion on strengthening the cooperation in publishing industry with 11 central and local publishing groups and 5 digital publishing enterprises from China. They reached the Nanning Consensus on the exchanges and cooperation in the book publishing industry between China and

ASEAN.

Taking "Pragmatism & Innovation: China–ASEAN Regional Economic Growth & Financial and Fiscal Cooperation" as its theme, the China–ASEAN Summit Forum on Financial Cooperation & Development (Financial Forum) had discussion and reached broad consensus on promoting bilateral financial cooperation. This was the third session of the Financial Forum this year, again concluded with great success. Based on the successful experience of the previous Financial Forums, this Financial Forum placed more importance to pragmatism and financial services. Targeting regional currency settlement, financial control of the regional economic development, financial cooperation and development and other problems, this Financial Forum discussed hot topics with common interests, including financial support for the China–ASEAN cooperation in economy and technology, regional currency settlement and financial cooperation in the CAFTA , financial cooperation and regional economic development, fund–raising and listing of enterprises and regional diversification of the development of capital market, and relevant policies and service support for economic and financial development in the CAFTA. Those high–end talks and dialogues of financial elites helped both sides reach broad consensus. Besides, a host of investment promotion programs were arranged during the fair period, building a platform to support the Chinese enterprises to Go Globe, and making financial services play a more important role in regional economic development. Those programs included Seminar on Financial Support for Chinese "Go Global" Enterprises, Enterprise Equity/ Debts Financing Fair and Project Financing Seminar, etc. The Financial Exhibition also arranged a China–ASEAN think–tank dialogue on the financial cooperation and development mechanism and released relevant research findings in this regard, which had provided theory basis and reference for the long–term mechanism for regional financial cooperation, and for the commercial and financial communities of both sides to pragmatically enhance exchanges and cooperation.

As the earliest concurrent forum held before the 8th CAEXPO, the China–ASEAN Forum on Population & Family Development was inaugurated on October 11. It aimed at pushing forward the China–ASEAN cooperation and exchange in population and family development, thus to jointly promote family development capacity and boosting the construction of the resource–saving, environmental friendly and harmonious society of sustainable development with more balanced population.

With the theme "China–ASEAN cooperation in the new context" , and centering on the first year after the CAFTA establishment, the 4th China–ASEAN Think Tank Strategic Dialogue Forum had discussion on pragmatically expanding bilateral cooperation in politics, economy and culture and deepening regional industry–to–industry cooperation, thus to achieve common development and prosperity. The participating experts believed that since China and ASEAN established dialogue relations 20 years ago, the two sides had always seen "peace and friendship and common development for win–win results" as objectives, "friendly cooperation" as basis, and jointly witnessed the bilateral relations growing from dialogue partners and good–neighborly partners to strategic partners. The two sides have established a whole set of cooperation mechanism including meetings of state leaders, ministers, senior officials and liaison officials on a regular basis. Those cooperation mechanisms have covered more than 20 fields including trade, investment, agriculture, finance, ICT and infrastructure construction. Besides, the two sides have established a free trade area with the largest population and territory in the world. The participating experts also suggested that after the CAFTA establishment, both sides should take full advantage of the rules of origin, expand the bilateral cooperation in investment and trade, attach importance to the quality of products and the sustainable development, and strengthen the construction of connectivity, in a bid to achieve a higher goal of building the China–ASEAN economic community.

The 2011 China–ASEAN Cultural Industry Forum aimed at forming an official cooperation mechanism in the field, so as to effectively promote the growth and development of cultural industry in the countries concerned and push forward the CAFTA construction. The theme of the forum was "operation and management of museums and the creative development of cultural products". More than 200 cultural officials, museum curators and experts had discussion on multiple topics, including "the operation and management of museums in the context of globalization and cultural industry development", "creative development of cultural products in museums", "suggestions on cooperation and exchange among museums of different countries".

The 2011 China–ASEAN Forum on Drug Safety & China–ASEAN Meeting for Heads of Drug Regulation Agencies themed on "enhancing exchanges and guaranteeing safety for common development & drug safety cooperation in CAFTA". Officials of the food and drug administrations and experts of China and the 10 ASEAN countries exchanged views on the laws and regulations on drug safety and relevant supervision system. .

At the China–ASEAN Tourism for Promoting Poverty Reduction Seminar, all parties concerned reached wide consensus on introducing private capitals to explore tourism resources for poverty alleviation.

Other forums, conferences and activities all harvested sound outcomes, providing institutional guarantees for China and ASEAN to enhance bilateral cooperation in trade and people–to–people exchanges.

V. Innovative Promotion Campaigns Running the Whole Course of the CAEXPO Have Effectively Enhanced the Recognition of the CAEXPO

As an important program to celebrate the 20th anniversary of ASEAN–China dialogue relations, the 8th CAEXPO drew wide attention from Chinese and foreign media. Through promoting the commemorative programs of the 20th anniversary of ASEAN–China dialogue relations, the CAEXPO promotion campaigns have effectively enhanced the recognition of the CAEXPO.

Before holding the 8th CAEXPO, Guangxi sponsored or organized a host of programs to celebrate the 20th anniversary of ASEAN–China dialogue relations, including Commermorative Reception on the 20th anniversary of ASEAN–China Dialogue Relations, China–ASEAN Friendship Knowledge Contest, China–ASEAN

Strategic Seminar on Connectivity, China–ASEAN Media Rally, Economic & Trade Seminar for ASEAN Journalists and foreign language speaking competition, etc, All of those programs have given a full play of Guangxi and the CAEXPO in China–ASEAN cooperation. The reception banquet & theatrical performance achieved a complete success. Chinese State Councilor Dai Bingguo. leaders of Guangxi, including Guo Shengkun, Ma Biao, Chen Wu and Yu Yuanhui, leaders of China–ASEAN Association, competent ministries and commissions of China and ASEAN envoys in China joined the banquet and all spoke highly of the performance. Participants had in–depth discussion on the cooperation and the development direction of connectivity of the two sides at the China–ASEAN Strategic Seminar on Connectivity, which promoted the role played by Guangxi in this regard. The China–ASEAN Friendship Knowledge Contest enhanced the mutual understanding of Chinese and ASEAN youngsters, consolidated bilateral good–neighborly relations, and again promote the role played by Guangxi and the CAEXPO in the China–ASEAN cooperation.

The 8th CAEXPO, as always, drew eyeballs of mainstream media and professional media from home and abroad. The participating media and journalists were more than the previous session. The 8th CAEXPO attracted 1738 journalists from 275 media, up by 19.2% and 38.19% respectively. Among them, 69 were ASEAN media, up by 20%, making it the event of such kind held in China that attracted the largest number of ASEAN media. According to the incomplete statistics, there were over 8300 reports released on newspapers, magazines and televisions and over 3,800,000 entries of relevant internet reprints or links. The influence of the CAEXPO was further enlarged.

During the fair period, CCTV, Hong Kong Phoenix TV, Hong Kong Asia TV, Guangxi TV and media from ASEAN and other countries/regions adopted on–the–spot reporting, exclusive interviews and other forms to broadcast the event. H.E. Dato' Sri Mohd Najib Tun Abdul Razak, prime minister of Malaysia, H.E. Dr. Surin Pitsu–wan, secretary–general of ASEAN and other political dignitaries received exclusive in–terviews by many media. According to incomplete statistics, Chinese and foreign media published more than 8,300 reports; 160,000 news articles were published on the in–ternet (inclusive of reprinted ones), along with 31780 pictures and 415 videos, making the search result top 3,800,000; new broadcasting channels like microblogs and mobile phone newspapers also contributed to promoting the event and enhance its recogni–tion.. The wide–range coverage made by Chinese and foreign media made a strong impression on the participants.

Major programs of the 8th CAEXPO were live broadcasted by many mainstream media. CCTV, Xinhua.com, People.com and Chinanews.com made live broadcast on the opening ceremonies of the 8th CAEXPO and the 8th CABIS and live web casting on the Roundtable Dialogue between Malaysian Prime Minister Dato' Sri Mohd Najib Tun Abdul Razak and Chinese CEOs and the Meeting between Thai Deputy Prime Minister Kittiratt Na–Ranong and Chinese/Thai entrepreneurs.

Media from ASEAN and other countries also paid keen attention to the 8th CAEXPO. Mainstream media from ASEAN countries like Thailand, Brunei Darussalam, Indonesia, the Philippines and Vietnam, U.S. and Japan all published the

CAEXPO–related news on the front or important pages.

The 8th CAEXPO adopted many measures to provide faster and more convenient services for the media to make relevant coverage. News materials like pictures and text of such major programs as the opening ceremony and VIP's inspection tours to the exhibition pavilions were available at the Press Center 30 minutes after the conclusion of those programs, and materials like pictures, text and videos of other programs were available at the CAEXPO official website 2 hours later.

Targeting the new characteristics of the China–ASEAN cooperation, the 8th CAEXPO arranged a series of promotion campaigns with new highlights for a long time, which exerted huge influence in the region. Guangxi sponsored or organized a host of programs to celebrate the 20th anniversary of the ASEAN–China dialogue relations, which laid a sound foundation for the promotion on the 8th CAEXPO. Before the inauguration of the 8th CAEXPO, we produced the CAEXPO Music Album, designed more mascot and souvenirs, to promote the brandname of the event.

VI More Professional Business–friendly Services are Provided for Participants.

Supporting services of the 8th CAEXPO such as booth building, on–site administration and customer service were further optimized.

Booth decoration highlighted the Theme of the Year and more exhibitors custom–built their booths. Design of the exhibition halls reflected this year's special background and the main theme, i.e., environmental protection cooperation. Custom–built booths occupied 64% of the total area of the Nanning International Convention & Exhibition Center, the CAEXPO main venue, much more than that of the previous sessions.

On–site administration was improved and more scientific. In line with the Theme of the Year of the 8th CAEXPO, we adopted green administrative measures like green office and smoke–free control at the venue for the very first time. The "MEGA EYES" was introduced to monitor all the exhibition halls. The Joint Law Enforcement Group was empowered to supervise a wider range of areas. Customs clearance, logistics, cleaning and other services were further improved. Direct chartered flights between Nanning and major cities of the 10 ASEAN countries were opened during the fair period as usual. More standardized regulations helped volunteers better serve the event.

VII. Using CAEXPO as a Platform to Propel the Socio–economic Development of Guangxi.

The 8th CAEXPO has brought much closer friendly exchanges between Guangxi and the ASEAN nations. During the event, provincial leaders of Guangxi Zhuang autonomous region held 12 meetings with state leaders of ASEAN countries, delegations of different countries and delegates from the sister cities, reaching broad consensus on issues like building the Guangxi Beibu Gulf Economic Zone, advancing the Pan–Beibu Gulf economic cooperation, the Greater Mekong Sub–regional cooperation, Nanning–Singapore economic corridor and cross–border economic zones, and promoting the development of China–ASEAN Free Trade Area. H.E.

Thiha Thura U Tin Aung Myint Oo, vice–president of Myanmar personally visited the Yulin city of Guangxi and attended the China (Yulin) SME Expo. The 8th CAEXPO was of good service to cities and government departments in Guangxi. For instance, it showcased the image of China–Malaysia Qinzhou Industrial Park and the Qinzhou's achievements in developing foreign cooperation. The signing ceremony for projects located in the Qinzhou Industrial Park was also held to secure the implementation of the key projects. Enterprises in Nanning High–tech Industrial Development Zone were organized to participate in investment promotion activities. Malaysian delegations were afterwards arranged to visit those enterprises. The CAEXPO Secretariat also held, in partnerships with the relevant cities in Guangxi, the China–ASEAN (Liuzhou) Automobile, Engineering Machinery and Spare Parts Expo, the China–ASEAN (Baise) Modern Agriculture Showcase and Trade Fair, China (Yulin) SMEs Expo and Wuzhou Precious Stones Festival, driving forward the development of the Guangxi's exhibition industry. Guangxi's government departments in charge of commerce, investment promotion, science and technology, agriculture, tourism, press and publications at the CAEXPO held a series of exchange activities oriented towards cooperation with ASEAN and produced significant results.

The 8th CAEXPO boosted the development of service industry in Nanning. According to the Guangxi Statistics Bureau, from October 20 to 26, the average occupancy rate of hotels in Nanning was 51.03% and a cumulative of 86200 guests were received, including 11900 foreign guests, up 6.47% over last year. The 12 large shopping malls in Nanning reported a total sales revenue of RMB154 million, averaging RMB 22.05 million on daily basis. The five highway bus stations in Nanning recorded 50632 times of bus arrival and departure cumulatively. 171,500 passengers were carried to and 168,100 ones traveled from Nanning by train. The Nanning Wuxu International Airport reported 1286 times of take–offs and landings. The number of coming–in passengers and leaving ones by air were 68,000 and 71,000 respectively. All the figures showed a big increase on daily basis as compared to those in usual days. By the end of 2011, the number of passenger handled by the Nanning airport was over 6 million, hitting a record high.

After the 8th CAEXPO, the Guangxi Statistics Bureau conducted a survey to find out how the local people thought about the event, and turned out that 83.84% felt satisfied, of whom 33.22% felt very satisfied.

第八届中国—东盟博览会
THE 8TH CHINA-ASEAN EXPO

第一章

1 对话合作二十载 携手共办迈新程

——第八届中国—东盟博览会的筹备

2011年，中国和东盟迎来了建立对话关系20周年，已建成运行1周年的中国—东盟自由贸易区欣欣向荣，走过第八个年头的中国—东盟博览会更加生机勃勃。

展示20周年合作成果，继续推动中国—东盟自由贸易区向前发展，是第八届中国—东盟博览会新的使命，也是中国和东盟各国共同的目标。

中国总理温家宝2011年4月访问马来西亚期间，邀请第八届中国—东盟博览会主题国马来西亚总理纳吉布出席博览会，欢迎马来西亚企业参会。中国10多个国家部委大力支持办好第八届中国—东盟博览会，中国各省（区、市）政府部门及企业界积极参与第八届中国—东盟博览会。

东盟各国政府、商协会、企业加强与中方合作，共同做好博览会的筹备工作，各共办方的组织力度进一步增强，共办机制得到进一步完善。

广西壮族自治区继续举全区之力承办第八届中国—东盟博览会。全区上下以高度的责任感和创新的精神，精心组织，全力以赴，各项承办工作更加机制化、常态化，进一步展示了广西人民搭建平台，服务中国—东盟友好合作的信心和决心。

Two Decades of Dialogues and Cooperation, a New Starting Point for Co-sponsorship

—Preparations for the 8th China-ASEAN Expo

The year 2011 witnessed the 20th anniversary of ASEAN-China dialogue relations and the energetic growth of the China-ASEAN FTA which was just completed one year ago. In the meanwhile, the 8-year-old China-ASEAN Expo (CAEXPO) is enjoying momentum.

The 8th CAEXPO carries a new mission, which is to well display the rich fruits of the China-ASEAN cooperation in the past two decades and to push forward the growth of the young China-ASEAN FTA, a common goal of China and the 10 ASEAN member states.

During his visit to Malaysia in April, 2011, H.E. Wen Jiabao invited the Right Honorable Dato' Sri Mohd Najib Tun Abdul Razak, prime minister of Malaysia to personally visit the 8th CAEXPO, bringing with him the Malaysian-based enterprises. Competent ministries and departments of Chinese central government have all granted full support to the event, not to mention the active participation of the provincial/municipal governments and local enterprises in China.

The ASEAN government departments, major chambers of commerce and trade associations, as well as the enterprises have worked closely with the Chinese side, and invested more efforts to enhance the existing co-sponsoring mechanism for the preparation of the CAEXPO. The ASEAN countries all put more efforts in the CAEXPO-related work.

As the organizer of the event, Guangxi continues to pool all needed resources to guarantee the success of the CAEXPO. Departments concerned work closely to ensure the efficient running of the preparation, making it an effective mechanism and more regular. All these efforts well display Guangxi's confidence and determination in building a good platform for the friendly exchanges and cooperation between China and the ASEAN side.

CHAPTER ONE

一　第八届中国—东盟博览会筹备的背景

2011年是中国—东盟建立对话关系20周年、中国—东盟友好交流年、中国—东盟自由贸易区建成1周年，第八届中国—东盟博览会在这一背景下举办，意义重大。

（一）中国—东盟建立对话关系20周年

1991年，中国同东盟建立对话关系，开启了中国与东盟关系的历史进程，体现了双方顺应时代潮流，探索区域合作的战略远见和勇气，具有里程碑意义。

20年来，双方在政治上平等相待，睦邻互信，中国已经与所有东盟成员国确立了合作伙伴关系，并率先与东盟建立了战略伙伴关系；在经济上双方互惠互利，共同发展，双方都相互视对方为重要合作伙伴，是好邻居、好伙伴、好朋友。

20年来，中国—东盟关系始终以和平发展为主题、以友好合作为主线，见证了从全面对话伙伴、睦邻互信伙伴到战略伙伴的发展历程。双方建立了包括领导人、部长、高官和工作组在内的一整套合作机制，在经贸、投资、农业、金融、信息通讯、基础设施建设等20多个领域开展务实合作，建成了全球覆盖人口最多、区域最广的自由贸易区，搭建了中国—东盟博览会平台。

近10年，中国与东盟的贸易额以年均20%以上的速度递增，特别是中国—东盟自贸区全面建成后，双方贸易实现了突破性的发展，2010年双边贸易额达到2928亿美元，增长37.5%，呈现出快速发展的势头。

2010年10月29日，中国国务院总理温家宝在越南河内举行的第十三次中国与东盟领导人会议发表讲话时提议："将2011年确定为'中国—东盟友好交流年'，双方共同举办丰富多彩的活动。"

（二）中国—东盟自由贸易区深入发展

2010年1月1日，中国—东盟自由贸易区如期建成。中国—东盟自由贸易区建成一年来，给双方企业和人民带来了实惠。它拥有多个“第一”：中国对外建立的第一个自由贸易区、东盟作为整体对外建立的第一个自由贸易区、最大的由发展中国家组成的自由贸易区、惠及人口最多的自由贸易区。

中国—东盟自由贸易区建成后，双方对超过90%的产品实行零关税。中国对东盟平均关税从9.8%降到0.1%，东盟6个老成员国对中国的平均关税从12.8%降到0.6%。关税水平大幅降低有力地推动了双边经贸合作快速增长。

一是双边贸易增长快。2010年，中国与东盟双边贸易额同比增长37.5%，高出中国对外贸易总体增幅2.8个百分点。

二是相互投资规模不断扩大。截至2011年6月，双方累计投资总额超过800亿美元。中国对东盟的投资方兴未艾，累计超过130亿美元，其中一半左右是在最近两年实现的。东盟已成为中国企业“走出去”的重要目的地之一。

中国—东盟自由贸易区建成使双方业已密切的经贸合作关系得到了进一步加强，双方经济一体化程度提升至前所未有的水平。双方合作已由最初的单一货物贸易形式，扩展到服务贸易、相互投资、信息通讯、湄公河开发、交通、能源、文化、旅游等众多领域。

2011年8月12日，第十次中国—东盟（10＋1）经贸部长会议在印度尼西亚万鸦老举行，来自中国和东盟10国的经贸部长出席会议并回顾了经贸合作历程。会议积极评价中国—东盟建立对话关系20年来的经贸合作成果，特别是实施《中国—东盟全面经济合作框架协议》所取得的成效，探讨了进一

2010年1月1日，中国—东盟自由贸易区正式建成

China-ASEAN Free Trade Area (CAFTA) was due established on January 1, 2010

步加强合作的具体措施。

中国商务部部长陈德铭在会上表示，自2010年1月1日中国—东盟自贸区全面启动以来，双方经贸关系发展迅速。中国已成为东盟第一大贸易伙伴，东盟也成为中国第三大贸易伙伴。当前，世界经济不确定性增加，发达国家需求可能下降，东盟与中国扩大经贸合作，对双方抵御外部经济不确定性、保持经济稳定发展有很大帮助。

印尼贸易部长冯慧兰说，2010年，中国与东盟贸易额接近3000亿美元，同比增速高达37.5%。2011年上半年，双边贸易额同比又增长25%，延续了快速增长势头。美国和欧洲的债务问题给世界经济增添了新的重大不确定性。在世界经济又处在新的十字路口的时刻，东盟与中国加强合作，对双方尤为关键。

会后，与会部长们发表《联合新闻声明》。《声明》对中国—东盟自贸区框架下的卫生和植物卫生措施/技术贸易壁垒等问题达成共识，并表示期待第八届中国—东盟博览会于2011年9月在中国南宁举行。在《声明》中，部长们欢迎《泛北部湾经济合作可行性研究报告》，并将其提交当年的中国—东盟领导人会议讨论。

二　中央领导关怀和国家有关部委指导支持

第八届中国—东盟博览会的筹备工作一如既往地得到了党中央、国务院的关怀指导，得到了中央有关部委的大力支持。

（一）中央领导的关怀，极大地鼓舞了广西承办好第八届中国—东盟博览会的信心和决心

应马来西亚总理穆罕默德·纳吉布、印度尼西亚共和国总统苏希洛·班邦·尤多约诺邀请，中国国务院总理温家宝于2011年4月27日至30日对上述两国进行正式访问。在马来西亚访问期间，温家宝邀请马来西亚总理纳吉布出席第八届中国—东盟博览会。

温家宝在中马经贸合作论坛致辞时表示，马来西亚是2011年第八届中国—东盟博览会的主题国，希望马方企业积极参会，推介产品和交流经验。温家宝在致辞中还提议双方共建中马钦州产业园。他指出，中马钦州产业园区是双方在中国西部地区合作的第一个工业园，具有示范意义，中国政府欢迎马方有实力的企业积极参与园区的规划和开发建设。马来西亚总理纳吉布表示，马方将支持中马钦州产业园区项目。

党中央、国务院对广西经济社会发展十分关心。从2011年初至第八届中国—东盟博览会开幕前，吴邦国、贺国强、周永康等中央领导同志分别到广西考察指导工作，充分肯定近年来广西各项建设取得的成绩，对广西经济社会发展作重要指示，极大地促进了广西各项工作，鼓舞了广西承办好第八届中国—东盟博览会的信心和决心。

（二）中央有关部委加大支持力度，国内各省区市积极参与

商务部作为博览会主办方，对广西承办博览会工作给予大力支持。2011年4月7日下午，商务部国际贸易谈判代表兼副部长高虎城莅临桂林指导第八届中国—东盟博览会筹备工作。高虎城与广西壮族自治区党委常委、自治区

副主席陈武举行了会谈，就第八届中国—东盟博览会筹备工作交换了意见。

陈武感谢商务部对广西经济社会发展，特别是对中国—东盟博览会承办工作的指导和大力支持。他说，过去的七届中国—东盟博览会成效显著，得到了国家和东盟各国领导人的高度评价，11国共办机制不断深化和完善。陈武表示，广西将进一步完善筹备工作的机制化建设，继续做好第八届中国—东盟博览会筹办工作，塑造博览会政治外交品牌，扩大影响力，提高经贸实效，服务国家战略。

高虎城对广西壮族自治区党委、政府为中国—东盟博览会连续成功举办所作出的突出贡献表示感谢，对广西扩大开放合作取得的巨大成绩表示祝贺。他说，中国—东盟博览会举办七届以来，广西作为承办方承担了大量繁重而具体的工作，博览会办得一届比一届好，得到11国政府和中外企业的普遍支持和肯定，让东盟10国得到了实惠。

高虎城表示，商务部对第八届中国—东盟博览会筹备工作高度重视，将一如既往地支持广西承办好博览会。高虎城要求努力把博览会打造成著名品牌展会，为国内各省区市扩大与东盟合作提供更好的服务。同时进一步加强投资促进工作，把促进中国与东盟投资合作作为博览会今后很长一段时期的一项重要工作抓好抓实。

4月8日，第八届中国—东盟博览会筹备工作会议在桂林召开。商务部国际贸易谈判代表兼副部长高虎城，广西壮族自治区党委常委、自治区副主席陈武，商务部相关司局、全国31个省（区、市）商务系统和中央直属企业派员出席了此次会议。会议对在中国—东盟建立对话关系20周年等新形势下，充分发挥博览会在“走出去”等方面的平台作用，促进中国和东盟经贸合作

2011年4月8日，第八届中国—东盟博览会筹备工作会议在广西桂林举行
The 8th CAEXPO Working Meeting held in Guilin, Guangxi, China on April 8, 2011

作了重要部署。

高虎城在会上强调，在新形势下，要充分利用好博览会平台，进一步发展与东盟的政治经贸合作，不断巩固和发展我国周边外交战略成果，推动区域经济一体化。他指出，要抓住中国—东盟自贸区建成的机遇，把中国与东盟经贸合作提高到新的水平，尤其要加大对企业的宣传力度，提高自贸区政策的利用效率。一是落实自贸区《货物贸易协议》，进一步提高贸易规模，优化贸易结构。二是落实自贸区《投资协议》，进一步扩大相互投资，加快“走出去”步伐。三是落实自贸区《服务贸易协议》，提升与东盟服务贸易合作水平。

陈武表示，广西将努力把中国—东盟博览会越办越好，不断深化以东盟为重点的开放合作，继续推进广西北部湾经济区开放开发，为各省（区、市）与东盟在各领域的合作提供更好的平台。

7月8日，商务部对外投资和经济合作司在贵阳召开第八届中国—东盟博览会国际经济合作展区筹备工作会议。 商务部合作司副司长刘迎军、中国对外承包工程商会秘书长于晓虹、中国—东盟博览会秘书处副秘书长王雷出席筹备会。来自全国33个省市，56家单位，包括商务、外经主管部门、投资促进机构和中直企业代表参加了会议。会议就第八届博览会国际经济合作展区、博览会投资合作专题和投资促进活动的筹备工作进行了部署。

7月26日，国务院新闻办公室举办中国—东盟建立对话关系20周年经贸关系成效暨第八届中国—东盟博览会、第八届中国—东盟商务与投资峰会新闻发布会。这是中国—东盟博览会连续第八年在国务院新闻办召开新闻发布

2011年7月26日，中国—东盟建立对话关系20周年经贸关系成效暨第八届中国—东盟博览会、第八届中国—东盟商务与投资峰会新闻发布会在北京举行

Press Conference on the 20th Anniversary of ASEAN-China Dialogue Relations, the 8th CAEXPO and the 8th CABIS held in Beijing ,on July 26,2011

会。

商务部国际贸易谈判代表兼副部长高虎城，广西壮族自治区党委常委、自治区副主席陈武，中国国际贸易促进委员会副会长王锦珍分别介绍中国—东盟建立对话关系20周年取得的经贸成效、中国—东盟自由贸易区建设成果以及第八届中国—东盟博览会、第八届中国—东盟商务与投资峰会等方面情况，并回答了记者提问。新闻发布会由国务院新闻办新闻局副局长华清主持。《人民日报》、新华社、中央电视台、中央人民广播电台、中国国际广播电台、中国新闻社、《澳门日报》、澳亚卫视、香港经济通通讯社、凤凰卫视有限公司、香港电台以及道琼斯金融通讯社、美国国际市场新闻社、路透社、日本经济新闻、越南通讯社、越南之声广播电台等国内外共计49家媒体81人到会采访报道。文莱、柬埔寨、印尼、缅甸、菲律宾、泰国、越南驻华使馆商务参赞等官员出席发布会。

8月24日，第八届中国—东盟博览会和中国—东盟商务与投资峰会组委会会议在北京召开。会议围绕在中国—东盟建立对话关系20周年、中国—东盟友好交流年、中国—东盟自由贸易区建成1周年以及当前国际新的形势下，进一步办好博览会、商务与投资峰会，为加强中国与东盟在多领域的合作搭好平台、做好服务进行了研究部署。博览会组委会主任、商务部部长陈德铭，广西壮族自治区党委书记、自治区人大常委会主任郭声琨，博览会组委会副主任、自治区主席马飚出席会议并分别讲话。

博览会组委会副主任、商务部国际贸易谈判代表兼副部长高虎城主持会议。博览会组委会副主任兼秘书长、广西壮族自治区党委常委、自治区副主席陈武，广西壮族自治区党委常委、秘书长余远辉，外交部部长助理刘振民，国家旅游局副局长祝善忠，国家食品药品监督管理局副局长边振甲，公

2011年8月24日，第八届中国—东盟博览会、中国—东盟商务与投资峰会组委会会议在北京举行

Working Meeting of the 8th CAEXPO and the 8th CABIS Organizing Committee held in Beijing on August 24, 2011

安部警卫局副局长张智文少将，中国贸促会副会长于平，以及中宣部、国务院办公厅、发展改革委、科技部、财政部、环保部、交通运输部、海关总署、质检总局、国务院新闻办等组委会成员单位和自治区有关部门负责人等出席会议。广西壮族自治区人民政府秘书长王跃飞出席会议。

陈德铭说，中国—东盟博览会是面向东盟、多国共办且永久落户中国的政治、外交、经贸多领域合作机制，担负着重要的政治外交使命，性质不同于一般展会。7年来，组委会各成员单位齐心协力，积极创新，为确保历届博览会圆满成功发挥了重要作用。同时，博览会已逐步形成“各部委支持办好博览会、博览会积极为各部委工作搭好平台”的工作机制，为各部委和各省（区、市）扩展与东盟的合作发挥了很好的作用，也确保了博览会长效发展，增进了中国与东盟国家友好互信，深化了双边互利合作。第八届博览会是中国—东盟建立对话关系20周年系列纪念活动的重要组成部分，意义重大。第八届博览会要充分展示20周年合作成果，深化共办共赢；加大创新力度，提高经贸实效；做好主题内容和活动的策划，不断形成新的亮点，确保本届博览会办得更有特色，更有实效，为深化中国—东盟战略伙伴关系，深入实施自贸区战略，推动区域经济一体化提供示范，进而推动经济发展方式加快转变。

郭声琨说，举办好第八届中国—东盟博览会和中国—东盟商务与投资峰会意义十分重大。特别是国家“十二五”规划纲要明确提出：“把广西建成与东盟合作的新高地”，“推动广西北部湾经济区加快发展、培育新的经济增长极”。广西将坚持服务国家周边外交战略，在中国—东盟自由贸易区框架下拓展新的开放领域和空间，形成参与国际合作与竞争的新优势；加强办好中国—东盟博览会和中国—东盟商务与投资峰会的机制化建设，更加有效地发挥合作平台作用；积极参与和推进大湄公河次区域合作、泛北部湾经济合作、中越“两廊一圈”合作、南宁—新加坡经济走廊、中越跨境经济合作区建设，推进交通、电力、电讯、信息网络等互联互通，完善保税物流体系，加快建设面向东盟的南宁商务总部经济基地等，形成与东盟国家互利共赢的全方位、多领域开放合作格局。广西壮族自治区党委、政府对承办好第八届博览会和峰会高度重视，自治区党委常委会专题研究有关事项，明确提出要继续举全区之力，全力以赴办好2011年博览会和峰会，确保取得圆满成功。目前博览会和峰会各项筹备工作正在积极有效推进。希望中央各部委继续支持办好中国—东盟博览会和中国—东盟商务与投资峰会，确保长期举办下去，进一步办出特色、办出实效。同时，博览会和商务与投资峰会也要为各部委和兄弟省（区、市）扩展与东盟的交流合作搭好平台，做好服务。

马飚说，前七届博览会和商务与投资峰会成果丰硕，影响深远，搭建了友好交流和经贸合作的平台，形成了中国—东盟合作的“南宁渠道”，带动了广西全方位对外开放，有力促进广西经济社会加快发展。在新形势下，广西将全力以赴做好第八届博览会和商务与投资峰会的各项筹备工作，加强统筹协调，创新展会形式和内容，突出经贸实效，加大宣传推介力度，营造良好氛围，做好保障工作。希望各部委更多地把部门主管的中国—东盟交流合作项目放在广西，拓宽中国—东盟博览会的合作平台，使博览会在我国与东盟的交流合作中发挥更大的作用，为服务国家周边外交，为中国—东盟自由贸易区发展，为各部委、各省（区、市）与东盟合作作出新的应有贡献。

高虎城说，要抓住中国—东盟建立对话关系20周年的新机遇，办好博览会。博览会要在内容和形式上加大创新力度，推动企业“走出去”。希望各部委继续支持办好博览会，博览会也要积极为各部委扩大与东盟合作搭好平台。

陈武通报了中国—东盟博览会、商务与投资峰会举办以来取得的成效，尤其是在推进我国与东盟各领域合作交流中发挥的作用，以及第八届博览会、商务与投资峰会的主要特点和亮点。

于平介绍了第八届中国—东盟商务与投资峰会的主题和筹备情况。

外交部介绍了东亚形势，环保部通报了中国—东盟环境合作论坛筹备工作情况，科技部介绍了关于将“科技合作”作为第九届博览会重点主题（含主题论坛）的提议和工作设想。组委会各成员单位在发言中表示，继续支持博览会、商务与投资峰会长远发展，并充分利用这一平台加强与东盟在各领域的交流合作，为促进中国—东盟全面合作作出新的贡献。

三　东盟10国携手共办

第八届中国—东盟博览会筹备工作得到了东盟10国政府部门及东盟秘书处、东盟各国主要商协会和企业界的高度重视，东盟方与中方加强合作，完善共办机制，提高共办水平。

（一）东盟10国加大共办力度

第八届中国—东盟博览会筹备期间，东盟秘书长素林对办好博览会提出了积极建议。中国和东盟各国共办方密切合作，召开了中国—东盟博览会高官会，各国根据本国实际情况，推动各项举措，组织更多更优的本国企业参展参会，提高共办水平。

1. 东盟秘书长素林支持办好第八届中国—东盟博览会。

2011年4月16日，广西壮族自治区党委书记、自治区人大常委会主任郭声琨在海南博鳌会见了东盟秘书长素林。

郭声琨对东盟秘书处及东盟秘书长素林一直以来对中国—东盟博览会的成功举办，以及对广西发展与东盟友好合作关系给予的极大关心和支持表示衷心感谢，衷心希望东盟秘书处为本届博览会的成功举办发挥更加积极有效的作用。郭声琨诚挚邀请素林秘书长出席第八届博览会，并继续推动东盟各国参展参会，特别是推动东盟国家高层领导人出席博览会。

素林愉快地接受郭声琨对其出席第八届中国—东盟博览会的盛情邀请。他说，中国—东盟博览会在推动中国—东盟自贸区如期建成和运行方面发挥了巨大作用。东盟秘书处将以各种适当的方式，尽力邀请并积极推动更多东盟国家领导人及贵宾参展参会，充分运用好博览会这个平台，促进中国与东盟在各方面的交流合作。

素林就举办好第八届中国—东盟博览会提出四点建议：一是邀请更多东盟10国的新闻媒体参与博览会，通过媒体广泛宣传报道，让更多人了解博览会、参与博览会。二是围绕2011年博览会“环保合作”的主题，邀请从事环保方面的专业机构和人士参加博览会，深入探讨环保合作相关问题。三是充分利用博览会这一很好的合作机制和交流平台，邀请更多更高层次工商界人士参展参会，特别是有效整合中国国内资源，把中国中西部省区与东盟各国工商界人士集聚南宁，探讨合作领域，寻找互赢商机，这必将使博览会的价值得到更好体现，博览会对东盟国家的吸引力也将得到进一步提升。四是建议加强中国与东盟在软实力特别是文化方面的交流合作，在本届博览会期间可以邀请主题国马来西亚文化艺术团体到南宁来开展丰富的文化交流活动。

2. 举办第八届中国—东盟博览会高官会及中国—东盟博览会投资促进高官会。

2011年6月1日，第八届中国—东盟博览会高官会议在北海召开。商务部亚洲司副司长梁文洮和东盟秘书处经济一体化合作司司长苏柏什共同主持会议，商务部投资促进事务局副局长张迎新及东盟各国经贸主管部门和投资主管部门高官出席了会议。会上，各方就第八届中国—东盟博览会筹备工作及举办中国—东盟博览会投资促进圆桌会达成广泛共识。会议期间，商务部投资促进事务局主持召开了中国—东盟博览会投资促进高官会；会前，广西壮族自治区党委常委、自治区副主席陈武会见了与会代表。

中国商务部亚洲司副司长梁文洮在高官会上，充分肯定了前七届中国—东盟博览会的成效。他表示，中方愿与东盟方一道，进一步巩固和发展中国—东盟博览会平台，使之更好地服务于中国—东盟经贸合作，促进中国—东盟自由贸易区建设，促进共同发展，共同繁荣。

与会的东盟10国高官认为，在11国共同努力下，前七届中国—东盟博览会成效显著，充分显示了中国—东盟自贸区的广阔前景，表示将与中方一道，进一步发展和完善已形成的博览会共办机制，全面、深入地推动各项筹

2011年6月1日，第八届中国—东盟博览会高官会议在广西北海举行

The Senior Officials Meeting for the 8th CAEXPO held in Beihai, Guangxi, China on June 1, 2011

备工作，确保第八届中国—东盟博览会取得圆满成功。

会上，中国商务部亚洲司副司长梁文洮代表中方对第八届博览会提出总体要求；商务部投资促进事务局副局长张迎新提出了进一步利用博览会平台加强中国—东盟投资合作的建议；中国—东盟博览会秘书处秘书长郑军健介绍了第八届博览会筹备工作目标、主要措施及总体设想；中国—东盟博览会秘书处副秘书长农融对第八届博览会招商招展、贸易投资、展务工作等工作安排作了详细说明。东盟方高度认可第八届博览会总体安排和各项工作建议，表示将按照筹备工作要求，积极做好本国博览会的相关事宜。

6月3日，第八届中国—东盟博览会高官会投资促进工作会议在北海召开，来自中国和东盟10国投资促进部门的官员一致表示，将充分发挥各自优势，共同努力，把中国—东盟博览会打造成为双方投资合作的最佳展会。

与会的各国高官认为，中国—东盟博览会既有商品贸易，也有投资合作和服务贸易，是为东盟国家与中国开展经贸合作“量身订制”的绝佳平台。博览会举办7年来，11国博览会共办机构已经建立了常态化工作联系，形成博览会贸易、投资促进机制，尤其在贸易促进方面成效显著。在此基础上，11国投资促进机构的共同参与，将进一步充实和加强博览会投资促进工作。这既符合中国—东盟经贸关系深入发展的需要，也将极大地满足各国企业通过博览会开拓市场的需要，势必成为第八届中国—东盟博览会的亮点之一。

会议确定，从2011年起，在每届中国—东盟博览会期间举办中国—东盟博览会投资促进圆桌会议。会议还提出共同发展完善博览会投资促进机构定期会晤机制，积极组织和动员本国相关机构、企业参加博览会，共同做好博览会投引资信息发布工作、会期投引资项目对接工作以及博览会投资专题在本国的宣传推介，进一步巩固和完善博览会投资促进工作机制。

3. 举办中国—东盟经贸关系研修班。

2011年6月14日，由中国商务部主办、中国—东盟博览会秘书处承办的中国—东盟经贸关系研修班在南宁开班。东盟国家贸易投资主管部门的官员参加了研修班的学习和实地考察等活动。

此次研修班课程内容包括中国—东盟区域经济合作、中国对外投资合作及相关政策、中国与东盟环境保护合作、中国—东盟博览会回顾及第八届中国—东盟博览会介绍等。本届研修班还专门增加了中国与东盟国家重点投资合作项目专题研讨板块，并对学员带来的各自国家的项目信息及时进行收集和整理，通过博览会官方网站对外发布，吸引投资，提高撮合成功率，进一步促进中国与东盟的双边投资合作。

中国—东盟博览会秘书处秘书长郑军健在开班仪式上表示，本次研修班有助于让东盟各国经贸官员深入了解双方经贸合作现状、博览会运行架构和中国经济建设情况，并在今后的工作中加强合作，共同把博览会办得更好，让东盟各国通过博览会更好地分享中国经济高速发展的成果。

据了解，中国—东盟经贸关系研修班自2006年以来已成功举办5届，共有来自东盟10国贸易投资和外交部门，以及东盟秘书处的100多位学员参加了学习。本次研修班授课时间14天，中国商务部、菲律宾驻广州总领馆贸易投资中心、中国—东盟博览会秘书处等机构的负责人和专家为学员授课，学员们到广西有关地市及海南进行了实地考察。

（二）马来西亚担任第八届中国—东盟博览会主题国，积极筹备主题国活动。

马来西亚是第八届中国—东盟博览会主题国。为做好主题国筹备工作，马来西亚通过组建跨部门专门机构，积极策划主题国活动。第八届博览会筹备之初，马来西亚成立了由马来西亚对外贸易发展局（MATRADE）、马来西亚投资促进局（MIDA）、马来西亚旅游局等组成的跨部门筹备委员会，由MATRADE负责总协调和商品贸易专题的组展，由MIDA负责组织投资合作专题的国家推介会及其他相关活动，由旅游局负责组织“魅力之城”专题的展览及活动。包括领导人双边会见、投资签约仪式、领导人与企业家见面会以及其他文化活动等都在跨部门筹备委员会的工作计划中。马方与中方保持紧密联系，共同筹备好主题国活动。

马来西亚作为主题国，在展览组织上加强对重点龙头企业的邀请。参展的重点行业为食品饮料、木材家具、服务业产品、大宗商品及品牌企业产品等。

为抓住担任主题国的机会，取得更好的参展参会成效，马来西亚深挖重点行业资源，向相关商协会推介博览会。马来西亚家具工业理事会、马来西亚家具同业联合总会就组展等事宜进行了深入谈论。两家行业协会均对博览会木材展表示了浓厚的兴趣，表示与博览会秘书处进行网络链接，并向会员企业推介博览会，得到了企业界的积极响应。

四　广西继续举全区之力承办

广西壮族自治区党委、自治区人民政府高度重视第八届中国—东盟博览会承办工作，加强组织领导，积极争取各方支持，全区上下齐心协力，做好各项筹备工作。

（一）积极争取各方支持

广西壮族自治区党委书记、自治区人大常委会主任郭声琨，自治区主席马飚，自治区党委常委、自治区常务副主席李金早，自治区党委常委、自治区副主席陈武等自治区领导多次利用赴京出差或出席会议的机会，拜会国务院和有关部委有关负责人，争取对中国—东盟博览会承办工作的支持，并率团出访东盟国家，推动东盟国家共同办好中国—东盟博览会。

2011年4月3日，以广西壮族自治区党委书记、自治区人大常委会主任郭声琨为团长的广西代表团启程对马来西亚进行为期5天的友好访问。马来西亚副总理丹斯里慕尤丁、房屋与地方政府部部长曹智雄、贸工部副部长耶谷·沙岸等马来西亚政要会见了代表团一行，双方就共同办好博览会、共建中马钦州产业园区等许多方面达成了广泛共识。出访期间，代表团举办了广西—马来西亚企业座谈会、广西国际教育展，与马来西亚霹雳州建立了友好区州关系，并见证了中马钦州产业园合作协议签署。

4月4日下午，郭声琨在吉隆坡拜会了马来西亚副总理兼教育部长丹斯里慕尤丁。郭声琨感谢丹斯里慕尤丁副总理拨冗会见广西代表团。他说，此次访马，主要目的之一就是邀请总理和副总理阁下出席第八届中国—东盟博览会。马来西亚是第八届中国—东盟博览会主题国。这届博览会恰逢中国—东盟建立对话关系20周年，又是中国—东盟自由贸易区如期建成和运行1周年，因此具有重大而特殊的意义。我们将按照中国—东盟博览会的会议机制，提供场地、创造条件、搞好服务，特别给予主题国8个方面的优惠安排。我们将大力支持中国—马来西亚钦州产业园项目建设。希望副总理阁下予以关注并积极支持这一项目建设。

丹斯里慕尤丁感谢郭声琨的盛情邀请。他说，中国—东盟博览会给马来西亚提供了一个很好的机会。通过博览会，我们可以向全世界展现马来西亚的经济社会发展状况，展现我们正在经历的转型和变化，展示我们的产品和服务，展示我们的政策和合作的诚意。我们不仅是要参加博览会，而且更要借此参与并推进对广西贸易、投资等方面的合作。实际上，广西给予主题国的条件非常优惠，服务非常周到，博览会的作用非常突出，这让我们难以拒绝这一盛情邀请。纳吉布总理从国外访问回来后，我将亲自把您的邀请向他转告。

2011年4月4日，广西壮族自治区党委书记、自治区人大常委会主任郭声琨在吉隆坡会见马来西亚贸工部副部长耶谷·沙岸

H.E. Guo Shengkun, secretary of the Communist Party of China (CPC) Guangxi Committee and chairman of the Standing Committee of the Guangxi People's Congress, meets with H.E. Datuk Jacob Dungau Sagan, deputy minister of international trade and industry of Malaysia on April 4, 2011 in Kuala Lumpur, Malaysia

4月4日上午，郭声琨在吉隆坡会见了马来西亚贸工部副部长耶谷·沙岸。郭声琨介绍了第八届中国—东盟博览会及马来西亚主题国筹备工作情况，希望马来西亚贸工部与广西一道，共同做好马来西亚主题国的相关工作。特别是推动马来西亚国家领导人出席本届博览会，尽快确定马来西亚主题国的相关活动方案，推动更多的马来西亚工商界参展参会。耶谷·沙岸说，东南亚经济发展与中国经济发展紧密相关，中国—东盟自贸区的如期建成和顺利运行，有力地推动了双方的贸易与发展。马来西亚很高兴担任第八届中国—东盟博览会的主题国，贸工部一定会尽力推动马来西亚国家领导人参加本届博览会。同时，我们已授权MATRADE（马来西亚对外贸易发展局）为博览会进行积极的筹备工作。我们将推动更多马来西亚企业参加博览会，并在此期间举办推介会，希望广西方及博览会组委会给予大力支持。马来西亚商界人士对参与中国发展很感兴趣，特别是希望加强在食品、建材、房地产，以及信息通信、教育、环境保护、金融服务等服务领域的合作。马方鼓励和支持钦州产业园建设，将鼓励更多商界人士在钦州产业园投资。

4月4日下午，郭声琨在吉隆坡会见了马来西亚房屋与地方政府部部长曹智雄。郭声琨感谢曹智雄为推动广西与霹雳州建立友好区州关系积极牵线搭桥，诚挚地邀请马来西亚国家领导人和曹智雄再次率团出席博览会。马来西亚是东盟各国中综合实力、发展后劲、发展前景最好的国家之一。广西企业要“走出去”，马来西亚是最合适的选择地之一。我们还将推动双方在文化、教育、旅游、经贸、产业等方面务实合作，实现互利双赢。曹智雄说，霹雳州跟广西签订建立友好区州关系协议，对双方来说都是值得鼓励的事情。我们将继续支持双方进一步加强务实合作。中国—东盟博览会对东盟国家来讲意义重大。马来西亚政府和商界高度重视中国—东盟博览会，房屋与地方政府部将会尽力推动马来西亚国家领导人出席第八届博览会。相信在双方的共同努力下，双方合作一定能够取得更加丰硕的成果。

4月15日上午，广西壮族自治区党委书记、自治区人大常委会主任郭声琨在海南博鳌拜会了中共中央政治局原委员、国务院前副总理、中国国际经济交流中心理事长、博鳌亚洲论坛副理事长曾培炎。

曾培炎说，本次博鳌亚洲论坛规格高、规模大、影响广泛。广西是国内唯一受邀参加的省区。这说明近年来广西北部湾经济区开放开发确实是风生水起，广西在中国—东盟自贸区建设中的地位日益突出，广西在区域合作中的影响力大大增强。希望广西利用好这一平台，发挥自身优势，不仅与东盟各国，同时也与世界其他国家开展更为深入的合作与交流。

郭声琨说，曾培炎理事长长期以来对广西经济社会发展倾注了大量心血，在推动广西北部湾经济区建设、重大项目审批等方面都给予广西巨大支持，广西人民永远铭记。现在中国国际经济交流中心的“智库”可以说是阵容豪华、影响巨大。我们恳请曾培炎理事长能够担任广西咨询委员会顾问，为广西经济社会发展出谋划策，把更多“广西题材”、“广西板块”推向全国、推向全球。博鳌亚洲论坛和中国—东盟博览会同为国家外交战略服务，郭声琨请求曾培炎理事长能够为论坛和博览会牵线搭桥，实现互利共赢。

2011年 5 月11日，广西壮族自治区主席马飚率广西代表团对文莱进行为期 4 天的正式访问。期间，拜会了文莱苏丹哈桑纳尔·博尔基亚，会见了文莱工业与初级资源部部长叶海亚，就全面加强广西与文莱在经贸、农业、渔业、文化、旅游、青年交流等方面的合作达成广泛共识。马飚在拜会文莱苏

2011 年 5 月 11 日，广西壮族自治区主席马飚在文莱拜会了文莱苏丹哈桑纳尔·博尔基亚

H.E. Ma Biao, governor of Guangxi Zhuang autonomous region at an audience with His Majesty Sultan Haji Hassanal Bolkiah Mu'izzaddin Waddaulah, the Sultan and Yang Di-Pertuan of Brunei Darussalam on May 11, 2011 in Brunei Darussalam

丹哈桑纳尔·博尔基亚时说，广西与文莱有很强的互补优势和很多的相似性，加强广西与文莱的交流合作前景十分美好。广西代表团已经与文莱工业和初级资源部举行了会谈，双方达成了广泛共识，一致认为应进一步推进广西和文莱在经贸、农业、渔业、旅游、文化、卫生、科技、教育、青年交流等方面的合作。

苏丹对马飚率团访问文莱表示欢迎，他说，他曾到访广西，在南宁受到了广西人民热情友好的接待。文莱非常重视发展与中国的关系，也非常重视加强与广西的交流合作。很高兴得知这次文莱工业与初级资源部与广西代表团就加强交流合作交换了意见。文莱政府有关部门此前已就加强农业、渔业、旅游等领域的合作与广西方面签订相关协议和备忘录，希望双方进一步推进各领域的合作，加强高层互访，加强两地青年之间的交流。

文莱工业与初级资源部部长叶海亚、中国驻文莱大使馆临时代办孙向阳、广西代表团全体成员参加拜会。访问期间，代表团与文中友协和当地知名社团进行了座谈交流。为庆祝中文建交20周年而举行的“魅力广西”文艺晚会在当地引起极大反响。

2010年11月16—23日，广西壮族自治区党委常委、自治区副主席陈武率领广西代表团访问老挝和缅甸，分别拜会了老挝政府总理波松·布帕万、常务副总理宋沙瓦·凌沙瓦及缅甸国家和平与发展委员会第一秘书长吴丁昂敏乌，就进一步推动广西与老挝、广西与缅甸在各个领域的务实合作，巩固和加强广西与老挝、广西与缅甸的友好合作关系进行了会谈和交流。

在拜会老挝总理波松时，陈武对波松为推动老挝与广西在各个领域的务实合作，特别是为推进中国—东盟博览会发展所作出的积极努力和重要贡献表示衷心感谢。陈武向波松简要介绍了广西经济社会发展以及近年来广西与老挝的友好交往情况，并就双方继续共同举办好第八届中国—东盟博览会和商务与投资峰会，做好2011年中老建交50周年系列庆祝活动，进一步深化双边在商贸、农业、教育、矿产资源开发利用等领域的合作，提出了一些建设性的意见和建议。

波松表示，中国—东盟博览会越办越好，反响也越来越大，博览会已经成为老挝企业与中国企业交往的最重要的平台和载体。老挝与广西气候相近，双方发展的互补性强，尤其是在农业生产、矿产资源开发利用等领域，广西有很强的实力，而这正是老挝目前急需的。波松对陈武就增进双边交流与合作所提出的意见和建议表示赞同，并表示将积极引导和促成有关方面加强与广西在各个领域的务实合作，共同造福两地人民。

陈武与老挝常务副总理宋沙瓦·凌沙瓦就推进双方的务实合作进行了深

入探讨和交流，并对老挝农业示范园区建设、农业技术人才培训、矿业合作开发等具体合作项目深入交换了意见。宋沙瓦表示，自己身兼老中合作委员会主席，非常乐意见到通过双方的共同努力，使双方在经贸往来、农业技术推广应用、矿产资源开发利用以及教育、人才培训等方面的合作交流不断得到巩固和提高。

在拜会缅甸国家和平与发展委员会第一秘书长吴丁昂敏乌时，陈武代表广西壮族自治区党委、政府对缅方为推动历届博览会的成功举办所做的大量卓有成效的工作表示高度赞赏和衷心感谢，并就继续共同举办好第八届博览会，进一步推进广西与缅甸在商贸、农业、矿产等领域的务实合作与吴丁昂敏乌进行了广泛深入的交流和会谈。

吴丁昂敏乌表示，缅甸与广西有着长期良好的合作基础，双方合作的空间很大，发展前景非常广阔。特别是广西有中国—东盟博览会这样一个重要的交往平台，相信不断通过双方的共同努力，缅甸与广西在各个领域的合作一定会在现在的基础上得到更大、更快的发展。

（二）加强组织领导

广西壮族自治区党委、自治区人民政府不断加强对中国—东盟博览会承办工作的组织领导。自治区党委常委会多次召开专题会议，自治区人民政府多次召开专题会议，对办好2011年中国—东盟博览会、中国—东盟商务与投资峰会（以下简称“两会”）进行了认真研究部署。自治区党委、自治区人民政府专门召开动员大会和“两会”广西领导小组会议。广西与东盟开放合作领导小组及其统筹协调办公室加强领导，积极统筹各方力量，全力以赴办好盛会。

1. 召开自治区党委常委会会议。2011年4月20日，广西壮族自治区党委常委会召开会议，研究部署经济工作。自治区党委书记郭声琨主持会议并作重要讲话。会议要求着力深化改革开放。突出办好第八届中国—东盟博览会和商务与投资峰会、泛北部湾经济合作论坛、桂台经贸文化交流合作论坛等重大活动，健全完善南宁保税物流中心、钦州保税港区、凭祥综合保税区、北海出口加工区等保税物流体系，充分发挥各类开放平台和载体的作用。

8月26日，广西壮族自治区党委常委会召开会议，听取第八届中国—东盟博览会、中国—东盟商务与投资峰会筹备工作情况的汇报，研究相关问题。自治区党委书记郭声琨主持会议并作重要讲话。

会议指出，在有关部委的大力支持下，中国—东盟博览会、商务与投资峰会已成功举办七届，取得了显著成效，形成了集政治、外交、经贸、人文为一体与东盟合作的新模式，建立了集合中央各部委和东盟10国资源、协调全区对东盟开放合作的工作机制，形成和增强了自我发展能力，实现了服务国家战略，服务中国—东盟自贸区建设，服务各部委、各省（区、市）与东盟交流合作，服务广西对外开放和经济社会发展“四个服务”的目标。第八届中国—东盟博览会、商务与投资峰会既面临新机遇，又面临新情况：东盟各国对博览会期望更高，希望中方动员更多广西周边省份的企业参加博览会，以便东盟企业扩大与中方企业的交往与合作；国家部委希望通过博览会，帮助企业了解自贸区优惠政策，不断完善各部委支持博览会的工作机制，把更多的中国—东盟合作项目放在博览会，放在广西。2011年博览会、商务与投资峰会筹备工作起步早，做得实，取得明显成效，总体形势很好。

会议强调，办好2011年中国—东盟博览会、商务与投资峰会意义重大，要充分认识2011年博览会面临的新形势、新特点、新考验和对我们提出的新要求，充分利用2011年是中国—东盟建立对话关系20周年、中国—东盟友好交流年和中国—东盟自由贸易区建成1周年的有利节点。从现在开始，各层面、各部门都要更加紧张地进入角色，发扬办好前七届博览会的拼搏精神，切实增强责任感和紧迫感，扎实做好各项筹备工作，再创佳绩、再立新功。

会议强调，第八届中国—东盟博览会、商务与投资峰会已经到了筹备工作关键阶段。要深入贯彻落实胡锦涛总书记关于把博览会“长期办下去，办出特色，办出成效”的重要指示精神，紧紧依靠博览会中方组委会的力量，把准广西自身定位，创新工作，强化措施，举全区之力办好“两会一节”，进一步提升博览会的规格、规模和成效。要继续做好国内外嘉宾、企业领导人和兄弟省（区、市）领导出席会议的邀请工作。要下大力气营造更加良好的环境氛围、文化氛围和社会氛围，为办好博览会打下更加坚实的基础。要发挥广西的区位优势和博览会的平台作用，进一步做好开展跨境贸易人民币结算试点工作，深入推动中国与东盟各国互联互通，深化开放合作，创造更多、更好“走出去”的条件，突出更多“走出去”的内容，动员更多的区内外企业走向东盟，使企业“走出去”取得更加务实丰硕的成果。要更加高标准、严要求地抓好安保工作，强化工作落实、责任落实，采取更加积极有效的安全保卫措施。要更加广泛、深入、创新地做好宣传报道工作，推动博览会办得更有特色，更有实效。要通过办好这次博览会，认真总结成功举办博览会的成果，推动和完善中国—东盟博览会、商务与投资峰会机制化工作，进一步提高承办工作的机制化、常态化、科学化水平。

2. 召开动员大会。2011年10月14日，第八届中国—东盟博览会和中国—东盟商务与投资峰会暨全区深化与东盟开放合作动员大会在南宁召开。广西壮族自治区党委书记、自治区人大常委会主任郭声琨在会上作重要讲话，自治区主席马飚主持会议。

郭声琨在讲话中强调，我们要站在全局和战略高度，充分认识进一步办好“两会”的重大意义。在党中央、国务院的亲切关怀和国家有关部委的大力支持下，经过全区上下艰苦努力，“两会”已经连续成功举办了七届，取得了显著成效。办好“两会”，关系到我国周边外交大局和对外开放战略的实施，是党中央、国务院交给我们的一项重要政治任务，有利于进一步发挥广西在中国—东盟合作中的前沿和窗口作用。2011年恰逢中国—东盟建立对话关系20周年、中国—东盟友好交流年、中国—东盟自由贸易区建成1周年，在新的形势下进一步办好“两会”，具有更加重要的意义。

郭声琨要求，充分发挥“两会”平台作用，进一步全面深化广西与东盟开放合作。一要加强统筹协调，有效集合各种资源和信息，不断完善广西与东盟开放合作常态化工作机制。二要突出工作重点，不断深化广西与东盟务实合作。要有效利用“两会”平台作用，加快推进广西北部湾经济区开放开发，推进大湄公河次区域合作、泛北部湾经济合作、中越“两廊一圈”合作、南宁—新加坡经济走廊和跨境经济合作区建设。特别是要以推进交通、电讯、信息网等互联互通，完善保税物流体系，加快建设面向东盟的南宁商务总部经济基地，不断扩大文化、教育、卫生、体育、广播影视、新闻出版等人文领域交流合作为重点，形成与东盟国家互利共赢的全方位、多领域开放合作格局。三要加快工作进度，不断推动广西与东盟全面开放合作行动计划有效实施。广西已在交通建设、农业资源、工业优势产业、港口物流、旅

2011年10月14日，第八届中国—东盟博览会和中国—东盟商务与投资峰会暨全区深化与东盟开放合作动员大会在广西南宁召开

Theme conference for promoting Guangxi's opening-up and cooperation with the ASEAN countries & preparations for the 8th CAEXPO and the 8th CABIS held in Nanning, Guangxi, China on October 14, 2011

游、经济合作区、人力资源培训、文化、体育等10个方面，制定了与东盟全面开放合作的行动计划。各级各部门要积极有效实施行动计划，全面开展与东盟的务实合作。四要狠抓项目落实，加快广西北部湾经济区开放开发。要利用好“两会”平台，全力推进北部湾经济区与东盟有关重大合作项目建设，切实做好项目的跟踪和服务工作，力保取得实实在在的效果。特别是要推动中马钦州产业园建设取得新进展。同时，大力招商引资，引导更多企业和投资者进入广西北部湾经济区。

郭声琨指出，2011年的“两会”，背景特殊，意义重大。我们要突出中国—东盟建立对话关系20周年合作共赢、突出中国—东盟自贸区建设显著成果、突出博览会常办常新，继续举全区之力，确保2011年“两会”办得更加隆重、更加热烈、更有实效、更具影响力。一要加强组织领导，严格落实责任。各地各部门要把参与和服务“两会”作为当前头等大事来抓。二要加强统筹协调，抓好重点环节，确保各项活动有序、顺畅运行。同时，安排好顺访活动，促进广西对外开放。三要积极探索创新，提高经贸实效。四要办好系列论坛，拓宽“南宁渠道”。五要强化安全保卫，确保万无一失。六要坚持周到细致，做好接待服务，做到文明、好客、友善。七要加大宣传力度，营造良好氛围，使博览会和商务与投资峰会的影响力走向全国、走向东盟、走向世界。

郭声琨特别强调，广西一定要站在大局和全国的高度来维护社会稳定，严防出现影响社会稳定的群体性事件。要做到强化领导，各级领导特别是党政一把手要坚守岗位，落实责任，守土有责；要深入基层、深入群众了解情况、化解矛盾；如因情况分析不透、措施不得力而引发重大问题，要严格追究领导责任。要做到密切配合，形成合力。要做到维护稳定与解决问题相结合。要做好应对预案措施，提高应对处置的能力。希望各地一把手和全体领导干部高度重视，保持广西社会和谐稳定、民族团结和睦的良好局面。

马飚在主持会议时要求，各级各部门要及时传达学习贯彻落实好会议精神，让广大干部群众充分认识到办好“两会”的重要意义，切实增强责任感和紧迫感，做好各项工作部署，进一步完善、细化具体的工作方案。要加强领导，落实责任单位，落实责任人，切实做好安保和服务接待工作，展示广西承办大型国际性活动的能力和水平。特别是做好安全维稳工作，为当前和“两会”营造安全祥和的气氛和环境，以办好“两会”为平台，全方位推动广西与东盟开放合作。

自治区领导车荣福、温卡华、陈武、石生龙、余远辉、周新建、刘新文、莫永清、陈章良、杨道喜、高雄、梁胜利、李达球、蒋培兰、苏道俨，自治区人民检察院检察长张少康，武警广西总队总队长李勇出席会议。

3. 召开“两会”广西领导小组会议。2011年9月29日，中国—东盟博览会、中国—东盟商务与投资峰会广西领导小组在南宁召开会议，听取筹备工作进展汇报，研究部署有关工作。广西壮族自治区主席、“两会”广西领导小组组长马飚主持会议并讲话。自治区领导、“两会”广西领导小组副组长李金早、沈北海、余远辉、梁胜利参加会议。

2011年9月29日，中国—东盟博览会、中国—东盟商务与投资峰会广西领导小组会议在南宁召开

The CAEXPO and the CABIS Guangxi Leaders' Group has a meeting in Nanning on September 29, 2011

马飚在听取“两会”及南宁国际民歌艺术节（以下简称“两会一节”）筹备工作汇报后给予充分肯定。他说，中央对于办好2011年的“两会”非常重视，国家相关部委继续给予大力支持，东盟国家积极参与。在自治区有关部门的团结协作下，2011年“两会一节”各项筹备工作正按预定方案有序推进，整个筹备工作扎实有效。各级各部门要充分认识办好2011年“两会一节”的重大意义，克服麻痹松懈思想，做到思想上更加重视、态度上更加认真，措施上更加有力、方案上更加具体，确保2011年“两会一节”圆满成功，确保取得良好成效。

马飚强调，当前要加强“两会”指挥中心的组织领导，抽调人员进驻指挥中心集中办公，落实国庆期间值班值守。要进一步细化方案，注重细节。要加强演练，通过演练发现问题，及时纠正，进一步完善方案。要进一步明确工作重点，统筹策划好一系列重点活动。要进一步加强安全保卫工作，确保万无一失。要做好市容市貌整治，加强“城乡清洁工程”实施力度。要加强宣传报道工作，营造良好氛围，同时有关部门要做好对媒体的服务和接待。

广西壮族自治区人民政府秘书长王跃飞等“两会”广西领导小组成员，“两会”指挥中心各工作部负责人，各有关单位负责人参加会议。

4. 召开“两会”广西指挥中心工作会议。2011年9月16日，广西壮族自治区党委常委、自治区副主席、中国—东盟博览会和中国—东盟商务与投资峰会广西指挥中心总指挥陈武主持召开会议，听取第八届中国—东盟博览会、中国—东盟商务与投资峰会有关筹备工作情况汇报，并对下一阶段工作作出重要部署。会议强调，要抢抓中国—东盟建立对话关系20周年带来的重大历史机遇，增强责任感，服务大局，努力把第八届博览会、商务与投资峰会办得更有特色，更有实效。

陈武要求指挥中心各部门要按自治区党委、政府的部署，抓住中国—东盟建立对话关系20周年、中国—东盟友好交流年、中国—东盟自贸区建成1周年的契机，把“两会”推向新的高潮，在中国和东盟产生更大的影响，为广西对外开放作出新的贡献。要增强责任感，增强大局观念，全力以赴团结拼搏，高效有序，高标准严要求，扎扎实实，认真细致，做好“两会”筹备工作的每一项工作。

陈武强调，当前要着重抓好以下各项工作：加强与国家部委和东盟方联系，跟踪和落实好各项工作；围绕重大活动安排，策划和组织好各场活动；做好采购商邀请工作，加强广西与东盟合作项目的组织，提高经贸成效；加强展览管理，营造良好洽谈交易环境；做好峰会各项工作；突出重点，提高水平，做好接待工作；确保安全，体现便利，做到安全保卫万无一失；加强宣传策划，结合中国—东盟建立对话关系20周年系列纪念活动，扩大影响；做好南宁市氛围营造和保障工作；做好“两会”市场开发工作，促进“两会”持续发展。

会上，“两会”指挥中心各工作部有关负责人汇报了第八届中国—东盟博览会、第八届中国—东盟商务与投资峰会筹备工作进展情况。

（三）举全区之力办盛会

广西继续举全区之力办好盛会。全区各级各地、各行各业上下动员，全力投入，第八届中国—东盟博览会各项筹备工作紧锣密鼓、如火如荼展开。

1. 华南城签约成为中国—东盟博览会轻工产品展览会场。

2011年7月11日，中国—东盟博览会秘书处与南宁华南城正式签订战略合作备忘录，南宁华南城展览中心正式成为第八届中国—东盟博览会轻工产品展览会场。从此，地处南宁市江南区的南宁华南城轻工展馆与南宁国际会展中心主展馆及广西展览馆农业展馆一起，成为第八届中国—东盟博览会的展区。

南宁华南城是一个以打造东盟商贸物流城为目标，立足南宁、服务北部湾、辐射东盟的一个品种齐全、现代化程度高的工业原料及产品展示交易中心、现代综合商贸物流中心和高端生产服务业基地。在这里设立轻工展会

南宁华南城外景
South China City (Nanning)

场，为中国—东盟自由贸易区搭建了一个集展示与交易于一体的国际化轻工业平台，有利于展会和市场的结合，彰显商贸交流效应，充分体现中国—东盟自贸区建成带来的利益。中国—东盟博览会与南宁华南城牵手，南宁华南城轻工展会场作为第八届中国—东盟博览会的分会场，可谓是水到渠成，应势而生。这不仅丰富了中国—东盟博览会的展示领域，扩展了客商层面，还有利于进一步提升中国—东盟博览会的影响力，推动和促进中国与东盟各国的商贸流通。

本届展会规模在2010年中国—东盟轻工产品展的基础上进一步增加，分为珠宝首饰工艺品、日用消费礼品、消费电子及境外展区等四个展区，重点突出展示与市民日常生活密切相关的轻工产品，旨在通过重点展示中国与东盟各国的优质轻工产品，整合和优化泛北部湾区域和东盟10国轻工业采购资源。

中国—东盟博览会秘书处副秘书长王雷表示，博览会将华南城作为轻工展会场，不但可以满足博览会规模扩大的需要和专业化发展的需要，更能进一步促进南宁市的经济发展。今后，秘书处将深化博览会的带动作用，适应国际展会专业化发展的趋势，探索在中国—东盟博览会品牌下，选择中国与东盟最具合作潜力的行业领域，举办更多专业展，促进双方行业对接，提高中国与东盟的产业合作水平。博览会与华南城将在更多领域、更深层次开展合作，共同打造中国—东盟博览会专业展，为南宁市会展业、服务业和南宁市地方经济的发展增添活力和动力，实现互利共赢的目标。

2. 广西国际博览事务局与广西大学签订战略合作框架协议。

2011年5月6日，广西国际博览事务局与广西大学战略合作框架协议签字仪式暨中国—东盟博览会秘书处研究中心揭牌仪式在广西大学君武馆第二会议室举行。这是继2010年11月5日广西大学与广西国际博览事务局共建艺术人才培养教学研究基地之后，双方合作的又一个成果。

广西国际博览事务局局长郑军健、副局长农融等领导，广西大学党委书记梁颖、校长唐纪良及相关部门负责人出席仪式。广西大学副校长陈保善主持仪式。

本着优势互补、资源共享、互利共赢的合作原则，双方签署了战略合作框架协议，协议主要内容包括中国—东盟研究院的共建、“中国—东盟博览会秘书处研究中心”名称的使用、科研合作、咨询服务、网站建设、人才培养、信息交流等方面。

梁颖在致辞中指出，广西大学将加强与广西国际博览事务局合作，做大做强中国—东盟研究院，力争使之成为研究和解决中国—东盟经济社会发展重大问题和关键技术、承担重大科技任务和提供重大战略咨询的重要基地，在服务广西、服务全国乃至服务东盟中发挥重要作用。

郑军健希望合作双方把握新机遇，不断探索合作新模式，使合作向更深、更广领域拓展，更好地服务国家战略、服务自贸区建设、带动广西发展。

3. 第八届中国—东盟博览会主题口号诗词楹联征集活动。

2011年8月11日，第八届中国—东盟博览会主题口号诗词楹联征集活动启动，中国和东盟国家的广大应征者热情参与，积极投稿。此次活动共收到应征作品共3000多份，其中主题口号应征作品1000多条，副主题口号应征作品2198条；诗词、楹联应征作品1000多首。

活动要求主题口号类的应征作品应紧扣2011年中国—东盟建立对话关系20周年、中国—东盟友好交流年、中国—东盟自由贸易区建成1周年和博览会的内容。诗词楹联类的应征内容要反映2011年中国—东盟建立对话关系20周年、中国—东盟友好交流年、中国—东盟自由贸易区建成1周年建设成就，展望中国—东盟合作前景、自贸区前景以及中国—东盟博览会成功举办等内容的诗词楹联作品。

据统计，征集活动历时1个月，参赛作者来自全国24个省（区、市），近自广西，远至哈尔滨、上海、昆明等地，东盟国家友人也积极投稿；应征者中有国家公务员、在校大中专学生、企业职工、教师、军人、退休干部，以及文联、楹联学会会员等，其中业余创作人员占了很大比例。

在应征投稿中，不少作者在作品之后附上创作构思以及参赛感想，有些在校学生寄来的作品，一笔一画书写工整。还有的作者意犹未尽，自己动手将文字作品设计成书法绘画一同寄送。一位来自新加坡的作者还用不太熟练的中文完成了作品创作。来自四川地震灾区的应征者在字里行间寄托了对自贸区和博览会美好将来的憧憬。

活动最后确定了四条第八届中国—东盟博览会口号，分别是：

二十年合作拓展　自贸区成果显著　博览会常办常新

中国—东盟博览会　10+1>11

博览会让自贸区明天更美好

精彩博览会　繁荣自贸区

4. 第八届中国—东盟博览会指定接待宾馆授匾仪式。

2011年9月22日，“两会”指挥中心为第八届中国—东盟博览会指定宾馆授匾，荔园山庄、沃顿国际大酒店、明园新都酒店、邕江宾馆、南宁饭店、锦华大酒店、明园饭店、南宁圣展酒店、凤凰宾馆、南宁西园饭店、南宁桂景大酒店、鑫伟万豪酒店、南宁跨世纪大酒店、翔云大酒店、运德旅游大酒店等15家宾馆获得本届博览会指定接待宾馆荣誉称号。

为了做好出席第八届博览会的中外领导人、各国嘉宾以及参展参会客商的接待服务工作，进一步规范“中国—东盟博览会指定接待宾馆”称号的使用，培育博览会接待品牌宾馆（酒店），中国—东盟博览会秘书处从2011年6月就开始启动第八届博览会指定接待宾馆评审工作，依据国家标准《旅游饭店星级的划分与评定》、广西地方标准《旅游饭店服务质量规范》，并结合博览会的具体情况，制定了《中国—东盟博览会指定宾馆评定标准》及《中国—东盟博览会指定宾馆服务规范》，为南宁宾馆行业树立了服务新标杆。

第八届中国—东盟博览会指定宾馆评审活动得到了南宁市各酒店积极响应，纷纷递交申请材料。博览会秘书处专门成立了评定工作小组，对递交申请材料的酒店进行了实地考察，并邀请由自治区旅游局、自治区接待办、自治区外办、自治区物价局、南宁市外办等单位组成的专家小组进行了评审。为确保指定宾馆的消防安全，确保接待质量，博览会秘书处还要求各指定的接待宾馆签署《第八届中国—东盟博览会消防安全承诺书》，把消防安全落实到宾馆接待的各项工作环节中，把消防安全落到实处，责任到人。

“两会”副总指挥、中国—东盟博览会秘书处秘书长、广西国际博览事务局局长郑军健，“两会”指挥中心统筹协调部副部长、中国—东盟博览会秘书处副秘书长、广西国际博览事务局副局长李文杰出席授匾仪式并分别为荣获指定接待宾馆称号的15家宾馆授匾。指挥中心统筹协调部、接待工作部相关领导出席仪式。参加授匾仪式的有15家指定接待宾馆的代表，多家驻广西媒体应邀观摩。万豪酒店餐饮总监Alfred Spieler代表指定接待宾馆发言并宣誓，将严格遵照中国—东盟博览会指定接待宾馆规范要求，继续做好本职工作，为中国—东盟博览会的接待服务工作，作出更加突出的贡献。

会后，参加授匾仪式的各家新闻媒体考察了荔园山庄等指定宾馆，亲身感受了盛会服务人员饱满的工作热情和高质量的服务水平。

5. "携手共进35天"启动仪式。

2011年9月16日，第八届中国—东盟博览会、中国—东盟商务与投资峰会"携手共进35天"启动仪式在南宁国际会展中心举行。广西壮族自治区主席马飚出席启动仪式，宣布第八届中国—东盟博览会、中国—东盟商务与投资峰会"携手共进35天"活动启动，标志着第八届"两会"筹备工作进入最后冲刺阶段。

自治区党委常委、自治区常务副主席李金早，自治区党委常委、宣传部部长沈北海，自治区党委常委、南宁市委书记车荣福，自治区党委常委、自治区副主席陈武，自治区副主席、自治区公安厅党委书记、厅长梁胜利，东盟国家驻南宁外交使节，自治区政府秘书长王跃飞出席启动仪式。

陈武在仪式上讲话。他说，第八届中国—东盟博览会、商务与投资峰会作为20周年系列纪念活动的重要组成部分，是20年辉煌成就的体现，将展示双方合作的美好前景，意义重大。广西作为承办方，将发挥共办优势，加大创新力度，把本届博览会、商务与投资峰会办得更有特色、更有实效，并以此为平台，积极参与和推进大湄公河次区域合作、泛北部湾经济合作、中越"两廊一圈"合作、南宁—新加坡经济走廊、跨境经济合作区建设，大力推进广西北部湾经济区开放开发，加快推进交通等基础设施的互联互通，为服务中国—东盟友好合作作出新的更大贡献。

越南驻南宁总领事范星梅在仪式上发言说，中国—东盟博览会、中国—东盟商务与投资峰会已成为东盟与中国合作框架下最重要的活动之一，为广西与东盟国家各个地方乃至东盟与中国发展全面合作关系起到了推动作用。东盟各国驻南宁总领事馆将一如既往地与承办方广西紧密合作，携手共进，

2011年9月16日，第八届中国—东盟博览会、中国—东盟商务与投资峰会"携手共进35天"启动仪式在南宁国际会展中心举行

35-Day Countdown Ceremony for the 8th CAEXPO and the 8th CABIS held in Nanning International Convention & Exhibition Center on September 16, 2011

为东盟—中国友谊和全面合作关系深入发展作出贡献。

东盟参展参会企业代表也在仪式上发言。参加启动仪式的还有自治区有关部门负责人、各界代表共300多人。

6. 首席战略合作伙伴、战略合作伙伴和合作伙伴一如既往支持第八届中国—东盟博览会。

2011年10月10日，中国有色矿业集团有限公司（以下简称“中国有色集团”）与中国—东盟博览会秘书处签约合作，成为第八届中国—东盟博览会首席战略合作伙伴，这也是第一家中央企业成为博览会的首席战略合作伙伴。

2009年起，中国有色集团已连续两年成为中国—东盟博览会的战略合作伙伴。中国有色集团总经理罗涛说：“我们重视中国—东盟博览会这个平台。与博览会建立首席战略合作伙伴关系，正是要向东盟国家传递一个信息：中国与东盟是可以互惠互利的。依托中国—东盟博览会的桥梁作用，中国有色集团进一步扩大了与东盟国家的合作，已与东盟10国中的8国建立了良好的业务往来。”

中国—东盟博览会秘书处秘书长郑军健在仪式上说，中国有色集团是大型央企，是我国有色金属工业“走出去”的排头兵，也是成为第八届博览会首席战略合作伙伴的首家央企。中国有色集团在2009年、2010年连续两年成为战略合作伙伴，给予了博览会战略性的支持。中国有色集团高度重视博览会的平台作用，充分利用博览会搭建的便捷渠道，扩大了与东盟的交流合作，加强了与广西的友好合作，取得了丰硕的成果。郑军健表示，第八届博览会作为20周年系列纪念活动的重要组成部分，将为企业创造商机，特别是在推动企业“走出去”方面推出一系列新举措。会期期间还将举行东盟国家领导人与企业家座谈会等出题国系列活动，并安排更多政商高端对接活动。

在签约仪式上，广西壮族自治区副主席林念修与中国有色集团总经理

2011年10月10日，第八届中国—东盟博览会首席战略合作伙伴签约仪式在广西南宁举行

Signing Ceremony of the 8th CAEXPO Chief Strategic Partner held in Nanning, Guangxi, China on October 10, 2011

罗涛还共同为中国有色集团（广西）平桂飞碟股份有限公司、中国有色（桂林）矿产地质研究院有限公司两个项目揭牌。

10月12日下午，第八届中国—东盟博览会战略合作伙伴签约仪式暨合作伙伴授牌仪式在广西南宁举行。来自矿产、农业、金融、通信等多个行业的50多家优秀企业成为本届博览会的战略合作伙伴和合作伙伴。在签约仪式上，广西投资集团、广西农垦集团、广西柳州钢铁集团、广西有色金属集团、中国移动广西公司等5家企业，成为第八届中国—东盟博览会战略合作伙伴。

而此次与第八届中国—东盟博览会签约的合作伙伴，是各领域、各行业的优秀企业，包括中国银行广西分行、广西北部湾银行、广西区农村信用社、中国电信广西分公司等40多家知名企业，涵盖食品、机械制造、金融投资、工艺品等多个行业。

本届中国—东盟博览会所有的战略合作伙伴和合作伙伴为博览会的顺利举办起到了推进作用。

7. “两会”指挥中心举行综合演练。

为确保第八届中国—东盟博览会、中国—东盟商务与投资峰会开幕式、巡馆、欢迎宴会等重要专场活动的顺利进行，同时确保“两会”各重要活动场所准备到位、安全有序，2011年10月17日，“两会”指挥中心组织各方进行综合演练，并对“两会”重要活动现场进行检查。广西壮族自治区党委常委、自治区常务副主席李金早参加演练，现场检查指导工作。

李金早强调，各部门要以高度的责任感、科学的态度、严密的组织，做好“两会”的筹备工作，各重要专场活动要做到安全、准时，要注重细节，确保效果。针对演练中发现的问题要及时整改，进一步完善工作方案，加强各部门之间的衔接、配合，确保各项工作有序、顺畅开展。同时要明确责任，落实专人保障各重要场馆和活动现场的电、水供应，确保各项配套设施的供应和服务万无一失，确保“两会”顺利召开。

此次演练以出席中国—东盟博览会开幕式、中国—东盟商务与投资峰会开幕式的重要贵宾转场为重点，演练内容包括活动的统筹安排和通知、安全保卫组织、交通组织、新闻记者组织、车辆配备及调度、外事礼宾协调、通讯技术保障、巡馆演练等，此外还重点检查了转场活动内部的筹备工作和各场活动之间的衔接工作。综合演练结束后，立即召开了评估总结会，对各场活动反映出的不足和问题，及时进行总结并提出整改意见。

“两会”信息通讯技术保障也举行了应急综合演练。10月15日，第八届中国—东盟博览会、中国—东盟商务与投资峰会指挥中心信息通讯技术保障组组织自治区通信管理局、自治区工信委、中国电信广西公司、中国移动广西公司及中国联通广西分公司等5家单位，在南宁国际会展中心开展了2011年“两会”信息通讯技术保障应急综合演练。该演练从实战角度出发，检验了应急通信队伍的快速响应、跨专业联动、有效应对及快速保障的能力。此次演练与往年相比具有规模大、参演人员多、技术全面等特点。

8. 第八届中国—东盟博览会志愿者上岗，志愿者卡通形象揭晓。

2011年10月15日上午，第八届中国—东盟博览会、第八届中国—东盟商务与投资峰会志愿者培训上岗暨志愿者卡通形象揭幕仪式在广西民族大学举行。据了解，共有1300多名志愿者服务本次盛会。

“两会”指挥中心招募的志愿者分别来自广西大学、广西民族大学等全区8所高校。在“两会”期间，他们将承担开幕式现场、新闻中心、宾馆咨询等300多个岗位的场馆翻译、礼仪接待、后勤保障、应急支援等志愿服务工作。

在仪式上，身穿白色或黄色志愿者服装的志愿者举手宣誓，立志为即将召开的“两会”提供热情周到的服务。“累，并快乐着。”来自广西大学2008级日语专业的罗良吉同学已经参加过三届中国—东盟博览会志愿服务工作。他说：“在志愿活动中，自己的处事能力和管理能力得到很大提高，外语能力得到锻炼，最重要是社会责任感得到增强。”为了做好这次志愿服务工作，罗良吉在语言、东盟国家背景资料搜集、礼仪等方面都做了准备。

为不断激发广西志愿者参与“两会”志愿服务的热情，2011年“两会”指挥中心统筹协调部推出了可爱的志愿者卡通形象。“两会”志愿者卡通形象为一男一女，分别身着第八届“两会”志愿者的服装，挥手向大家致意，寓意青年志愿者朋友们手拉手、用真心的微笑迎接国内外宾客、共同努力服务好“两会”。

小结　强大合力推动筹备工作机制化

中国—东盟博览会是11国共办的盛会，体现了中国和东盟共同的需要、共同的目标、共同的利益。因此，博览会始终得到中国和东盟各国领导人的高度重视，亲自推动，11国政府部门、商界和社会各界紧密合作，确保了博览会越办越有成效。第八届中国—东盟博览会的筹备工作在前七届基础上，11国共办机制更加深化，形成了强大合力。

一是国家层面的支持力度加大。中国国务院总理温家宝2011年4月出访马来西亚期间，邀请马来西亚总理纳吉布参加第八届中国—东盟博览会。博览会中方组委会10多个成员单位及其他国家部委加大对博览会的支持力度。不仅有商务部、外交部、中国贸促会等部委在展会组织上大力支持，而且有环保部、科技部、国家质检总局、文化部、新闻出版总署等多个部委在博览会的框架下举办多领域交流活动，完善了"各部委支持办好博览会、博览会积极为各部委工作搭好平台"的工作机制，这为博览会的成功举办提供了强大的组织保障。

二是11国共办机制进一步深化。文莱苏丹哈桑纳尔·博尔基亚、时任老挝总理波松、马来西亚副总理丹斯里慕尤丁以及多位东盟国家部长级官员在会见到访的广西代表团时，均表示支持办好第八届中国—东盟博览会。东盟秘书长素林对办好第八届中国—东盟博览会提出了4点建议。东盟各国建立了跨部门的博览会组委会。其中，越南、老挝成立了包括贸易、投资、旅游等部门的跨部门的组委会。印尼、柬埔寨成立了跨部门工作机制。东盟各国在动员和推动本国贸易、投资、旅游、金融、物流、新闻、文化、教育等政府部门及地方政府支持和参与博览会方面，积累了很多好经验，取得了良好成效。马来西亚作为第八届博览会主题国，成立了由本国贸易、投资、旅游等多个部门组成的跨部门筹备委员会，精心筹备展览组织和主题国系列活动。

每年举办的中国—东盟博览会高官会办得更加务实，2011年的高官会还首次举办有11国投资促进部门官员参加的博览会投资合作工作会议，使博览会的共办机制从贸易部门向投资促进主管部门延伸；举办面向东盟经贸官员的中国—东盟经贸关系研修班，增进了博览会与东盟各国贸易部门的日常工作联系；举办面向东盟新闻官员和新闻记者的东盟经贸记者培训班，增进了博览会与东盟新闻界的相互了解和交流。这些举措，都体现了第八届博览会的共办机制在前七届基础上更加务实、更加具体、更加深化。

三是承办方广西继续举全区之力办好盛会。广西壮族自治区党委、自治区人民政府高度重视第八届博览会承办工作。自治区党委书记、自治区人大常委会主任郭声琨多次主持召开自治区党委常委会会议，研究部署博览会工作。自治区主席马飚多次听取博览会工作汇报，并主持召开“两会”广西领导小组会议等，加强对筹备工作的领导。郭声琨、马飚等自治区领导率广西代表团出访东盟国家，会见东盟国家领导人、部长和商界人士，继续加强与东盟方高层和商界的交流，完善博览会的共办机制。其中，2011年4月，郭声琨率团出访马来西亚，拜会了马来西亚副总理丹斯里慕尤丁和相关部长，邀请纳吉布总理和丹斯里慕尤丁副总理出席博览会。5月，马飚率团出访文莱，拜会了文莱苏丹哈桑纳尔·博尔基亚，会见了文莱工业与初级资源部部长叶海亚，并邀请苏丹和叶海亚部长出席第八届博览会。2010年11月，自治区党委常委、自治区副主席陈武率团访问老挝和缅甸，分别拜会了老挝政府总理波松·布帕万、常务副总理宋沙瓦·凌沙瓦及缅甸国家和平与发展委员会第一秘书长吴丁昂敏乌，邀请老挝和缅甸领导人出席第八届博览会。以上访问都得到东盟方的积极回应。在自治区党委、自治区人民政府的领导下，广西全区上下万众一心、全力以赴办盛会。

四是社会各界热情参与。在第八届中国—东盟博览会筹备工作中，社会各界人士积极参与，献策献力。第八届博览会口号、诗词楹联征集活动启动后，退休干部、公务员、企业职工、教师、学生等广西各行各业人士踊跃参加。每年的博览会志愿者招募，都吸引数以万计的市民、学生报名，本届报名人数比往届更多。举办地南宁积极为盛会的举办营造喜庆、热烈的氛围，包括对重点场所、重点路线进行装点，对博览会分会场广西展览馆和广西民族博览馆进行重点装饰，以及集全市园林系统力量，在公园、广场等重要户外场地及道路布置鲜花等。

第二章

2 高层聚首盛会隆重热烈 政商互动对接促进共赢

——第八届中国—东盟博览会开幕

每一届中国—东盟博览会的开幕式，都是对源远流长的友好交往历史的回顾和日益深化的合作成果的演绎，也是对中国—东盟自由贸易区美好未来的展望。

中国和东盟各国领导人率团高规格出席第八届中国—东盟博览会。第八届中国—东盟博览会开幕式以“二十年合作拓展、自贸区成果显著、博览会常办常新”为主题，形象地表达出博览会11国共办、领导人亲自推动的特点，反映中国—东盟建立对话关系20周年的辉煌成就，展示博览会促进中国—东盟友好交流、推动自贸区建设取得的成果和作出的贡献。

会期举行了双方领导人、部长、地方负责人之间的会见。中国总理温家宝与马来西亚总理纳吉布见证了中马钦州产业园区签约仪式并为该园区揭牌，共同出席了主题国“魅力之城”开馆仪式。马来西亚举办了主题国系列活动。各国领导人、部长、代表团团长巡视了展馆。会期还举行了22场政要与商界的高端对接活动，带动了商家的务实合作，推动了多领域交流。

第八届中国—东盟博览会规格高，多层次交流活动丰富务实，表明在中国—东盟建立对话关系20周年的特殊历史背景下，面对复杂的世界经济形势，中国和东盟更加重视博览会的平台作用，进一步加强互利合作，继续共同推进自贸区建设，实现共同发展、共同繁荣。

A Grand Gathering of Top Leaders, a Series of Government–to–Business Interactions for Win–Win Results

—The 8th CAEXPO Opening Ceremony

The opening ceremony of each of the previous CAEXPOs has turned out to be a wonderful and ingenious showcase of the historical and time–honored China–ASEAN friendly exchanges, and the rich fruits of the increasingly closer bilateral cooperation in recent years. It also forecasts a brighter future for the newly–completed China–ASEAN FTA.

Heads of state/government of China and the 10 ASEAN member states have headed their high–profiled delegations to the 8th CAEXPO, whose opening ceremony takes "20 Years' Cooperation, Fruitful CAFTA and Ever–growing CAEXPO" as its theme. The program well displays CAEXPO's unique feature, i.e., a grand trade event, which is co–sponsored by China and the 10 ASEAN member countries, gains full support from the state/government leaders. It also showcases the grand achievement gained in the past two decades of ASEAN– China dialogue relations, and CAEXPO's contribution to the promotion of bilateral friendly exchanges and the CAFTA construction.

During the 8th CAEXPO, meetings were arranged for state leaders, ministers and local executives. H.E. Wen Jiabao, premier of the State Council of China joined the Right Honorable Dato' Sri Mohd Najib Tun Abdul Razak, prime minister of Malaysia to witness the signing of China–Malaysia Qinzhou Industrial Park and also unveiled the plate for it, besides participating in the inaugural ceremony of the City of Charm of Malaysia, the Country of Honor of the 8th CAEXPO. In the meanwhile, Malaysia hosted a series of programs and activities to promote itself as the 8th CAEXPO Country of Honor. State leaders, ministers and heads of government delegations visited the CAEXPO exhibition pavilions. During the fair period, 22 high–end meetings were arranged for political and business leaders, which had injected new vigor for the pragmatic cooperation of businesses, thus fueling the exchanges of different areas.

The 8th CAEXPO has attracted high–profiled participants and arranged programs in diverse forms, which is good evidence that, against the backdrop of the 20th anniversary of ASEAN–China dialogue relations and the increasingly complex world economic situation, both sides are willing to use the CAEXPO as a platform to further strengthen the bilateral win–win cooperation and push forward the CAFTA construction, for common development and prosperity.

一 中国和东盟国家参加第八届中国—东盟博览会

2011年10月21日，第八届中国—东盟博览会在中国广西南宁隆重开幕。本届中国—东盟博览会作为中国—东盟建立对话关系20周年系列纪念活动的重要组成部分，意义重大。

（一）中国和东盟政要高规格出席第八届中国—东盟博览会

中国和东盟各国政府高度重视本届中国—东盟博览会，各国均派出高规格代表团出席盛会。中国总理温家宝、马来西亚总理纳吉布、柬埔寨首相洪森、缅甸副总统吴丁昂敏乌、老挝副总理宋沙瓦、泰国副总理吉滴叻、越南副总理阮春福、文莱工业与初级资源部部长叶海亚、新加坡贸工部部长林勋强、菲律宾贸工部副部长珍艾达·马拉雅、印度尼西亚贸易部部长助理穆赫达塔尔、东盟秘书长素林率团出席本届博览会。

中国商务部国际谈判贸易代表兼副部长高虎城，财政部部长谢旭人，海关总署署长于广洲，国家质量监督检验检疫总局局长支树平，中国贸促会会长万季飞，国务院副秘书长、总理办公室主任项兆伦等中方组委会成员单位领导，中国有关部委领导以及中国和东盟国家环保、金融、电信等多个领域的部长出席本届盛会。出席本次博览会的部长级贵宾有240人，其中中方141人，东盟和其他国家部长级贵宾99人。

中国和东盟各国领导人率团高规格出席本次盛会，表明在中国—东盟建立对话关系20周年的特殊历史背景下，面对复杂的世界经济形势，中国和东盟更加重视博览会的平台作用，显现出进一步加强互利合作，继续共同推进自贸区建设，实现共同发展、共同繁荣的信心和决心。

（二）中国和东盟商家和世界知名企业参展参会

第八届中国—东盟博览会上中外企业参展参会更加踊跃，实际安排展位4700个。参展企业总数2300家，同比增长4.6%。

东盟及区域外国家参展更加踊跃，共办特色更加鲜明。东盟及区域外国家使用展位数达到历史最高水平。印尼、老挝、马来西亚、缅甸、泰国、越南等6个东盟国家包馆，40多家东盟知名品牌企业参展。

中国国内企业参展空前高涨，博览会在区域内外的市场吸引力进一步增强。国内企业申请展位数超过计划数的30.2%。

本届博览会参展的名优企业多。台北世界贸易中心、日本首次分别组织企业整体参展。

本届博览会中外采购团组有70多个，多于往届。其中，东盟采购商报名热情空前高涨，有600多家东盟采购商参会，东盟采购商团组数比上届增加20%以上。意大利、法国、德国、埃及、日本、韩国等国家和地区的采购商积极到会采购。

（三）中外媒体积极参会报道

第八届中国—东盟博览会吸引大批中外记者参会报道。据统计，前来采访报道“两会一节”的中外媒体和记者共275家1738名，分别比上届增加38.19%和19.23%。其中，国外媒体77家记者138名，港澳台媒体17家记者56名，中央媒体和国内行业媒体91家记者378名，外省媒体15家记者23名，广西媒体58家记者1022名。参会记者中的外国媒体、中央涉外媒体和港澳台媒体、网络媒体记者所占比重较往届呈普遍增多的趋势。

《人民日报》、新华社、《光明日报》、《经济日报》、中央人民广播电台、中央电视台、中国国际广播电台、中国新闻社等中央新闻单位都派出强大的报道团队参会报道。

文莱《婆罗洲纪事报》、柬埔寨国家电视台、柬埔寨国家电台、印尼安塔拉通讯社、老挝《人民报》、马来西亚《新海峡时报》、《缅甸时报》、菲律宾《星报》、新加坡亚洲新闻台、新加坡新传媒广播、泰国国家电台、泰国国家广播电台、越南之声广播电台、胡志明之声等东盟国家媒体，以及朝日新闻、香港《文汇报》、《大公报》、《商报》、《澳门日报》、香港亚洲电视、凤凰卫视等境外媒体都派记者到会报道。

二　第八届中国—东盟博览会开幕式

2011年10月21日上午，万众瞩目的第八届中国—东盟博览会在南宁国际会展中心朱槿花厅隆重开幕。

中共中央政治局常委、国务院总理温家宝，第八届中国—东盟博览会主题国马来西亚总理纳吉布，柬埔寨首相洪森，缅甸副总统吴丁昂敏乌，老挝副总理宋沙瓦，泰国副总理吉滴叻，越南副总理阮春福，文莱工业和初级资源部部长叶海亚，新加坡贸工部部长林勋强，菲律宾贸工部副部长马拉雅，印度尼西亚贸易部部长助理穆赫达塔尔，广西壮族自治区党委书记郭声琨，广西壮族自治区主席马飚，东盟秘书长素林出席开幕式。

开幕式会场气势恢弘，主舞台造型别致、庄重、大气。与往年博览会开幕式不同的是，主席台正上方，“庆祝中国—东盟建立对话关系20周年”的横幅格外醒目。环廊四周，八棵金色大树枝叶相连，象征着中国—东盟博览会举办八届，生机盎然。绿色背景将会场装点得绿意盎然，体现了本届博览

2011年10月21日，第八届中国—东盟博览会在广西南宁隆重开幕

The 8th CAEXPO grandly opens in Nanning, Guangxi, China on October 21, 2011

会“环保合作”的重点主题。

2011年10月21日，中国国务院总理温家宝宣布第八届中国—东盟博览会开幕

H.E. Wen Jiabao, premier of the State Council of China declares the open of the 8th CAEXPO on October 21, 2011

2011年恰逢中国—东盟建立对话关系20周年、中国—东盟友好交流年、中国—东盟自贸区建成1周年，在此背景下举办第八届中国—东盟博览会具有特殊而深远的意义。20年来，中国—东盟合作领域不断拓展深化，双方关系从对话关系上升为战略伙伴关系；中国—东盟博览会走过8年，常办常新，推动中国—东盟自贸区加速发展，成果显著。中国与东盟友好交流、合作共赢，给双方人民带来巨大福祉，为本地区和平稳定与繁荣发展作出了重要贡献。

上午9时，开幕式正式开始。马来西亚总理纳吉布、广西壮族自治区主席马飚、中国商务部国际贸易谈判代表兼副部长高虎城分别在开幕式上致辞。第八届中国—东盟博览会主题国马来西亚国际贸易和工业部部长穆斯塔法、东盟秘书长素林共同主持开幕式。

2011年10月21日，马来西亚总理纳吉布在第八届中国—东盟博览会开幕式上致辞

Right Honourable Dato' Sri Mohd Najib Tun Abdul Razak, prime minister of Malaysia addresses the 8th CAEXPO opening ceremony on October 21, 2011

纳吉布说，我们为马来西亚作为本届博览会的主题国深感荣幸。2011年的博览会尤为重要，因为2011年恰逢东盟与中国建立对话关系20周年。20年来，在共同发展理念的支撑下，双边关系蓬勃发展。我们努力推进经济一体化进程，通过实施中国—东盟自贸区协议来促进区域合作及全球融合。这一协议让来自中国与东盟的商家均可从贸易中获得更大收益并扩展投资机会，从而在本地区和世界其他地方产生更大影响。纳吉布对中国提出将双边贸易额在2015年增至5000亿美元由衷赞赏。他指出，双方更应加强沟通和相互理解。他认为，本届博览会将环保和可持续发展作为重点主题，意义也在于改变我们自己的行为方式，发展更清洁环保的技术，降低排放，确保我们的子孙能从我们手里继承一个清洁、安全和健康的星球。

马飚说，8年来，由中国和东盟10国共办的中国—东盟博览会常办常

2011年10月21日，广西壮族自治区主席马飚在第八届中国—东盟博览会开幕式上致辞

H.E. Ma Biao, governor of Guangxi Zhuang autonomous region addresses the 8th CAEXPO opening ceremony on October 21, 2011

新，硕果累累，搭建了中国和东盟友好交流、经贸合作和深化友谊的重要平台，形成了中国—东盟“南宁渠道”，成为中国—东盟自贸区建设发展的助推器，成为中国与东盟友好合作的象征。5年前，中国—东盟建立对话关系15周年纪念峰会在广西南宁与博览会同期举办。今天，第八届中国—东盟博览会作为中国—东盟建立对话关系20周年系列纪念活动的重要内容，将创造更多商机，进一步提升友好合作水平，加深传统友谊，谱写共赢发展的新篇章。我们愿与各方加强合作，共同开创中国—东盟友好合作的美好未来。

2011年10月21日，中国商务部国际贸易谈判代表兼副部长高虎城在第八届中国—东盟博览会开幕式上致辞

H.E. Gao Hucheng, China international trade representative & vice-minister of commerce of China addresses at the 8th CAEXPO opening ceremony on October 21, 2011

高虎城说，中国和东盟建立对话关系20年来，各领域友好互利合作不断推进，经贸合作成效尤其显著。我们携手合作，实现了全面建成中国—东盟自由贸易区的目标。我们共同搭建了中国—东盟博览会平台，增进企业间的交流与合作，促进了双边贸易和投资，为双方企业和人民带来了实实在在的利益。本届博览会将充分反映20年来双方合作的辉煌成就，展示中国—东盟自贸区广阔商机和美好前景，为双方企业创造更多的合作机会。

剪彩仪式前，播放了精彩的短片，回顾了中国与东盟友好交往的历史，展示了中国与东盟友好合作的丰硕成果。双方建立对话关系20年来，友好合作快速发展，特别是中国—东盟博览会的举办，加快了自贸区建设进程，为双方友好合作注入新的动力。在博览会的推动下，中国与东盟双边贸易额2004年提前一年实现1000亿美元目标，2007年提前三年实现2000亿美元目标，2010年接近3000亿美元；双方在农业、信息产业、人力资源开发、相互投资、湄公河流域开发、交通、能源、文化、旅游、公共卫生和环保等11大重点领域的合作取得显著成果。短片结束后，来自中国和东盟的青少年走上舞台，分别用本国语言介绍自己，这使博览会开幕式显得既端庄又活泼，且有特色，引起了中外嘉宾的共鸣，全场掌声雷动。

随后，剪彩嘉宾上台，剪彩台升起，红绸飘落，露出“中国—东盟青少

第八届中国—东盟博览会开幕式剪彩仪式

Ribbon-cutting moment of the 8th CAEXPO opening ceremony

年交流活动中心”牌匾。11国的青少年向剪彩嘉宾献上了象征友谊与希望的绣球和表达庆贺与祝福的花朵。14位剪彩嘉宾将象征喜庆与祝福的花朵，放在剪彩台上，共同庆祝中国—东盟合作交往取得的成就，共同祝愿中国与东盟友好合作代代相传。

9时30分，中国国务院总理温家宝宣布：“第八届中国—东盟博览会开幕！”这时，舞台两侧的大屏幕上，出现“10+1＞11”标语，寓意中国与东盟10国携手同行、共创辉煌。

主席台上，一幅印有中国与东盟10国标志性建筑和博览会会徽的大型画卷瞬间展开，如飞瀑直下，大气磅礴。主席台上红色“火焰”欢快地跳跃，寓意中国—东盟自贸区的红红火火、蒸蒸日上。

在本届博览会开幕式上揭牌的“中国—东盟青少年交流活动中心”，是由中国国务院总理温家宝亲自倡议建立的，目前已在广西落户，即将投入使用。它是中国—东盟20年对话合作的重要成果之一，为中国与东盟国家青少年合作交流提供了具体平台和场所，并将进一步拓展和深化中国与东盟国家青少年间的合作交流。

温家宝总理一向关心呵护青少年。5年前，温家宝总理和东盟10国领导人在南宁出席中国—东盟建立对话关系15周年纪念峰会和第三届博览会开幕式时，当年15岁的女孩丁钰谨为他捧上剪彩用的珍珠。5年后的今天，在博览会开幕式贵宾室里，温总理听说丁钰谨在礼仪队伍中，主动走上前，亲切地和她握手，并详细询问她的学习、生活情况。

11国少年心心相连，友好情谊代代相传。5年后的今天，来自中国与东盟10国的青少年，带着美好的祝福和期待来到博览会开幕式现场。他们是传递中国—东盟友谊的接力者，代表着未来，让人们看到了中国与东盟美好的明天。

伴随着漫天飞舞飘扬的礼花、彩带和雷鸣般的掌声，第八届中国—东盟博览会正式拉开序幕。

开幕式前，各国领导人一道步入贵宾室，饶有兴致地观看了中国—东盟建立对话关系20周年成就展、中国—东盟博览会成果展和主题墙。在精心设计的题词本上，各国领导人分别用本国文字为中国—东盟博览会题写会名及寄语。

中国财政部部长谢旭人，人力资源和社会保障部部长尹蔚民，住房和城乡建设部部长姜伟新，卫生部部长陈竺，国务院研究室主任谢伏瞻，国务院副秘书长、总理办公室主任项兆伦，外交部副部长傅莹，国家发改委副主任穆虹，中国贸促会会长万季飞，民政部副部长姜力，国务院研究室副主任田学斌等中方组委会成员单位领导，国家其他有关部委领导，广西壮族自治区党政军领导马铁山、陈际瓦、李文潮、李金早、沈北海、车荣福、温卡华、陈武、石生龙、黄道伟、余远辉、周新建、吴恒、刘新文、莫永清、荣仕星、文明、陈章良、杨道喜、李康、梁胜利、林国强、蒋济雄、李达球、蒋培兰、彭钊、李彬，自治区高级人民法院院长罗殿龙，自治区人民检察院检察长张少康，以及世界知名企业家、商协会会长、区域经济研究专家与参展参会客商代表共1000多人参加开幕式。

出席第八届中国—东盟博览会的各国嘉宾

Heads of state/government and ministers of China and ASEAN at the 8th CAEXPO opening ceremony

三　中外贵宾巡视展馆

2011年10月21日上午，在第八届中国—东盟博览会开幕式结束后，中共中央政治局常委、国务院总理温家宝在广西壮族自治区党委书记、自治区人大常委会主任郭声琨，自治区主席马飚以及有关部委领导的陪同下，兴致勃勃地巡视了第八届中国—东盟博览会国际经济合作展区、“魅力之城”专题展区以及农业先进适用技术暨高新技术专题展区。

国际经济合作展区在前七届的基础上更加突出展示中国企业在对外承包工程和各行业投资合作领域中的整体实力和核心竞争力，进一步突出宣传“走出去”的成果。温家宝依次走过中国有色矿业集团有限公司、北京建工集团、中国水利电力对外公司等国内知名企业的展位，鼓励国内企业结合中国—东盟自贸区建成的新形势新机遇，积极稳妥实施“走出去”战略，实现更好更快发展。

2011年10月21日，中共中央政治局常委、国务院总理温家宝巡视第八届中国—东盟博览会展馆

H.E. Wen Jiabao, premier of the State Council of China inspects the 8th CAEXPO exhibition pavilions on October 21, 2011

“魅力之城”展区独具特色，让人流连忘返。温家宝微笑着巡视展区，向各国参展人员亲切地挥手致意。他走进中国“魅力之城”海南国际旅游岛展区，勉励海南省利用好博览会平台，不断深化与东盟各国的旅游产业合作，加快推进海南国际旅游岛建设。温家宝对博览会“魅力之城”展区给予高度评价，认为这个展区集中展示了各国“魅力之城”的风土人情和发展优势，有利于各方促进交流，深化友谊。这种模式很有意思、很有意义。

农业先进适用技术暨高新技术专题展区集中展示了适合东盟国家需求的农业技术和高新技术。温家宝在高产优质木薯新品种、太阳能集热系统等展位前驻足停留，与参展人员亲切交谈。温家宝表示，中国—东盟博览会为中国—东盟双边推广农业先进适用技术，促进高新技术合作交流搭建了一个很好的平台，希望大家继续努力，实现共赢。

在欢乐热烈的气氛中，温家宝与马来西亚总理纳吉布来到本届博览会的主题国马来西亚魅力之城——“柔佛州”的展馆，共同为极具特色的“柔佛”馆开馆。

马来西亚国际贸易和工业部部长穆斯塔法，自治区领导李金早、沈北海、余远辉、梁胜利陪同巡馆或参加马来西亚魅力之城开馆仪式。

10月21日，率团前来南宁出席第八届中国—东盟博览会的东盟各国政要，兴致勃勃地巡视了博览会展厅展馆。

马来西亚总理纳吉布在广西壮族自治区党委常委、宣传部部长沈北海

2011年10月21日，马来西亚总理纳吉布巡视第八届中国—东盟博览会展馆

Right Honourable Dato' Sri Mohd Najib Tun Abdul Razak, prime minister of Malaysia inspects the 8th CAEXPO exhibition pavilions on October 21, 2011

的陪同下，出席了本届博览会主题国马来西亚商品馆开馆仪式并巡视了本国商品馆。马来西亚商品馆内先后奏响马来西亚和中国两国国歌，在电脑屏幕前，纳吉布手按触摸屏，随着两根蓝白两色的牛角柱向两边开启，马来西亚商品馆正式开馆。2011年马来西亚已是连续第六次包馆参展，商品馆以白色为主基调，参展商品既有中国消费者熟悉的白咖啡、燕窝、榴莲、巧克力等饮料、食品，又有保健用品、医疗产品、教育咨询服务及精致的乐器。看到本国琳琅满目的展品，纳吉布十分高兴。他饶有兴致地参观了教育、医疗护理服务、餐饮、保健等各个展位，鼓励马来西亚参展商利用中国—东盟博览会这个平台，大力开拓中国市场，与中国客商共拓商机。巡馆过后，纳吉布和沈北海还共同见证了马来西亚隆基马中国际集团公司与中国湖南永州市政府的合作项目协议书交换仪式。

柬埔寨首相洪森在广西壮族自治区党委常委车荣福的陪同下，来到南宁国际会展中心巡视博览会展馆。作为南宁市的荣誉市民，这是2004年以来洪森第六次率团出席中国—东盟博览会和商务与投资峰会，并巡视博览会展馆。在柬埔寨包用的展馆里，洪森兴致勃勃地参观多个摊位，一会儿停下观看琳琅满目的商品，一会儿询问产品的性能价格，并同摊主一一握手问候，并对柬埔寨本届有那么多的商品参展感到非常满意。在柬埔寨的“魅力之城”拉达那基里省展厅，用树枝编制成的小村落以及村民现场织布、演员载歌载舞等，引起了洪森的极大兴趣。他向大家挥手致意，并嘱咐大家充分利用中国—东盟博览会这个平台，促进柬中双方在贸易、文化、旅游等各领域的合作和发展。

2011年10月21日，柬埔寨首相洪森巡视第八届中国—东盟博览会展馆

H.E. Samdech Hun Sun, prime minister of Cambodia inspects the 8th CAEXPO exhibition pavilions on October 21, 2011

越南副总理阮春福在广西壮族自治区党委常委、政法委书记温卡华的陪同下，进入南宁国际会展中心越南馆巡馆，受到越南参展商的热烈欢迎。阮春福驻足展区，了解越南商品参展情况，盛情邀请温卡华等品尝越南咖啡、干果等特色食品；并欣然题词，赞叹越南展台漂亮、展品丰富，鼓励参展商提供更多更好的商品，加强与中国企业的经贸往来，进一步扩大双方在多领域的交流与合作。以越南会安古城特色建筑为原型装饰的越南“魅力之城”会安展厅显得分外古色古香，身着民族传统服饰的越南姑娘跳起极具民族风情的舞蹈，迎接阮春福一行的到来。以自然风光、传统手工艺、特色食品扬名的会安曾是东南亚地区最繁荣的商港之一，历史文化悠久，1999年被列入世界文化遗产名录。在会安古楼模型前，阮春福邀请温卡华及展馆人员合影留念。在先进技术展厅，阮春福饶有兴致地了解了广西特产罗汉果的生产情况。

2011 年 10 月 21 日，越南副总理阮春福巡视第八届中国—东盟博览会展馆

H.E. Nguyen Xuan Phuc, vice-prime minister of Vietnam inspects the 8th CAEXPO exhibition pavilions on October 21, 2011

缅甸副总统吴丁昂敏乌在广西壮族自治区党委常委、自治区纪委书记石生龙的陪同下，首先来到东盟商品馆缅甸馆，驻足观看玉器、家具等展台；并与客商亲切交谈，鼓励他们利用中国—东盟博览会这一平台，把缅甸的特色商品，推销到中国市场。随后，吴丁昂敏乌与石生龙等来到“魅力之城”缅甸馆，吴丁昂敏乌向石生龙介绍了缅甸的旅游业、运输业、农业、林业、渔业等方面的发展情况，还特意介绍了缅甸的投资环境及优惠措施。他欢迎石生龙一行到缅甸考察、访问。最后，吴丁昂敏乌饶有兴致地参观了农业产品深加工区，并对广西大学培育出的高产优质木薯新品种——新选048表现出浓厚的兴趣，希望缅甸能引进这一新品种。

2011年10月21日，缅甸副总统吴丁昂敏乌巡视第八届中国—东盟博览会展馆

H.E. Thiha Thura U Tin Aung Myint Oo, vice- president of Myanmar inspects the 8th CAEXPO exhibition pavilions on October 21, 2011

老挝副总理宋沙瓦在广西壮族自治区党委常委、自治区统战部部长黄道伟的陪同下，首先来到位于14号展馆的老挝商品展区进行巡视。古色古香的原木家具、色彩缤纷的首饰品、做工精致的手工纺织品等具有浓郁老挝特色的展品，让人目不暇接。宋沙瓦仔细询问展品的价格、制作工艺、市场销售情况等，与参展企业人员亲切交谈、合影，并兴致勃勃地见证了老挝东南亚集团股份有限公司建立驻中国华东地区办事处的签约仪式。随后，宋沙瓦一行参观了“魅力之城”老挝馆，听取工作人员对此次参展的巴塞省在农作物种植、旅游观光等方面的情况介绍。走进农业先进技术展厅参观，宋沙瓦对中国企业在节能减排环保技术方面取得的成就表示赞赏。

2011年10月21日，老挝副总理宋沙瓦巡视第八届中国—东盟博览会展馆

H.E. Somsavat LENGSAVAD, deputy prime minister of Lao PDR inspects the 8th CAEXPO exhibition pavilions on October 21, 2011

泰国副总理吉滴叻在广西壮族自治区人大常委会副主任吴恒的陪同下，和着泰国经典传统民族音乐的节拍巡视泰国馆。首先映入眼帘的是泰国茉莉香米的展位，展台上的电磁炉里已煮好雪白的茉莉香米饭，吉滴叻和吴恒一起饶有兴趣地围上围裙，现场抄起锅铲，放鸡蛋、火腿肠、胡萝卜等配料炒起米饭来，随后与陪同人员分享"劳动成果"。接着，吉滴叻参观了泰国手工艺品、药品、保健品等展台，分别跟参展商亲切交谈并合影留念。他希望参展商能通过此次博览会获得更多的商机。之后，吉滴叻一行又高兴地来到"魅力之城"泰国馆。四位赤足且盛装打扮的泰国姑娘翩翩起舞欢迎贵宾，并给吉滴叻、吴恒戴上了象征友谊长存的手链。吉滴叻一行还在环保展示台前观看了泰国环保工作的成果宣传。吉滴叻说，环保是全球关注的热点，泰国对此很重视，希望下一步跟中国在环保方面开展环境领域的高层对话，促进政策交流，搭建合作平台，建立伙伴关系，为区域可持续发展共同努力。

文莱工业与初级资源部部长叶海亚一行在广西壮族自治区人大常委会副主任莫永清的陪同下，参观了中国—东盟投资合作、"魅力之城"、先进技术展厅和文莱商品展区。文莱"魅力之城"斯里巴加湾展区，是一座极具民族风情的乡间度假屋，享有"东方威尼斯"之美誉。步入先进技术展厅，叶海亚一行便被广西大学的木薯新品种吸引。叶海亚说，文莱也有木薯，此行必须多了解广西在木薯多功能利用方面的技术。叶海亚还对太阳能交流水渠系统、农村净水材料设备、苗木修剪机、污水处理器等现代农业技术表现出浓厚兴趣。他表示，2011年是中国与文莱建交20周年，两国关系一直发展良好，希望双方能利用中国—东盟博览会这个平台，加深农业技术、经贸旅游等多方面的交流合作。

2011年10月21日，文莱工业与初级资源部部长叶海亚巡视第八届中国—东盟博览会展馆

H.E. Pehin Dato Awang Haji Yahya, minister of industry & primary resources of Brunei Darussalam inspects the 8th CAEXPO exhibition pavilions on October 21, 2011

新加坡贸工部部长林勋强在广西壮族自治区人大常委会副主任文明的陪同下，巡视了中国—东盟博览会展馆。林勋强一行驻足了解新加坡参展商品内容，向企业家了解项目推介情况，和企业家亲切交谈并合影，表示要利用好中国—东盟博览会这个平台，把新加坡的特色商品推向广阔的中国市场。随后，林勋强一行还巡视了“魅力之城”展厅以及先进技术数字展厅。

2011 年 10 月 21 日，新加坡贸工部部长林勋强巡视第八届中国—东盟博览会展馆

H.E. Lim Hng Kiang, minister of trade and industry of Singapore inspects the 8th CAEXPO exhibition pavilions on October 21, 2011

印度尼西亚贸易部部长助理穆赫达塔尔在广西壮族自治区政协副主席蒋济雄的陪同下，先来到印尼“魅力之城”西巴布亚省展馆，印尼舞蹈演员跳起欢快的舞蹈，淋漓尽致地演绎了印尼的民族风情。在农产品深加工区，中国的先进节能减排环保新能源技术、罗汉果深加工产品等深深吸引了印尼客

2011 年 10 月 21 日，印度尼西亚贸易部部长助理穆赫达塔尔巡视第八届中国—东盟博览会展馆

H.E. Dr. Muchtar, chairman of the Indonesian Anti-dumping Committee and the assistant minister of trade sector policy of Indonesia inspects the 8th CAEXPO exhibition pavilions on October 21, 2011

人。在一台养着金鱼的污水处理技术演示装置旁，穆赫达塔尔饶有兴趣地听取了工作人员的讲解，并走向各展台收集名片。在印尼商品展区，穆赫达塔尔驻足了解印尼的工艺品、食品等参展商品，与参展商人亲切交谈，询问参展情况，并鼓励印尼企业加强与中国企业的交流与合作，进一步扩大双方经贸往来。

菲律宾贸工部副部长马拉雅一行在自治区政协副主席李达球的陪同下，来到菲律宾馆，向参展商了解产品情况，并向李达球介绍了菲律宾的旅游、农业、工业、自然资源等方面情况。随后，在菲律宾“魅力之城”普林塞萨港市展厅，马拉雅向李达球介绍了普林塞萨港市的旅游资源、地理奇观、社会经济发展和环境保护等方面情况，两人还与展区工作人员合影留念。在广西农业产品深加工区，马拉雅被展区门口高达3米多的高产优质木薯吸引。当工作人员介绍说用木薯制取乙醇可生产乙醇汽油时，她表现出浓厚兴趣，希望将来菲律宾从广西引种木薯优良品种，在木薯生物质能源科研和技术开发方面扩大双方的交流与合作。

2011 年 10 月 21 日，菲律宾贸工部副部长马拉雅巡视第八届中国—东盟博览会展馆
H.E. Ms. Zenaida Cuison-Maglaya, under secretary of the Department of Trade and Industry of the Philippines inspects the 8th CAEXPO exhibition pavilions on October 21, 2011

四　主题国活动

马来西亚是第八届中国—东盟博览会主题国。展会期间，马来西亚举行了主题国开馆仪式、中马钦州产业园区签约暨揭牌仪式、专场推介会等一系列丰富多彩的主题国活动。

1. 主题国开馆仪式。2011年10月21日上午，第八届中国—东盟博览会主题国马来西亚“魅力之城”柔佛州开馆仪式在南宁国际会展中心2号展厅隆重举行。作为第八届中国—东盟博览会主题国，中方对马来西亚出任主题国予以高度重视和特别礼遇安排，中共中央政治局常委、国务院总理温家宝和马来西亚总理纳吉布共同出席马来西亚“魅力之城”的开馆仪式。当日，马来西亚商品馆同时开馆。

第八届中国—东盟博览会主题国马来西亚“魅力之城”柔佛州开馆仪式

Inaugural ceremony of the pavilion of City of Charm (Johor) of Malaysia , Country of Honor of the 8th CAEXPO

9时45分，温家宝总理来到马来西亚“魅力之城”柔佛州展馆，马来西亚总理纳吉布热情迎接。两国领导人共同触摸开馆仪式的水晶球，马来西亚“魅力之城”正式开馆。中马两国领导人共同在开馆仪式纪念牌上签名，纪念这一历史性的时刻。

随后，温家宝总理和纳吉布总理兴致勃勃地参观了马来西亚柔佛州“魅力之城”展厅。展厅中，屹立海边的石柱壁雕、美丽的海滩、奇形怪状的小岛等自然景观的展示牌，展现了柔佛州浓浓的异域风情。曾经是世界最高建筑的马来西亚标志“双子塔”，则充满现代感。

马来西亚作为本届博览会主题国，继续独立包馆，并展示更多特色商品，重点展示品牌展品，以及食品、家具家居、工艺品及珠宝饰品等特色商品，首次设置形象展区，展示马来西亚的棕榈油、橡胶、矿产品等。

素有“亚洲珍宝柔佛”美称的柔佛州，是马来西亚13个州之一，位于马来西亚西部的最南端，也是亚洲大陆最南端的陆地。东面是南中国海，是“天赐”的滨海旅游胜地；西面是马六甲海峡，南面隔着柔佛海峡与新加坡毗邻，这里有马来西亚保护的最好的红树林，是著名的海岸线旅游区，保存无数个黄金沙滩及美丽迷人的岸外岛屿，海水清澈。

马来西亚政府对出任博览会主题国非常重视，精心准备，搭建了展示马来西亚深厚文化底蕴和巨大经济潜力的“魅力之城”展区，展示柔佛州的文化，吸引中国的游客到柔佛州旅游。

2. 中国—马来西亚钦州产业园区签字暨揭牌仪式。10月21日，中国—马来西亚钦州产业园区签字暨揭牌仪式在南宁举行。中共中央政治局常委、国务院总理温家宝和马来西亚总理纳吉布见证签约并共同揭牌。

中国—马来西亚钦州产业园区签字仪式
China-Malaysia Qinzhou Industrial Park Signing Ceremony

该项目是温家宝2011年4月28日在出席中国—马来西亚经贸投资合作论坛时提议建立的，马方表示支持。

中马钦州产业园区毗邻30万吨级航道、钦州保税港区和北部湾集装箱干线港，东临西南出海大通道——六景至钦州港高速公路和钦州进港铁路，北接南宁至北海高速公路，区位独特，交通便利。园区规划总面积55平方公里，其中启动区6平方公里，规划总人口47万人。

中马钦州产业园区将由中国商务部和马来西亚贸工部共同合作，按照“政府搭台、园区支撑、企业运作、项目带动、利益共享”的合作开发模式，建立双边合作框架，以综合制造业、信息技术产业和现代服务业为主导，携手面向中马两国以及世界其他国家和地区招商引资，致力建设成为中国—东盟区域性先进制造基地、信息智慧走廊、文化生态新城和合作交流窗口，打造一个集工业、商业、居住三位一体的产业新城，成为中马两国经贸合作的标志性项目和中国—东盟自贸区合作共赢的示范区。

中国商务部国际贸易谈判代表兼副部长高虎城，马来西亚国际贸易和工业部部长穆斯塔法分别代表中马两国在“中马钦州产业园区项目”文本上签字。

广西壮族自治区党委书记、自治区人大常委会主任郭声琨，自治区主席马飚，自治区党委常委、自治区常务副主席李金早，中国驻马来西亚大使柴玺，国务院副秘书长、总理办公室主任项兆伦，外交部副部长傅莹，国家发改委副主任穆虹及钦州市主要领导参加仪式。

五　中国和东盟国家领导人会见

2011年10月20日，国务院总理温家宝在南宁分别会见柬埔寨首相洪森、老挝副总理宋沙瓦、越南副总理阮春福、泰国副总理吉滴叻和缅甸副总统吴丁昂敏乌。温家宝欢迎东盟国家领导人出席第八届中国—东盟博览会和第八届中国—东盟商务与投资峰会，相信中国与东盟的经贸合作会取得更加丰硕的成果。

温家宝积极评价中国同上述东盟各国的双边关系，表示中国愿同各国一道，落实好达成的各项共识，推动双边关系取得新进展。东盟国家领导人均认为，发展同中国的友好关系至关重要，前景广阔，愿与中方一道，推动双边框架下的互利合作深入发展。

温家宝对柬埔寨和泰国遭受罕见的严重洪灾表示深切慰问，两国领导人

2011 年 10 月 20 日，中国国务院总理温家宝在南宁会见柬埔寨首相洪森
Bilateral meeting between Chinese Premier Wen Jiabao and Cambodian Prime Minister Samdech Hun Sun held in Nanning on October 20, 2011

2011年10月20日，中国国务院总理温家宝在南宁会见泰国副总理吉滴叻

Bilateral meeting between Chinese Premier Wen Jiabao and H.E. Kittiratt Na-Ranong, deputy prime minister of Thailand held in Nanning on October 20, 2011

感谢中方及时提供物资援助和帮助。

温家宝希望有关国家政府切实做好在湄公河遇难中国船员的善后事宜，加快案件调查处理工作，共同采取行动，加强在湄公河的执法合作，确保人民生命和财产安全。泰国等有关国家领导人对中方人员遇害深表哀悼，表示愿与中方密切合作，做好案情调查及善后工作，共同维护湄公河航运安全。

温家宝在会见吴丁昂敏乌时表示，实施好中缅重大合作项目符合双方的共同利益，双方要认真落实两国领导人达成的各项共识，切实履行承诺，加强协调沟通，妥善解决出现的问题，确保中缅经贸合作健康顺利发展。吴丁昂敏乌表示，缅方高度重视缅中全面战略合作伙伴关系，将与中方保持密切沟通，积极寻求解决问题的办法，维护共同利益。

2011年10月20日，中国国务院总理温家宝在南宁会见缅甸副总统吴丁昂敏乌

Bilateral meeting between Chinese Premier Wen Jiabao and Myanmar Vice-President Thiha Thura U Tin Aung Myint Oo held in Nanning on October 20, 2011

2011 年 10 月 20 日，中国国务院总理温家宝在南宁会见老挝副总理宋沙瓦

Bilateral meeting between Chinese Premier Wen Jiabao and Lao Deputy Prime Minister Somsavat LENGSAVAD held in Nanning on October 20, 2011

在谈到即将举行的东亚领导人系列峰会时，温家宝说，东盟联合自强，在东亚合作中发挥了主导作用。“10+1”和“10+3”合作分别构成东亚合作的基础和主体，取得了丰硕成果。面对国际金融危机以及各种严峻挑战和复杂因素，这次东亚领导人系列峰会仍要以发展、合作、互利共赢为主题，坚持东盟主导，进一步做实、做强“10+1”和“10+3”合作，推动东亚合作健康发展，达到更高水平。中国坚定奉行睦邻友好的周边外交政策，愿与有关各国一道，妥善处理海上争议，共同为维护地区和平与稳定做出不懈努力。

东盟五国领导人表示，愿巩固“10+1”、“10+3”机制，加强同中国在经济、文化、教育等领域的友好交流与互利合作，夯实东亚合作的基础。

2011 年 10 月 20 日，中国国务院总理温家宝在南宁会见越南副总理阮春福

Bilateral meeting between Chinese Premier Wen Jiabao and Vietnamese Vice Prime Minister Nguyen Xuan Phuc held in Nanning on October 20, 2011

东盟感谢中国长期以来支持东盟主导东亚合作，愿与中方密切沟通配合，推动本次东亚领导人系列会议取得成功，维护共同利益，促进地区和平、稳定与繁荣。

广西壮族自治区党委书记郭声琨、自治区主席马飚、外交部副部长张志军、商务部国际贸易谈判代表兼副部长高虎城等会见时在座。

10月21日，国务院总理温家宝在南宁会见出席第八届中国—东盟博览会和第八届中国—东盟商务与投资峰会开幕式的马来西亚总理纳吉布和东盟秘书长素林。

2011年10月21日，中国国务院总理温家宝在南宁会见马来西亚总理纳吉布

Bilateral meeting between Chinese Premier Wen Jiabao and Malaysian Prime Minister Dato' Sri Mohd Najib Tun Abdul Razak held in Nanning on October 21, 2011

在会见纳吉布时，温家宝表示，近年来，中马传统友谊得到巩固和加深，两国战略性合作不断取得进展，马来西亚成为中国在东盟内最大的贸易伙伴。面对当前错综复杂的国际和地区形势，加强中马合作不仅对两国有利，对中国与东盟关系和东亚合作也有重要意义。双方要继续加强经贸、投资、金融、科技等领域的合作，密切在重大问题上的沟通协调，共同推动两国关系继续向前发展。

纳吉布表示，当前马中关系发展良好，两国相互信任，相互支持，维护了共同利益。马方高度重视对华关系，愿进一步深化两国各领域互利合作，使马中传统友谊发扬光大。马方将与中方密切配合，推动东盟—中国关系和东亚合作健康、稳定发展。

在会见素林时，温家宝表示，中国—东盟建立对话关系20年来，双方各领域合作日益紧密，取得丰硕成果，前景广阔。中方将发展同东盟的战略伙伴关系作为周边外交政策的重要基石，坚定支持东盟一体化建设，支持东盟

2011年10月21日，中国国务院总理温家宝在南宁会见东盟秘书长素林

Meeting between Chinese Premier Wen Jiabao and Dr. Surin Pitsuwan, secretary-general of ASEAN held in Nanning on October 21, 2011

在东亚合作中发挥主导作用，愿与东盟密切配合，推动中国与东盟关系发展迈入新阶段。

素林表示，东盟与中国的关系很好，20年来的友好合作给双方带来实实在在的利益。“10+1”、“10+3”机制成果丰硕，应继续成为东亚合作的基础。东盟感谢中方的支持，希望中方进一步扩大对东盟的投资。东盟愿与中方共同努力，全面推进各领域互利合作，加强在重大地区事务中的协调配合，将东盟与中国关系和东亚合作提升到新的高度。

六　广西壮族自治区领导人会见东盟国家领导人、东盟秘书长及其他重要贵宾

2011年10月20日，自治区党委书记、自治区人大常委会主任郭声琨，自治区主席马飚在南宁会见了柬埔寨首相洪森。

郭声琨说，阁下是广西人民的老朋友、好朋友。特别是您从2004年至2008年连续五年出席中国—东盟博览会和商务与投资峰会，2011年又再次率团出席，我们对此表示衷心感谢。希望柬埔寨政府继续对广西的承办工作给予大力支持，共同办好中国—东盟博览会和商务与投资峰会。建议进一步加强双方在农业、经贸、文化、教育、旅游等领域的合作，进一步加强高层往来，继续加强国际友城交流。

柬埔寨近期遭受历史罕见的严重洪涝灾害，郭声琨向洪森首相并通过他向灾区人民表示深切慰问，相信柬埔寨人民一定能战胜灾害，早日重建家园。

2011年10月20日，广西壮族自治区党委书记、自治区人大常委会主任郭声琨，自治区主席马飚在南宁会见柬埔寨首相洪森

H.E. Guo Shengkun, secretary of the CPC Guangxi Committee and chairman of the Standing Committee of the Guangxi People's Congress and H.E. Ma Biao, governor of Guangxi Zhuang autonomous region at an audience with H.E. Samdech Hun Sun, prime minister of Cambodia in Nanning on October 20, 2011

洪森表示，作为南宁市的荣誉市民，自己非常高兴再次回到广西南宁。他完全赞同郭声琨关于深化双方各领域交流合作的建议，对广西为柬埔寨遭遇洪涝灾害给予的慰问和支持表示衷心感谢，对博览会在促进中国与东盟合作交流发挥的积极作用给予高度赞赏，表示将为促进中柬之间的传统友谊作出新的贡献。

柬埔寨国务兼商业大臣占蒲拉西，柬埔寨驻华大使凯·西索达，中国驻柬埔寨大使潘广学，广西壮族自治区领导李金早、车荣福、余远辉参加会见。

10月20日，广西壮族自治区党委书记、自治区人大常委会主任郭声琨，自治区主席马飚在南宁会见了老挝副总理宋沙瓦。

郭声琨为与宋沙瓦欢聚在南宁感到格外高兴，对老挝政府连续8年组织高规格代表团出席博览会表示衷心感谢。他说，中国和老挝是好朋友、好邻居、好伙伴、好同志。老挝对博览会的高度重视和大力支持，充分体现了双方兄弟般的友谊和真诚的感情。

郭声琨表示，近年来广西与老挝高层往来密切，各领域友好交流与合作不断深化，特别是进出口贸易快速增长、态势良好。今后，希望通过副总理阁下的积极推动，使双方在工作层面上进一步沟通，在农业、经贸、文化、教育以及其他加工领域达成更多合作协议。广西将充分发挥自身的优势，将老挝的资源优势转变为经济优势，帮助老挝逐步建立和完善自身的工业体系。只要有利于双方，有利于改善老挝人民生活水平的事，广西都会全力以赴，抓紧落实，务实推进。我们一定要把上世纪60年代结下的中老友谊代代相传，不断发展，不断提升。

2011年10月20日，广西壮族自治区党委书记、自治区人大常委会主任郭声琨，自治区主席马飚在南宁会见老挝副总理宋沙瓦

H.E. Guo Shengkun, secretary of the CPC Guangxi Committee and chairman of the Standing Committee of the Guangxi People's Congress and H.E. Ma Biao, governor of Guangxi Zhuang autonomous region at an audience with H.E. Somsavat LENGSAVAD, deputy prime minister of Lao PDR in Nanning on October 20, 2011

宋沙瓦为再次率团参加博览会感到高兴，对广西为老挝参展参会给予的便利表示感谢，对广西经济社会发展取得的成绩给予赞赏。他说，老挝与中国的友谊源远流长，广西与老挝地缘相近，通过中国—东盟博览会平台，双方的交流合作日益深化。当前，中国已进入“十二五”发展的新时期，老挝也在实行开放政策，双方应继续落实两党两国领导人达成的共识，将老中全面战略伙伴关系提高到新的水平。他希望广西与老挝在经贸、文化等方面进一步加强交流合作，并预祝本届“两会”取得圆满成功。

广西壮族自治区领导黄道伟、余远辉参加会见。

10月20日，广西壮族自治区党委书记、自治区人大常委会主任郭声琨，自治区主席马飚在南宁会见了越南副总理阮春福。

2011年10月20日，广西壮族自治区党委书记、自治区人大常委会主任郭声琨，自治区主席马飚在南宁会见越南副总理阮春福

H.E. Guo Shengkun, secretary of the CPC Guangxi Committee and chairman of the Standing Committee of the Guangxi People's Congress and H.E. Ma Biao, governor of Guangxi Zhuang autonomous region at an audience with H.E. Nguyen Xuan Phuc, vice-prime minister of Vietnam in Nanning on October 20, 2011

郭声琨对阮春福率团参加第八届中国—东盟博览会和商务与投资峰会表示感谢。他说，中国与越南有着源远流长的传统友谊和根深蒂固的深厚感情。广西与越南更是山连山，水连水，亲上加亲。近年来，广西与越南双方高层往来密切，双方在经贸、农业、交通、教育、文化、体育、旅游等各领域的交流蓬勃开展，越南已连续12年成为广西的第一大贸易伙伴。目前，广西已接收越南留学生4000多人，成为在华越南留学生最多的省区。这些都为我们双方友谊代代相传奠定了良好基础。只要有利于增进双方友谊，有利于促进两国经济发展，有利于提高两国人民生活水平的合作项目，我们都要奋力推进，并在原有的合作基础上，进一步拓展双方在各领域的交流合作。

阮春福对广西方面给予的热情接待表示感谢，并预祝第八届中国—东盟博览会和商务与投资峰会圆满成功。他说，广西与越南是同志加兄弟的关系。越南和广西合作前景广阔，合作潜力巨大。就进一步加强越南与广西的友好合作，阮春福提出四点建议：一是继续加强双方高层往来，促进地方经贸、旅游、教育、文化等领域交流合作。二是继续推进广西与越南边境四省联委会合作机制。三是积极推进中越“两廊一圈”框架下的合作项目。四是加强双方民间团体的交流，为进一步发展彼此兄弟般的友谊打下良好基础。

郭声琨十分赞同阮春福提出的合作建议，表示将进一步加强双方沟通，增进友谊，促进广西与越南边境四省的友好合作关系，更加务实地推动双方全方位合作，取得更大实效，实现互利共赢。

越南驻华大使阮文诗，广西壮族自治区领导温卡华、余远辉参加会见。

10月20日，广西壮族自治区党委书记、自治区人大常委会主任郭声琨，自治区主席马飚在南宁会见了缅甸副总统吴丁昂敏乌。

郭声琨为与吴丁昂敏乌副总统在南宁相聚感到高兴，对副总统阁下率团出席“两会”表示热烈欢迎和衷心感谢。他说，近年来广西与缅甸高层往来不断，有力地促进了双方在经贸、农业、教育、文化等各领域的交流与合作。这充分说明我们的友谊是真诚的，是源远流长的，是根深蒂固的。我们认为，只要有利于双方友谊增进，有利于两国人民生活水平提高，有利于双方经济社会发展的事，就要加强沟通、加快推进。建议双方以本届博览会为新的起点和契机，在原来的合作基础上，进一步拓展合作领域，丰富合作项目，加大推进力度，务求取得实效。

郭声琨说，2012年缅甸将成为第九届中国—东盟博览会主题国，我们将积极支持贵国做好相关参展参会工作，使第九届博览会办得更精彩，成效更显著。相信在缅甸新政府领导下，缅甸的经济发展会越来越好，人民生活水平会越来越高。

2011年10月20日，广西壮族自治区党委书记、自治区人大常委会主任郭声琨，自治区主席马飚在南宁会见缅甸副总统吴丁昂敏乌

H.E. Guo Shengkun, secretary of the CPC Guangxi Committee and chairman of the Standing Committee of the Guangxi People's Congress and H.E. Ma Biao, governor of Guangxi Zhuang autonomous region at an audience with H.E. Thiha Thura U Tin Aung Myint Oo, vice-president of Myanmar in Nanning on October 20, 2011

吴丁昂敏乌表示很高兴能率团参加本届博览会，来到南宁就像回到了自己的家一样。他对广西为缅甸代表团参展参会及参观考察所作的精心安排和热情接待表示感谢。缅甸政府一定精心组织、精心安排，当好2012年博览会的主题国。吴丁昂敏乌对广西为缅甸驻南宁总领事馆开馆及日常工作给予的支持表示感谢，强调缅方高度重视缅中全面战略合作伙伴关系，将一如既往地与广西加强合作交流，增进传统友谊，取得共同发展。

缅甸国家计划与经济发展部部长吴丁乃登、科技部部长吴埃敏、商务部部长吴温敏、外交部副部长吴貌敏、铁道部副部长吴当伦、农业灌溉部副部长吴翁丹，缅甸驻华大使吴丁吴，广西壮族自治区领导余远辉、李彬参加会见。

10月20日，广西壮族自治区党委书记、自治区人大常委会主任郭声琨，自治区主席马飚在南宁会见了东盟秘书长素林。

郭声琨说，秘书长阁下是广西的好朋友、老朋友，也是我们亲密的合作伙伴。长期以来，您致力于发展中国与东盟的友好关系，致力于办好中国—东盟博览会，并给予了悉心指导和大力支持。特别是2011年4月我与阁下在海南博鳌会面时达成了共识，充分利用中国—东盟博览会这个平台，加强中国内陆各省区与东盟的合作交流，而且您亲自出席本届“两会”，并积极推动东盟国家领导人和更多贵宾前来出席，我们对此表示衷心感谢。

郭声琨说，当前广西已成为中国经济增长最快、最富有活力和潜力的地区之一，这也为广西深化与东盟的合作奠定了坚实基础。经过各方的共同努力，本届“两会”的整个筹备工作已经就绪。本届“两会”规格很高，主题鲜明，内容丰富，合作务实，大家都抱以很高的期望。广西一定做好东道

2011 年 10 月 20 日，广西壮族自治区党委书记、自治区人大常委会主任郭声琨，自治区主席马飚在南宁会见东盟秘书长素林

H.E. Guo Shengkun, secretary of the CPC Guangxi Committee and chairman of the Standing Committee of the Guangxi People's Congress and H.E. Ma Biao, governor of Guangxi Zhuang autonomous region meet with Dr. Surin Pitsuwan, secretary-general of ASEAN in Nanning on October 20, 2011

主，使参会各方感到更加满意，收获更多成果。

素林代表东盟各国，诚挚感谢广西壮族自治区党委、政府和各族人民在历届博览会中给予东盟各国人民的最好接待，这充分体现了双方的深厚友谊。2011年适逢中国—东盟建立对话关系20周年，博览会正是中国与东盟友谊与合作的最好象征。得益于博览会，东盟已成为中国第三大贸易伙伴，博览会也办得越来越成功，越来越全面。东盟秘书处诚挚希望中国进一步增加对东盟国家的投资，希望广西在投资中发挥主导作用。希望博览会为进一步增进中国与东盟经贸、文化、社会、人文等各领域交流合作创造更多的机会。同时希望博览会进一步发挥平台作用，进一步帮助中国其他省份特别是西部省份利用这个平台，加强与东盟各国的合作交流。

广西壮族自治区领导李金早、余远辉、林国强参加会见。

10月21日，广西壮族自治区党委书记、自治区人大常委会主任郭声琨在南宁会见了率团出席第八届中国—东盟博览会和商务与投资峰会的新加坡贸工部部长林勋强。

郭声琨说，新加坡与中国一直保持着深厚的友谊和良好的贸易往来，与广西有着很好的合作基础和广阔的发展前景。近年来，广西与新加坡高层往来日益密切，双方在深化经贸、城市建设、港口物流、文化教育等各领域交流与合作不断发展，特别在生态、环保、教育、石化等领域，新加坡拥有先进技术和丰富管理经验，双方合作取得明显成效。

郭声琨希望以此次林部长率团出席博览会和峰会为契机，为双方政府、大型企业之间搭起交流合作的桥梁，进一步加强双方在经贸、投资、港口物流、教育培训、旅游业等领域的务实合作，不断提升双方的合作水平，不断增进双方友谊，不断扩大双方的合作成果。

林勋强对广西方给予的热情接待表示感谢。他说，广西是中国所有省区市中与东盟距离最近的省区，这为东盟与广西开展经贸、投资等领域合作提供了很好的平台。中国—东盟博览会和商务与投资峰会举办得非常好，每年都有创新，开幕式非常成功，令人振奋。越来越多的新加坡企业前来广西投资，来参加博览会和峰会并寻找商机。近年来，广西经济社会快速发展，特别是在环保、城市建设等方面取得很大成绩。新加坡愿意与广西加强交流与合作，相互学习借鉴，分享彼此的好经验、好做法，进一步加强双方在港口物流、项目建设、教育培训等各领域的合作，实现互利共赢，共同发展，迎接更加美好的未来。

新加坡贸工部政务部长张思乐、外交部高级政务次长陈振泉，广西壮族自治区领导李金早、余远辉、文明参加会见。

10月23日上午，广西壮族自治区主席马飚在南宁会见前来出席第八届中国—东盟博览会、中国—东盟商务与投资峰会的文莱工业与初级资源部部长叶海亚一行。

马飚对叶海亚部长再次率团出席中国—东盟博览会和商务与投资峰会表示欢迎，并请他转达对文莱苏丹陛下的问候与祝福，同时对文莱工业与初级资源部近年来给予广西的大力支持表示感谢。他说，叶海亚部长是广西人民的老朋友、好朋友，已经多次率团出席中国—东盟博览会，对广西的承办工作一直给予大力支持。广西代表团2011年4月访问文莱取得了圆满成功，留下了美好回忆，是与叶海亚部长的精心组织和周到安排分不开的。随着中国—东盟博览会连续成功举办，广西和文莱之间的来往进一步密切，了解进一步加深，合作进一步加强。希望双方进一步加强在经贸、农业、渔业、旅游、文化等方面的交流合作，继续共同举办好中国—东盟博览会、商务与投资峰会和泛北部湾经济合作论坛。

叶海亚表示一定把马飚主席的问候转达给苏丹陛下，感谢广西给予文莱代表团的热情款待。他说，每次来南宁都像回家一样，第八届中国—东盟博览会和商务与投资峰会举办得很成功。展望未来，文莱希望与广西在加强农业合作的同时，进一步加强贸易投资、旅游、航运等各领域的合作，并探讨开通文莱到广西的飞机直航，希望更多的广西朋友能到文莱参观旅游。

文莱驻中国大使张慈祥，自治区领导李金早、莫永清，自治区政府秘书长王跃飞等参加会见活动。

10月22日下午，广西壮族自治区党委常委、自治区常务副主席李金早在南宁会见了前来参加第八届中国—东盟博览会的新加坡外交部兼社会发展、青年及体育部高级政务次长陈振泉。

李金早表示，第一届中国—东盟博览会举办以来，广西与新加坡经贸往来逐年增多，人才交流日益频繁，每年从自治区层面到各市都输送许多人才前往新加坡学习城市规划建设、社会管理等内容，希望广西与新加坡的友好关系继续推进。

陈振泉对中国—东盟博览会给予了高度评价。他说，广西作为对接中国—东盟的重要枢纽门户，拥有优越的地理环境和经济政策，他将推荐新加坡企业界和工商界大举到广西来考察投资创业。除了日益频繁的商贸往来，广西与新加坡在文化上还有密切交流。陈振泉介绍，2012年春节，广西文化厅将参与新加坡举办的“春到河畔”大型春节联欢晚会，把刘三姐的歌声带给新加坡人民。

七　政商高端对接活动

第八届中国—东盟博览会政商互动比往届更多，更有实效。除了马来西亚总理纳吉布与中国企业CEO圆桌对话会外，还举行了泰国副总理与中泰企业家见面会、中国—缅甸企业家座谈会等活动。会期政商高端对接活动共22场，各场对接活动取得了良好实效，签署了一系列合作协议，促进了务实合作。

1. 泰国副总理与中泰企业家见面会暨中泰合作项目签约仪式。

2011年10月21日，泰国副总理吉滴叻与中泰企业家见面会暨中泰合作项目签约仪式在南宁举行。广西壮族自治区党委副书记陈际瓦、自治区人大常委会副主任吴恒出席见面会。

吉滴叻在主旨发言中说，当前，泰国正处于经济社会快速发展变化的阶段，也面临着世界经济的不稳定性居高不下等危机的影响和自然灾害，泰国能否渡过此次难关，主要在于和亚洲各国尤其是中国的合作。泰国政府非常支持泰国经济均衡发展，特别是在开发产品、进出口贸易和投资等领域发展。2011年前8个月，泰中双边贸易额接近400亿美元。泰中两国政府计划到

2011年10月21日，泰国副总理与中泰企业家见面会暨中泰合作项目签约仪式在南宁举行

Thai Deputy Prime Minister Kittiratt Na-Ranong meets with Chinese/Thai CEOs in Nanning on October 21, 2011

2015年双边贸易额达到1000亿美元。旅游业方面，目前泰国到中国旅游的游客以及中国到泰国旅游的游客均约为110万人。希望借助此次见面会，促进泰中两国企业家携手迈进，促进商业投资各领域的成功合作。泰国政府将继续支持两国企业家加强合作，确保泰中经济目标计划如期实现。

陈际瓦在致辞中，对出席见面会的嘉宾表示热烈欢迎和衷心感谢。她说，中国与泰国人民的友谊源远流长。特别是自2006年泰国在广西设立驻南宁总领事馆以来，双方友好交往不断增多，高层互访日益频繁，在经贸、文化、教育、旅游等方面的交流与合作取得了积极进展。广西与泰国经济各有优势、互补性强，合作潜力巨大。举办此次见面会，将为深化拓展广西与泰国的经贸合作开辟广阔空间，展现美好前景，提供无限商机。我们将以此次见面会为契机，鼓励更多的广西企业到泰国投资，深化农业、能源资源、化工、卫生、服务等领域的合作；也诚挚欢迎泰国的企业到广西投资，共同深化双方企业间的合作，实现互利共赢、共同发展。

泰国两仪糖业集团公司董事、中国区业务总裁汪鸿洲，安徽桑铌科技股份有限公司董事长李德峰分别在见面会上发言。见面会结束后，还举行了中泰合作项目签约仪式。

2. 中国—缅甸企业家座谈会。

10月22日下午，中国—缅甸企业家座谈会在南宁国际会展中心举行。缅甸商务部部长吴温敏出席并致辞，30多位中缅企业代表参会。

中方企业家代表、中国电子进出口总公司副总裁徐世伟介绍了公司在缅甸的投资情况。他表示，在中缅两国政府的支持下，中方企业很愿意与缅方企业加强合作，为缅甸的基础设施建设、社会经济发展、人民生活改善作出贡献。

2011年10月22日，中国—缅甸企业家座谈会在南宁举行
China-Myanmar Business Seminar held in Nanning on October 22, 2011

缅方企业家代表、缅甸工商联合总会副主席吴佐敏温则表示，缅甸作为发展中国家，在自然资源和人力资源方面具有得天独厚的优势，能够为外来投资方提供大量的机会。缅甸政府正致力于改革和完善外来投资的政策规则，积极鼓励引进外商投资。中国—东盟自由贸易区为中缅双方的深化合作提供了一大契机，缅方非常期待中国投资商到缅甸投资。

缅甸商务部部长吴温敏充分肯定了中缅两国良好的经贸合作现状。他表示，中缅双方企业的投资合作应该由传统领域向多领域发展，保持现有的上升势头。

小结　政治外交影响力带动经贸合作

中国—东盟博览会与一般商业性展会的区别之一，在于博览会得到了中国和东盟各国政府的高度重视，各国领导人亲自推动，年年出席。每届博览会期间，各国领导人之间及部长之间举行双边或多边会晤，共同出席博览会开幕式、巡视展馆等重要活动，增进政治互信，体现了博览会的政治外交影响力不断增强，为不断深化中国—东盟战略伙伴关系作出了贡献。

中国—东盟博览会与一般商业性展会的另一个区别，在于博览会每年都安排领导人、部长与企业家或地方政府负责人之间的政商高端对接活动，以政治外交影响力带动经贸等领域的合作。

第八届中国—东盟博览会作为中国—东盟建立对话关系20周年纪念活动的重要组成部分，中国和东盟10国高度重视，各国领导人均派出高规格代表团出席，会期举行了更多的政商高端对接活动，进一步促进了经贸等领域的务实合作，呈现以下特点：

一是政治外交规格高。第八届博览会共有7位中国和东盟国家领导人出席。其中，中国总理温家宝是第二次出席，柬埔寨首相洪森是第六次出席，缅甸副总统吴丁昂敏乌是第二次出席。出席本届博览会的部长级贵宾有240位，为历届最多。这表明在中国—东盟建立对话关系20周年的特殊历史背景下，面对复杂的世界经济形势，中国和东盟更加重视博览会的平台作用，显现出进一步加强互利合作，继续共同推进自贸区建设，实现共同发展、共同繁荣的信心和决心。

二是政要活动密集，内容丰富。本届博览会期间举行了6场国家领导人会见，各国政要巡视了展馆，共同出席了博览会开幕式。主题国马来西亚举行了丰富多彩的主题国活动，中国和马来西亚领导人见证了中马钦州产业园区签约仪式并为该园区揭牌，共同出席了主题国“魅力之城”开馆仪式。马来西亚总理纳吉布还出席了马来西亚商品馆开馆仪式等活动。老挝副总理宋

中国—马来西亚钦州产业园区展区
China-Malaysia Qinzhou Industrial Park

沙瓦出席了“庆祝中老建交50周年‘北部湾之声’节目落地老挝万象”活动。会期还举行了中国—东盟经贸部长晚餐会，促进了友好交流。

三是政商高端对接更多，务实推动经贸等领域合作。会期成功举行了马来西亚总理纳吉布与中国企业家CEO圆桌对话会、泰国副总理吉滴叻与中泰企业家见面会、中国—缅甸企业家座谈会等政商高端对接，共22场。既有东盟国家领导人与中国地方政府领导、企业家的会见和对话，也有中国有关部委领导、各省（市）领导与中外企业家的会见和交流。在这些活动中，领导人介绍了本国的贸易投资政策，对企业关心的热点问题进行了解答，释放了互利合作的政策信号。通过对接活动，企业家及时获得高端信息，掌握了经济发展的风向标。在各场对接活动上，企业家之间签署一系列的合作协议，取得了务实成果。

四是博览会开幕式隆重热烈，反映了中国—东盟合作和博览会的成果。开幕式形象地表达出博览会11国共办、领导人亲自推动的特点，反映中国—东盟建立对话关系20周年的辉煌成就，展示博览会促进中国—东盟友好交流、推动自贸区建设取得的成果和作出的贡献。开幕式上举行了有11国青少年参加的中国—东盟青少年交流活动中心揭牌仪式，展示了中国与东盟友谊代代相传的深刻寓意，博览会取得的成果得到更具体的展现。

五是会议提出的实质建议更多。中国和东盟各国领导人在会期活动中分别发表了讲话，充分肯定了双方20年合作成果，深入分析了当前形势，指明了下一步合作的方向。

中国总理温家宝在本届商务与投资峰会主旨演讲中提出了共同建设好自贸区、大力推进互联互通、扩大双方投资合作、深化区域经济合作和拓展人文领域交流等五件重点办好的大事。

马来西亚总理纳吉布在与中国企业CEO圆桌对话会上提出，希望中国企业更多地进入高科技，包括电信、水利、污水处理、绿色技术、生物医药等领域。

柬埔寨首相洪森在本届商务与投资峰会讲话中说，希望中国可以向东盟欠发达的成员国转让绿色科技，以增加农业产量。

泰国副总理吉滴叻在与中泰企业家见面会上说，希望借助此次见面会，促进泰中两国企业家携手迈进，促进商业投资各领域的成功合作。

第三章

3 深化区域合作　实现共同繁荣

——第八届中国—东盟商务与投资峰会开幕

中国—东盟自由贸易区从建设到建成运行的实践证明，它给双方企业和人民带来了福祉，体现了互惠、互利、共赢。中国—东盟商务与投资峰会作为中国与东盟开展高层对话、深化区域经贸合作、实现共同发展繁荣的重要平台，在推动中国—东盟自由贸易区建设中发挥了重要作用。

在新形势下，如何进一步促进区域合作，让双方企业和民众更好地享受自贸区合作成果，实现共同发展，是中国和东盟各国的共同愿望，也是第八届中国—东盟商务与投资峰会新的使命。

2011年10月21日，第八届中国—东盟商务与投资峰会在南宁成功举办。第八届中国—东盟商务与投资峰会主题是：“深化区域合作，实现共同繁荣”，主要活动有开幕式、马来西亚总理纳吉布与中国企业CEO圆桌对话会、中国—东盟商品交易中心启动暨签约仪式、2011中国—东盟矿业合作论坛暨推介展示会、中国—东盟电信高峰论坛、中国—东盟商会领袖论坛、商务早餐会、商务国际书画展示会等，体现了“论”与“实”的更好结合。

Enhance Regional Cooperation for Common Prosperity

—The 8th CABIS Opening Ceremony

The due completion and the healthy development of the CAFTA have brought blessings and benefits for the business circles and people of both sides, which displays the bilateral reciprocal cooperation for win–win results. The China–ASEAN Business & Investment Summit (CABIS), a concurrent event and also an important platform for high–end dialogues, has helped promote the economic and trade cooperation in the region for common development and prosperity, thus playing a good role in the CAFTA construction.

In this context, it is the common wish of both sides, and also the new mission for the 8th CABIS, to further promote regional cooperation, bring more CAFTA benefits for the business circle and general public, thus to achieve common development.

On October 21, 2011, the 8th CABIS was successfully held in Nanning, taking Enhancing Regional Cooperation and Achieving Common Prosperity as its theme. Major programs include the opening ceremony, meeting of Right Honorable Dato' Sri Mohd Najib Tun Abdul Razak, prime minister of Malaysia with Chinese CEOs, launching and signing ceremony of China–ASEAN Plaza, 2011 China–ASEAN Mining Cooperation Forum & Exhibition, China–ASEAN Telecommunication Summit Forum, China–ASEAN Business Leaders Forum, Business Breakfast, International Art Exhibition by Business Professionals, are all gaining more pragmatic outcomes.

CHAPTER THREE

一 第八届中国—东盟商务与投资峰会主题和议题

（一）主题："深化区域合作，实现共同繁荣"

2011年是中国—东盟建立对话关系20周年、中国—东盟友好交流年和中国—东盟自由贸易区建成1周年，本届峰会紧扣这一形势，围绕进一步深化区域行业之间的务实合作、实现共同发展和繁荣进行讨论和展望。

（二）马来西亚总理纳吉布与中国企业CEO圆桌对话会

邀请马来西亚总理纳吉布与中国和东盟企业家，围绕双边经贸关系特别是双方高度重视的重大合作项目开展建设性对话，促进政府与企业的沟通，加强企业之间的互动，为项目的顺利建设打下良好基础。

（三）中国—东盟商品交易中心启动暨签约仪式

该交易中心作为东盟各国向中国出口和中国向东盟市场出口产品的一个集散地，将有效地服务东盟各国供应商和采购商，打造世界级工业原料及商品展示交易平台、商贸物流中心。

（四）2011中国—东盟矿业合作论坛暨推介展示会

在新的区域合作形势下，中国—东盟矿业合作将迎来前所未有的机遇。此次论坛作为中国—东盟商务与投资峰会系列活动，为中国与东盟矿业搭建了一个新的交流与合作平台，旨在推动中国与东盟矿业的共同发展。

（五）中国—东盟电信高峰论坛

论坛以"提升中国—东盟域内通信与信息领域合作，更好服务中国—东盟自贸区"为主题，通过开展与东盟各国电信运营企业间的对话与交流，拓宽合作领域，挖掘合作机会，营造互利共赢合作空间。

（六）中国—东盟商会领袖论坛

邀请中国和东盟重要行业商会领袖，就区域和全球贸易发展进行交流，

第八届中国—东盟商务与投资峰会会场
The 8th China-ASEAN Business & Investment Summit

以提高对双边贸易发展的共识，加强中国和东盟国家行业商会组织之间的合作关系。

（七）商务早餐会

为加强中国和东盟企业的直接交流与互动，举办商务早餐会，为双方企业开展企业推介、商务配对、样品展示等活动提供场地和机会。

（八）商务国际书画展示会

为中国和东盟书画艺术家的作品交流提供平台，促进区域文化交流。

二　第八届中国—东盟商务与投资峰会开幕式

2011年10月21日上午，第八届中国—东盟商务与投资峰会在广西南宁荔园山庄国际会议中心隆重开幕。中共中央政治局常委、国务院总理温家宝，马来西亚总理纳吉布，柬埔寨首相洪森，缅甸副总统吴丁昂敏乌，老挝副总理宋沙瓦，泰国副总理吉滴叻，越南副总理阮春福，文莱工业和初级资源部部长叶海亚，新加坡贸工部部长林勋强，菲律宾贸工部副部长马拉雅，印度尼西亚贸易部部长助理穆赫达塔尔，东盟秘书长素林，中国国际贸易促进委员会会长万季飞，广西壮族自治区主席马飚，中国商务部国际贸易谈判代表兼副部长高虎城等出席开幕式。广西壮族自治区党委书记郭声琨主持开幕式并致欢迎辞。

温家宝在开幕式上发表题为《深化合作　共同繁荣》的主旨演讲。他说，全球经济格局正在发生深刻变化，亚洲的地位和作用日益重要。中国和东盟都是最具活力的经济体，都处在发展转型的关键时期。要抓住难得的历

2011年10月21日，第八届中国—东盟商务与投资峰会在广西南宁隆重开幕
Opening ceremony of the 8th CABIS held in Nanning, Guangxi, China on October 21, 2011

2011 年 10 月 21 日，中国国务院总理温家宝在第八届中国—东盟商务与投资峰会上发表主旨演讲
H.E. Wen Jiabao, premier of the State Council of China delivers keynote speech at the opening ceremony of the 8th CABIS on October 21, 2011

史机遇，推动经济持续平稳较快发展，就要进一步加强区域合作。为了推动双方经贸合作再上水平，当前要重点办好几件大事：一是共同建设好自贸区。中国—东盟自贸区的建成，使中国和东盟经济在更大范围、更高层次上实现优势互补。中方愿意继续扩大东盟国家优势产品的进口，在南宁建设中国—东盟商品交易中心，作为双方产品的展示交易平台和商贸物流基地。二是大力推进互联互通。我们将与东盟方面密切合作，加强对中国与东盟有关国家互联互通的投入，为促进本地区商品、资本、信息的自由流通、人员往来和经济社会发展创造更好条件。三是扩大双方投资合作。中国政府欢迎东盟各国企业来中国投资兴业，特别是到中西部投资。中方也鼓励本国优秀企业扩大对东盟的投资。四是深化区域经济合作。中方将鼓励企业参与东盟东部增长区、大湄公河、泛北部湾等次区域合作，给予金融、技术、市场等方面的有力支持，推动形成若干经济增长极。中方愿与东盟密切合作，进一步深化现有各项区域财金合作，进一步增强本地区应对国际金融风险的能力。五是拓展人文领域交流。要以办好“中国—东盟友好交流年”为契机，继续加强文化、教育、旅游、青年等领域的交流与合作，努力实现2015年双方人员往来达到1500万人次的目标。温总理的讲话高度阐述了在新形势下，中国政府对进一步加强中国—东盟战略伙伴关系和经贸合作关系的政策和战略性建议，具有重大的现实指导意义和重要的影响。

柬埔寨首相洪森代表东盟方在开幕式上讲话。他在讲话中高度赞扬了中柬、中国—东盟的友好合作关系，对在全球金融危机中，中国在区域经济乃至世界经济的复苏所起的重要作用作了积极的评价，对中国和东盟关系的不断拓展和加深表达了坚定的信心，并对进一步落实自贸区协议、加强互联互通和支持私营经济参与区域合作等提出了建设性建议。

2011年10月21日，柬埔寨首相洪森在第八届中国—东盟商务与投资峰会上发表讲话

H.E. Samdech Hun Sun, prime minister of Cambodia addresses the opening ceremony of the 8th CABIS on October 21, 2011

广西壮族自治区党委书记、自治区人大常委会主任郭声琨在主持开幕式时对出席峰会的中国和东盟国家领导人以及嘉宾表示热烈欢迎和衷心感谢。他说，由中国和东盟各国领导人共同确定的中国—东盟商务与投资峰会，自2004年在广西南宁举办以来，在中国和东盟各国的共同努力下，在东盟秘书处的大力支持下，峰会紧扣中国—东盟自贸区建设主题，突出区域经济合作特色，秉持互利共赢理念，不断创新内容与形式，取得了互惠共利的显著成效，收获了务实合作的丰硕果实，成为中国与东盟开展高层对话、深化区域经贸合作、实现共同发展繁荣的重要平台，在推动中国—东盟自由贸易区建设中发挥了重要作用。广西作为峰会的举办地，将继续努力为各方深化友好交流合作做好服务、提供便利。

2011年10月21日，广西壮族自治区党委书记、自治区人大常委会主任郭声琨主持第八届中国—东盟商务与投资峰会开幕式并致欢迎辞

H.E. Guo Shengkun, secretary of the Communist Party of China Guangxi Committee and chairman of the Standing Committee of the Guangxi People's Congress hosts the opening ceremony of the 8th CABIS and makes opening remarks on October 21, 2011

中国国际贸易促进委员会会长万季飞在致辞中说，中国与东盟建立对话合作伙伴关系20年来，中国与东盟携手共进，互利共赢，经贸关系全面发展。我们很高兴地看到，在中国与东盟各国政府、商协会组织的大力支持和企业的积极参与下，峰会经过7年的成功实践，不断创新会议内容和办会形

式，在为中国和东盟之间开展部门和行业合作构建新的载体和机制，促进中国—东盟自由贸易区的如期建成，加强中国与东盟的战略合作伙伴关系中，发挥了不可替代的作用。中国贸促会愿意与中国以及东盟各国工商界一起为深化中国—东盟的务实合作，不断提供更为有效的服务。

2011年10月21日，中国国际贸易促进委员会会长万季飞在第八届中国—东盟商务与投资峰会上致辞

H.E. Wan Jifei, chairman of the China Council for the Promotion of International Trade (CCPIT) addresses the opening ceremony of the 8th CABIS on October 21, 2011

中国财政部部长谢旭人，人力资源和社会保障部部长尹蔚民，住房和城乡建设部部长姜伟新，卫生部部长陈竺，国务院研究室主任谢伏瞻，国家质检总局局长支树平，中华全国供销总社理事会主任杨传堂，国务院副秘书长、总理办公室主任项兆伦，广西壮族自治区领导马铁山、陈际瓦、李文潮、李金早、沈北海、车荣福、温卡华、陈武、石生龙、黄道伟、余远辉、周新建、吴恒、刘新文、莫永清、荣仕星、文明、杨道喜、梁胜利、林国强、蒋济雄、李达球、蒋培兰、彭钊、李彬，自治区高级人民法院院长罗殿龙，自治区人民检察院检察长张少康等，以及东盟各国代表团主要成员、外交使节、中国政府有关部门和各省、自治区、直辖市的领导，中国和东盟各国商协组织的负责人，中国和东盟企业界代表、专家学者和新闻界人士，区域外的贵宾共1000多人参加了开幕式。300多名中外媒体记者到现场报道了此次盛会。

三　第八届中国—东盟商务与投资峰会专题会议

（一）马来西亚总理纳吉布与中国企业CEO圆桌对话会

2011年10月21日下午，马来西亚总理纳吉布与中国企业CEO圆桌对话会在南宁市广西人民会堂五楼会议室举行。

马来西亚总理纳吉布出席对话会并发表演讲，中国国际贸易促进委员会会长万季飞致开幕辞，广西壮族自治区党委常委、宣传部部长沈北海致欢迎辞，中国商务部国际贸易谈判代表兼副部长高虎城作了总结发言。马方出席对话的还有：马来西亚国际贸易和工业部部长穆斯塔法，马来西亚能源、绿色科技与水务部长陈华贵，马来西亚驻华大使萨鲁汀，马来西亚政府代表团成员。中马双方工商组织负责人和政府官员，以及企业家、专家学者等300多人出席了会议。在本次圆桌对话会上，中国技术进出口总公司和马来西亚

2011年10月21日，马来西亚总理纳吉布与中国企业CEO圆桌对话会在广西南宁市广西人民会堂举行

Right Honorable Dato' Sri Mohd Najib Tun Abdul Razak, prime minister of Malaysia meets with Chinese CEOs in Guangxi People's Hall on October 21, 2011

捷硕集团，中国机械设备进出口总公司和马来西亚KLS能源公司，华泰企业集团和马来西亚宝腾汽车集团，厦门金龙汽车集团有限公司和马来西亚联合巴士服务有限公司举行了合作项目签约仪式，合同金额达30亿美元。此次对话会推动的中马合作项目金额共近100亿美元。

马来西亚总理纳吉布在发言中介绍了马来西亚经贸的基本情况和近期的发展目标。他说，在当今世界经济面临着很大的不确定性的背景下，我们希望和中国、东南亚以及东盟进行紧密合作。中国和东亚地区为马提供了许多商机，我们应该更加重视马中经济贸易关系的发展。马中经贸中最引人瞩目的是双边贸易增长率。在此，我们承诺给予来马投资的中国企业办理快捷审批手续。我们同时提供便捷基金来帮助外资项目更好地立足发展。影响力大的项目将获得马来政府提供的便捷基金方面的支持。我们将尽量为来马投资的企业提供便利，以此表明马来政府在提高国家竞争力，跻身世界经济强国的决心。他提出，希望中国企业更多地对马来西亚的电信、水利、污水处理、绿色技术、生物医药等领域进行投资。马来西亚全力支持钦州产业园的发展，希望两国的私营部门能够更多地参与合作，促进双边经贸关系的进一步发展。

中国国际贸易促进委员会会长万季飞在致辞中表示马来西亚是与中国最早建交的东盟国家，30多年来，两国经贸关系持续稳定快速发展。中马双边贸易、投资和经济合作已形成多层次、多领域、多形式的互利合作格局。2010年两国双边贸易额达到742亿美元，是10年前的9倍，是建交时的40倍。目前，中马双边贸易额已占中国和东盟10国贸易总额的四分之一，中国已成为马来西亚最大的贸易伙伴，马来西亚是中国在东盟最大的贸易伙伴。现在，两国央行签署了中国与东盟国家间第一个本币互换协议，中国工商银行（马来西亚）有限公司在马来西亚首都吉隆坡隆重开业，两国政府已签署高等学历互认协议，中马共建的广西钦州产业园已经启动。这些互利的政策和项目必将推动中马经贸持续、健康、快速发展。万季飞希望企业能够把握机会，开展合作，实现共赢。同时，他希望两国政府为中马双方企业家在政策、机制和环境等方面创造更加有利的条件。

广西壮族自治区党委常委、宣传部部长沈北海在致辞中指出，推动中国与东盟在商务与投资的高层对话，深化区域经贸关系，促进企业界的务实合作，是中国—东盟商务与投资峰会的办会宗旨，我们相信，这次圆桌会议的成功举办，必将进一步增进中马双方的友谊和相互的了解，把双方的经贸关系提高到一个新的水平。广西历来高度重视加强与马来西亚的交流合作，2010年，广西与马来西亚双边贸易额接近3亿美元，马来西亚在广西投资项目已达到104个，在东盟国家中，合同外资额排第二位，马来西亚也成为广西在东盟的第四大贸易伙伴。他还特别提到中马双方签署了建设中国—马来西亚钦州产业园的协议，中国国务院总理温家宝指出要把这个产业园区建设成为中国向东盟经济合作的一个典范区，这为双方加深合作开拓了更加广阔的前景。

中国商务部国际贸易谈判代表兼副部长高虎城在闭幕致辞中指出，纳吉布总理亲自出席本次对话，体现了马来西亚政府对两国经贸合作的高度重视和积极的态度。中马两国是友好近邻，又互为重要的经贸伙伴。中马两国双边的贸易保持良好的发展势头，首先，目前中国是马来西亚的第一大贸易伙伴，第二大出口市场和第三大进口来源地，也是马来西亚棕榈油和天然橡胶最大的出口市场。其次，中马相互投资取得积极进展，两国总理关心的中马钦州产业园区的合作正在稳步推进，该项目将为中马经贸合作注入新的活力。再次，中马双方人员互访稳步增长，中国已成为马来西亚在东盟之外的第一大客源地。纳吉布总理亲自率团出席本届中国—东盟博览会和商务与投资峰会，见证了两国经贸合作取得的丰硕成果。他强调，中马两国经贸前景十分广阔，相信在两国领导人的关心和双方企业的共同努力下，两国经贸合作一定会向互利共赢、共同发展的目标不断迈进。

（二）中国—东盟商品交易中心启动仪式

2011年10月22日上午，中国—东盟商品交易中心启动仪式在南宁华南城举行。

中国国际贸易促进委员会会长万季飞，东盟秘书处秘书长素林，广西壮族自治区党委常委、自治区副主席、南宁市委书记陈武，华南城控股有限公司董事许扬出席活动并讲话。

万季飞在致辞中说，近年来，随着中国与东盟经济贸易的快速发展，特别是中国—东盟自由贸易区实施以来，中国与东盟企业界相互了解、相互开展经济贸易和投资的愿望越来越强烈，建设一个中国和东盟区域性商贸、物流基地成为共同的需求。在中国与东盟各方的努力下，中国—东盟商品交易中心在南宁华南城终于落成。今天举行启动仪式就组织上百家企业签约，可喜可贺。广西与东盟国家有着先天的地缘优势，并得到了自治区政府的大力支持，在南宁建立中国与东盟商品交易中心是正确的选择。他希望中国与东盟双向贸易中有特色、有品牌、有竞争力的产品都能在南宁华南城进行展示交易，也希望中心能够为企业家提供贴心、全面、周到的服务，尽快成为服务中国与东盟各国供货商和采购商的世界级工业原料及商品展示交易平台、

2011年10月22日，中国—东盟商品交易中心启动仪式在广西南宁举行

Launching ceremony of the China-ASEAN Plaza at South China City in Nanning, Guangxi on October 22, 2011

现代商贸物流中心。

东盟秘书处秘书长素林在发言中表示，东亚地区已成为世界经济新的增长极，而东盟正处在这一新经济增长极的核心位置。中国—东盟建立了自由贸易区，自贸区的建立创建了本地区内最大的贸易交流区域，在这一区域中，有19亿消费者。双方的工商界领袖今天聚集一堂，因为经贸合作的主体是工商企业界。必须抓住双方合作的机遇，深挖潜力，把东盟—中国合作、互联互通提升到新的高度，创造更多商机，推动双方的交流和合作进一步向前迈进，造福于19亿人民。此外，我们还需要在中国和东盟之间进行更多的人员、资源和技能交流，以实现共同繁荣。

广西壮族自治区党委常委、自治区副主席、南宁市委书记陈武祝贺交易中心建成并表示，2011年是中国—东盟建立对话关系20周年，也是中国—东盟友好交流年和中国—东盟自由贸易区建成1周年，中国与东盟的战略伙伴关系和经贸合作已进入一个新的阶段。广西是中国面向东盟开放合作的前沿和窗口，当前正以独特的优势加快构建国家区域经济合作新高地、形成中国沿海经济发展新一极。南宁市作为中国—东盟博览会、中国—东盟商务与投资峰会的永久举办地，正着力打造成为区域性商贸物流基地、加工制造基地和国际综合交通枢纽中心、信息交流中心、金融中心，不断提升城市国际化、现代化水平。我们将以更加优惠的政策、更加高效的服务、更加良好的环境，全力支持中国和东盟的工商界在广西及南宁的商务与投资活动，促进共同繁荣、共同发展。

华南城控股有限公司董事许扬说，经过一年多的筹备和准备，中国—东盟商品交易中心在南宁华南城正式挂牌成立了，这是中国—东盟商界的一件大喜事。南宁华南城建设总面积接近500万平方米，总投资超过120亿元人民币，将建成立足南宁、面向西南、服务东盟的工业原料产品展示交易中心、综合商贸物流中心和高端的生产服务业基地，为中国和东盟10国采购商和供应商提供全产业链的一站式的服务平台。在过去一年里，东盟国家政府组团、新闻机构、商家朋友以及东盟驻中国使领馆官员近30批200多人到南宁华南城实地考察，纷纷表示希望能够尽早入驻华南城。东盟商家入驻华南城后，能够共享华南城在中国各地分支机构数十万个客户资源和中国广阔市场，同时一年一度的中国—东盟博览会也将为所有商家提供无限商机。

启动仪式当天，近100家来自东盟10国的商家在现场签署了入驻中国—东盟商品交易中心协议。

（三）中国—东盟矿业合作论坛暨推介展示会

2011年5月30日—6月1日，中国—东盟矿业合作论坛暨推介展示会在南宁国际会展中心举行。

中国国土资源部副部长汪民，中国国际贸易促进委员会秘书长徐沪滨，自治区领导郭声琨、马飚、陈武、黄道伟、杨道喜、林念修，柬埔寨矿产部部长述赛、老挝矿产部副部长宋本·拉沙松本、菲律宾矿产部前部长拉莫斯、马来西亚地矿总局局长拉扎克、缅甸地矿总局局长叶明水、越南地矿局

2011年5月30日—6月1日，2011 中国—东盟矿业合作论坛暨推介展示会在广西南宁举行

2011 China-ASEAN Mining Cooperation Forum and Exhibition held in Nanning，Guangxi from May 30 to June 1, 2011

副局长郑春边等20位司局级高官和5位驻华总领事出席了论坛的有关活动。

大会举行了开幕式、签约仪式、巡馆、高官会议、企业高峰论坛、4个专业论坛、高层会见、欢迎宴会、展览会、项目推介会、企业考察等33项专项活动。参展参会单位410家、1100多人，签约项目25个、总投资额214亿元。

中国—东盟矿业高官会议是这次论坛的一大亮点。中国和东盟8个国家部局级高官出席会议，东盟商协会代表列席会议，与会代表共50人。会议一致通过了《中国—东盟矿业合作论坛南宁宣言》。这一成果将对今后开展中国与东盟的矿业合作产生重要影响。

2010年矿业论坛的成功举办，确定了中国一南一北两个国际矿业大会的地位。2011年的矿业论坛，进一步提升了规格、规模和效益。高官会议确定的框架协议，为今后深化中国与东盟双边或多边矿业合作奠定了重要基础；会上签约的中国与缅甸、老挝、越南、印尼等国的合作项目，凸显了矿业论坛的平台作用；矿业和机械展览会的贸易成交，取得了展贸结合的好效果；中央和广西、香港18家主流媒体到会采访报道，扩大了本届矿业论坛的影响。

（四）中国—东盟电信高峰论坛

2011年10月22日下午，中国—东盟电信高峰论坛在广西人民会堂举行。

广西壮族自治区工业和信息化委员会主任束华主持论坛。中国工业和信息化部副部长尚冰、广西壮族自治区副主席杨道喜、中国联合网络通信有限公司副总裁韩志刚、缅甸邮政电信总局董事长Mr. Eaik Di Hla、印度尼西亚Matrix Networks公司董事长Pangestu Tjuhendra和泰国True Move公司国际业务总裁Mr. Supoj Mahapan出席了本届论坛并致辞。

中国工业和信息化部副部长尚冰在致辞中表示，信息通信业是中国国民经济的基础性、先导性和战略性产业。“十二五”期间，中国将大力发展新一代信息技术产业等战略性新兴产业，在信息通信领域重点发展新一代移动通信、物联网、云计算等，加快建设宽带、融合、安全、泛在的下一代国家信息基础建设，推动信息化和工业化深度融合。中国—东盟自由贸易区是由发展中国家组成的惠及人口最多、区域最广的自贸区，自贸区的全面建成使双方资金、资源、技术和人才等生产要素的流动效率显著提高。他还就“提升中国—东盟区域内信息领域合作，更好地服务中国—东盟自贸区”这一论坛主题提出四点建议：第一，加强信息通信基础设施的互联互通；第二，加强信息技术应用的交流与合作；第三，加强新一代信息技术领域的交流与合作；第四，持续开展网络安全领域的合作。

2011年10月22日，中国—东盟电信高峰论坛在广西南宁举行

China-ASEAN Telecommunications Forum held in Nanning, Guangxi on October 22, 2011

广西壮族自治区副主席杨道喜在论坛上致辞时表示，中国政府明确提出要把广西北部湾经济区建成中国—东盟信息交流中心。中国电信、中国移动、中国联通三大电信运营商进一步加大了在广西投资与合作。其中，中国联通3年内将投资5亿元在广西南宁建设中国第四个国际通信业务出入口，并配套投资30亿元，建设国际信息服务外包中心、国际互联网数据储存中心、国际云计算中心及国际直达数据专用通道。这些项目的实施，对完善中国国际通信网络的总体布局，提升面向东盟的国际化信息提供能力，推动中国—东盟自贸区发展具有重要的支撑作用。广西将以本次论坛为契机，加快推动中国电信、中国移动、中国联通三大电信运营商与东盟各大电信运营企业合作，为中国与东盟经贸发展提供高效服务。

中国联合网络通信有限公司副总裁韩志刚在演讲中说，经济全球化的深入发展、中国对外开放的不断深化，为电信运营商的国际业务开辟了巨大的发展空间。无论是全球经济和中国经济的发展，还是信息通信产业的转型，都为国际电信业务开辟了更加广阔的发展空间。融合重组后的中国联通的国际网络和业务资源更加丰富。聚焦中国—东盟区域，开展电信运营商间的双边和多边合作大有可为。他表示，中国与东盟国家山水相连，双方在经贸、文化、人文方面交往密切，特别是随着2010年中国—东盟自由贸易区的正式建立，中国与东盟的经济贸易发展驶入了快车道。我们相信，中国联通南宁区域性国际通信业务出入口以及相关国际通信基础设施的起用，将架起中国联通与东盟各电信运营商深化合作的桥梁，为中国—东盟区域内的电信用户提供更加优质、可靠的信息与通信服务，造福中国—东盟自由贸易区内的19

亿人口。

缅甸邮政电信总局董事长Mr. Eaik Di Hla在演讲中表示，中国已成为东盟重要的对话伙伴，同时也已成为缅甸最大的贸易伙伴。中国—东盟商务与投资峰会的召开也在不断加强中国与东盟之间双边与多边的合作。同时，我们也认识到东盟与中国双方应秉持发展长期战略伙伴关系的理念，促进区域和平与繁荣。缅甸在ICT领域的发展处于落后状态。目前电话普及率刚刚超过5%，而互联网普及率不到1%。我们正采取必要措施增加全国电话的普及率。他还向中国政府，中国电信、中国联通、中兴通讯、华为、上海贝尔阿尔卡特股份有限公司与缅甸的继续合作表示感谢。他建议所有的成员国和有关公司应共同努力，加强信息领域的合作，更好地服务中国—东盟自贸区。

印度尼西亚Matrix Networks公司董事长Pangestu Tjuhendra在演讲中介绍了印尼及印尼电信业的现状。他还特别介绍了Matrix Networks公司的线缆系统，并且详细列举了Matrix公司是电信领军企业的首选合作伙伴的具体优势：一是较强的可靠性；二是运营方的中立性；三是一站式服务。他还提出因为现在印度尼西亚外围严重缺少国际频带宽度能力，并且使用者要支付的费用太高，所以印度尼西亚需要更多的海底电缆。Pangestu Tjuhendra董事长表示，Matrix将在这个领域继续投资，我们相信通过自我检验与自我超越，我们会满足用户对服务越来越高的需求。

泰国True Move公司国际业务总裁Mr. Supoj Mahapan在演讲中表示，电信对于泰国的发展尤为重要，他希望通过他的介绍让大家更好地交流，在未来有更多的合作。True Online公司是泰国最大的宽带供应商，同时也是最大的无线网络运营商，拥有最大的市场份额。泰国仍然是一个发展中国家，因此互联网以及个人电脑普及率随着社会发展仍不断增长。来自国内外市场的价格竞争将使更多人在将来可以使用互联网。除了True Online外，True Move公司提供True Vision数字卫星电视、电缆光纤电视以及互联网协议电视服务，True Money公司提供网上金融交易服务，而True Life 则是生活的聚合体。

来自马来西亚、印度尼西亚、缅甸、老挝、菲律宾、新加坡、泰国、越南等国家的电信运营企业60多位负责人和250多位代表参加了会议。论坛举行了中国联通与缅甸邮政电信总局、老挝ETL公司、Unitel公司以及越南移动公司合作项目签约仪式，金额达8亿美元。论坛还举行了中国联通南宁区域性国际通信业务出入口、中国联通南宁国际直达数据专用通道、中国联通东盟国际漫游创新平台等项目启用仪式。

（五）中国—东盟商会领袖论坛

2011年10月22日上午，第二届中国—东盟商会领袖论坛在南宁华南城举行。

马来西亚前驻WTO总代表苏帕曼大使，马来西亚国家工商会副会长钟廷森，香港工业总会名誉会长孙启烈，文莱国家工商会副会长卡玛鲁丁，柬埔寨总商会总干事阮明德，老挝国家工商会副会长萨南，菲华新联公会会长王书侯，新加坡中华总商会秘书长林三顿，越南工商会副会长范家足，中国广西钦州市市长肖莺子，中国—东盟商务理事会中方秘书长许宁宁出席论坛并发言。中国和东盟各国商协会负责人共同探讨了在自贸区建成背景下如何加强区域行业合作，如何利用好中国—东盟商品交易中心服务于区域商贸物流发展，以及对共建中马钦州产业园等广泛交换了意见，并进一步达成合作共识。

2011年10月22日，第二届中国—东盟商会领袖论坛在广西南宁举行

The 2nd China-ASEAN Business Leaders Forum held in Nanning, Guangxi on October 22, 2011

马来西亚前驻WTO总代表苏帕曼在发言中介绍说，中国与东盟可以共享各自不同的资源、技术以及高端人才，从而提升核心竞争力，为本国经济发展服务，使其在区域和全球市场中茁壮成长。在地区乃至世界经济发展中，中国和东盟的一些重要工业以及服务业扮演着重要角色。中国和东盟在这些领域中促使双方的市场将不仅扩大到地区，而且发展到世界各地。在个别领域的竞争者应该考虑通过共同努力来站稳脚跟，获得更多的市场份额。中国—东盟自贸区拥有巨大潜力为竞争者进行战略定位，不断提高竞争者的供应链、产品质量以及销售网。中国代表了“一个很大的市场”，而且未来中国人均收入还会在当前基础上大幅增长。他指出：“中国未来具有很高的消费力，会消费大量的进口品，对我们而言蕴涵着丰富的商机。”

马来西亚国家工商会副会长钟廷森在发言中提到，自从2010年“10+1”共同市场成立以后，很多产品都可以自由出入各国，这是一个好事，因为贸易可以增加。不过东盟10国里面有某些行业制造成本没有办法跟中国比较，中国的技术各方面都很先进，所以各国生产制造的产品没有办法跟中国竞争。当然我们需要各国的出口继续增加。希望中国今后的投资也要关注东盟各个国家的成长，增加他们的收入，变成一个真正的共同市场，大家互相支援，互相供应。

香港工业总会名誉会长孙启烈在发言中提到，2010年中国—东盟自贸区的建成为中国—东盟区域的繁荣和发展设计了一个充满魅力的蓝图。在中国—东盟货物零关税的实施下，中国和东盟各国的合作进入了一个新纪元，大大推进了自贸区的经济发展，为区域企业带来了巨大的商机。为了向自贸区的建设在不同的领域注入更多的商机，本次盛会将进行不同的展示活动。本次盛会将为公司企业提供一个直面世界各地买家的绝佳平台，一个进入潜力无限的东盟市场的高速通道。

文莱国家工商会副会长卡玛鲁丁在发言中介绍说，中国与文莱签署了“中文双边协议”，而作为东盟成员国，文莱还与澳大利亚、新西兰、中国、印度、韩国签署了“自由贸易协议”，与日本签署了“全面经济伙伴协议”。同时，文莱也是“泛太平洋战略经济伙伴关系协议”的缔约方之一。文莱还与阿曼、德国、中国、韩国和乌克兰签订了“双边投资协定”。他看好中国这个巨大的市场带给文莱的机会。他说：“文莱有信心能够继续向中国市场提供相关产品。”

柬埔寨总商会总干事阮明德在发言中说，比起欧盟和北美自贸区，中国—东盟自贸区论其价值毫不逊色，论其人口规模略胜一筹。长期以来，双方彼此合作缔造了更大的繁荣。然而我们也看到了世界的纷繁变化，尤其是西方世界的经济萧条。我们将更加彼此信赖，加倍努力以求共同繁荣。

老挝国家工商会副会长萨南在发言中提到，只要双方遵循平等互利原则和本着相互谅解的态度，将会为中国—东盟的经贸合作带来巨大的发展潜力和美好的未来。为此，我们需要有完善的基础设施作为依托，如建设较好的公路、铁路、海运、航空以及通畅的电信服务业等。除了改善基础设施之外，我们还需要消除海关官僚主义，因为这对我们的增长至关重要。这样才能在中国和东盟间的商务活动中互惠互利。

菲华新联公会会长王书侯在发言中介绍说，菲律宾是一个风景秀丽而且能源丰富的千岛之国，有世界新七大自然奇观美誉的巴拉湾地底河，有海滩细如面粉的长滩岛，椰子生产和出口占世界第一位，是世界市场蕉麻的主要供应国。广西拥有得天独厚的地理位置和宜人气候，正在吸引越来越多的投资客商前往投资和考察。加强菲律宾与广西之间的经贸合作，将使双方进入一个共同繁荣的新阶段。菲华新联公会成立30年来，积极推动菲中经贸、科技、文化等方面的交流和发展。2011年已是第三次组团参加中国—东盟博览会，取得非凡效果，受到菲中两国政府的一致好评。我们希望通过论坛整合中国与东盟商会资源，构建中国—东盟商会网络平台，增进了解，顺势而为，推动菲律宾与中国商会经贸合作，不断向纵深发展，以促进全球经济复苏和持续稳定的繁荣，拓展和加深双方区域性经济合作，真正实现共同繁荣和发展。

新加坡中华总商会秘书长林三顿在发言中提到，在当前欧美面对经济衰退，以及国际市场动荡的不稳定情况下，中国—东盟自由贸易区的设立，尤其显得迫切和重要。为维持东盟各成员国的持续与稳定发展，我们必须团结一致，尽心尽力，尽快落实各个有效的商贸平台和服务体系，让大家从中受惠。新加坡中华总商会很高兴地获悉，在中国国际贸易促进委员会、中国国际商会和广西壮族自治区人民政府的鼎力支持下，中国—东盟商务与投资峰会秘书处和华南城控股集团展开合作，将在南宁设立一个中国—东盟产品展示交易中心，以实际行动和免租金的优惠条件，为东盟各成员国提供5000平方米的场地，展示各地独特的产品与服务产业，以便开拓中国与东盟区域广大的市场。

越南工商会副会长范家足在发言中介绍说，越南是一个拥有9千万人口的东南亚市场经济国家。年轻的劳动力和优越的地理条件，有助于促进越南和中国及东盟其他国家之间的贸易与投资。越南的投资环境也更加灵活、透明和便利，这有利于投资者和投资公司获益。越南的经济日益与世界经济融为一体。越南政府明确表示，我们和其他国家是和平、友谊、合作、发展、平等互利的关系，我们是值得信任的合作伙伴。越南将坚持对国际社会的承诺。作为代表工商界和越南雇主的国家组织，同时也是越南最大的经济、贸易、投资、科技促进机构，越南国家工商会在中国和越南以及越南和其他东盟国家的工商合作中一直起着桥梁和纽带作用。

中国广西钦州市市长肖莺子在发言中介绍，从4月28日温家宝总理访问马来西亚提出了倡议到10月21日这短短的半年时间，中马钦州产业园区就取得如此重要的进展，应该说商会发挥了非常重要的作用。所以这一次的商会领袖论坛，对搭建东盟各国企业合作交流平台、服务区域经济发展和繁荣将起到非常重要的推动作用。肖莺子还在发言中介绍了钦州：第一，钦州是广西北部湾获得国家支持最多的城市。钦州是一座与中国—东盟自贸区共同成长的城市，钦州享有国家赋予的全国第五个保税港区、第六个整车进口口岸、国家级的钦州港经济技术开发区、国家级的台湾农民创业园、中马钦州产业园等。第二，钦州也是北部湾发展最好、后劲最足的城市。第三，钦州也是北部湾合作商机最多的城市。第四，钦州是投资环境最优的城市。

中国—东盟商务理事会中方秘书长许宁宁在发言中说，我们均已意识到，面对全球经济的不确定性和不稳定性，唯有加强我们双方的经济合作，才能获得新的发展。我们均强调，商会在中国与东盟经贸合作中已经发挥、正在发挥并将进一步发挥重要而积极的促进作用，双方商会将密切合作关系，充分发挥好自身优势和桥梁作用，协助双方企业创新合作、深入合作、互利合作。

与会嘉宾还围绕利用自贸区平台，推进商协会务实合作；加强商贸物流合作等议题进行了充分的交流和探讨。

（六）商务早餐会

2011年10月22日上午，商务早餐会在南宁市新都酒店举行。中国国际贸易促进委员会会长万季飞、广西壮族自治区副主席高雄出席商务早餐会并致辞。中外政界、商界以及国际和区域组织200多位代表出席早餐会。为加强中国和东盟企业的直接交流与互动，早餐会提供场地和机会，以便双方企业开展企业推介、商务配对、样品展示等活动。

（七）国际商务书画展

2011年10月20—23日，第八届中国—东盟商务与投资峰会首届中国（南

2011年10月20—23日，第八届中国—东盟商务与投资峰会首届中国（南宁）国际商务书画展在广西南宁举行

The 8th China-ASEAN Business & Investment Summit 1st China (Nanning) International Art Exhibition held in Nanning, Guangxi on October 20-30, 2011

宁）国际商务书画展在广西科技馆举行，这是由中国国际贸易促进委员会、广西壮族自治区人民政府指导，中国—东盟商务与投资峰会秘书处主办，为庆祝中国—东盟建立对话关系20周年举办的一次书画展览。来自中国、马来西亚、新加坡、美国、法国等多国的艺术家、书画家出席。本次展览共展出80多位书画家作品共计200多幅，艺术家和观众踊跃参会，还有书画家的现场作画表演，促进了中国与东盟的人文交流。

小结　凝聚共识的对话　务实合作的成果

第八届中国—东盟商务与投资峰会是在中国—东盟建立对话关系20周年、中国—东盟友好交流年、中国—东盟自贸区建成1周年的历史背景下召开的。中国和东盟国家领导人高规格出席。本次峰会主题和议题具有鲜明的时代性、务实性。各场活动亮点多，共识多，取得了务实成果。

一是对20年来中国—东盟友好关系的发展历程进行了总结和定位，对新形势下进一步深化中国—东盟战略伙伴关系和经贸合作关系提出了战略性建议。中国国务院总理温家宝在开幕式上全面回顾了20年来中国—东盟关系发展的历程，对新形势下进一步深化中国—东盟战略伙伴关系和经贸合作关系提出了战略性建议。中国和东盟国家领导人充分利用此次出席峰会的机会展开对话，对中国—东盟携手合作，巩固和加强双方战略伙伴关系表示高度重

第八届中国—东盟商务与投资峰会会场
The 8th China-ASEAN Business & Investment Summit

视并达成一致共识。与会代表围绕主题，集思广益，献计献策，就进一步发挥中国—东盟自贸区作用，扩大双方经贸合作和相互投资，改善双方经贸关系，实现互利共赢，提出建设性举措，推动中国—东盟互利合作进一步向广度和深度发展。

二是马来西亚总理纳吉布与中国企业CEO圆桌对话会取得了积极成效，通过创新举办系列专题活动，建立起区域行业合作机制，实效性强。“务实、创新、可持续发展”，是中国—东盟商务与投资峰会筹备工作所坚持的办会思路。在这个思路指导下，峰会不断创新办会形式，丰富办会内容，取得令人瞩目的成果，实现了促进中国—东盟商务与投资峰会由“论”向务实合作方向发展的目标。实践证明，本届中国—东盟商务与投资峰会举办圆桌对话会、商会领袖论坛等活动，已经有效地建立起政府与企业圆桌对话机制，为中国与东盟开展高层次、深领域的合作提供有力保证。

三是本次峰会宣布在南宁建立中国—东盟商品交易中心并正式启动。温家宝总理在峰会开幕式讲话中指出：我们将在南宁建设中国—东盟商品交易中心，作为双方产品的展示交易平台和商贸物流基地。至此，经过一年筹划和建设的中国—东盟商品交易中心作为政府的决策正式建立。该中心是自贸区建成后第一个大型的区域性商贸物流和交易平台，对于把广西建设成为中国和东盟交往的“三基地一中心”具有重要意义。

四是通过峰会平台建立了中国—东盟在矿业领域的合作机制。作为峰会系列活动之一，中国—东盟矿业合作论坛暨推介展示会已在中国南宁成功举办了两届，促成了300亿元人民币的合作，签署了中国和东盟矿业合作《南宁宣言》，形成了中国—东盟矿业合作机制，成果斐然。目前，论坛已被国土资源部确定为国家在矿业领域年度举办的两项国际活动之一，并成为中国和东盟矿业合作的一个新平台，对于促进区域内矿产和资源领域的优势互补、互利共赢、共同发展作出了新的贡献。

五是中国—东盟电信高峰论坛宣布了中国第四个国际网络出入口的建立，对于把广西建设成为中国与东盟信息交流中心具有重要作用。2011年，国家授权中国联通在南宁建设我国第四个国际网络出入口。为加强区域信息领域合作，更好服务于自贸区的建设，峰会举办了中国—东盟电信高峰论坛，论坛上中国联通南宁区域性国际通信业务出入口、中国联通南宁国际直达数据专用通道、中国联通东盟国际漫游创新平台等项目举行了启用仪式。中国联通将在3年内投资5亿元在广西南宁建设中国第四个国际通信业务出入口，并配套投资30亿元，建设国际信息服务外包中心、国际互联网数据储存中心、国际云计算中心及国际直达数据专用通道。这些项目的实施，对完善中国国际通信网络的总体布局，提升面向东盟的国际化信息提供能力，推动中国—东盟自贸区发展具有重要的支撑作用。

正如中国国际贸易促进委员会会长万季飞在峰会开幕式致辞上指出的，在中国与东盟各国政府、商协会组织的大力支持和企业的积极参与下，峰会经过七年的成功实践，不断创新会议内容和办会形式，为中国和东盟之间开展部门和行业合作构建新的载体和机制，促进中国—东盟自由贸易区的如期建成，为加强中国与东盟的战略伙伴关系，发挥了不可替代的作用。第八届峰会取得了空前成功。峰会的政治成果对下一阶段的中国—东盟经贸合作关系的发展具有重要的指导意义。峰会在务实合作方面取得了新的突破，通过峰会活动推动达成合作项目和贸易签约共计140多亿美元，为峰会的可持续发展打下新的基础。

第四章

4 务实创新拓平台 专业特色显实效

——第八届中国—东盟博览会展览和洽谈活动

展览，是中国—东盟博览会的核心内容。

第八届中国—东盟博览会的展览活动在中国—东盟自由贸易区蓬勃发展的潮流中，依靠更加专业的品质和不断增强的市场服务能力，彰显出新的活力和生机。

一方面，尽管世界经济形势由于美国和欧洲的债务问题增添了新的重大不确定性，但中国与东盟的经贸合作在中国—东盟自由贸易区建成的强力推动下，保持稳定快速增长。因此，第八届中国—东盟博览会的展览必须满足双方企业强信心、促合作、谋实效的实际需要。

另一方面，2011年的中国展览市场发展迅猛，展览业的竞争更加激烈。据《中国会展经济蓝皮书》统计，2011年中国共举办展会7333场，同比增长18.21%，居世界第二位。中国—东盟博览会的展览要在7000多个展会的竞争中独树一帜、保持优势，必须坚持创新、提高实效、优化服务。

为此，第八届中国—东盟博览会紧扣中国—东盟合作形势，推出一系列创新举措：优化展览内容，突出展示双方互补性强的商品，行业特色更加鲜明；投资合作内容更有针对性，首次举办中国—东盟博览会投资合作圆桌会议，为投资合作特别是中国企业“走出去”投资东盟提供更好平台。这些措施得到了企业广泛认同，各国企业参展参会更加踊跃，企业重复参展率进一步提高，博览会的市场吸引力进一步增强。

Pragmatic Innovations to Build a Better Platform, Specialized Exhibitions to Yield Richer Outcomes

— The 8th CAEXPO Exhibitions and Business Promotion Programs

Exhibition has always been the core focus of the CAEXPO.

Keeping close pace with the fast developing CAFTA, CAEXPO exhibition has also gained new vigor with more professional management and stronger business-friendly supports.

On one side, though the world economic situation is now curved with major uncertainties due to the debt and banking problems in the US and Europe, economic and trade cooperation between China and the ASEAN member nations still maintains fast growth, thanks to the strong drive of the newly-established CAFTA.

On the other hand, the convention and exhibition industry in China has gained momentum in 2011, causing more severe competition in the sector. In accordance with China C&E Industry Blue Book, there were 7333 exhibitions and conventions of different forms held in China in 2011, an increase of 18.21%, and ranking second in the world. To be outstanding among its competitors, CAEXPO has no choice but to adopt more innovative measures, increase its economic outcomes and provide more business-friendly services for its participants.

To this end, the 8th CAEXPO, keeping close pace with the China-ASEAN cooperation, has adopted a series of innovative measures, including better arranging its exhibition contents, highlighting the products that enjoy complementary advantages in bilateral trade and displaying more distinctive industrial sectors. It also designed more targeted showcase of investment cooperation, and held the first-ever CAEXPO Roundtable Meeting on Investment Cooperation, making a better platform for the bilateral investment cooperation, in particular, the overseas investing of Chinese enterprises in the ASEAN countries. All these measures have gained positive feedback from the business circles, attracting more enterprises to the event as exhibitors and trade visitors. It is worth noting that, the CAEXPO is seeing more repeat exhibitors, which means that the event has now increased its market appealing.

CHAPTER FOUR

一 第八届中国—东盟博览会展览活动的特点

第八届中国—东盟博览会作为双方建立对话关系20周年系列纪念活动的重要组成部分，集中展示双边经贸合作的成果和商机，进一步促进互利共赢。

本届博览会设商品贸易、投资合作、服务贸易、先进技术、“魅力之城”等五个专题，采用“一会三馆”的形式，同时使用南宁国际会展中心、广西展览馆、南宁华南城展览中心三个展区，规模比往届扩大。

本届博览会展览活动具有以下特点：

（一）展览内容更有针对性，行业特色更加突出

中国商品展区主要展示机械设备、电子电器、建筑材料、农业及食品、轻工业品等优势产品，推动了更多国内商品出口东盟。

东盟国家展品进一步向食品农产品、家具家居、特色工艺品及珠宝饰

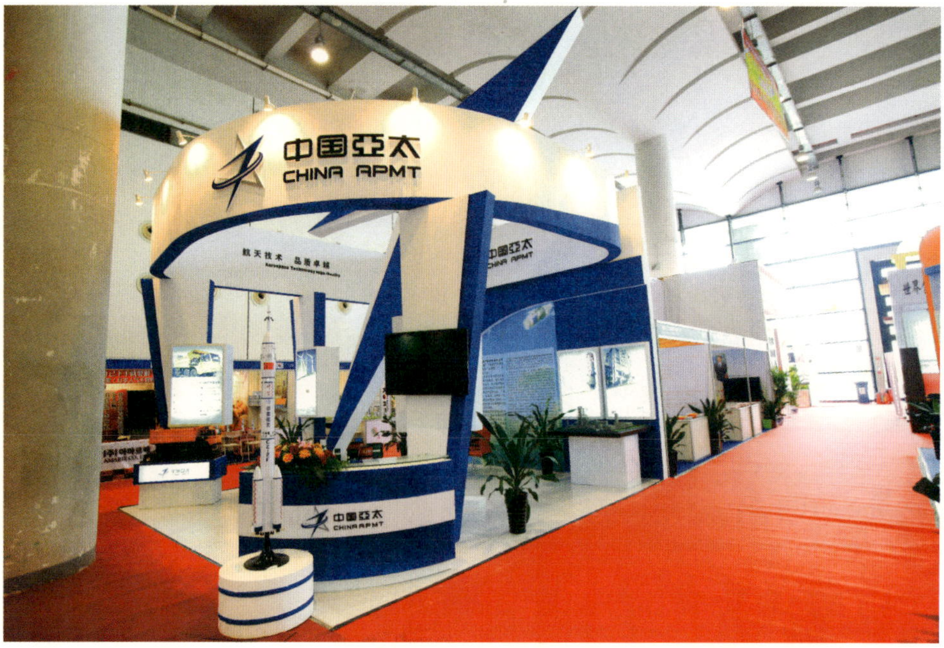

中国商品展区
Chinese Commodities Section

品、日用消费品等优势行业集中，本届博览会继续设立东盟品牌展区，首次设立大宗原材料展示区。

（二）企业参展十分踊跃，展位供不应求

本届博览会国内外预订展位4943个，超出计划数的23.6%。实际安排参展企业2300家，比上届增长4.6%，共设展位4700个。中国国内省（区）报名的规模和质量比上届明显提高。台北世界贸易中心首次组织台湾企业整体参展。

东盟10国和其他国家、地区使用展位1210个。其中，东盟10国使用展位1161个，均为历届新高。印度尼西亚、老挝、马来西亚、缅甸、泰国、越南等6个东盟国家包用独立展馆展示本国商品。40多家东盟品牌企业参展，参展企业质量进一步提高。日本、韩国、加拿大、芬兰等区域外国家积极参展。

（三）企业重复参展率进一步提高，博览会的市场吸引力进一步增强

东盟国家企业重复参展率高，缅甸达71.9%，新加坡、柬埔寨均达55%。中国企业在国际经济合作展区和工程机械、运输车辆展区重复参展率高达90%，电力设备展区企业重复参展率接近35%，这表明博览会对企业的市场吸引力不断增强。

（四）采购商数量质量好于往届，商贸配对更有针对性

本届博览会采购团组更多更专，采购意向更加明确和集中。东盟国家有600多家东盟采购商报名参加博览会贸易配对活动，东盟采购商团组数比上届增加20%以上。中国各省（区、市）采购商踊跃参会。广东、上海、福建、厦门、山东、安徽等省（市）组织采购团组及投引资企业参会。青岛有20多家企业专门采购东盟国家橡胶，上海有50多家企业专门采购东盟轻工产品和包装食品。意大利、法国、德国、瑞士、西班牙、英国、瑞典、卢森堡、阿尔巴尼亚、埃及、日本、韩国等国家和地区的采购商积极参会。

本届博览会各项商贸促进活动丰富多彩，更有针对性。包括举办大型采购对接会，为东盟国家和国内各省（市）采购团与博览会境内外参展企业进行对接，提供面对面的洽谈机会；根据行业特点举办专场小型对接会，为采购商和参展企业提供洽谈见面机会；与联合国采购机构合作举办联合国采购说明会。

（五）投资合作更加务实，着力打造“走出去”最佳展会。

第八届博览会着力提高投资促进实效，强化“走出去”特色，打造“走出去”最佳展会，加快中国企业“走出去”到东盟投资步伐，促进中国和东

盟双向投资。

会期首次举办有11国投资促进部门参加的中国—东盟博览会投资合作圆桌会，完善博览会的“10+1”投资合作机制，发布中国和东盟国家的项目信息，帮助企业及时了解东盟10国投资环境，以及中国政府鼓励企业“走出去”相关政策。

东盟各国及中国各省分别举办投资推介会，各国投资贸易部门、地方政府、经济走廊和园区在会上进行推介，博览会秘书处对投资项目进行撮合，各国部长见证重大项目签约。

会期专门组织了“走出去”企业与金融机构对接活动，包括金融支持企业洽谈会、中国—东盟基本设施投融资合作论坛、投融资项目对接会等，为企业投资东盟提供了务实的金融支持。

二 商品贸易专题

本届博览会商品贸易专题设在南宁国际会展中心。同时，在广西展览馆举办农业展，在南宁华南城展览中心举办轻工展。

南宁国际会展中心各商品展厅展出内容如下：

4号展厅是泰国的独立商品展区，这是泰国连续第五次包用独立展厅参展，主要展示泰国的优势和特色商品，包括食品农产品、工艺品及珠宝饰品、日用消费品等。参展的知名企业有：PSN国际集团有限公司、泰国双莲有限公司等。

5号展厅是马来西亚的独立商品展区。马来西亚是本届博览会的主题国，这是马来西亚连续第六次包用独立展厅参展，主要展示马来西亚的优势和特色商品，包括食品饮料、大宗商品、保健产品、专业服务综合产品、环保产品、生活时尚、教育经营连锁等。参展的知名企业有：马来西亚森那美集团、马来西亚商峰控股有限公司、马来西亚双威集团、马来西亚泰莱大学等。

东盟商品展区
ASEAN Commodities Section

6号展厅是越南的独立商品展区。这是越南连续第六次包用独立展厅参展，主要展示越南的优势和特色商品，如咖啡、手工艺品、木制家具等。参展的知名企业有：越南边和威拿咖啡股份有限公司、越南平仙日用品生产有限公司、越南平新日用品生产有限公司等。

7号展厅是机械设备（食品加工和包装机械）展区。食品加工和包装机械是中国—东盟合作潜力巨大的行业。中国食品和包装机械工业协会连续七届组织本行业有实力的企业和名牌产品参展。主要展品有：全自动包装机、喷码机、贴标机、饮料生产设备等。参展企业大部分是历届博览会多次重复参展的企业，如无锡华明机械、江阴三本科技、济南赛信、武汉吉美粮油、柳州粮油等已连续五年参展。

8号、9号展厅是建筑材料展区，展示在建材和设备方面有优势、产品适合东盟市场的中国建材企业。展示的商品包括：新型环保化学建材、室内装饰材料、门窗幕墙、卫浴洁具、铺装材料等。参展的知名企业有中宇建材集团有限公司、中轻资源集团、广东东方雨虹防水公司、南南铝业股份有限公司、平果铝业集团。

10号展厅是电子电器展区，由深圳市包馆，集中展示与东盟市场有互补性、需求量较大的电子电器类产品。主要展品有：手机及周边产品、笔记本电脑、DVD、液晶显示屏等电子数码产品。参展的知名企业有：深圳朗科电器有限公司、深圳神舟电脑股份有限公司、深圳多彩实业有限公司等。

电子电器展区
Electronics & Electrical Appliances Exhibition

11号展厅是电子电器展区，优选中国优质的降税电子和家电精品，集中展示优质的降税电子和家电精品，其中绿色家电区将主推LED节能灯、太阳空气能热水器、环保空调等。参展的知名企业有CEC、老板电器、江苏春兰空调、澳兰空调、福建南孚电池、天津通广集团等。

12号展厅是电力与新能源设备展区，参展企业大部分是多次重复参展的企业。本展厅集中了中国在电力与新能源设备领域的重要生产基地和骨干企业参展。展品主要有发电设备、输/配/变电设备、电线电缆、风能、太阳能、核能等新能源发电设备。参展企业有：中国南方电网、大唐集团、中广核、国家核电二三建设公司、江苏远东电缆、英利集团、浙江永达集团等。

电力与新能源设备展区
Electrical Power & New Energy Equipment Exhibition

13号展厅是文莱、柬埔寨、菲律宾、新加坡4个东盟国家商品展区。文莱在本展厅参展商品有：食品、工艺品、杂志、服务信息等，参展企业有Sabli Food、联利广告项目公司（文莱）、Mazfel enterpris等。柬埔寨在本展厅参展商品包括珠宝和工艺品、家具和木制品、食品和农产品、日用品、纺织服装、服务贸易等。参展企业有老汉兴酒业（集团）有限公司、加华银行等。菲律宾在本展厅参展商品包括农产品、食品、特色工艺品等。参展机构有椰来香、巧克弗龙公司等。新加坡在本展厅参展商品包括食品、服务业产品等。参展企业有星展银行、康元饼干厂、新加坡工商联合总会等23家企业。

14A号展厅是缅甸的商品展区，这是缅甸连续第五次包用独立展厅集中展示本国商品。本展厅主要展示缅甸的优势和特色商品。展品包括珠宝、玉器等。参展机构有：OK翡翠珠宝有限公司、缅甸联邦工商联合会等。

14B号展厅是老挝的独立商品展区。这是老挝连续第三次包用独立展厅集中展示本国商品。本展区主要展示老挝的优势和特色商品，展品包括木材与木制品、珠宝、手工艺品、食品及服务咨询等。参展企业有：老挝东南亚有限公司、丹萨旺木业有限公司等。

15号展厅是印度尼西亚的独立商品展区。这是印度尼西亚连续第五次包用独立展厅参展。本展厅主要展示在中国市场广受欢迎的印尼优势和特色商品，包括汽车配件、橡胶、农产品、木材家具、传统手工艺品等。参展机构有：印尼贸易部、印尼农业部、印尼投资协调署、印尼地方政府、印尼各参展商协会等。

16号展厅是港澳台地区及其他国家展区。本届博览会首次为港澳台及其他国家地区企业与东盟合作提供了专门展区。参展展品包括LCD/CED数字电视、摄像机等。参展企业有：香港富士康实业有限公司、广西钦州同方数字技术有限公司（港资）、广西钦州宇欣电子科技有限公司、台湾合济工业股份有限公司、台湾通天股份有限公司等。

室外展场是工程机械与运输车辆展区，连续多届参展企业占90%以上。本展区主要展品有：工程机械、建筑机械、矿山机械、农用机械、运输车辆。参展知名企业有：柳工集团、玉柴集团、长城汽车、江淮汽车、山东临工、重汽集团、东风汽车、大宇客车、恒通客车。

工程机械与运输车辆展区
Engineering Machinery & Vehicles Exhibition

中国—东盟博览会农业展设在广西展览馆。整个展馆分为A、B两个区域，一层前厅A区主要是水果、茶叶、食品及农用生产资料等。一层后面B区球厅，主要展示各省名优特色食品、土特产等。

参展企业和商品中，有众多知名企业、行业龙头企业和知名品牌。如：海南椰树集团、浙江古越龙山绍兴酒、山西水塔老陈醋企业等。本届博览会农业展还吸引众多外国知名企业参展，如：咖啡特食品（马来西亚）有限公司、乳业集团（新西兰）公司等，成为博览会农业展的一大亮点。

本届农业展期间，中国农业部举办优质水果推介活动，主要展示广西、山西、陕西、江西四省水果，具体活动包括：（1）优质水果展示。在农业展会场设立“中国优质水果”主题展位，展区面积约300平方米，布局、视觉和运行上既有统一性又有独立性，各地分别以省（区）名义参展，集中展示陕晋赣桂水果产业情况，以鲜果为主，辅以加工品。（2）中国优质水果交流洽谈会。2011年10月22、23日在广西南宁举行中国优质水果交流洽谈会，主要包括推介活动启动仪式、四省（区）水果情况交流、贸易洽谈和签约活动。（3）成交货物出口发车仪式。2011年10月24日在广西凭祥市举行成交货物发车仪式。

轻工产品一直是中国与东盟之间互补性强、市场需求量巨大的贸易品类。本届博览会首次增设轻工展，满足专业客商开展轻工业品贸易需求。中国—东盟博览会轻工展设在南宁华南城展览中心，分为珠宝首饰及工艺品展区、数码电子展区、日用消费品展区、境外特色精品展区。本届博览会轻工展具有以下亮点：

一是展品琳琅满目，涵盖轻工领域整个产业链。轻工展汇集轻工领域内符合中国与东盟市场需求的日用商品，突出展示高附加值和高技术产品，满足不同层次群体的采购需求。

珠宝展区内展品精致美观，极具地域和行业代表性，有缅甸翡翠原石、新疆和田玉、浙江珍珠、浦江水晶、上海金器、云南翡翠、河南玉石、梧州宝石；此外，新疆、香港和国内一线城市也携珠宝玉器设计名师的作品参展，彰显名贵风格。

日用消费品展区汇集浙江、福建、广东等国内一线品牌的高端办公和户外用品进行展示，涵盖体育器材、文化创意、文教办公用品、家居用品、和日化用品等多个领域精品。

二是国际化程度高，境外参展规模超1/4。境外特色展区以东盟各国、日本、香港和台湾组织的展团为主，展览面积超过总展览面积25%，此外尼泊尔、马达加斯加等国也组团参展，带来各国极具特色的精致商品展示。

第八届中国—东盟博览会轻工展开展仪式
The 8th CAEXPO Light Industrial Exhibition Openning Ceremony

三　服务贸易专题

设在南宁国际会展中心2号展厅的本届博览会服务贸易专题展，旨在落实中国—东盟自贸区《服务贸易协议》，主要展示中国和东盟金融服务和旅游服务。

金融服务展区重点展示了中国各类金融管理机构的金融政策、主要职能、服务理念、信息资讯等内容，以及信用贷款、国际结算、企业理财、资产管理、证券发行、投/融资、金融信息服务及技术等金融服务。参展机构有：中国建设银行、中国信用保险公司、广西北部湾银行、中国农业银行、中国工商银行、广西农村信用合作社等。

旅游服务展区以展示墙形式整体展示了广西的旅游资源、旅游城市、旅游合作项目以及东盟国家的旅游资源。旅游服务展与各国“魅力之城”形象展示相得益彰，充分展示了中国与东盟的文化旅游资源和城市形象。

金融服务展区
Financial Services Exhibition

四　投资合作专题

本届投资合作专题总体上呈现三个特点：第一，形式新。强化板块互动，“展”“会”“谈”相结合，专题表现形式更加系统周全；第二，内容针对性强。金融服务力促企业“走出去”，充分利用参会资源，活动更具针对性；第三，更富有实效。国内外投资促进工作机制逐步建立，信息来源和企业组织渠道更广泛，投资促进活动更富实效。

（一）国际经济合作展区

本展区以促进中国企业“走出去”到东盟国家开展投资和国际经济合作为特色。 这是中国对外承包工程商会第八次承办“国际经济合作展区”。本届展区延续和发扬了上届展区的几个特点：一是展会结合。围绕中国—东盟自贸区建成一年来双方合作面临的新机遇，来自政府主管部门、行业协会、承包商和投资商、金融保险法律等咨询机构的代表100余人参加了论坛，就进一步发挥投融资对基础设施合作的促进作用达成共识。二是东盟专业观众

国际经济合作展区
International Economic Cooperation Exhibition

增加。承包商会与东盟建筑商联合会（ACF）合作，邀请东盟各国相关部门和企业参加展览和论坛，扩大了专业观众队伍，为企业与相关方面建立联系与沟通创造条件，促进展览取得实效。三是展览展示水平全面提升。在继续坚持100%特装搭建的基础上，更加凸显“国际经济合作”主题，进一步加强展区整体布展工作，打造展区和展台、整体与个体的和谐统一。

本展厅参展企业有中国中央直属企业及各省（市）外经企业，涉及机械、电子、冶金工程、路桥建设、水电等行业，知名企业有：中国电子信息产业集团、中国铝业、中国有色金属集团、中国通用技术公司、中国水利电力对外公司等。

（二）投资合作圆桌会

2011年10月22日上午，第八届中国—东盟博览会投资合作圆桌会在广西南宁国际会展中心举行。本次投资合作圆桌会由中国商务部投资促进局主办。中国商务部国际贸易谈判代表兼副部长高虎城出席并致辞。来自东盟各国投资促进机构、香港贸易发展局、澳门贸易投资促进局及国内企业代表约70人参加会议。

会议以“凝聚共识，合作共赢”为主题，重点探讨如何以中国—东盟博览会为平台，加强中国与东盟投资促进相关机构的联系，建立投资合作长效机制，进一步推动中国与东盟在投资领域的合作。

高虎城在致辞中表示，中国政府鼓励有实力的中国企业对东盟投资，并为此提供各种支持。他说，近年来，中方设立了规模为100亿美元的中国—东盟投资合作基金，并向东盟国家提供150亿美元的信贷，为双方投资合作提供金融支持。中方愿与东盟国家一道，积极创造条件，争取在5年内与每

2011年10月22日，第八届中国—东盟博览会投资合作圆桌会在广西南宁举行

The 8th CAEXPO Roundtable Meeting on Investment Cooperation held in Nanning, Guangxi, China on October 22, 2011

个东盟成员国构建一个经贸合作区，为企业在东盟国家开展各类集群式生产性投资创建平台。

高虎城表示，随着中国—东盟自贸区《投资协议》深入实施，中国商务部愿与东盟各国投资机构一道，共同推动交通、通信等基础设施的互联互通，加强技术和标准合作，扩大投资规模和领域，发挥中国—东盟博览会的平台作用，推动双方投资合作更加深入，更有成效。

中国商务部合作司、亚洲司、中国—东盟投资合作基金介绍了中国与东盟投资合作的现状及鼓励投资的相关政策，东盟各国投资促进部门的官员介绍了本国投资促进工作经验。双方就如何以中国—东盟博览会为平台，加强中国与东盟投资促进相关机构的联系，建立投资合作长效机制，进一步推动中国与东盟在投资领域的合作进行了深入探讨。

圆桌会上，28位中国企业家就各自企业在赴东盟投资过程中面临的问题和情况，与所在国官员进行了面对面的交流。有东盟国家的投资促进部门官员表示，他们将致力创建一个稳固、安全的政治和社会环境，确保中国企业和企业家在该国的投资利益。

本次会议取得以下主要成果：

1. 首次举办圆桌会，标志着在中国商务部指导框架下，通过博览会这一平台，中国与东盟投促机构合作迈上新台阶。

2. 首次将中国和东盟国家投促机构召集在一起，在圆桌会上探讨有关促进中国与东盟投资合作的设想。

3. 达成多项共识，为中国与东盟今后更好地利用博览会这一平台进行合作打下良好基础，中国与东盟投促机构之间建立了便利的工作联系。

4. 基本形成博览会投资合作机制，即每年至少举行两次会议——高官会投资促进工作会议以及会期的投资合作圆桌会。

（三）投资促进活动

本届博览会期间举行了一系列投资促进活动，取得了显著成效。

1. 举行多场高端对接、政企互动，从政府层面推进投资合作。会期举办东盟国家领导人、政府部长等官员和相关商会会长与国内重点“走出去”企业负责人的对话活动，如：中国对外承包工程商会与东盟建筑商联合会会长会面、海南省领导与老挝计划投资部副部长会谈、中国—东盟旅游官员座谈会、中国—缅甸企业家座谈会、马来西亚玻璃市政府与南宁市高新区管委会和企业对接、广西壮族自治区发改委与马来西亚广州领事馆的会谈等。

2. 举办“走出去”企业与金融机构对接活动，为企业投资东盟提供务实的金融支持。会期举办中国—东盟基础设施投融资合作论坛，由中国对外承包工程商会主办，商务部合作司和博览会秘书处共同支持，众多中央直属企业和金融企业参会。会议探讨为企业“走出去”提供投融资服务，以及金融政策支持、风险管理分析、投资保险、法律保障等各方面服务，为中国企业“走出去”提供切实的协助和支持。举办金融支持企业“走出去”洽谈会，邀请出席第三届中国—东盟金融合作与发展领袖论坛的金融机构和中央企业、各省外经企业代表进行银企对话。

3. 中外政要共同见证重大项目签约，项目签约仪式规格更高。本届博览会期间，中外政要见证重大项目签约，提升了签约仪式的层次和影响力，对重大项目的启动和实施具有重要推动力。例如中国总理温家宝和马来西亚总理纳吉布共同见证中国—马来西亚钦州产业园项目签约、老挝南椰2水电站（BOT）投资项目等。

除政要见证的签约仪式外，本届博览会期间还举行了国际合作项目签约仪式和国内合作项目签约仪式。

2011年10月22日上午，第八届中国—东盟博览会国际合作项目集中签约仪式在南宁举行。广西壮族自治区领导陈际瓦、荣仕星、高雄出席签约仪式。

本次集中签约共签订国际经济合作项目63个，合同总额54.1亿美元。其中，中国企业对东盟国家投资和承包工程等“走出去”项目24个，合同总额17.5亿美元；中国利用外资项目39个，总投资36.6亿美元。

集中签约活动呈现出六大特点：

一是国际合作成效显著。签订的合同总额比上届增长64%，增幅居历届

2011年10月22日，第八届中国—东盟博览会国际合作项目集中签约仪式在南宁举行
The 8th CAEXPO Project Signing Ceremony held in Nanning on October 22, 2011

博览会第一。涉及的产业行业有：工业制造、基础设施、交通能源、农业及农产品加工、商贸物流、住宿和餐饮业等。

二是中国—东盟经贸合作广泛性增强。主要体现在：中国与东盟国家签约合作项目32个，合同总额24.7亿美元，比2010年增长1倍多。中国与东盟9个国家都有合作项目签约。中国有10个省（区、市）和8家中央企业与东盟国家有合作项目，分别比上届增加了6个省（区、市）和7家中央企业。

三是中国—东盟博览会“走出去”平台作用凸显。“走出去”签约项目24个，合同金额17.5亿美元，比上届增长3倍以上。项目包括基础设施建设、建材制造、农业合作等。

四是广西的前沿和窗口作用突出。广西签订国际合作项目51个，合同总额36.3亿美元，占集中签约总额的67%。

五是主题国优势明显。本届博览会主题国马来西亚成为2011年中国—东盟双向投资的新亮点。本次集中签约活动中，中国和马来西亚双向投资项目5个，合同投资额6亿多美元。

六是金融机构积极参与中国—东盟投资合作。国家开发银行与中国建筑股份有限公司、中国技术进出口公司、中国路桥工程有限责任公司和海外柬华投资有限公司等国内外公司签订高达35亿美元的融资合作协议，支持中国企业到东盟开展投资合作。

10月22日上午，第八届中国—东盟博览会国内合作项目集中签约仪式在南宁举行，广西壮族自治区领导陈际瓦、高雄等出席签约仪式。

本场签订国内投资合作项目87个，项目投资额691.3亿元。参加签约的企业分别来自北京、山东、江苏、上海、浙江、福建、广东、湖北、湖南、四川、河北、云南、辽宁、黑龙江、安徽、新疆、广西等17个省（区、市）和中央直属企业。签订项目涉及制造业、基础设施、交通能源、农业及农产品加工和商贸物流仓储等行业。

本次集中签约项目突出四大特点：

一是国内投资合作持续升温。在上届博览会国内合作项目合同投资额增长9%的基础上，本届增长比率继续坚挺，达8.4%。

二是北部湾经济区建设千帆竞发。投资广西北部湾经济区建设的项目24个，合同投资额258亿元，比上届增长2.4倍，占本场签约项目投资总额的37%，比上届高出20个百分点。

三是“三基地”建设投资吸引力增强。本次签约的制造业、商贸和物流项目合计47个，合同投资额385亿元，占签约项目投资总额的46.2%。

四是投资合作趋于多样化。参与本场签约的国内省（区、市）达17个，其中广西与广东、北京、山东、江苏、浙江、上海等11个东部省（市）签订合作项目77个，签约金额612亿元，两者均占本场合作项目数和总投资额的88.5%。广西与湖南、安徽、湖北等3个中部省份签订合作项目5个，签约金额24.7亿元；与四川、云南、新疆等3个西部省（区）签订合作项目3个，签约金额36.5亿元。

4. 服务贸易活动更丰富，促进金融、教育、旅游等合作。本届博览会投资合作与服务贸易专题相互结合更紧密，内容更丰富。除金融支持企业“走出去”洽谈会等金融服务活动外，由商务部服务贸易司举办企业服务外包宣讲会，宣传自贸区服务外包的有关政策与知识。举办中国“魅力之城”海南省旅游产业推介会、海南与东盟国家旅游主管部门官员座谈会，以及国际教育交流活动等，促进中国与东盟金融、旅游和教育合作发展。

5. 投资推介活动丰富多彩，洽谈对接更富成效。在中国—东盟自贸区框架下，博览会期间举办的各种有关中国—东盟次区域合作、投资领域合作的各类促进性、展示性会议，是投资促进活动的重要载体。

本届博览会投资促进活动共举办各类会议61场，数量之多创历届之最。其中，东盟10国全部举办会议，实现了全覆盖，范围之广为历届首次。东盟各国主办或参与主办各类会议共16场，其中泰国4场，新加坡、马来西亚各2场，其他东盟国家各1场。中国北京、上海、江苏、湖南、山西、海南、甘肃、宁夏等省（区、市）举办的各类投资推介会议达22场，其中宁夏回族自治区自首届参与以来，本届已是连续第八次举办投资推介会。加拿大也在本届博览会举办投资加拿大说明会。这些会议都吸引了众多客商的目光。

本届博览会投资促进活动规格高，权威性强，马来西亚总理纳吉布出席了与中国企业CEO的圆桌对话会，泰国副总理吉滴叻出席了与中泰企业家的座谈会，其他多场会议也有部长级官员出席。

本届博览会投资促进活动内容务实，紧扣中国—东盟自贸区建成后双方合作的热点和企业关注的问题，设计和安排各类会议。

一是以整体推介国家或地区投资环境、投资机会作为会议主要内容。如：印尼、泰国、缅甸、文莱、新加坡等东盟各国举办的国家推介会和甘肃、宁夏等国内省（区）举办的会议。

二是以推介重点领域、优势产业、重大园区和项目作为会议主要内容。如：中国商务部合作司主办的中国境外经贸合作区推介会、中国—东盟太阳能政策对话与技术洽谈会、安徽企业与中国印尼经贸合作区对接会、海南国际旅游岛专场推介会、广西重点产业招商推介会等会议。

三是以宣讲解读自贸区有关政策，促进投资合作为会议内容。如：中国

中国—东盟投资合作基金和面向东盟信贷资金说明会
Orientation Session on China-ASEAN Investment Cooperation Fund and Credit Facilities for ASEAN Countries

商务部服务贸易局主办的服务外包政策宣讲及企业交流会，由中国进出口银行和广西壮族自治区人民政府联合主办的中国—东盟投资合作基金和面向东盟信贷资金说明会等。

四是以深化中国—东盟合作关系作为会议内容。例如，由中国对外承包工程商会主办的中国—东盟基础设施投融资合作论坛、中国商务部国际贸易经济合作研究院主办的泛北部湾经济合作发展规划研讨会和由中国商务部、泰国工业部、联合国工业发展组织主办的首届中泰橡胶产业发展合作研讨会等。

本届博览会投资促进活动不仅在投资推介和项目撮合方面取得良好成效，而且更在推动自贸区深入发展、促进次区域经济合作、提升中国—东盟全面战略合作等方面成果丰硕。具体是在跨境经济合作、泛北部湾合作、投资促进机制化建设、境外经贸合作区建设、中国—东盟投资合作基金及面向东盟国家信贷资金的投资促进、服务外包合作等六个方面，取得了新的成果。

五　先进技术专题

中国科技部主办的先进技术专题展设在南宁国际会展中心3号展厅，分为“农业先进技术”和“高新技术”两个板块，集中选取了中国和东盟国家推荐的380家企业、388个农村先进适用技术暨高新技术项目参加展示。

农业先进技术板块有249个项目，涉及农业种养殖、农产品深加工、现代农业装备、农业生物肥料和农村民生科技等领域。

高新技术板块有123个项目，涉及节能环保技术、机电一体化技术和高新材料技术等领域。

本届博览会还有东盟国家参展项目16项，展示东盟国家农业技术成果。

部分参展项目有：华南农业大学的“水稻航天生物育种技术”；贵州省生物技术研究所的“彩色马铃薯技术”；湖南农夫机电有限公司研发的“半喂入微型联合收割机”；广西汽牛农业机械有限公司的“汽牛多功能微耕机”；柳州理工尚迪太阳能科技有限公司的“高聚光抗冻型太阳能集热器”；广西神达新能源公司的“太阳能种植系统”；桂林兴安太阳能光伏产业园；海南立升净水科技公司的“PVC合金超滤膜”；广西农科院的“杂交水稻优质新品种”和“葡萄一年两收栽培技术”；云南农科院的“甘蔗新产品及产业技术”；广西大学与南宁市合辰科技公司的“全自动多功能绿篱苗木修剪机”；贵港市智鸿环境科技公司的“双膜式水处理装置”。

农村先进适用技术暨高新技术展区
Agricultural Advanced Technology & High-tech Exhibition

六 “魅力之城”专题

“魅力之城”专题设在南宁国际会展中心2号展厅。“魅力之城”是每届博览会的亮点，由各主办国选择本国具有代表性的城市作为“魅力之城”，综合展示其在贸易、投资、科技文化、旅游等方面的发展和商机。“魅力之城”使中国和东盟合作由国家层面延伸到城市层面，进一步深化中国与东盟的友好关系。

本届博览会11个“魅力之城”的简要内容介绍如下（按展位实际排列顺序，即从1号展厅往3号展厅方向）：

1. 印度尼西亚西巴布亚省。西巴布亚省位于印度尼西亚新几内亚岛西北部，拥有丰富的矿产资源，包括金、铜、铀、镍、铁、煤、石油天然气、森林、渔产等资源。本展区展示了该省旅游业的勃勃生机。

印度尼西亚西巴布亚省
West Papua Province, Indonesia

2. 柬埔寨拉达那基里省。位于柬埔寨金边北部，与越南、老挝接壤，该省具有得天独厚的山林、瀑布和矿物资源，矿产业、农业、旅游业的开发前景都相当广阔。本展区展示了拉达那基里的旅游和其他领域合作商机。

柬埔寨拉达那基里省
Rattanak Kiri Province, Cambodia

3. 越南会安市。位于越南中部，距岘港30公里处海边，原为占婆国的对外贸易港口，古称“大占海口”，是越南4个“世界文化与自然遗产”之一，也是越南中部著名旅游景点。本展区展示了会安市旅游合作商机。

越南会安市
Hoi An, Vietnam

文莱斯里巴加湾市
Bandar Seri Begawan, Brunei Darussalam

4. 文莱斯里巴加湾市。文莱首都，原为沿河分布的几十座水上聚落，现为现代化城市，有豪华宫殿、体育馆、博物馆和巨大清真寺等。本展区展示了斯里巴加湾市在区域经济合作中的商机。

5. 中国海南省。海南省位于中国最南端，是我国唯一的热带岛屿省份。海南集自然风光、民族风情、热带温泉、文化古迹、珍稀动植物为一体，拥有一批高品位的景区景点，滨海沙滩、蓝色海洋、热带雨林、珍禽异兽、黎苗风情构成奇特的热带生态景观和人文景观，形成了中国不可复制的环海密集型热带旅游资源。这里四季无冬、空气清新、水质纯净，被誉为“一个未受污染的长寿岛”，是无与伦比的休闲胜地，宜居之地。本展区展示了海南省独特的自然资源和生态环境、优质的环保设施与项目、社会发展状况、经济合作和文化交流成果。

中国海南省
Hainan Province, China

6. 马来西亚柔佛州。柔佛州位于马来西亚半岛的最南端，经济迅速发展，以农业、制造业和旅游业为主，本展区展示了柔佛州旅游方面的特色。马来西亚是本届博览会主题国，马来西亚政府高度重视，精心准备，搭建了展示本国深厚文化底蕴和巨大经济潜力的“魅力之城”展区。中方对马来西亚出任主题国予以高度重视和特别礼遇安排，中国和马来西亚领导人共同出席马来西亚“魅力之城”的开馆仪式。

马来西亚柔佛州
Johor, Malaysia

7. 老挝占巴塞省。老挝省级行政区，位于国境南端西侧，土壤肥沃，雨量充沛，河网众多，是老挝南部的鱼米之乡、热带经济作物重点发展区与养畜业基地。本展区展示了占巴塞省在区域经济合作中的商机。

老挝占巴塞省
Champasack Province, Laos

8. 新加坡新加坡城。新加坡位于新加坡岛南端，南距赤道136.8公里，面积约98平方公里，有“花园城市”之称，是世界上最大港口之一和重要的国际金融中心。本展区充分展示新加坡“我行由我新加坡”和“立足狮城、通商环球”的理念。

新加坡新加坡城
Singapore

9. 泰国孔敬府。泰国孔敬府的府会和泰国东北部的政治、商业、金融、交通、教育、医疗和稻米贸易中心。当地浓郁的民族风情、秀丽的自然风光和便捷的交通，加上孔敬府境内发掘出土的恐龙化石，使得孔敬市及周边地区拥有丰富的旅游资源和很大的发展潜力。本展区集中展示泰国孔敬的人文、旅游资源及商务与投资机会。

泰国孔敬府
Khon Khan, Thailand

10. 菲律宾普林塞萨港。菲律宾巴拉望省中东部的一个港口城市，以鳄鱼养殖、地底河流以及潜水景点等特色闻名。本展区展示普林塞萨港环境、经济发展和地理位置及旅游、风土人情等。

菲律宾普林塞萨港
Puerto Princesa, the Philippines

11. 缅甸内比都。缅甸首都，农业和林业为支柱产业，主要作物有稻米、黄麻、柚木、蔬菜、水果等。本展区展示内比都经济社会发展成就及独特的旅游风光。

缅甸内比都
Naw Pyi Taw, Myanmar

七 商贸对接活动

第八届中国—东盟博览会举办了多场专场配对会，并组织东盟国家采购商团组到中国商品展区进行巡馆，让采购商到展位与中国商家直接进行交流。如泰国国家工商会采购商团组，专门到中国食品包装机械展厅巡馆；泰国东北三府采购商团专门到中国电力设备馆巡馆，与事先配对的展商进行洽谈；越南采购商团组专门到工程机械展区巡馆并洽谈。

本届博览会创新组织国别专场贸易配对会。其中，越南采购商专场配对会，越南共办方副秘书长谢煌灵专程参加了配对会并发言。博览会秘书处还与马来西亚出口促进局合作，邀请广东益华百货公司举行进口食品论坛（马来西亚展商专场采购会）。受到中外客商的普遍欢迎。这表明博览会的专场贸易配对会的形式已经逐渐深入人心，成为共办方、商协会和企业家越来越重视的一个重要经贸活动。

本届博览会创新举办大宗商品的研讨会——首届中泰橡胶研讨会，并组织中国—东盟大宗商品（橡胶）专场配对会、中马大宗商品配对会。博览会秘书处根据中国—东盟之间大宗商品交易活跃的特点，配合大宗商品展示区的设置，并结合中国采购企业的需求，与中国商务部、联合国工发组织和泰国工业部共同举办了首届中泰橡胶研讨会，同时，结合研讨会，组织了多家泰国橡胶工业促进机构、协会、会员企业及东盟国家其他橡胶生产企业，与中国约30家青岛、上海等地的橡胶采购企业举行了大宗商品采购配对会（橡胶）。该项活动受到参会各方代表的高度评价，务实推动了橡胶行业各方的供需对接。

此外，与马来西亚沙巴棕油局、马来西亚中华总商会、马来西亚中国经济贸易总商会共同举办了中马大宗商品配对会。60多家马来西亚和中国的棕油、橡胶企业出席了会议。会上，专家就棕榈油的发展前景作了演讲，同时中马企业进行了互动交流，取得良好效果。

本届博览会期间，联合国项目服务厅（UNOPS）、联合国世界粮食计划署、联合国开发计划署（UNDP）、世界卫生组织（WHO）等联合国机构举办了联合国采购说明会。

联合国每年在全球的采购金额达150亿美元，采购内容包括货物和服务两大部分，涉及近万种商品。进入联合国采购市场，有利于利用联合国遍布全球的网络推广企业的商务和服务，拓宽出口渠道，从而推动企业外贸出口的增长。

在本次说明会上，联合国项目服务厅、联合国世界粮食计划署、联合国开发计划署、世界卫生组织的采购官员详细介绍了各自机构的采购规则、主要商品及数量、产品标准等，并与参会企业进行了一对一的洽谈对接。通过这次会议，增进联合国有关组织机构对中国和东盟国家企业及其商品和服务能力的了解，同时也为博览会的参展参会企业创造了解和参与联合国采购的机会，有效提升了博览会的经贸成效。

联合国采购说明会
UN Procurement Presentation

八　公众开放日

2011年10月26日是第八届中国—东盟博览会公众开放日，吸引了数万名公众前来观展。琳琅满目的各国展品、独具特色的异国风情，给观展公众留下了难忘的经历。

当天上午，现场公众兴奋地发现，“杂交水稻之父”袁隆平院士也在参观者的行列中。袁隆平院士在本届博览会农村先进适用技术暨高新技术展厅，对木薯、罗汉果、境外杂交水稻等农作物生产技术进行详细调研，并向来自国内外涉农生产的商家和农业专家了解相关情况。袁隆平院士称

赞说："中国—东盟博览会办得很好。"他表示，希望今后与广西农科院的专家一起密切合作，实现亩产水稻1000公斤的目标。

与往届博览会公众开放日一样，吸引公众的还是各具特色的东盟商品。例如，泰国的香米，香气四溢，引得不少公众前去品尝。越南的红木制品，有各种造型，栩栩如生，惟妙惟肖，深受公众喜爱。马来西亚的白咖啡，热气飘香，久久不散。在中国商品展区，通讯及通信设备、软件及IT服务、厨房电器、制冷设备、音像视听及数码产品等，也吸引了很多民众争相采购。

在"魅力之城"展区，公众穿梭在各国城市之间，这里有国际旅游岛海南岛的旖旎风光，柬埔寨的竹制小屋，老挝的瓦普寺模型。在泰国孔敬展区，大厨们正忙着现场烹饪，木瓜沙拉、烤扒鸡、糯米饭……让公众享受泰国大餐。在马来西亚柔佛展区，舞狮表演展示了马来西亚的风采，舞蹈演员成了热情观众争相合影的对象。印度尼西亚的西巴布亚省展区人气也很旺，在这里，观众可以看到西巴布亚部落皮肤黝黑的原住民，头插羽毛，身画油彩，赤脚坐在地上，现场雕刻他们的图腾木雕。一些兴致勃勃的观众走上舞台，与当地原住民共舞。

公众开放日
CAEXPO Public Open Day

九　2011年中国—东盟博览会林产品与木制品展

2011年11月18日，2011年中国—东盟博览会林产品与木制品展（下称“林木展”）在南宁国际会展中心隆重开幕。博览会在专业化道路上迈出新的步伐。中国国家林业局党组副书记、副局长赵树丛，广西壮族自治区副主席陈章良参加开幕式并巡馆。参加开幕式的还有国家林业局领导、南宁市政府领导、广西林业厅领导、中国林产工业领导以及越南贸易促进局出口促进中心官员等。柬埔寨、老挝、缅甸、泰国、越南等东盟国家驻南宁总领事馆代表也出席了开幕式。

林木展是中国—东盟博览会在主展以外不同时间举办的第一个专业展，目的是进一步促进中国—东盟林木企业合作。本次林木展由中国—东盟博览会秘书处、中国林产工业协会、广西壮族自治区林业厅承办，这是继2010年成功举办首次林木展之后的又一届展会。本次林木展得到了中国和东盟国家林木业管理部门的大力支持，来自中国、柬埔寨、老挝、缅甸、越南等国家的林木企业积极报名参展。

2011年中国—东盟博览会林产品与木制品展开幕式
2011 China-ASEAN Forest & Wood Products Expo Opening Ceremony

本次林木展展览面积为3万平方米，集中展示木门、木地板、木楼梯、红木家具、木工机械等特色林木制品。其中，木工机械，东南亚红木家具、藤制家具等产品成为亮点。会期还将举办2011年国际林产品贸易论坛等系列活动。

林木展为中国—东盟林木企业合作搭建平台。陈章良在致辞中强调，中国与东盟国家林木业资源互补性强，地缘优势明显，合作潜力大。近年来，中国与东盟各国开展了各种林木相关项目的合作，譬如广西与泰国、越南合作开展油茶、八角、桉树等技术合作，还积极推进中国—东盟（南宁）林业产业物流园项目建设。林木展为双方的合作交流提供了很好的机会。

林木展是中国—东盟林木业领域交流的重要活动。中国林产工业协会执行会长王满在致辞中强调，林木产品是中国与东盟国家最重要的进出口货物之一，双方在林木产品的需求和产业结构上互补性强，迫切需要进一步拓宽国际市场。林木展将为双方林木业企业创造更多商机。

开幕式上，赵树丛、陈章良等领导亲自为2011年通过中国林产工业“行业新产品鉴定”的五家企业颁发鉴定证书。行业新产品鉴定是中国林产工业协会贯彻落实国家林业局、国家发改委、财政部、商务部、国家税务总局共同发布的《林业产业振兴规划》的一项新举措。

小结　专业品质赢得强大市场吸引力

中国—东盟博览会经过八年的探索创新，内容不断适应中国—东盟自由贸易区发展趋势，适应企业开拓市场的需求。第八届博览会展览内容更加专业，吸引更多更优的中国和东盟及其他国家地区企业参展参会，重点行业展区继续保持较高的重复参展率，表明博览会的专业化得到了市场的认可，博览会服务企业的能力也进一步提高。

第一，专业品质赢得强大市场吸引力。2011年是中国展览业快速发展的一年，展览数量持续增加。据中国会展经济研究会发布的《中国会展经济蓝皮书》统计，2011年中国共举办展会7333场，同比增长18.21%，居世界第二位；总展出面积8173万平方米，同比增长5.59%。在展览市场竞争日趋激烈的情况下，中国—东盟博览会仍然受到越来越多企业的青睐，报名参展参会企业有增无减，展位仍供不应求。

博览会强大的市场吸引力，来自其不断提升的专业品质。在展览内容上，本届博览会东盟国家展品进一步向其优势行业集中，东盟国家在本国展区内继续设立东盟品牌展区，首次设立大宗原材料展示区。中国展品更加契合东盟市场需要。这样的设置既突出了双方的优势行业，又满足了企业专业采购的需求。因此，企业报名十分踊跃，报名展位数比规划展位数多11.3%。其中，湖南省报名展位数比上届接近翻番，福建报名展位数比上届增加20%，广东省报名参展的知名企业也比上届更多。本届博览会重复参展企业继续保持高比例，名优企业增多。

第二，专业服务提升经贸实效。本届博览会举办了多场政商高端对接活动，从更高层面推进务实合作；围绕东盟棕榈油、橡胶和其他特色行业举办了多场配对活动，以及东盟各国投资推介会、投融资项目对接会等，为东盟商品找到买家，帮助东盟项目引进国际资本。

本届博览会加强了对中国各省（区、市）企业的服务，积极组织广东、上海、福建、山东、安徽、北京、江西等省（市）采购团组和投引资项目参会；为本届博览会中国“魅力之城”海南举办了开馆仪式、领导人特别参观、专场旅游产业推介会、海南省领导与老挝计划投资部副部长会谈等活动，充分展示了海南形象；为各省（区、市）举办专场推介活动，如甘肃投资环境说明暨葡萄酒品鉴会、宁夏回族自治区投融资说明会、安徽企业与中国印尼经贸合作区项目对接会、山西运城市代表团项目签约仪式等。

本届博览会对企业的市场服务水平更优，贸易配对、投资项目撮合服务做得更细更实，现场对接活动更有效。例如，安排专人引领采购团组参观展区、参加采购活动；现场设置“客商资讯服务区”，实时公布采购和投资清单及相关信息，协助客商获取产品信息及联系供应商，为客商提供现场配对和商贸促进活动的宣传引导服务，取得了很好的效果。

第三，首次举办投资合作圆桌会，为建立投资促进长效机制夯实基础。首次由商务部投资促进局牵头在会期举办中国—东盟博览会投资合作圆桌会。邀请中国和东盟国家政府的投资促进机构高层官员出席，共商中国与东盟投资合作大计，还发布了中国和东盟国家的项目信息，为企业提供与各国投促机构直接交流互动的机会，使企业及时了解东盟国家的投资环境和政策，建立起与东盟国家投资合作联系，降低企业在东盟国家和更大范围内寻找投资项目的成本，为中国企业“走出去”投资东盟搭建便捷通道。

总之，本届博览会以更加专业的品质、更优质的市场服务，在服务中国—东盟合作、服务中国—东盟自由贸易区建设、服务中国国内各省（区、市）与东盟合作等方面，取得了新成效，使企业得到了实惠。

第五章

5 推动多领域交流 促进全方位合作格局

——第八届中国—东盟博览会系列会议、论坛和交流活动

中国—东盟经贸合作的持续快速发展，离不开金融、海关、质检、物流等相关服务配套领域的支撑。同时，经贸合作与人文交流的结合，有利于推动形成全面持久稳定的友好关系格局。

中国—东盟博览会举办以来，每年都围绕多个领域，举办一系列会议论坛和交流活动，研究双方在各领域合作中的热点问题，形成一系列合作机制，为双方全面合作提供保障。例如，中国和东盟10国质检部长定期在博览会期间举行会议，在食品安全、动植物检验检疫等多个方面达成共识，促进了贸易便利化。在其他领域的交流活动中，各国部长级官员、企业家、专家学者深入研讨交流，形成了越来越多的合作机制，达成了越来越多的共识，产生了越来越多的务实合作成果。

第八届中国—东盟博览会继续举办系列会议论坛和交流活动。其中，围绕“环保合作”主题，举办中国—东盟环保合作论坛，同时还围绕质检、金融、太阳能、药品安全、智库、人口与家庭发展、文化产业论坛、出版、森林、物流等领域，举办了相关会议和交流活动。各场活动规格高，针对性强，各方围绕各领域的热点议题，展开了深入研讨和对话，形成了一批务实成果。

Promote Bilateral Exchanges and Cooperation on All Fronts

— Concurrent Forums and Conferences of the 8th CAEXPO

China–ASEAN economic and trade cooperation has enjoyed fast growth in recent years, which can not be possible without the support of relevant authorities/sectors including finance, customs, quality inspection & quarantine as well as logistics, etc. In the meanwhile, enhanced economic & trade ties, combined with more frequent people–to–people exchanges, will help establish a pattern of long–lasting and stable friendly relations between the two sides.

Since the first session of the CAEXPO, concurrent conferences and forums on diverse fields have been held, to talk about issues of common interests in different areas, and to shape a series of working mechanisms for cooperation, aiming to provide guarantee for bilateral comprehensive cooperation. To name just a few, ministers of quality inspection and quarantine of China and the 10 ASEAN member countries met at each of the previous CEXPOs, reaching common grounds on many fields including food safety and fauna & flora inspection & quarantine, and promoting trade facilitation. At the exchange programs held for other fields, ministers, entrepreneurs, scholars and experts have had in–depth discussions, promoting the shaping of diversified mechanisms and consensus, thus yielding rich and pragmatic outcomes.

During the 8th CAEXPO, concurrent conferences and forums were also held, including ASEAN–China Environmental Cooperation Forum 2011, which was held to echo the 8th CAEXPO Theme of the Year, i.e., Environment Protection Cooperation, and those on inspection & quarantine, finance, solar energy, drug safety, think tank, people & family development, cultural industry, press & publishing, forestry, logistics and more. All these events feature high–profiled participants and targeted topics. Participants gather and discuss hot issues of their own sector, yielding pragmatic results.

CHAPTER FIVE

一　2011中国—东盟环保合作论坛

2011年10月22日，2011中国—东盟环保合作论坛在广西南宁成功举办。本次论坛以“创新与绿色发展”为主题，由广西壮族自治区人民政府和中国环境保护部共同主办、东盟秘书处支持、中国—东盟博览会秘书处协办，广西壮族自治区环境保护厅和中国—东盟环境保护合作中心承办。

中国环境保护部副部长李干杰、广西壮族自治区副主席林念修、广西壮族自治区政协副主席李彬、东盟秘书处副秘书长米斯然·卡尔梅、亚洲开发银行副行长宾度·洛哈尼以及东盟各国高级代表、联合国机构高级代表等来自中国、东盟各国及其他国家和地区的政府机构、企业、协会等环保领域的220多位代表参加论坛，30多位演讲嘉宾围绕“创新与绿色发展的国家政策”和“绿色创新与产业合作”两大主题展开精彩演讲和热烈讨论。

中国环境保护部副部长李干杰在致辞中充分肯定过去的十年中国—东盟环境合作取得的丰硕成果，并就进一步推动中国—东盟环保合作提出了三点建议

2011年10月22日，2011中国—东盟环保合作论坛在广西南宁举行
ASEAN-China Environmental Cooperation Forum 2011 held in Nanning, Guangxi on October 22, 2011

和希望：第一，积极落实《中国—东盟环境保护合作战略》，实施好《中国—东盟环境合作行动计划》，共同促进绿色发展。第二，不断创新合作模式，丰富合作内涵。第三，完善环境合作机制，为绿色发展注入新的动力，进一步推动中国—东盟环境合作在区域环境合作中发挥更为积极的影响与示范作用。

东盟秘书处副秘书长米斯然·卡尔梅说，东盟非常赞赏中国和东盟在环境方面的合作，尤其是在绿色发展的合作，论坛会提供一个非常好的平台，使得中国和东盟在这方面合作的意识能够进一步提高，使双方在环境友好问题上进行更多的合作，并且在技术上和政策上也可以进行进一步的合作。双方都希望能够实现在这个地区的创新与绿色的发展。

亚洲开发银行副行长宾度·洛哈尼说，环保论坛是一个非常及时也非常重要的论坛。中国—东盟环保合作战略的建立，对于这个地区起着非常重要的作用。为了实现绿色发展的目标，我们也必须进一步加强环境方面的合作，这对亚洲的未来是至关重要的，而且对世界的未来也是至关重要的。

广西壮族自治区副主席林念修在主题发言中说，随着中国—东盟自贸区的建成，广西在促进中国与东盟双边合作关系，特别是在经贸等领域合作与交流方面，发挥了重要作用。广西愿意与东盟国家在绿色技术研究、技术交流和人员培训等方面加强合作，共同开展先进绿色实用绿色技术和环保产品的研发和推广。开展双边生物多样性保护，同时充分利用中国—东盟自贸区和中国—东盟博览会这一重要平台，建立节能环保技术及节能环保产业的合作机制，共同开拓节能环保产业市场，进一步加强生态保护与减贫、跨境地区生物廊道建设等合作，构建自然保护区网络，共同保护好区域生态环境。

论坛的成功举办，取得多项积极成果：

1. 论坛达成了多项共识。各方一致认为，应加强国家间在绿色发展方面的合作，充分发挥政策、法规、市场、金融等各种因素对绿色创新的激励作用，加速绿色创新；积极推动绿色产业发展，优化产业结构，大力推进企业节能环保改造，使绿色产业成为推动经济增长的新生力量；制定和完善促进绿色技术的政策，利用金融等手段，扶持和鼓励绿色发展与技术创新，使绿色经济显现出勃勃生机。

2. 启动了中国—东盟绿色使者计划。绿色使者计划是中国—东盟环保合作的旗舰项目，必将以丰富的内涵和多样的形式，为中国—东盟的环保合作注入新的活力。在唤醒中国和东盟各国公众的环保意识，推进环境教育，促进区域绿色发展合作步入稳定、可持续的发展轨道过程中发挥积极的作用。

3. 初步建立了中国—东盟环保产业合作网络。来自环保领域的代表们在论坛上就“创新与绿色发展”主题发表了真知灼见，分享先进理论和绿色成长的宝贵经验，为中国—东盟环保产业合作与技术交流建立了网络，搭建了平台与桥梁。

4. 为中国—东盟环保合作机构在中国建立打好基础。马来西亚总理纳吉布表示："今后数年里，随着《中国—东盟环保合作战略（2009—2015年）》的实施，中国—东盟环保合作机构有望在中国成立。"通过本次论坛，中国与东盟各国探讨了环保合作大计，彼此增加了理解，形成了共识，为中国—东盟环保合作机构在中国的建立奠定了基础并产生积极的推动作用。

论坛期间还举办了中国—东盟环境保护合作图片展和广西环境保护成就图片展。

二 第三届中国—东盟金融合作与发展领袖论坛

2011年10月22日，由广西壮族自治区人民政府、中国人民银行、中国银行业监督管理委员会、中国证券监督管理委员会、中国保险监督管理委员会（以下简称“一行三会”）共同主办，广西壮族自治区人民政府承办的第三届中国—东盟金融合作与发展领袖论坛在广西南宁成功举行。

论坛以“务实与创新，中国—东盟区域经济发展的金融合作及财政合作”为主题，紧密围绕区域内货币结算、区域经济发展的金融调控、金融财政合作与发展等问题，分设“中国—东盟经济技术合作的金融与财政支持”、“区域内货币结算与中国—东盟自由贸易区的金融合作及财务合作”、“金融合作与区域经济发展”、“企业融资上市与区域多元化资本市场发展”及“中国—东盟自由贸易区经济金融发展的相关政策与服务支撑”等议题进行研讨，吸引了来自中国和东盟国家金融主管部门领导，中国和东盟国家及欧美亚太地区的国际金融、财会机构高层管理人员，国内外金融、财政等领域知名专家学者，企业界代表等300余人参加，其中包括总部/总行级领导28人（副部级以上贵宾15人）、73家境内金融机构、22家境外机构。

本届金融论坛呈现五个亮点：

1. 品牌效应进一步增强。本届论坛继续保持高规格、高层次、高水平，影响力得到不断扩大和提高，主要体现在以下方面：

一是继续保持高规格。论坛继续由广西壮族自治区人民政府和“一行三会”共同主办，中国人民银行行长助理金琦、中国银监会副主席蔡鄂生、中国证监会主席助理姜洋、中国保监会纪委书记陈新权均代表主办方出席论坛并作主旨演讲。

二是广西壮族自治区党委、政府领导高度重视。会期，广西壮族自治区党委书记、自治区人大常委会主任郭声琨，广西壮族自治区主席马飚，广西壮族自治区党委副书记陈际瓦，广西壮族自治区党委常委、自治区常务副主

2011年10月22日，第三届中国—东盟金融合作与发展领袖论坛在广西南宁举行

The 3rd China-ASEAN Summit Forum on Financial Cooperation & Development held in Nanning, Guangxi on October 22, 2011

席李金早分别会见并宴请了出席论坛的贵宾，成为广西至今举办的高层论坛中受自治区领导关注度最高的论坛。

三是论坛得到参会单位和嘉宾的积极肯定和支持。在两届论坛积累的基础上，本届论坛逐渐形成了一个相对比较稳定的客户群体，如中国进出口银行、中国银行、交通银行、华夏银行、北京银行、柬埔寨加华银行、德勤华永会计师事务所等18家机构连续三年参会，农业银行、建设银行、包商银行、天津银行、深圳证券交易所、澳门金融管理局、越南河内证券交易所等12家机构连续两年参会，重复参会的机构占31%。

四是金融论坛辐射面进一步扩大。参加论坛的东盟国家由2010年的6个增至9个，包括文莱、柬埔寨、印尼、老挝、马来西亚、菲律宾、新加坡、泰国、越南。

2. 进一步突出“走出去”内容，更加注重务实性和服务性。论坛期间举办了金融机构支持企业“走出去”交流洽谈会、企业股权（债券）投融资交易会、投融资项目对接会等一系列投资促进活动，使企业与金融机构得到有效衔接。这些活动进一步突出了“走出去”内容，强化金融对区域经济发展的服务作用。

3. 突出前瞻性，搭建中国—东盟专业互动平台。本届金融论坛期间举办中国—东盟经济金融合作智库对话，邀请金融界知名专家学者、金融机构及企业界代表进行专业互动。一是从学界、金融界、商界等各界不同的视角探讨和剖析中国—东盟经济金融合作的机制安排与实施途径，为区域金融合作谋划长远机制。二是对下一步金融论坛的主题议题设置进行探讨，促进金融论坛的可持续发展。

4. 继续利用金融论坛专业宣传渠道，不断扩大论坛影响力。在充分利用中国—东盟博览会、中国—东盟商务与投资峰会拥有的大众传媒资源基础上，继续利用论坛积累的专业宣传渠道，通过战略合作的方式，与《小康财智》、《金融时报》及和讯网等一批财经界知名媒体签约合作，得到12家合作媒体广告宣传版面的支持，和讯网继续以网络图文直播形式对论坛进行宣传，《小康财智》、《贸易金融》及和讯网等媒体对论坛贵宾进行了新闻专访，有效提高了论坛的影响力。

5. 连续两届实现市场化运作。本届金融论坛继续探索市场化运作方式，力求兼顾论坛的社会效益与经济效益，得到了广西北部湾银行的大力支持，自2010年开始，该行连续两届以联合承办的方式参与论坛工作。

本届金融论坛取得了以下主要成果：

1. 形成中国—东盟金融合作发展机制研究成果。本届金融论坛委托中国人民银行金融研究所向国内金融界知名专家学者征集了中国—东盟金融合作发展课题相关的研究成果，并在论坛上正式对外发布了研究成果摘要，论文集在论坛结束后结集出版，为中国—东盟的商界和金融界开展务实交流和合作提供理论依据和参考指导。

2. 不断深化政银、银企及金融机构间的交流，进一步提高了广西及博览会的知名度、美誉度和对外开放水平。论坛务实推动了政银、银企及金融机构间合作交流。一是通过举办金融机构支持企业“走出去”交流洽谈会、企业股权（债券）投融资交易会、投融资项目对接会等一系列投资促进活动，使企业与金融机构得到有效衔接。二是金融机构借此机会与广西金融部门进行深入交流，寻找合作机会。如北京银行表示正在积极筹建南宁分行，并以南宁分行为“桥头堡”，加强对自贸区经贸发展的金融支持，推进服务网络向东盟延伸；正信银行积极考察广西的金融投资环境，希望加快与广西政府、企业的合作；北京黄金交易中心计划在南宁设立其分支机构，积极配合广西及南宁市提出的金融业发展战略规划需求，树立北京黄金交易中心的品牌形象。

三　中国—东盟人口与家庭发展论坛

由国家人口计生委和广西壮族自治区人民政府联合主办，国家人口计生委国合司和广西壮族自治区人口计生委承办的中国—东盟人口与家庭发展论坛，于2011年10月11—12日在广西南宁举行。来自东盟、拉美、欧洲以及非洲等地区的20个国家、6个人口计生领域国际组织的官员，以及国际国内专家、人口计生工作者共130余人参加了论坛。论坛以人口与家庭发展为主题，围绕统筹解决人口与可持续发展，全球化城镇化背景下的家庭、健康与福利，增进人口与家庭发展领域交流合作等3个专题进行研讨，取得了圆满成功，得到了国际、国内嘉宾的一致好评。

会前，广西壮族自治区党委书记、自治区人大常委会主任郭声琨，广西壮族自治区主席马飚会见了国家人口计生委主任李斌一行；国家人口计生委主任李斌和广西壮族自治区主席马飚共同会见了与会的部级重要外宾和国际组织负责人，广西壮族自治区党委常委、宣传部部长、广西计生协会会长沈北海，广西壮族自治区党委常委、秘书长余远辉，广西壮族自治区副主席李康参加

2011年10月11—12日，中国—东盟人口与家庭发展论坛在广西南宁举行

China–ASEAN Forum on Population and Family Development held in Nanning, Guangxi on October 11–12, 2011

了会见。

李斌、马飚、沈北海与缅甸移民与人口部部长吴钦伊，印度尼西亚国家人口和计划生育委员会主任苏吉瑞·塞亚瑞夫，老挝卫生部副部长因拉文·凯博潘，柬埔寨卫生部副部长坦沃乘，国际计生联总干事特沃德斯·梅莱斯，人口与发展南南合作伙伴组织执行主任哈利·乔瑟里，联合国人口基金驻华代表处代理代表玛丽安等出席论坛。国家人口计生委副主任崔丽作了题为《坚持统筹解决人口问题，努力实现可持续发展》的主旨演讲。开幕式由李康主持。广西壮族自治区人口计生委主任黄丹代表广西在论坛上作了经验发言。

李斌在开幕式上指出，人口与家庭发展问题关系到世界各国人民的利益和整个人类社会的发展前途。中国和东盟国家在经济领域开展了积极合作，今后应在人口与家庭发展领域进行交流，共同提升家庭发展能力，促进人口均衡型、资源节约型、环境友好型的和谐可持续发展社会的建设。

广西壮族自治区主席马飚在致辞中说，广西与东盟国家山水相连、人文相通，是中国面向东盟开放合作的前沿和窗口。近年来，广西积极探索人口与家庭发展新机制，加强人口与家庭发展的前瞻性研究，完善以增强养老保障功能、促进家庭发展能力、抵御突发风险为核心利益导向政策体系，打造针对家庭、针对全人群生命全过程的家庭健康公共服务体系，加强新型家庭人口文化建设，创新有利于家庭发展的诚信计生民主管理模式，促进了人口工作的科学发展和家庭的和谐幸福，走出了一条西部民族地区人口与经济社会和谐发展的新路子。

国际计生联总干事特沃德斯·梅莱斯在发言中表示，中国和东盟国家共同面对大量农村人口涌入城市带来的潜在矛盾、婴儿死亡率较高、艾滋病防治服务的普及仍落后于世界总体目标等诸多挑战，应充分发挥国际合作与民间团体的力量，积极有效地应对这些问题。

人口与发展南南合作伙伴组织执行主任哈利·乔瑟里认为，要实现家庭发展，需要政府创造更好的政策，加大资金投入和医疗设施建设，进一步加强以社区为基础的行动方案，使妇女和青少年得到服务。中国从人口控制过渡到人口管理，有利于中国创造更和谐的家庭和社会，中国的成功经验值得其他亚洲、非洲、中东地区人口大国借鉴。

各国与会代表还介绍了本国在人口与家庭发展方面取得的经验。印度尼西亚代表介绍了该国以机构建设、预算编制和人力资源为核心的人口发展和计划生育项目；越南代表介绍了该国在促进人口发展和家庭幸福方面取得的成绩、面临的挑战以及今后方向；马来西亚代表介绍了在全球化、工业化时代，该国家庭和文化可持续发展面临的挑战、国家家庭政策以及以提升家庭发展能力为核心的国家项目；菲律宾代表介绍了“负责任父母运动”，该运动旨在帮助和动员夫妇做认真、负责和可靠的父母，发挥孩子最大的潜能；泰国代表介绍了国际合作经验，如经验共享、技术合作以及交流培训等。

论坛期间，与会代表实地参观考察了广西崇左市扶绥县渠黎镇碧蓍村、南宁市青秀区凤岭北社区、广西民族博物馆和广西药用植物园，了解广西城乡基层开展计划生育、家庭和社区服务情况以及文化建设、经济建设情况。

本次论坛围绕主题，通过主旨报告、案例介绍和点评讨论等形式，进行了交流研讨，取得了积极的成果，主要体现在以下几个方面：

一是搭建了各国交流共享经验智慧的平台。各国代表及专家学者在论坛上围绕三个具体主题，交流了在人口和家庭发展领域的成功经验和做法，开拓了视野，启迪了思路，增进了相互了解，促进了相互学习借鉴，将对中国与东盟各国贯彻落实国际人发大会行动纲领和联合国千年发展目标起到积极的促进作用。

二是形成了关注人口与家庭发展的共识。论坛以人口与家庭发展为主题展开交流研讨，重申人口与家庭在可持续发展中的重要地位和作用，促进人口长期均衡发展，促进提升家庭发展能力，将有助于进一步唤起各国政府、非政府组织及相关国际组织对人口和家庭发展的关注，推动落实人口与家庭发展领域的政治承诺和具体行动，切实促进人口均衡、环境友好和资源节约，确保发展的协调可持续性。

三是加强了人口与家庭发展领域的交流合作。论坛内容丰富，交流充分，使与会代表建立了有效的了解和沟通渠道，为深入开展交流合作奠定了良好基础，促进经验共享，推动共同发展。

四是进一步提升了广西的国际形象。论坛在广西举办，在人口发展领域把广西摆到了中国西部发展的前沿，而且推向国际舞台，加深了国际、国内对广西经济社会发展和人口工作的认识，扩大了广西的国际影响，提升了国际形象，对实现“富民强桂”新跨越起到积极的推动作用。国家人口计生委对本次论坛给予了高度评价，认为办出了新意，办出了特色，办出了水平，展示了广西在人口计生领域的新进展和新成就。

四　第四届中国—东盟智库战略对话论坛

2011年10月17—18日，第四届中国—东盟智库战略对话论坛在广西南宁举行。论坛由中国社会科学院国际研究学部、广西社会科学院、广西国际博览事务局、广西北部湾发展研究院联合主办，围绕“新形势下的中国—东盟合作”主题，围绕自贸区建成一周年，扩大中国—东盟政治、经济、文化合作领域，深化区域行业之间的务实合作，实现共同发展和繁荣进行讨论和展望。

广西壮族自治区人大常委会副主任刘新文，柬埔寨皇家科学院副院长宋春奔（Sum Chhum Bun），老挝社会科学院副院长坎飞(Khamphay Rasmy)，菲律宾企业领导人研究所总裁兼首席执行官，亚洲团结学会主席（菲律宾前任财政部长）约瑟思·艾思塔尼斯劳（Jesus Estanislao），中国社会科学院国际研究学部主任张蕴岭，以及来自中国和东盟及其他国家智库的专家、学者和嘉宾共100多人出席会议。

论坛开幕式由广西社会科学院副院长黄志勇主持。广西壮族自治区人大常委会副主任刘新文，柬埔寨皇家科学院副院长宋春奔，中国社会科学院国

2011 年 10 月 17—18 日，第四届中国—东盟智库战略对话论坛在广西南宁举行

The 4th China-ASEAN Think Tank Strategic Dialogue Forum held in Nanning, Guangxi on October 17-18, 2011

际研究学部主任张蕴岭以及广西社会科学院、广西北部湾发展研究院院长吕余生，广西国际博览事务局副局长宫起君等先后在开幕式上致辞。

刘新文在致辞中说，智库在中国—东盟交流合作中发挥着重要的作用。中国—东盟合作的丰富实践为各国智库交流合作及研究提供了广阔空间，中国—东盟关系的进一步发展和交流合作的具体实践也迫切需要各国智库和专家学者的理论创新和献计献策。她建议，广西在四个方面加强与各国智库的合作：一是搭建更多的交流平台，丰富和完善合作机制；二是加强信息沟通交流，共促中国—东盟互联互通信息网络建设；三是充分发挥智库作用，推进中国—东盟各项合作的具体落实；四是促进各国智库人才交流合作，共同培养促进中国—东盟关系发展急需的高端人才。

宋春奔（Sum Chhum Bun）在致辞中说，第四届中国—东盟智库战略对话将有利于推动亚洲地区的经济发展和加强中国与东盟之间积极和友好的伙伴关系，尤其是有利于深化和加强柬埔寨和中国的长期友好合作关系。

张蕴岭在致辞中说，2011年是中国—东盟建立对话关系20周年。20年来，中国与东盟坚持睦邻友好，坚持互利共赢，共同应对危机和挑战，共同创造了经济发展的“东亚奇迹”。20年来，双方政治互信和互利合作水平不断提升，共同利益不断扩大。同时，我们也应看到，中国与东盟的一些成员国之间还存在着一些问题和争议，但我们应把握中国—东盟合作的大局，不让这些问题成为影响中国—东盟友好关系的发展。

吕余生在致辞中说，多年来，中国和东盟国家的智库为各国和地区的发展，为中国与东盟的合作和友谊作出了重要的贡献。特别是近年来，各国智库机构紧密合作，发挥智库作用，为中国—东盟合作、泛北部湾经济合作、中国南宁—新加坡经济走廊建设，积极献计献策，贡献智慧力量。面对当前世界经济大变革、大调整、大发展的新形势，我们愿与东盟各国智库一道通过加强对话与交流，共同谋求应对挑战之策，共同维护友好合作大局，共同推动各方充分全面发展。

广西国际博览事务局副局长宫起君在致辞中说，即将于10月21日开幕的第八届中国—东盟博览会，被列为中国—东盟建立对话关系20周年系列纪念活动的重要组成部分，意义非凡。已经成功举办七届的中国—东盟博览会，搭建了中国—东盟友好交流、经贸促进和多领域合作的重要平台，成为中国—东盟自贸区具有广泛影响力的国际盛会，得到11国商界的广泛认可。

与会专家就论坛主题以及3个主要议题“中国—东盟建立对话关系20周年回顾与展望”、“中国—东盟自由贸易区建成后双边经贸合作的推进”、“广西在中国—东盟合作中的作用”进行了广泛而深入的研讨与交流。

与会专家认为，中国—东盟建立对话关系20年来，双方始终以和平友好，发展共赢为主题、以友好合作为主线，见证了从全面对话伙伴、睦邻互信伙伴到战略伙伴的发展历程。双方建立了包括领导人、部长、高官和工作组在内的一整套合作机制，在经贸、投资、农业、金融、信息通讯、基础设施建设等20多个领域开展务实合作，建成了全球覆盖人口最多、区域最广的自贸区。面对目前由于世界政治经济动荡对中国—东盟关系发展造成的一些问题和分歧，双方通过相互对话谈判和真诚合作是可以友好解决的。中国与东盟只要珍惜这来之不易的友好关系，本着求同存异、务实合作的精神，不断加强双方的交流合作，增信释疑，定能合力应对世界经济可能发生的动荡，构筑中国—东盟友好关系的未来。

与会专家认为，几年来广西充分发挥紧邻东盟的区位优势，大力实施以东盟为重点的多区域合作战略，日渐成为双向沟通中国与东盟的国际大通道、交流大桥梁、合作大平台。广西应充分发挥参与东盟国家区域经济的分工优势，抓住中国—东盟自由贸易区建成后的发展机遇，加强边境经济合作区、保税物流园区、出口加工区等的建设，加快与东盟国家的互联互通，扩大与周边东盟国家的经济贸易合作。

五 2011中国—东盟文化产业论坛

由中国文化部、国家文物局、广西壮族自治区人民政府主办，自治区文化厅承办的2011中国—东盟文化产业论坛，于2011年10月19—20日在广西南宁举行。中国文化部党组成员、国家文物局局长单霁翔，文化部对外文化联络局副局长张爱平，东盟秘书处文化官员阿利夫·毛拉纳，广西壮族自治区副主席李康出席开幕式并致辞。来自中国、东盟秘书处、东盟10国的代表以“博物馆运营管理与博物馆文化产品创意开发”为主题，就“经济全球化、文化产业发展背景下的博物馆运营管理”、“博物馆文化产品创意开发”和“促进国际间博物馆合作交流”等内容进行了探讨。

东盟10国国家博物馆馆长、专家，日本国立民族学博物馆专家以及中国国家博物馆、故宫博物院，各省、自治区、直辖市及计划单列市的博物馆馆长等出席了论坛。广西有关方面代表列席会议，论坛规模近200人。

单霁翔在致辞中说，当今世界正经历着复杂而深刻的变化，博物馆事业面临新的重要发展机遇。加强交流合作，积极适应新形势，加快改革和创新，进一步提升博物馆的专业化水平，激发博物馆可持续发展的活力，加快

2011年10月19—20日，2011中国—东盟文化产业论坛在广西南宁举行

2011 China-ASEAN Forum on Cultural Industry held in Nanning, Guangxi on October 19-20, 2011

博物馆融入社会生活的步伐，是各国博物馆界共同关注和积极实践的重大命题。本届论坛为来自东盟各国和中、日、韩的文化遗产及博物馆专业人员搭建了良好的交流平台。衷心期待论坛在增进中国与东盟各国博物馆界交流的同时，为各国文化产业发展带来新的灵感和启迪，为提升区域文化合作水平，增进中国与东盟各国友谊作出新贡献。

阿利夫·毛拉纳在致辞中说，通过这次论坛，中国与东盟国家及日韩可以拓展和深化其他领域的合作，使“10+3”地区成为世界上最具活力的地区和最有文化涵养的地区，让各国相互学习和分享彼此丰富多彩的文化遗产。

李康在开幕式上指出，中国—东盟文化产业论坛已经成为中国与东盟文化产业交流合作的重要平台。2011年正值中国—东盟建立对话关系20周年，又是中国—东盟友好交流年，本届中国—东盟文化产业论坛成功举办具有特殊的重要意义，通过东盟各国间的交流对话，相互借鉴，集思广益，共同探讨和分享文化产业发展的经验、理念、模式和路径，将对中国—东盟文化产业合作发展起到促进作用。

论坛报告会上，单霁翔作了题为《全球化视野下的博物馆运营管理》的主旨报告，广西文化厅厅长余益中作了题为《加快建设，提升管理，努力搭建与东盟博物馆合作交流平台》的主题发言，东盟秘书处文化官员、部分东盟国家代表以及部分国内省（市）博物馆馆长也先后作了专题发言。

2011中国—东盟文化论坛是在文化新时期、新形势和中国—东盟密切合作的背景下举办的。因此，论坛取得的成果显而易见。首先，论坛贯彻落实了党的十七届六中全会提出的“推动中华文化走向世界”的方针政策、为党的十七届六中全会召开献上了一份贺礼。其次，本届论坛最具特色的，在于它不仅仅是一个单纯以研讨为研讨的论坛，而是一个融入了交流、研讨、展示、考察、观演等多项内容的区域国际论坛。它在形式上既是“中国—东盟文化产业论坛”，又是“10+3人力资源开发与合作研讨班”；在内容上，既有论坛主旨报告和专题发言，又有“佛风梵韵——缅甸文化展”和“博物馆文化创意产品展”，还有实地考察活动；在礼遇上既有开幕仪式，又有欢迎晚宴和文艺表演。论坛的举办，配合了国家外交大局，整合了国内国外的文化资源，扩大了中国—东盟文化合作的效应。与会的东盟国家嘉宾看到了中国边疆的稳定及广西对外开放的文化风采和社会风貌。

六　中国—东盟太阳能政策对话与技术洽谈会

由中国科技部、东盟科学技术委员会共同主办，广西壮族自治区科学技术厅具体承办的中国—东盟太阳能政策对话与技术洽谈会于2011年10月21日在广西南宁举行。来自中国、柬埔寨、印度尼西亚、老挝、马来西亚、新加坡、泰国、越南等国的嘉宾围绕“太阳能政策对话”与“太阳能产业发展”主题，就中国与东盟成员国太阳能政策、太阳能技术与产品需求对接以及产业合作等方面的问题进行了深入交流与合作探讨。中国科技部国际合作司亚处处长徐捷、广西壮族自治区科学技术厅副厅长粟定成出席会议并致辞。

徐捷代表中国科技部在致辞时说，中国和许多东盟国家一样，面临共同的资源、能源和环境问题。大力发展新能源技术与产业，走绿色、低碳、环保、生态的可持续发展道路，是我们的共同选择。太阳能是一种清洁环保、取之不竭、用之不尽的能源。高效开发利用太阳能资源，是应对日益严峻的能源短缺、环境挑战的重要手段，受到各国政府的高度重视。绿色发展和可

2011 年 10 月 21 日，中国—东盟太阳能政策对话与技术洽谈会在广西南宁举行

China–ASEAN Solar Energy Cooperation Seminar held in Nanning, Guangxi on October 21, 2011

持续发展已成为当今世界发展的大势所趋。我们愿与东盟各国进一步拓展新能源领域的合作与交流，为促进区域内经济社会与环境的可持续发展作出更大的贡献。

粟定成在致辞中介绍了广西鼓励发展太阳能产业的相关政策。他指出广西是中国与东盟国家唯一海陆相连的省区，是中国与东盟双向开放、双向交流的桥梁和门户。希望通过此次太阳能政策对话与技术洽谈会，增进彼此了解，促进技术交流与合作，拓展和构建多种科技合作渠道和平台，营造有利于推进科技创新创业的服务环境、政策环境、社会环境和人文环境，实现互利共赢，共同发展。

科技部高新司能源处处长郑方能详细介绍了中国太阳能应用状况及相关政策，他指出，中国的太阳能产业近十年来发展迅猛，如何有效降低成本与提高能效成为当务之急。柬埔寨能源及非传统能源研究委员会的代表就“柬埔寨太阳能产业发展”作了主题演讲，让与会代表系统了解柬埔寨现有的产业状况；马来西亚国立大学代表作的“大型太阳能热水系统在马来西亚医院中的应用”讲演因其实用性而引发关注。新加坡国立大学代表以“太阳能在新加坡的发展”为题的讲演，因内容丰富生动引来现场代表的共鸣。中国和东盟各国太阳能方面的专家均发表演讲，就中国与东盟国家太阳能政策、太阳能产业发展现状及其适用技术开展交流与合作，并结合现有技术与产品对接各方需求，共同探讨太阳能产业趋势和对策。

与会的太阳能行业及关联行业的企业家围绕太阳能开发技术和产业合作开展专题研讨，热议中国—东盟太阳能合作，探寻和分享新能源技术发展所带来的新商机。

本届中国—东盟太阳能政策对话与技术洽谈会的成功举办，为中国和东盟国家搭建了信息交流的平台，加深了中国与东盟国家在太阳能政策和技术方面的交流，促进了太阳能技术与产品需求对接，共同推进中国与东盟国家太阳能领域双边和多边科技合作。

七　第二届中国—东盟物流合作论坛

2011年10月22日，第二届中国—东盟物流合作论坛在广西南宁举行。论坛由中国物流与采购联合会、中国—东盟商务理事会、广西壮族自治区人民政府主办，由广西物流与采购联合会、广西壮族自治区发展与改革委员会、广西投资促进局、广西物资集团有限责任公司共同承办。

广西壮族自治区政协副主席林国强致欢迎辞，中国—东盟商务理事会中方常务副秘书长许宁宁、中国物流与采购联合会副会长蔡进、北京交通大学物流研究院副院长王耀球、新加坡物流管理学院中国区教务主任杨喜春、广西物流与采购联合会会长张福利等出席本次论坛并发表演讲。

本届中国—东盟物流合作论坛以产业、物流、文化互动发展为主题，采用主题演讲、高峰对话、商务洽谈、项目推介、展览展示、参观考察等形式，为中国和东盟国家政府官员、工商领袖和专家学者提供了对话机会，为物流企业、金融机构、制造企业、流通企业搭建了合作平台。与会嘉宾围绕

2011年10月22日，第二届中国—东盟物流合作论坛在广西南宁举行

The 2nd China-ASEAN Logistics Cooperation Forum held in Nanning, Guangxi on October 22, 2011

中国—东盟自由贸易区内产业、物流与文化互动发展的主题进行深入探讨。

蔡进作了题为《中国物流发展格局与趋势》的演讲。他认为，社会的各个方面都需要物流，包括产业和文化等，物流体系的扩张和融合是今后十年一个重要的体现，所以必须加快物流一体化的建设。他表示，物流是服务于全社会的，无论是生产、生活甚至包括文化领域，都需要物流。物流在当前中国现阶段可能偏重于生产，随着经济生产方式和经济结构的变化，物流的发展也要转型。

张福利作了题为《中国—东盟物流一体化对产业、物流、文化互动发展的决定性影响》的主题演讲。他表示，物流一体化要求不断构筑整个中国—东盟自由贸易区的低成本、高效率、无障碍通关的实体物流网络和新的物流中心，因此要以区域经济一体化为突破口，加快经贸信息和文化交流，在产业、物流与文化互动基础上，促进中国和东盟各国经济快速发展。

许宁宁在发言中表示，互联互通是中国—东盟合作的着力点。目前，中国与东盟贸易进入了“零关税”时期，这为双方打造新的产业链提供了有利条件。而要打造具有更强生产力和竞争力的区域内产业链，则需要自贸区内各国尽快实施行业对接，通过优势互补，减少或消除东盟有些国家对中国产品冲击其产业的担忧。

会议期间举行了防城港投资项目推介会。防城港市委书记刘正东致欢迎辞，广西壮族自治区投资促进局领导作主题演讲，防城港市市长莫恭明介绍防城港市经济社会发展概况，防城港市副市长范宇新解读防城港市物流招商投资政策，防城港市副市长陈可猛作防城港物流及相关项目推介。

本届中国—东盟物流合作论坛的成功举办，对中国—东盟自由贸易区的发展起到积极推动作用，同时也将对广西物流发展以及物流周边产业发展产生推动作用。

八　中国—东盟药品安全论坛暨药品监督管理局局长会议

2011年10月21日，由中国国家食品药品监督管理局和广西壮族自治区人民政府主办的中国—东盟药品安全论坛暨药品监督管理局局长会议在南宁举行。中国国家食品药品监督管理局局长邵明立、广西壮族自治区副主席李康出席论坛并讲话，东盟各国药品监督管理局局长发表主旨演讲。中国国家食品药品监督管理局、中国各省（区、市）食品药品监督管理局领导及企业界约200人出席论坛。

此次论坛的主题是：加强交流，保障安全，共谋发展——中国—东盟自贸区发展形势下的药品安全合作。议题是：交流各国药品法律体系和药品监管体制、体系及监管机制等情况；建立中国和东盟药品监管机构之间的经常性联系，研究中国—东盟药品安全合作机制等相关问题（中国和东盟各国药用资源、产业发展、中药和传统药学基本情况及发展思路；中国和东盟药品进出口贸易合作发展态势研判及面临的安全课题）；商定高峰论坛组织方式

2011年10月21日，中国—东盟药品安全论坛暨药品监督管理局局长会议在广西南宁举行

China-ASEAN Forum on Drug Safety & China-ASEAN Meeting for Heads of Drug Regulatory Agencies held in Nanning, Guangxi on October 21, 2011

以及下一次高峰论坛的主题及相关活动内容。

论坛的主要目标是：建立中国—东盟药品安全合作平台，定期开展高层对话与磋商，建立全面的药品安全机制；利用中国—东盟自由贸易区已形成的优越环境，发挥中国—东盟博览会的平台作用，以中国—东盟药品安全论坛成果展为依托，提供更好的行政管理服务，营造更加优惠便利的营商环境；加强中国—东盟药品安全合作与交流，共同发展，促进中国—东盟药品经贸健康持续发展。

会上，邵明立作了题为《中国药品监管现状及展望》的主旨演讲，介绍了中国药品监管概况，以及未来中国药品监管的主要任务和措施。他指出，中国通过药品市场准入制度、药品质量管理规范认证制度、药品分类管理制度、特殊药品监管制度、国家基本药物制度等药品监管制度，加强药品研制、生产、流通各环节的监管，对药品实施严格的全过程质量控制。未来5年，中国药品监管部门将力争实现化学药品、生物制品标准与国际标准接轨，中药标准能引领国际标准的制定，医疗器械的国际标准采标率和转化率有明显提高。同时，进一步加强与世界各国以及相关组织机构的交流合作，推动与东盟各国的药品安全合作，坚定不移地推进医药市场的对外开放，深入推进与东盟各国药品监管领域的交流。

李康在致辞中说，广西政府一直高度重视药品安全监管和药品安全国际合作。近5年来，不断加大药品安全基础设施建设投入，建立了以自治区食品药品监管局为核心，覆盖全自治区各市、县的行政执法机构、药品不良反应监测、药物滥用监测系统，对特殊药品、疫苗、血液制品、中药注射剂及第二类精神药品实行电子监管。建立了中华人民共和国广西口岸药品检验所，药品安全风险预警能力得到很大提升，药品安全监管的部门协作机制不断完善。集中力量开展了药品和医疗器械专项整治，严厉打击药品违法犯罪行为。加强对药品进出口和边境贸易的监管，严肃查处药品和中药材跨国违法案件。2011年6月，国家食品药品监督管理局与广西壮族自治区人民政府在南宁签署了共建食品药品安全合作示范区备忘录，将加强中国—东盟药品安全合作作为重点内容，把广西推向了前沿，迎来了新的机遇。她表示，通过举办中国—东盟药品安全论坛，不断扩大与深化中国与东盟在药品安全领域的合作，共同推进药品安全以及其他各个方面的发展。

本届论坛由广西壮族自治区食品药品监督管理局、中国医药国际交流中心、中国—东盟博览会秘书处承办。

九　2011中国—东盟出版博览会

2011年10月22—24日，主题为“书香传友谊、和谐共发展”的2011中国—东盟出版博览会在广西民族博物馆举办。2011中国—东盟出版博览会由中国国家新闻出版总署和广西壮族自治区人民政府共同主办、广西新闻出版局和广西国际博览事务局承办、广西出版传媒集团和广西新华书店集团协办，是中国—东盟建立对话关系20周年、中国—东盟友好交流年和中国—东盟自由贸易区建成1周年重要系列纪念活动之一。这是中国首次举办中国—东盟出版博览会，为中国—东盟博览会注入了新的文化元素。

2011中国—东盟出版博览会组委会主任、中国国家新闻出版总署副署长邬书林，2011中国—东盟出版博览会组委会主任、广西壮族自治区党委常委、宣传部部长沈北海，2011中国—东盟出版博览会组委会主任、自治区副主席李康，全国政协委员、中国出版集团公司原总裁聂震宁，缅甸联邦共和国信息部副部长苏温等中国和东盟出版文化主管部门的领导和嘉宾出席博览会开幕式。邬书林、沈北海和苏温分别致辞。

邬书林在致辞时说，中国与东盟10国山水相连、唇齿相依，文化交流的历史源远流长。2008年以来，由中华人民共和国新闻出版总署主办，广西壮族自治区新闻出版局承办的中国图书展销暨版权贸易交易会已在越南、柬埔寨、印尼三国举办了三届，成为中国与东盟国家出版界开展交流合作的重要途径，逐步成为中国文化“走出去”、中国出版对外交流与合作的重要国家品牌。2011年是中国—东盟建立对话关系20周年，也是中国—东盟友好交流年和中国—东盟自由贸易区建成1周年。利用中国—东盟博览会这个大平台举办这次2011中国—东盟出版博览会，为中国与东盟各国出版文化界的交流与合作搭建了一个新的平台，为中国与东盟各国的经贸和各领域合作打好了文化基础，并将进一步加深中国与东盟各国人民的深厚友谊。

沈北海在致辞中说，2011中国—东盟出版博览会将为影响越来越广的

2011年10月22—24日，2011中国—东盟出版博览会在广西南宁举行

2011 China-ASEAN Publishing Expo held in Nanning, Guangxi on October 22-24, 2011

中国—东盟博览会增加丰富的文化内容，为中国与东盟出版界的交流与合作搭建重要平台，为中国—东盟自由贸易区的建设增添新的发展活力，必将对促进中国与东盟的出版交流与合作、推动构建互利互惠的经济文化合作新格局、增进中国与东盟国家的睦邻友好关系产生积极的推动作用。他相信，在东盟各国和国内出版界的大力支持下，大家携起手来，团结奋进，一定能把中国—东盟出版博览会办成为中国与东盟国家文化交流与合作的重要平台、版权贸易和出版物出口的重要渠道、各国读者交流的盛会，不断推动互利共赢合作深入发展，共同谱写中国—东盟出版交流合作的新篇章。

苏温表示，举办博览会将有助于东盟和中国互相学习、了解对方的人文历史、文化传统、风俗习惯、自然环境，促进东盟成员国与中国之间的友好关系，促进双方的理解、合作和共同发展。

本次出版博览会成果丰硕，展出1万多种中国和东盟国家的精品图书；举行中国—东盟出版合作签约仪式、中国—东盟出版论坛、数字出版论坛、中国—东盟出版合作成果展、《新越汉词典》首发式、媒体见面会、著名作家专题讲座及签名售书、中国—东盟青少年读书节等系列活动；中国和东盟出版界共达成版权贸易、合作出版、战略合作协议12项。其中最重要的成果是中方领导与东盟各国出版文化代表团团长及出版发行协会代表举行高层会晤，达成中国—东盟出版界合作《南宁共识》。其主要内容是：各方要利用中国—东盟出版博览会平台加强出版交流，推动在版权贸易、出版物进出口、读者阅读交流等方面的合作，鼓励用本国语言介绍、翻译、出版各方优秀文学作品，并积极鼓励和组织本国出版机构参加每年在中国和东盟国家举办的国际书展，建立出版交流与合作的长效机制。

来自缅甸信息部、柬埔寨文化艺术部、越南通信传媒部、泰国文化部、马来西亚国家图书理事会、亚太出版商协会、印尼出版商协会、新加坡华文出版协会、老挝驻南宁总领事馆、文莱—中国友好协会等东盟10国的36名出版文化界官员和代表，以及国内有实力和影响力的11家中央和地方出版发行集团、5家著名数字出版企业的代表和其他有关出版发行文化机构的代表500多人参加了博览会。

本届中国—东盟出版博览会充分展示了中国和东盟的历史文化和人文魅力，有力地促进传统与现代融合、内容与技术共生的数字出版等新兴业态的交流，实现了中国与东盟10国出版交流的历史性突破：中国和东盟10国的精品图书首次在中国同台集中展示展销，中国—东盟出版全面合作交流机制首次落户广西。本次出版博览会成为中国与东盟出版交流合作的主要平台和成果展示盛会、版权贸易和图书进出口的重要渠道、读者交流的乐园，为中国—东盟自由贸易区的繁荣发展提供了文化支持，得到国家新闻出版总署领导和广西壮族自治区领导的充分肯定和高度评价。

十　第一届中国—东盟TBT合作部长会议

2011年10月22日，由中国国家质检总局与东盟秘书处共同主办、广西出入境检验检疫局和中国—东盟博览会秘书处承办的第一届中国—东盟TBT合作部长会议在广西南宁召开，来自东盟成员国TBT工作主管部门部级领导和高官，中国国家发改委、科技部、工信部、商务部、国家质检总局、国家食药局、国家认监委、国家标准委8个部门的代表和国内质监机构负责人共80余人参加了会议。

TBT是标准、技术法规和合格评定的英文简称。此次会议是中国—东盟在TBT合作领域的首次部长级会议，主题是“产品质量与安全”。会议由中国国家质检总局局长支树平和马来西亚科技创新部部长翁凯里担任会议联合主席，共同主持会议。支树平、东盟秘书长素林、广西壮族自治区政协主席马铁山分别在会议开幕致辞。中国国家质检总局副局长、国家认监委主任孙大伟代表中方介绍了中国TBT管理的基本情况。

2011年10月22日，第一届中国—东盟TBT合作部长会议在广西南宁举行

The 1st ASEAN-China Ministerial Meeting on TBT Cooperation held in Nanning, Guangxi on October 22, 2011

支树平在致辞中指出，此次会议的召开，标志着中国和东盟在TBT和SPS两个领域部长级会议机制的正式建立，标志着2004年中国—东盟领导人所达成的关于加强检验检疫合作的共识即将从法律制度层面和部长级高层对话机制层面得到有效落实，也标志着中国与东盟在质检领域的合作将全面步入制度化和规范化轨道，对双方加强在产品质量与安全领域的合作，对全面开启中国—东盟在标准、技术法规、检验监管、认证认可等合格评定领域的合作具有重要的里程碑意义。支树平表示，中国愿与东盟各成员国一道，在7个方面加强合作：一是加强高层对话与互访，推进双方合作；二是加强信息与经验共享，促进共同提高；三是加强措施协调认可，便利双边贸易与投资；四是开展联合研究，促进关键问题解决；五是加强在国际规则和标准制定和修订方面的协调，维护共同利益；六是加强能力建设，缩小相互差距；七是加强管理，提高进出口产品质量安全水平。

素林对支树平的建议表示赞同。他说，希望双方以正式建立TBT领域的部长级会议机制为契机，共同努力解决保证产品质量安全方面所面临的问题，促进本地区产品质量与安全水平的提高，为完善中国—东盟自贸区建设、促进中国—东盟经贸往来、积极服务中国—东盟区域经济发展作出新的更大的贡献。

马铁山代表广西壮族自治区党委、政府对此次会议的召开表示热烈的祝贺。他说，随着中国、东盟经济社会的发展，消费者对产品质量和安全的关注程度不断提高，对产品质量与安全实行严格管理所需要的技术法规和标准也得到进一步加强和完善。中国与东盟各成员国有必要就各自的技术法规、标准与合格评定程序进行交流与合作，推动中国—东盟自由贸易区的健康发展，提升中国—东盟战略伙伴关系，实现互利共赢。

与会代表围绕“产品质量与安全”这一主题，进行广泛交流讨论，并审议通过了《中国—东盟关于加强产品质量安全合作的联合声明》（南宁联合声明）。《南宁联合声明》提出了双方在加强产品质量安全管理、技术法规、标准、合格评定程序领域的合作重点，同意采取联合行动，加强在产品质量安全领域的合作，共同提高产品质量安全水平，妥善处理不合格产品，保护消费者安全与健康，确保本地区贸易的健康发展。双方还将在相关国际规则和标准制定和修订中加强合作，维护本地区利益。会议决定，下次会议于2013年在东盟成员国举行，并通过了会议《联合新闻声明》。

此次会议审议批准了《TBT备忘录执行计划2012—2013》，标志着中国—东盟TBT合作部长级磋商合作机制正式建立，对全面开启中国—东盟在标准、技术法规、检验监管、认证认可等合格评定领域的合作具有重要的里程碑意义。

十一　中国—东盟城市森林论坛

2011年10月22—23日，由国家林业局、广西壮族自治区人民政府主办，南宁市人民政府、广西壮族自治区林业厅承办的中国—东盟城市森林论坛在广西南宁举行。国家林业局党组成员、中央纪委派驻国家林业局纪检组长陈述贤，缅甸联邦共和国环境保护及林业部部长温吞，广西壮族自治区党委常委、自治区副主席、南宁市委书记陈武，广西壮族自治区副主席陈章良，南宁市市长周红波等南宁市领导以及等东盟各国的代表出席论坛。陈章良在开幕式上致辞。

论坛以“中国—东盟共同推动森林城市、低碳城市、宜居城市建设”为主题，来自中国、柬埔寨、老挝、缅甸、菲律宾、泰国、越南等国家的林业官员代表在论坛上就加快推进中国—东盟自由贸易区和广西北部湾经济区的建设，进一步发展中国与东盟的睦邻友好关系，加强林业应对气候变化的合作等方面的问题进行了探讨。

陈述贤在论坛上宣读了《全国绿化委员会、国家林业局关于授予广西壮族自治区南宁市“国家森林城市”称号的决定》，《决定》认为，城市森林是现代林业建设的重要领域，是城市生态建设的主体。建设城市森林，已经成为落实科学发展观和建设生态文明的生动实践，成为打造低碳城市和扩展

2011年10月22—23日，中国—东盟城市森林论坛在广西南宁举行
China-ASEAN Urban Forest Forum held in Nanning, Guangxi on October 22-23, 2011

生态环境容量的重要途径，成为增进人民福祉和提高生活品质的重要内容，对于全面推进我国城市经济社会可持续发展具有不可替代的作用。长期以来，广西南宁市坚持把加快城乡绿化、发展城市森林摆在十分重要的位置，深入探索城市森林建设的特点规律，加强组织领导、科学规划发展、广泛宣传动员、积极部署推动，初步建成了以森林植被为主体、城乡一体、健康稳定的森林生态系统，城市生态环境面貌发生了显著变化，走出了符合当地经济社会发展实际、满足人民群众生态需求的城市森林建设之路，具有较强的区域代表性和示范带动作用。为在全国不同生态区域树立城市森林建设的典型，进一步推广城市森林建设的先进理念，全国绿化委员会、国家林业局决定授予南宁市“国家森林城市”称号。希望南宁市在新的起点上，认真总结经验，坚持科学做法，不断推动城市森林建设与时俱进，创新发展，为建设生态良好国家、推动生态文明建设作出更大的贡献。

中国—东盟城市森林论坛通过了《中国—东盟城市森林论坛南宁宣言》。该宣言认为，城市森林是城市文明发达的重要标志。人类文明发祥于森林，在人类发展的各个历史阶段，森林都发挥了不可替代的作用，森林繁盛则文明兴旺，森林枯竭则文明衰败。当前，在人类由工业文明向生态文明转型的重要历史时刻，必须把加强城市森林建设作为推进城市文明进程的基础性工作，城市森林是城市可持续发展的重要基础。发展城市森林是提高城市生态承载力的有效途径，是实现城市经济社会可持续发展的基础保障。没有绿色的城市就是没有生机的城市，也是没有希望、没有未来的城市。必须把加强城市森林建设，作为城市全面发展的重要内容，通过城市森林的可持续发展，推动城市经济社会的可持续发展。

十二　中国—东盟旅游促进减贫研讨会

由中华全国工商业联合会、大湄公河次区域（GMS）工商论坛联合主办，广西壮族自治区工商业联合会承办的中国—东盟旅游促进减贫研讨会于2011年11月1—3日在广西南宁举行。GMS工商论坛轮值主席、中华全国工商联常务副主席孙安民，广西壮族自治区政府副主席杨道喜，GMS工商论坛秘书长、亚太经合组织工商理事会副主席、东盟旅游协会副主席、老挝国家商会副主席欧迪特·苏旺那旺等出席开幕式并致辞。来自中国、越南、老挝、缅甸、柬埔寨、泰国、新加坡、文莱、马来西亚、印尼等国的政府旅游和扶贫部门、商会、旅游企业的代表和专家学者等近110人参加了研讨会。

中华全国工商联副秘书长、经济部部长欧阳晓明，广西壮族自治区工商业联合会主席磨长英分别主持研讨会开幕式、专题研讨会和旅游促进减贫圆桌研讨会。来自各国的19位代表在大会上作了发言。本次研讨会以“旅游让生活更美好”为主题，就区域内民间资本如何进入旅游业、旅游业如何促进

2011年11月1—3日，中国—东盟旅游促进减贫研讨会在广西南宁举行

The China-ASEAN Tourism for Promoting Poverty Reduction Seminar held in Nanning, Guangxi, on November 1-3, 2011

减贫、如何发挥商会组织推进旅游减贫中的作用等相关问题进行深入探讨，并对中国—东盟自贸区内的政府部门、民间机构、企业相互衔接的问题提出了具体意见和建议。

本次会议呈现出三大特点：

一是参与研讨人员范围广、代表性强。参加本次会议的代表既有中国和东盟国家政府主管旅游和扶贫部门的官员，又有民间机构组织和商会的负责人；既有旅游业和扶贫工作投资、发展、规划的专家学者，又有在业界有影响力的企业精英和准备做相关投资的企业代表。此外，还特别邀请了大湄公河次区域五国驻南宁总领馆总领事出席研讨会。

二是主题鲜明、活动丰富。会前，孙安民会见了部分国外嘉宾；开幕式上，孙安民、杨道喜、欧迪特·苏旺那旺分别致辞；在主题演讲环节，各国专家学者、政府官员分别阐述旅游促进减贫对中国—东盟自由贸易区人民生活的影响，对自贸区经济发展的影响等的意见和建议；在圆桌研讨会上，商会及企业交流分享旅游业对当地经济社会的促进作用的经验，探讨投资旅游项目和联合开发的现状，分析存在问题，提出解决办法；在实地考察环节，国外嘉宾考察了南宁花花大世界园林产业示范园，国内企业赴崇左市、百色市开展“旅游投资减贫老区行”活动。

三是成果显著。各国专家学者以前瞻性的眼光分析旅游事业在减贫中的作用；政府相关部门的领导除介绍本国在此项工作的基本情况外，还分别介绍了本国政府此项工作努力的方向；旅游投资企业以自己亲历的体会与与会者分享在此项工作中取得的成绩及成功经验，同时也指出了影响此项工作开展的一些问题。与会者认为，会议要实现的目的就是政府要支持企业发展，企业再推动当地的发展，为生活在这些待开发的地区的人们，保护他们的生活环境，推动可持续的旅游发展。

研讨会准备充分，组织周密，取得了良好的效果：

一是以沟通交流为纽带，提高推动旅游促进减贫工作的认识。本次会议为中国—东盟国家的专家学者、政府官员、民营机构组织、企业四方共同参与、共同探讨关于旅游促进减贫工作的认识和意见创造了一个良好的机会，为今后建立一个广泛参与、多方协作的以旅游业发展为架构的联合推动减贫减困工作的组织打下了良好的基础。

二是思想开放，观点鲜明，集思广益。与会代表形成了如下共识：旅游业是中国和东盟合作及消除贫困的重要途径之一，旅游可以增进就业机会，推动减贫；旅游业是提高贫困地区人口素质的重要途径之一，通过旅游为媒介，带动发达地区与欠发达地区人们的广泛接触与交流，有利于快速提升贫困地区的人口综合素质；发展旅游业可以带动基础建设、食品业、手工业、农产品加工业、乡村旅游业等相关产业的发展，有利于加速推动贫穷地区的经济发展；推动旅游促进减贫工作必须加强公私部门的合作，特别是要推动中国与大湄公河次区域，以及中国与整个东盟国家在这方面的合作；旅游促进减贫工作要加强人才培训，提高中小型企业的经营管理能力，更好地使用社会媒体进行宣传和引导；推动旅游促进减贫工作要充分发挥商会组织的桥梁和纽带作用，提供良好的平台来吸引更多的私营企业共同发展贫困地区的旅游产业。

三是在推动GMS国家旅游促进减贫工作中充分发挥大湄公河次区域工商论坛的作用。《大湄公河次区域的发展规划2011—2015年纲要》中提出要加快推动减贫的旅游业发展，关注点是要发展大湄公河次区域，发展大湄公河次区域旅游走廊，这个战略也同时写进了2011—2015年东盟旅游发展战略规划中。本次会议的主办方之一GMS工商论坛以此次会议为契机，进一步推动GMS国家经济社会的发展，GMS商会组织要加强协作，其中包括建立大学教育机构，以进一步加强人才的培养，从而提升旅游业方面的发展水平。

十三　亚洲及大洋洲地区大众体育合作发展论坛暨中国—东盟大众体育合作发展论坛

由中国国家体育总局、广西壮族自治区人民政府、亚洲及大洋洲地区大众体育协会（简称“亚太群体协会”）主办，国家体育总局群体司、广西壮族自治区体育局、广西民族大学承办的亚洲及大洋洲地区大众体育合作发展论坛暨中国—东盟大众体育合作发展论坛于2011年11月21—23日在广西南宁召开。

2011年11月21—23日，亚洲及大洋洲地区大众体育合作发展论坛暨中国—东盟大众体育合作发展论坛在广西南宁召开

Asia and Oceania Sport for All Cooperation and Development Forum & China-ASEAN Sport for All Cooperation and Development Forum held in Nanning, Guangxi, on November 21-23, 2011

中国国家体育总局副局长、亚洲及大洋洲地区大众体育协会主席冯建中，广西壮族自治区副主席李康出席会议并致辞。来自亚洲及大洋洲地区大众体育协会、东盟10国、港澳台地区及国内的体育官员和专家学者共300多人出席了论坛，就亚太地区大众体育合作发展进行广泛交流、深入研讨。

中国国家体育总局群体司副司长、亚洲及大洋洲地区大众体育协会执委兼司库刘国永、广西壮族自治区体育局长容小宁以及部分国内外官员和专家，围绕“大众体育、健康和谐、合作发展”的主题，作了27个关于大众体育的高端专题演讲。论坛还收到数十篇学术论文，代表了亚太地区国家大众体育理论研究和实践操作的最高水平。这些专家学者和政府部门官员以自身的资源、掌握的信息，全方位、多角度展示对大众体育发展的高见，分享推进大众体育可持续发展的成功案例和经验，具有很强的针对性、思想性和权威性。

本次论坛内容丰富，特色鲜明，以国际化的视角设置了具有前瞻性和指导性的重大议题，重点解读亚太地区、中国及东盟国家大众体育发展面临的机遇和挑战，探讨大众体育交流合作对推动区域经济社会发展的影响，分析和展望中国与亚太地区国家大众体育发展的趋势。论坛注重虚实结合，既有务虚的研讨又有务实的交流合作，以虚促实，注重实效，通过主题演讲、议题发言、大会交流、板报展示等活动形式，把国内外各层面、各层次大众体育发展的做法、经验、模式和理念进行有效的推介宣传、互动交流，让参会者扩展视野、有所借鉴。同时，论坛形成的专用标识、论文文献等会务成果，为打造国际论坛品牌创造了良好条件。

本次论坛的成功举办，打造了本地区大众体育信息交流、产品展示和项目合作的新平台，通过论坛开展战略性对话，探讨中国与亚太地区国家体育发展，推进了国际区域性体育交流合作，改善了中国与亚太地区国家之间的关系，特别是提升我国体育在东盟地区的影响，树立体育强国的新形象，服务中国—东盟友好合作打牢友谊之基。同时，也将有力推动包括体育在内的我国社会主义文化的繁荣发展，特别是对于广西重振体育雄风、建设西部体育强区、加快推进体育产业城建设产生积极影响。

本次论坛得到中央和广西主流新闻媒体积极关注，《人民日报》、新华社、《广西日报》及香港《大公报》等20多家媒体通过网络报道、专题专栏、新闻评论、系列报道等形式，多角度、全方位报道了论坛的盛况及取得的成效。国内外嘉宾云集和境内外媒体对论坛成功举办的大力报道，进一步提升了我国大众体育在国际上的影响力，也大大提高了广西的知名度和美誉度。

十四　2011中国—东盟传统医药高峰论坛暨传统医药展

2011年12月8—9日，中国国家中医药管理局、国家民族事务委员会、广西壮族自治区人民政府共同主办的2011中国—东盟传统医药高峰论坛暨传统医药展在广西南宁举行。

2011年12月7日下午，广西壮族自治区主席马飚，自治区副主席高雄、李康在南宁荔园山庄会见了前来出席2011中国—东盟传统医药高峰论坛的中国卫生部副部长、国家中医药管理局局长王国强，国家民族事务委员会副主任丹珠昂奔，中国工程院院士、自治区主席顾问姚新生等有关部门领导、专家，并就推进中国—东盟传统医药交流合作、加快广西中医药民族医药发展进行了交谈。

12月8日，2011中国—东盟传统医药高峰论坛隆重开幕。王国强、丹珠昂奔、李康与东盟秘书处副秘书长米斯然·卡梅，柬埔寨卫生部国务秘书欧库·摩那出席开幕式并致辞。中国国家中医药管理局副局长于文明主持开幕式，世界卫生组织发来贺电。中国国家中医药管理局人事教育司负责人、东盟秘书处健康与传染病部代表以及姚新生院士分别作了论坛专题报告。中国、东盟秘书处和东盟国家、俄罗斯、澳大利亚、新西兰、香港、澳门、台湾等国家和地区的官员、专家学者、行业和企业代表500多人出席论坛。

论坛的主题是“传统医药创新发展”，涉及中国—东盟传统医药交流合作机制、传统医药教育与科技合作、传统医药理论传承与创新、传统医药外治法、药用资源可持续利用和传统医药产业发展等多项专题内容。论坛既有以演讲、主题报告形式开展理论研讨，也有以战略互动政府间官员对话等多种形式进行多边交流，堪称传统医药界的一次盛会。论坛确定了中国与东盟在传统医药方面遵循“求同存异、优势互补、循序渐进、互利共赢”的原则，通过了《南宁宣言》，并确定每两年举办一届中国—东盟传统医药高峰论坛。

2011 年 12 月 8—9 日，2011 中国—东盟传统医药高峰论坛暨传统医药展在广西南宁举行

2011 China-ASEAN Summit Forum on Traditional Medicine & Exhibition held in Nanning, Guangxi, on December 8 9, 2011

12月9日上午，中国—东盟传统医药展在广西药用植物园举行隆重剪彩仪式。中国—东盟传统医药展以图文展示、实物展示、现场演示、现场体验、信息发布、洽谈咨询等方式，多方位、多层次交流各国传统医药在医疗、保健、教育、科技、文化、产业等领域的优秀成果，让参观者认识到各国源远流长的传统医药发展历史，感知各国保护、扶持、发展传统医药事业的政策方略，现场亲身体验传统医药医疗保健和健康养生服务，留下深刻印象。

本届论坛具有以下特点：

1. 论坛规格高、规模大、代表性广。来自中国、东盟以及俄罗斯、澳大利亚等18个国家、地区和组织的约500位嘉宾参加了论坛，与会代表具有广泛代表性。

2. 政府主导、兼顾学术。论坛是由政府主导的官方会议，体现了在建设中国—东盟自由贸易区大背景下，中国与东盟各国进行深入合作的意愿。论坛除了有官方战略性商讨，同时还兼顾学术，为构建双方传统医药合作长效机制发挥了积极作用。

3. 内容丰富、形式多样、信息量广。论坛除开幕式外，有以“传统医药创新发展”为主题的大会专题报告，还分设了政府论坛和5个专题进行研讨，给与会者留下深刻印象。

4. 新闻宣传及时到位，营造良好舆论氛围。设立了中国—东盟传统医药高峰论坛网站，链接主办、承办单位网站，共有30多家中央、地方媒体和网站报道论坛信息，扩大了论坛的社会影响。

本次论坛以中国—东盟博览会为平台，把传统医药纳入中国与东盟经济、社会合作的重点领域，拓展了中国—东盟交流合作空间，全面提升了中国与东盟各国传统医药的交流合作水平，促进了彼此间经济社会的发展，取得了可喜的成果：

1. 交流了经验、增进相互间的了解。论坛研讨的主题集中，领域宽广、形式多样，内容丰富精彩。大家分享了信息，交流了经验，启发了思维，增进了了解。大大拓展了中国与东盟国家的交流对话，为推动务实合作打下了良好基础。

2. 提供了直观有效的信息资源交流平台。中国—东盟传统医药展让与会领导和代表能够比较全面地了解中国和东盟各国传统医药的基本概况和优秀成果，为进一步深化交流合作提供更直接、更有效的信息资源平台。

3. 见证了“世界最大药用植物园”。在中国—东盟传统医药展剪彩仪式上，出席论坛的领导和嘉宾共同见证了“世界最大药用植物园”吉尼斯世界纪录的诞生。

4. 考察了社区，体会到中国深化医改的初步成果。中国—东盟国家以及香港、澳门、台湾地区的嘉宾参观了社区卫生服务中心，对富有中国特色的传统医疗服务和医改取得的成果表示认同，部分嘉宾表示把要这种服务模式带回去推广。

5. 推进了广西壮族自治区人民政府一揽子出台了四个重要文件，为今后一段时期全区的中医药民族医药工作发展规划了宏伟蓝图。在论坛的筹备工作期间，高层领导多次会晤，共商广西加快发展中医药民族医药大计。论坛前夕，广西壮族自治区人民政府出台了《关于加快中医药民族医药发展的决定》、《广西壮族自治区壮瑶医药振兴计划（2011—2020年）》、《广西壮族自治区中医药民族医药发展十大重点工程实施方案（2011—2015年）》等重要文件。这些文件对加快广西中医药民族医药的发展，尤其是对促进中国广西与东盟传统医药的交流与合作具有重要的意义。

小结　论坛越办越实　社会人文交流成为新亮点

在第八届中国—东盟博览会框架下，会期举办了14个高层次会议论坛和交流活动。这些会议论坛和交流活动与往届相比，在内容和形式上进一步创新，更加贴近中国—东盟自贸区发展的需要，更加务实，解决了各领域合作的热点问题，形成了更多的合作机制，为中国与东盟经贸和人文等多领域合作提供更好的机制保障，促进双方友好关系全面持久稳定发展。

近年来，中国—东盟经贸合作快速发展，双方对海关、检验检疫、金融、港口、物流、信息、通讯等相关领域的服务配套提出了新的需求。例如，双方货物贸易快速增长，需要双方海关和质检加强合作，提高便利化水平。双方相互投资规模扩大，需要双方加强金融合作，给企业投资提供更好的支撑。双方贸易和投资的增长，都需要双方在交通、物流、通讯等多领域加强合作，完善基础设施支撑。同时，经贸合作与文化、教育、体育等人文领域交流相结合，才能形成经济社会发展的持续推动力。第八届中国—东盟博览会顺应这一形势需要，以中国—东盟建立对话关系20周年为契机，精心组织了14个会议论坛和交流活动。各场活动的主题鲜明，内容丰富务实，形成了许多亮点。

一是主题鲜明。第八届中国—东盟博览会以“环保合作”为主题，主题论坛为中国—东盟环保合作论坛。环保是中国与东盟最新确定的第十一大重点合作领域，双方合作潜力大，有利于推进节能减排和经济发展方式转变。从环保论坛举办的实际效果看，论坛达成了加强绿色技术创新与产业合作等多项共识，启动了中国—东盟绿色使者计划，初步建立了中国—东盟环保产业合作网络，为中国—东盟环保合作机构在中国的建立奠定了基础，达到了预期目标。

二是内容丰富，成果务实。第八届中国—东盟博览会的14场会议论坛和交流活动涉及环保、金融、人口与发展、智库、文化产业、太阳能、物流、药品安全、出版、质检TBT合作、城市森林、旅游促进减贫、体育、传统医药等十多个领域，内容十分具体，议题紧扣这些领域合作的重点、热点和难点，紧扣中国—东盟自贸区建设和发展进程，具有很强的现实意义，务实地推动了全方位合作。

例如，中国—东盟金融合作与发展领袖论坛已经是第三次举办，在前两届基础上，进一步议题集中到“区域内货币结算、区域经济发展的金融调控、金融财政合作与发展”等问题，特别是论坛期间举办了金融机构支持企业“走出去”交流洽谈会、企业股权（债券）投融资交易会、投融资项目对接会组织等一系列务实的交流活动，使企业与金融机构得到有效衔接，强化金融对区域经济发展的服务作用。金融论坛已经成为博览会系列会议论坛中的一个响亮品牌。

首届中国—东盟TBT合作部长会议是自2007年在中国—东盟博览会形成质检部长级会议机制以来，双方质检部长对话更加具体、更加务实的体现，标志着中国和东盟在TBT和SPS两个领域部长级会议机制的正式建立，对全面开启双方在标准、技术法规、检验监管、认证认可等合格评定领域的合作具有重要的里程碑意义。

各场会议论坛和交流活动取得了丰硕成果。其中，环保论坛启动了中国—东盟绿色使者计划。金融论坛形成中国—东盟金融合作发展机制研究成果。TBT合作部长会议通过了关于加强中国—东盟产品质量安全合作的《南宁联合声明》。城市森林论坛通过了《南宁宣言》，这些成果标志着中国—东盟多领域合作的机制化进一步健全，为双方友好合作的全面持续稳定发展作出了贡献。

三是社会人文交流成为新亮点。社会人文交流对于增进中国与东盟人民之间的相互了解和友谊，促进双方全面持久稳定的友好关系，具有独特作用，社会人文交流与政治互信、经贸合作一道，构成中国—东盟友好合作关系的重要内容。

第八届中国—东盟博览会成功举办了中国—东盟人口与发展论坛、中国—东盟文化产业论坛、中国—东盟药品安全论坛、中国—东盟出版博览会、亚洲及大洋洲地区大众体育合作发展论坛暨中国—东盟大众体育合作发展论坛、中国—东盟传统医药高峰论坛暨传统医药展等6个社会人文领域的会议、论坛和交流活动，取得丰硕成果，成为新的亮点。其中，人口与发展论坛形成了关注人口与家庭发展的共识，加强了人口与家庭发展领域的交流合作。文化产业论坛搭建了中国与东盟文化产业交流合作的重要平台。药品安全论坛对中国—东盟自由贸易区发展形势下的药品安全合作发展等领域进行了深入研讨。出版博览会展出1万多种中国和东盟国家的精品图书，达成中国—东盟出版界合作《南宁共识》。大众体育合作发展论坛打造了本地区大众体育信息交流、产品展示和项目合作的新平台。传统医药高峰论坛交流了各国传统医药在医疗、保健、教育、科技、文化、产业等领域的优秀成果，通过了《南宁共识》。

本届博览会在社会人文交流方面取得的成果，为中国—东盟友好合作注入了更加丰富的内容，展示了中国—东盟友好合作的美好前景。

第六章

6 纪念对话关系20周年 永做互利共赢好伙伴

——中国—东盟建立对话关系20周年系列纪念活动

中国同东盟国家山水相连，双方人民的友好交往源远流长。

1991年，中国与东盟建立对话伙伴关系；2003年，双方建立战略伙伴关系；2010年，中国—东盟自贸区全面建成；2011年，是中国—东盟建立对话关系20周年、中国—东盟友好交流年、中国—东盟自由贸易区建成1周年。

中国—东盟建立对话关系20年来，双方相互尊重，平等相待，睦邻友好合作全方位发展，给中国和东盟国家的人民带来巨大福利，实现了互利共赢，促进了双方各自经济社会发展，也为本地区的和平稳定与繁荣发展作出了重要贡献。

为纪念中国—东盟建立对话关系20周年，双方举行一系列丰富多彩的纪念活动。其中，第八届中国—东盟博览会被列为纪念活动的重要组成部分。博览会的举办地广西在国家有关部委的指导下，还参与主办或承办了多项纪念活动。包括：中国—东盟建立对话关系20周年纪念招待会文艺演出、中国—东盟互联互通战略研讨会、中国—东盟友谊知识竞赛、2011年东盟经贸记者研修班、2011中国—东盟国际汽车拉力赛暨中国—东盟媒体汽车拉力赛、纪念中国—东盟建立对话关系20周年“广西农垦杯”外语演讲比赛等。

中国—东盟建立对话关系20周年系列纪念活动得到了中国和东盟各国政府的高度重视，企业和社会各界积极参与，内容丰富，精彩纷呈，成果丰硕，影响深远，谱写了中国—东盟友好关系的新篇章。

To Celebrate the 20th Anniversary of ASEAN–China Dialogue Relations for Long–term Reciprocal and Win–win Collaboration

—Commemorative Programs to Celebrate the 20th Anniversary of ASEAN–China Dialogue Relations

China and the 10 ASEAN member countries are close neighbors linked by water and mountains. The two peoples enjoy time–honored friendship which can be traced back to ancient times.

In 1991, both sides established dialogue relations, which were upgraded to strategic partnership in 2003. In 2010, the CAFTA was completed as scheduled. The year 2011 is quite special since it witnessed the 20th anniversary of the establishment of ASEAN–China dialogue relations, the China–ASEAN Friendship and Exchange Year and the first anniversary of CAFTA completion.

In the past two decades, both sides have assumed equality and mutual respect, and the good neighborliness and friendly cooperation maintain growth. All these have brought blessings for the two peoples, ensuring the bilateral reciprocal cooperation, promoting the economic and social development of both sides and greatly contributing to the peace, stability, prosperity and development of the China–ASEAN region.

To celebrate the 20th anniversary of ASEAN–China dialogue relations, colorful programs and activities were held, with the 8th CAEXPO as an integral part. With the guidance of competent ministries and departments of Chinese central government, Guangxi, the CAEXPO organizer, has participated in the organization of diverse celebrations, including Commemorative Reception on 20th Anniversary of ASEAN–China Dialogue Relations, ASEAN–China Strategic Seminar on Connectivity, China–ASEAN Friendship Knowledge Contest, 2011 Economic and Trade Seminar for ASEAN Journalists, 2011 China–ASEAN International Touring Assembly & China–ASEAN Media Rally, and "Guangxi State Farms Cup" Foreign Language Speaking Competition Marking the 20th Anniversary of ASEAN–China Dialogue Relations, to name just a few.

The celebrations have attracted the attention of governments of both sides, and the active involvement of business circles and people of all walks of life. These colorful and splendid programs have yielded rich outcomes and exerted profound influence in all fields, opening a new chapter for the bilateral friendly relations.

CHAPTER SIX

一 中国—东盟建立对话关系20周年纪念招待会

为纪念中国—东盟建立对话关系20周年，2011年8月23日晚，外交部与东盟北京委员会在北京钓鱼台国宾馆举行中国—东盟建立对话关系20周年纪念招待会。国务委员戴秉国出席招待会并致辞。广西壮族自治区党委书记、自治区人大常委会主任郭声琨，自治区主席马飚，自治区党委常委、自治区副主席陈武，自治区党委常委、秘书长余远辉等领导应邀出席招待会。

戴秉国在致辞中代表中国政府向长期致力于中国—东盟友好事业的各界人士致以诚挚问候和良好祝愿，并高度评价中国与东盟国家关系发展。他说，这20年是世界大变化、大发展的20年，更是中国和东盟各国大发展、中国—东盟关系大发展并给各自的人民带来巨大利益的20年。双方睦邻友好不断巩固，经贸往来不断扩展，安全合作不断深化，团结精神不断增强。巩固和发展中国—东盟战略伙伴关系，是双方共同的战略选择。中国将坚定不移地支持东盟欠发达国家加速实现发展目标，坚定不移地支持东盟共同体建设和东盟在东亚合作中的主导地位。中国愿同东盟加强政治互信；拓展各领域

2011年8月23日，中国—东盟建立对话关系20周年纪念招待会在北京举行

Commemorative Reception on 20th Anniversary of ASEAN-China Dialogue Relations held in Beijing, China on August 23, 2011

互利合作，落实第二份五年行动计划，实现双边贸易额达5000亿美元等未来五年的具体目标；推进互联互通建设，中方愿同东盟方面积极推进海上互联互通，使其成为中国—东盟合作的新亮点；深化安全合作，使南海成为和平之海、友谊之海、合作之海；促进社会人文交流，推动东亚合作健康发展。

东盟北京委员会轮值主席、柬埔寨驻华大使西索达在致辞中表示，2011年是东盟—中国建立对话关系20周年、东盟—中国友好交流年以及东盟—中国自由贸易区建成1周年。东盟—中国自贸区覆盖19亿人口，潜力巨大，是仅次于欧洲和北美自由贸易区的世界第三大经济实体，作为新兴力量吸引了全世界的关注。东盟和中国将继续致力于推动和进一步发展东盟—中国对话关系，实现双方国家和人民的共同发展。

受外交部委托，根据广西壮族自治区党委、自治区人民政府统一部署，广西文化厅精心策划组织了广西歌舞剧院、广西杂技团的优秀演员，为出席招待会的贵宾表演了具有浓郁特色、丰富多彩的文艺节目。包括：展现广西"山美、水美、人美"的壮族歌舞《山歌好比春江水》，寓意中国与东盟各国友好相处、开放包容的歌曲《阿依莎娜·妮亚》，展现中国—东盟互惠互利、和谐共赢的歌舞《和谐大家园》，蕴含中国—东盟博览会精神的杂技《朱槿花开——女子造型》，极具广西民族特色、地域风格的广西民乐《壮乡春早》等。广西的舞蹈演员向戴秉国、郭声琨、马飚等领导和嘉宾敬献了绣球，得到了与会领导嘉宾的一致好评。陈武、余远辉等自治区领导以及中国东盟协会负责人、中方各部委有关负责人、专家学者、东盟各国驻华使节、东盟常驻代表委员会访华团及工商界代表等约500名贵宾观看了演出。招待会上，来自东盟国家的艺术家们还为宾客带来了富有异域风情的东南亚舞蹈节目。

本次广西文艺院团在北京钓鱼台国宾馆举行中国—东盟建立对话关系20周年纪念招待会文艺演出活动，向国家领导以及东盟各国驻华大使、外宾演出了广西民族特色浓郁、地域特征鲜明的艺术精品，宣传了中国—东盟友好合作，宣传了广西，树立广西的文化形象，展示了广西近年来文化高速发展的最新成果。

二　中国—东盟互联互通战略研讨会

为更好地借助东盟互联互通战略深化中国与东盟合作，由外交部和广西壮族自治区人民政府主办，外交学院与中国—东盟博览会秘书处承办的中国—东盟互联互通战略研讨会于2011年8月23日在北京召开。本次研讨会在中国—东盟建立对话关系20周年、中国—东盟友好交流年和中国—东盟自由贸易区建成1周年的背景下举办，具有特殊的重要意义。本次研讨会是中国—东盟建立对话关系20周年纪念活动之一。外交部部长助理刘振民，广西壮族自治区党委常委、自治区副主席陈武，东盟各国常驻代表、东盟驻华大使、东盟秘书处等代表出席了研讨会开幕式，中国和东盟10国政府、企业、银行、智库等代表约140人出席研讨会。

刘振民在致辞时说，中国—东盟建立对话关系20年来，在20多个领域开展了务实合作，搭建了中国—东盟博览会等一系列合作平台，促进了双方

2011年8月23日，中国—东盟互联互通战略研讨会在北京举行

ASEAN-China Strategic Seminar on Connectivity held in Beijing, China on August 23, 2011

经济社会发展。中国和东盟作为战略合作伙伴，双方的互联互通是全方位、深层次、战略性的，主要包括“硬件”和“软件”两方面。“硬件”方面，主要是基础设施和交通运输的互联互通，这几年双方陆路和航空的互联互通已取得重要成果，下一阶段要加强海上互联互通大通道的建设。“软件”方面，一是制度互联互通，重点是建设好中国—东盟自贸区，不断提高贸易便利化水平，促进区域内生产要素的自由流动。二是感情互联互通，通过民间友好组织、青年、妇女、媒体、非政府组织等渠道，积极加强人文领域的交流合作，营造良好舆论环境，加深彼此了解，夯实双方睦邻友好的社会基础。中国高度重视与东盟的互联互通建设。近年来，中国与东盟各国领导人多次强调要把互联互通作为合作的优先领域和重点方向，交通部门还制定了《中国—东盟交通合作战略规划》。

陈武在致辞中说，广西愿意以本次研讨会为契机，进一步发挥区位优势和中国—东盟博览会的平台作用，加强与东盟各国的互联互通合作，努力把广西建设成为中国与东盟合作的新高地，为进一步深化中国—东盟友好合作作出新的贡献。

研讨会上，代表们围绕中国—东盟互联互通与制度建设、产业对接、地方动议等议题，深入探讨中国—东盟互联互通合作和未来发展方向。

本次中国—东盟互联互通战略研讨会取得以下成果：

（一）促进中国—东盟互联互通战略合作交流

在研讨交流过程中，与会代表提出的一些创新性观点和对策建议，具有很强的针对性和可操作性，为相关部门决策提供了很好的参考和借鉴。主要有以下几点：

一是建议成立中国—东盟互联互通委常设机制，推动东盟互联互通总体规划与中国—东盟互联互通战略与规划的对接。比如柬埔寨常驻东盟代表提出应建立中国—东盟互联互通行动小组；越南代表提出可先行建立中国与东盟互联互通协调委员会（ACCC）定期对话机制。

二是建议扩大各方参与互联互通合作的渠道，打造成多行为体、多层面的合作模式，为地区、国家和地方层面的行为体提供参与互联互通合作的渠道，调动私营部门的参与积极性。

三是建议大力发展保税、仓储、物流等服务性设施，削减关税、消除非关税壁垒、对外来资本实行国民待遇，改善投资环境；提高各国海关和检疫部门的工作效率，实现通关便利化。

本次研讨会上这些建议对于抓住当前中国与东盟合作的良好机遇，深化中国—东盟自由贸易区成果，扩大中国—东盟博览会平台作用，促进互联互通战略合作交流、推动区域经济合作，促进合作共赢，具有积极作用。

（二）丰富和增强了中国—东盟博览会的平台作用

外交部部长助理刘振民在会上高度评价中国—东盟建立对话关系20周年取得的成果，肯定了中国—东盟博览会所发挥的平台作用。中国—东盟博览会秘书处秘书长郑军健在研讨会答记者问中介绍了中国—东盟博览会成功举办七届的成效。他说，博览会搭建了中国与东盟友好交流、经贸促进、多领域合作的平台，促进了双边金融、物流、港口、交通、科技、文化、教育等多领域的合作；并在中国—东盟自贸区中形成广泛影响力，成为中国与东盟、发展中国家与发展中国家共同发展的典范，服务了国家战略，带动了广西经济发展。

通过举办本次研讨会，既有利于中国—东盟互联互通的合作交流，也能为促进中国与东盟国家的交往从合作经贸活动延伸到互联互通的多领域合作层面，促进全方位、多层次、宽领域的合作作贡献，同时，也将进一步丰富博览会的平台作用。

外交部此次特别邀请自治区人民政府担任研讨会主办单位，正是对广西发挥中国—东盟“桥头堡”作用、博览会发挥中国—东盟自贸区“助推器”作用的肯定，也将进一步促进中国—东盟双方利用博览会的在互联互通领域的深化合作。

（三）展示广西近年来在中国—东盟互联互通领域取得的成效，为进一步发挥广西在中国—东盟互联互通领域的作用打下基础

广西壮族自治区党委常委、自治区副主席陈武在会上介绍了广西发挥区位优势和博览会平台作用，在促进中国—东盟互联互通方面取得的成效，提出了与各方共同推进互联互通的建议：

一是与东盟将积极携手共建国际大通道，加强在码头建设、仓储物流、航线航班、港口信息化和人才培训等方面的交流与合作，推进区域高等级公路、干线铁路的建设和改造，加快南宁—新加坡经济走廊建设，促进基础设施的互联互通。

二是共建合作平台。广西将继续充分发挥中国—东盟博览会、中国—东盟商务与投资峰会等平台的功能和作用，为互联互通做好服务。

三是共同推进区域经济合作。广西将继续推进大湄公河次区域合作、泛北部湾经济合作、“两廊一圈”合作、南宁—新加坡经济走廊建设，大力实施《广西北部湾经济区发展规划》，加快建设中国—马来西亚钦州产业园区

等重大项目，加快推进中越跨境经济合作区建设，努力为互联互通注入更加丰富的内容，产生更加务实的成果。

此外，本次研讨会专门设立了“中国—东盟互联互通与地方动议”专题，广西作为中国地方政府的唯一代表发言并研讨，大力宣传了广西的发展优势和博览会的平台作用。

本次研讨会对中国—东盟互联互通将产生积极作用和深远影响。随着中国与东盟区域经贸合作的更大发展，迫切需要一个涵盖交通、能源、信息等基础设施互联互通网络的强力支撑。特别是在全球经济金融形势持续动荡、欧美等发达国家正面临债务危机困扰的背景下，促进本地区基础设施网络互联互通是推进区域经济一体化的必要条件，也是东亚国家发掘区内经济增长动力，通过扩大区内贸易与投资增长来摆脱对欧美市场的依赖，更好发展区内经济的现实需要。中国—东盟互联互通网络建设正处在一个关键时刻，本次研讨会的圆满召开将为中国与东盟双方如何尽善尽美地实现这一重要规划提供一个良好的交流平台。为进一步拓展和加深中国—东盟互联互通合作起到了积极的推动作用。

三　中国—东盟友谊知识竞赛

为促进中国—东盟友好交流，增进双方特别是青少年之间的了解和友谊，推动双方文化交流，中国外交部、中国教育部、广西壮族自治区人民政府共同主办了中国—东盟友谊知识竞赛。此次竞赛是中国—东盟建立对话关系20周年系列纪念活动之一，也是第八届中国—东盟博览会的一项重要活动，由中国—东盟博览会秘书处、广西壮族自治区教育厅、中国—东盟中心承办。

本次竞赛已于2011年8—9月举办，分为初赛和决赛两个阶段。初赛采用网络答题的形式、通过中国—东盟中心官方网站进行。题目内容包括中国与东盟各国基本国情、中国—东盟友好合作、中国—东盟自贸区建设、中国—东盟博览会等。初赛吸引了中国和东盟各国高等院校学生积极参与，实现了11个国家全部参与的目标。决赛采用主题活动营的形式举行。从初赛中脱颖而出的来自中国和东盟10国25名选手，于9月24—28日在广西南宁参加决赛系列活动。广西壮族自治区人大常委会副主任莫永清、自治区副主席李康，中国驻东盟大使佟晓玲，中国教育部国际司副司长黄颖，中国—东盟博览会秘书长郑军健、副秘书长农融、郝志刚，柬埔寨、老挝、缅甸、泰国、越南驻南宁总领事馆代表等出席了决赛相关仪式。

此次竞赛形成了四个方面的鲜明特色：

1. 规格高，规模大，参与面广。中国外交部、中国教育部和广西壮族自治区人民政府共同主办充分体现了本次比赛的高规格。比赛覆盖中国和东盟10国，而且网络初赛吸引了欧美、南亚、中东等区域外青年参与，竞赛覆盖范围之广，这在中国—东盟青年友好交流的历史上是不多见的。

2. 内容丰富，隆重热烈，活动有序。比赛内容涵盖中国和东盟10国在历史、人文、音乐、发展等多方面。决赛期间每场活动都寓意深刻，反映了中国与东盟友好合作的主题。在浇灌友谊之林活动中，广西壮族自治区副主

中国—东盟友谊知识竞赛开营仪式

China-ASEAN Friendship Knowledge Contest Opening Ceremony

席李康与各国参赛选手一起共同浇灌中国和东盟国家领导人亲手种植的“友谊之林”，寓意中国和东盟友谊之树万古长青。在再注合作之水活动中，选手模拟首届中国—东盟博览会开幕式，将11国合作之水浇注在一起，寓意中国—东盟友好合作源远流长、生生不息。在开营仪式中，参赛选手逐一亮相并诵读友谊宣言，出席领导嘉宾授予选手决赛友谊旗帜，寓意中国—东盟友谊代代相传。在颁奖晚会上，通过电视演播、视频剪辑等先进技术，实现了场内与场外的互动，集中展示友好和谐氛围，把竞赛推向了高潮。各场活动在社会氛围营造、现场布置、舞台灯光等各方面都突出主题，办得隆重、热烈，始终洋溢着友好和谐的氛围。

3. 轻松和谐，寓宣于乐，给青年留下美好印象。在决赛阶段安排了户外趣味知识竞技与决赛晚会现场竞答的两大项，选手们在答题过程中既学到了中国—东盟友谊相关知识，又享受相互协作、互动表演的乐趣，留下了美好的印象。

4. 针对性强，形式新颖，达到效果。本次知识竞赛内容紧扣中国与东盟合作，采取青年喜闻乐见的网络平台作为初赛形式，采取主题活动营的形式进行决赛，使各国青年能够充分了解和交流，取得良好成效。

此次竞赛取得多方面的成果：

一是促进了中国—东盟友好交流与合作。竞赛紧扣中国—东盟友好合作，突出友谊联欢的性质，增强沟通交流，使中国与东盟青年在竞赛中相互协助，建立了深厚的友谊，重温了友好合作的历史，见证了友好合作的成就，展望了友好合作的美好前景，以实际行动把中国与东盟的友谊世代传承下去，巩固睦邻友好基础。

二是宣传了中国与东盟的友好合作和互利共赢。竞赛吸引了中国和东盟各大媒体广泛关注，共有40多家媒体参与报道，包括《人民日报》、新华社、中新社、中央电视台等国内媒体和柬埔寨之光、越南《西贡解放日报》等东盟媒体，宣传了中国—东盟友好合作。

三是增进了中国与东盟各国青年的相互了解。本次比赛在题目设置突出中国—东盟友谊知识的传播，选手们在轻松、有趣的氛围中学到了知识。通过实地观光考察，增进东盟青年对中国的了解。比赛之余，还组织歌唱联欢，让选手在轻松、愉快的氛围中增进友谊。

四是丰富了中国—东盟人文领域交流的形式和内容。竞赛通过交流、活动、联欢、参观、比赛等方式传导中国—东盟友好合作的信息，寓教于乐，务实推动了双方青年学生在中国—东盟人文领域的交流，丰富了合作的形式和内容。

五是进一步扩大了中国—东盟博览会的品牌影响力。竞赛是第八届中国—东盟博览会的一项活动，竞赛题目和活动内容也紧扣中国—东盟博览会宗旨、内容、开幕式、会歌等元素，体现了中国—东盟博览会在中国—东盟合作中的作用，提升了博览会的品牌影响力。

四　2011年东盟国家经贸记者研修班

为纪念中国—东盟建立对话关系20周年、中国—东盟友好交流年、中国—东盟自贸区建成1周年，2011年7月12日，由中国商务部主办、中国—东盟博览会秘书处承办的2011年东盟国家经贸记者研修班在南宁开班。这是在中国举办的首个面向东盟经贸记者的研修班。来自文莱《联合日报》、柬埔寨国家电视台、泰国《曼谷邮报》、印尼《商报》、越南《经济时报》等东盟10国知名媒体的22名新闻官员及经贸记者参加研修班。举办此次研修班，旨在帮助东盟各国媒体记者更深入地了解中国经济发展情况，了解中国—东盟自贸区建成后中国与东盟国家的经贸合作前景。

中国商务部投资促进局副局长张迎新在开班仪式上说，中国与东盟建立对话关系20周年来，经贸合作不断深化。特别是中国—东盟自贸区全面建成，中国—东盟博览会成功举办七届，给双方企业和人民带来了实实在在的好处。这是中国和东盟10国共同努力的结果，东盟各国媒体记者也为宣传中国—东盟经贸合作，宣传互利共赢，做了大量卓有成效的工作。希望各位记

2011 年 7 月 12 日，2011 年东盟国家经贸记者研修班在广西南宁开班

Inaugural ceremony of 2011 Economic & Trade Seminar for ASEAN Journalists held in Nanning, Guangxi, China on July 12, 2011

者积极参加研修班的课堂学习及相关活动，把东盟国家的成功经验和做法，带到研修班上来互相交流，取长补短，增强学习效果，使研修班在提供相互学习的机会的同时，在中国与东盟各国之间搭建起合作的桥梁，构建起联系的平台。

中国—东盟博览会秘书处副秘书长郝志刚在研修班开班仪式上致辞，向东盟各国学员介绍了中国—东盟博览会举办七年来取得的显著成效。

本次研修班具有三个方面的特色：

1. 内容丰富，针对性强。本次研修班注重讲授中国经济社会发展状况及中国—东盟经贸关系发展、自贸区、博览会的相关知识，同时融入更多中国文化的元素。期间，邀请专家、学者讲授了中国—东盟经贸关系发展、中国—东盟区域经济合作、中国—东盟博览会主要成就及平台作用等主要内容，还组织学员考察桂林阳朔的世外桃源并观看具有壮族文化特色的《印象·刘三姐》，这些内容针对性强，受到东盟学员的欢迎。

2. 形式生动，互动性强。研修班邀请了商务部投资促进局、商务部亚洲司、中国—东盟博览会秘书处、中国社会科学院亚太研究所研究员等专家授课，并安排互动讨论课，收到了良好的效果。

3. 开展实地考察，开拓视野。研修班组织学员考察了广西和海南，让东盟学员更直观地了解当地的经济社会发展情况及与东盟经贸合作的状况。

本次研修班取得五个方面的成果：

一是加深了学员对中国经济社会发展情况及中国—东盟经贸合作情况的了解。通过授课、考察等活动，学员对中国经济社会发展、中国—东盟双边经贸合作、中国—东盟自贸区、中国—东盟博览会等方面的知识有了基本的认识，进一步了解了中国的经济发展现状。

二是进一步扩大中国—东盟自贸区和中国—东盟博览会的影响力。本次研修班重点安排了中国—东盟自贸区、中国—东盟博览会的相关知识，组织了专题讨论，学员都纷纷表示回国之后会通过自己手中的笔更好地宣传中国—东盟自贸区和中国—东盟博览会。

三是进一步向东盟国家展示了广西和海南与东盟国家经贸合作的潜力和商机。配合授课内容，研修班实地考察了广西、海南的部分主要城市及具有代表性的工业园区。通过实地参观考察，学员进一步了解了广西和海南经济社会建设的成就以及与东盟国家经贸合作的潜力和商机。

四是进一步推动对中国—东盟友好合作的宣传。本次研修班受到各地新闻媒体的高度关注，共有35家媒体进行报道，报道新闻40多篇，并有大量媒体进行转载。海南电视台海南新闻栏目对研修班考察海南的行程进行了长达两分钟的新闻报道，海口市电视台、三亚电视台、北海电视台、柳州电视台等都对研修班的活动进行了报道。新闻媒体的大量报道，掀起了中国—东盟经贸合作宣传的小高潮。

五是增进了相互了解，建立了友谊。在为期14天的研修班生活中，中方人员与东盟学员之间建立了深厚的友谊。不管是教学、讨论还是实地考察，大家充分交流、积极沟通，增进了相互了解和友谊。

东盟学员对此次研修班给予积极评价。印尼《希望之光午报》记者TUTUT觉得这次研修班办得很好，通过学习、考察，她学到了中国发展经济社会的经验，回去她要把在中国的所见所闻告诉家人及朋友；缅甸记者Aye Kywe说，整个研修班的行程和内容非常完美，学到很多东西；文莱《联合日报》记者PUI/CHIN SIONG希望每年都能举办这样的研修班。

五　2011中国—东盟国际汽车拉力赛暨中国—东盟媒体汽车拉力赛

由中国国家体育总局、广西壮族自治区人民政府、东盟秘书处共同主办，中国汽车运动联合会、广西体育局、广西国际博览事务局等单位共同承办的2011“体育彩票杯”中国—东盟国际汽车拉力赛暨中国—东盟媒体汽车拉力赛于2011年9月20日在南宁发车并从东兴出关，车队由来自中国、越南、泰国、柬埔寨、老挝、马来西亚、新加坡等国的34辆车包括154名参赛车手、记者和工作人员组成，历时23天，行程约10000公里，途经越南、老挝、柬埔寨、泰国、马来西亚、新加坡六国，于10月12日从凭祥友谊关顺利回到南宁，安全、圆满地完成了拉力赛的各项任务。赛事秉承着“和谐之旅、友谊之旅、欢乐之旅”宗旨，在各方努力下，朝着一个更为专业化、国际化、多元化的方向发展。

2011年9月20日，2011中国—东盟国际汽车拉力赛暨中国—东盟媒体汽车拉力赛在广西南宁发车

Flag-off ceremony of 2011 China-ASEAN International Touring Assembly & China-ASEAN Media Rally held in Nanning, Guangxi, China on September 20, 2011

此次比赛得到了东盟各国官方与民间的积极参与和互动：越南国家体育总局副局长范文俊专程从河内赶到下龙，参加车队在下龙湾的活动，越南广宁省文化体育旅游厅专门为拉力赛准备了一台欢迎晚会；老挝国家体委两位副主任出席联谊酒会，并与广西体育局签署体育交流合作备忘录，老挝国立大学办公室主任出席活动并接受组委会赠送的书籍；在泰国素可泰府与拉力赛组委会共同主办的发车仪式上，素可泰府尹代表、泰国国家旅游局的代表、素可泰体育局局长、皇家汽车协会秘书长出席了发车仪式；在柬埔寨发车仪式上，柬埔寨国务秘书、教育青年体育部副部长邦索克先生发表了讲话并接受媒体采访，柬埔寨奥委会派出一名观察员参加后半部分的赛程；在新加坡体育理事会和汽车协会的共同协助下，发车仪式安排在新加坡F1赛道边上的新加坡地标建筑——摩天轮下举行，国会议员林伟杰博士等官方代表出席仪式并发表讲话；在马来西亚，体育旅游部非常重视拉力赛车队的活动，除副部长亲自出席联谊晚宴并发表讲话外，还组织了文艺表演节目，F1雪邦赛道的组织方给拉力赛车队提供场地和各种便利，马来西亚官方还破例允许拉力赛的车队到F1赛道上巡游一周。

2011年的竞赛内容丰富、形式多样、安排合理，并在规则和组织形式上进行了很多有益的尝试。本届拉力赛在境外举行了5场比赛：老挝场地趣味赛、马拉西亚卡丁车赛、老挝段集结赛和泰国段集结赛以及首次引进的老挝段定速赛。在文化内涵方面，车队途经中南半岛大部分的世界文化及自然遗产所在地，包括柬埔寨吴哥窟、老挝占巴塞华普、越南顺化古皇宫和河内市、泰国素可泰皇宫遗址和大城古皇城、马来西亚乔治城等7个世界历史文化遗产遗址和越南下龙湾1个世界自然遗产，让参赛者和媒体通过拉力赛平台感受东南亚的独特文化、历史和自然风光。2011拉力赛可谓东南亚世界历史文化及自然遗产之旅。

此外，国内活动也精彩纷呈，主要包括“三行一选秀”的系列活动（“三行”即东盟行、万里行和八桂行，“一选秀”即拉力赛形象大使选拔赛），为赛事在扩大内涵、提高品牌价值方面起了重要的作用。

六　纪念中国—东盟建立对话关系20周年“广西农垦杯”外语演讲比赛

根据外交部积极开展公共外交实践的要求，为配合2011中国—东盟友好交流年系列活动，隆重纪念中国—东盟建立对话关系20周年、广西农垦建垦60周年，宣传广西对外开放的巨大成就，广西壮族自治区外事办公室和广西农垦局共同主办了纪念中国—东盟建立对话关系20周年“广西农垦杯”外语演讲大赛。

大赛自2011年5月5日召开新闻发布会启动大赛，至6月19日完成决赛，前后历时46天，共11000余人参赛，其中外籍选手近3000名。6月20日晚，在简约而隆重的颁奖典礼上，广西壮族自治区党委常委、宣传部部长沈北海，自治区政协副主席黄日波，广西外事办公室主任范晓莉，中国—东盟中心秘书长马明强，以及广西外事办公室、广西农垦局、广西大学、广西民族大学等单位领导以及柬埔寨、老挝、缅甸、泰国、越南驻南宁总领事及印尼驻广州总领馆领事官员等，分别为获奖中外选手颁奖，大赛获得圆满成功。

纪念中国—东盟建立对话关系20周年“广西农垦杯”外语演讲大赛颁奖典礼

Awarding ceremony of "Guangxi State Farms Cup" Foreign Language Speaking Competition Marking the 20th Anniversary of ASEAN-China Dialogue Relations

本次外语演讲大赛分2个语种共3个组进行，其中汉语组面向在广西工作、学习和生活的外国籍人士，英语1组面向全自治区高中生，英语2组面向大中院校老师、学生和社会人员。3个组报名选手共11000余人，其中来自东盟、美国、加拿大、英国、法国、俄罗斯、乌克兰、乌兹别克斯坦、印度、韩国、巴基斯坦、纳米比亚、喀麦隆、阿尔及利亚等23个国家的外籍选手近3000人。初赛共设23个赛场，分别由南宁等14个地级市外事（侨务）办公室以及广西大学等9所高校承办。复赛、决赛和颁奖典礼则以自治区外办为主体，联合广西大学和广西民族大学共同承办。经过海选、初赛、复赛和决赛，共有21名外籍选手及40名区内选手分别夺得三个组别的一、二、三等奖及单项和优胜奖。获奖的外籍选手分别来自越南、老挝、缅甸、泰国、印尼、美国、喀麦隆等7个国家。

大赛着眼于提升广西为国家总体外交服务的能力，提高公众对公共外交工作的认识，吸引他们的积极参与和支持。通过外语演讲大赛，促进在桂中外人士学外语、用外语，增进其对广西参与中国—东盟合作交往情况的了解，进一步打造广西“人文外交软实力”。大赛始终由政府外事部门主导，规格高、规模大、规范性强。为了广泛宣传中国—东盟建立对话关系20年来广西对外开放取得的辉煌的经济社会发展成就，广西外事办公室通过网站、媒体登载了丰富的背景资料以及广西企业“走出去”的突出成绩，吸引各界人士和国内外选手阅读、浏览。

比赛中，各国选手紧紧围绕中国与东盟建立对话关系20年、广西与东盟国家开展各领域友好交流合作等主题，演讲内容明确，形式丰富多彩，既有讲述广西与东盟人员友好往来的感人事迹与体会、七届中国—东盟博览会和商务与投资峰会对广西对外开放及经济社会发展的影响、泛北部湾经济合作特别是现代农业技术合作对广西及东盟国家经济社会发展的影响，也有广西中学生“走出去”和“请进来”交流的案例、成果与展望，广西农垦建垦60年来的发展历程、成就和与东盟合作的成功范例和成果，还有对未来双边和多边合作前景的展望等。无论是自命题演讲，还是问答，选手们都发挥出色，展示了高水平的语言功底和良好的精神风貌。

广西选手讲东盟，外国选手讲广西，广西和东盟的人文历史、自然地理、风土人情、趣闻轶事、饮食文化呈现于评委和观众眼前；广西壮族自治区领导、中国和东盟高级外交官为获奖选手颁奖，给予选手们无比的荣耀和终身难忘的回忆；中外选手同台发表获奖感言，传递了浓浓的感情和友谊。中外选手之间，外国籍选手和中国籍指导老师之间，中外籍评委和工作人员之间，友好交流、打成一片，拉近了距离，提高了互信，交流了感情，增进了友谊。

各类媒体对大赛进行了广泛宣传报道。外国人说汉语的各级赛事，更是吸引媒体自主采访报道的热点。各市外（侨）办和宣传部门协调配合，充分利用公交视频、街道宣传窗、政府门户网站等多种媒体开展宣传活动，使大赛深入人心；《广西日报》全文刊发了大赛实施方案，方便读者了解掌握赛事规则和流程；广西新闻网开设大赛网站，发布赛事信息和有关背景资料，提供有关网站链接；中国国际广播电台网广西站记者主动积极和自治区及各地市外（侨）联系，对大赛进行了持续的深入报道；人民网、《中国日报》、搜狐滚动等网站转载了有关报道。

越南、老挝、缅甸、泰国、柬埔寨驻南宁总领事馆自初赛起就十分关注赛事的进程和本国选手的成绩，派出领事官员亲临赛场观摩比赛。大赛为广西政府部门、高校与东盟国家密切交往提供了新的平台，选手们之间，外交官、老师、学生之间加强了互动交流，为将来在不同领域不同岗位上开展合作交流打下了良好的人脉和感情基础。

小结　系列纪念活动精彩纷呈　营造友好和谐喜庆氛围

为纪念中国—东盟建立对话关系20周年、中国—东盟友好交流年、中国—东盟自贸区建成1周年，第八届中国—东盟博览会被列为20周年系列纪念活动的重要组成部分。在此基础上，中国—东盟博览会举办地广西还主办或参与主办承办一系列20周年纪念活动。包括：中国—东盟建立对话关系20周年纪念招待会文艺演出、中国—东盟互联互通战略研讨会、中国—东盟友谊知识竞赛、2011东盟经贸记者研修班、2011中国—东盟国际汽车拉力赛暨中国—东盟媒体汽车拉力赛、纪念中国—东盟建立对话关系20周年外语演讲比赛等。这些活动主题突出，特色鲜明，内容精彩，参与面广，隆重热烈，影响力大，始终洋溢着友好和谐喜气的气氛，为第八届中国—东盟博览会成功举办营造了良好氛围，形成以下亮点。

一是主题突出，体现互利共赢。中国总理温家宝在2010年10月29日举行的第十三次中国—东盟领导人会议上提议将2011年确定为“中国—东盟友好交流年”，双方共同举办丰富多彩的活动。为落实这一倡议精神，中国—东盟友好交流年的主题确定为“互利共赢的好伙伴”，共举行30多项交流活动。其中，广西主办或参与主办承办的系列活动，始终紧扣“互利共赢的好伙伴”这一主题，从经贸、文化、互联互通、青年、新闻、体育、外语等多个领域，展示了双方20周年合作的成就，展示了友好合作的美好前景。

二是内容精彩，区域特色鲜明。中国—东盟建立对话关系20周年系列纪念活动围绕中国与东盟友好合作，展开多层次多领域的交流，是中国—东盟“10+1”合作的一次生动展示，形成了鲜明的区域特色。例如，20周年纪念招待会文艺演出内容突出展现中国—东盟互惠互利、和谐共赢，弘扬中国—东盟博览会精神。中国—东盟互联互通战略研讨会深入研讨了中国—东盟互联互通合作。中国—东盟友谊知识竞赛增进青年一代对中国—东盟合作的了解和相互之间的友谊。2011年东盟经贸记者研修班组织东盟各国的新闻官员和经贸记者深入到中国与东盟合作的前沿地区，使他们更直观了解双方合作的现状和前景。2011中国—东盟国际汽车拉力赛暨中国—东盟媒体汽车拉力赛以汽车运动为载体，增进中国和东盟人民之间的友好往来。纪念中国—东盟建立对话关系20周年外语演讲比赛为广西与东盟国家密切交往提供了新的平台。

三是参与面广，多层次宽领域交流广泛而深入。广西主办或参与主办承办的中国—东盟建立对话关系20周年系列纪念活动，参与人员层次多，覆盖面广，既有政府官员，也有企业界人士、记者、学生、运动员和普通民众等。其中，20周年纪念招待会有中方各部委有关负责人、专家学者、东盟各国驻华使节、东盟常驻代表委员会访华团及工商界代表等约500人出席。互联互通战略研讨会有中国和东盟各国政府官员、东盟各国常驻代表、东盟驻华大使、东盟秘书处等代表出席。友谊知识竞赛面向中国和东盟各国大学生。东盟经贸记者研修班面向东盟各国新闻官员和经贸记者。汽车拉力赛面向各国车手和记者。纪念中国—东盟建立对话关系20周年外语演讲比赛面向中国和东盟官员、学生和普通民众。各方围绕多领域开展了全方位友好交流，巩固了睦邻友好基础。

四是各方高度重视和积极评价，影响力大。广西主办或参与主办承办的中国—东盟建立对话关系20周年系列纪念活动，隆重热烈，各方高度重视，

第八届中国—东盟博览会气氛隆重热烈
The grand 8th CAEXPO

给予积极评价。媒体聚集报道，营造了友好和谐喜庆的良好气氛。中国国务委员戴秉国与东盟北京委员会轮值主席、柬埔寨驻华大使西索达分别在中国—东盟建立对话关系20周年纪念招待会上致辞。中国外交部部长助理刘振民，广西壮族自治区党委常委、自治区副主席陈武在中国—东盟互联互通战略研讨会上致辞。中国—东盟友好知识竞赛得到了各国选手的积极评价。马来西亚的选手吴彩宝说，这次活动中不仅收获了快乐和知识，更重要的是增进了彼此间的友情。缅甸记者Thet Swe在参加东盟经贸记者研修班后说，此次行程让他受益良多，终身难忘。中外媒体对上述活动进行了充分报道，宣传了中国—东盟互利共赢，彰显了系列活动的影响力。

第七章

7 文化盛宴 友谊桥梁

——第八届中国—东盟博览会文化交流活动

国之交在于民相亲，民相亲在于心相通。中国与东盟友好关系长期稳定发展的根本在于人民之间的相互了解、相互信任。文化交流是中国与东盟各国人民增进了解和友谊的重要桥梁。

文化的交流和发展对于推动各国经济社会可持续增长、促进本地区的共同繁荣具有重要意义。

中国与东盟山水相连、文化相近，近年来，不仅在政治、经济、文化等方面保持着良好的合作关系，而且文化交流日益密切，为促进双方睦邻友好关系作出了积极贡献。

中国—东盟博览会是文化交流的大舞台。每届博览会期间，都举办丰富多彩的文化交流活动。第八届中国—东盟博览会期间，举办了2011南宁国际民歌艺术节暨第八届中国—东盟博览会开幕晚会系列文化活动、2011南宁 东南亚国际旅游美食节、中老建交50周年“北部湾之声”节目落地老挝万象系列活动、高尔夫名人邀请赛、国际精英邀请赛、“网球之友”联谊活动、第五届中国—东盟青年艺术品创作大赛获奖作品暨五周年成果展等。

各场文化交流活动展示了中国与东盟各国多姿多彩的文化魅力，展现了一幅中国人民和东盟各国人民文化交流合作的生动画卷。

A Feast of Culture, a Bridge of Friendship

—Cultural and Sport Programs during the 8th CAEXPO

The connection of countries is strengthened via the exchanges among their peoples, and the good will of communication always lies in the hearts of our people. The long-lasting and stable friendly exchanges between China and the ASEAN member countries are attributed to the mutual understanding and trust of the peoples. Among all the communication channels, cultural exchange is one of the most popular and effective ways for people to enhance understanding and friendship.

The exchanges and development of culture is good and vital for promoting the sustainable growth of economic and social development of the countries concerned, and the common prosperity of the whole region.

China links the ASEAN countries both by sea and land, and their cultures share similarities. In recent years, both sides have kept close touch in political, economic and cultural areas. In particular, the bilateral cultural exchanges are increasingly enhanced, effectively promoting the good neighborliness and friendly relations of both sides.

CAEXPO is a huge stage for cultural exchanges. During each of the previous sessions, colorful and splendid cultural programs were held concurrently. During the 8th CAEXPO, diverse programs were staged, including 2011 Nanning International Arts Festival of Folk Songs & Gala Show for the Inauguration of the 8th CAEXPO, 2011 Nanning–Southeast Asia International Tourism & Food Festival, Launching Ceremony of "Voice of Beibu Gulf "in Vientiane, Laos to celebrate the 50th anniversary of China–Laos diplomatic relations and related celebrations, Golf Masters' Invitational, Golf Elites' Invitational, tennis games and the 5th China–ASEAN Youth Artwork Creativity Contest Award–winning Works & Fifth Anniversary Achievement Exhibition.

All these cultural events has well showcased the charms of the splendid Chinese and ASEAN local cultures, which make a fine picture of the cultural exchanges and cooperation of both sides.

CHAPTER SEVEN

一　2011南宁国际民歌艺术节暨第八届中国—东盟博览会开幕晚会系列文化活动

（一）2011南宁国际民歌艺术节暨第八届中国—东盟博览会开幕晚会

2011年10月21日晚，“大地飞歌·2011”第13届南宁国际民歌艺术节暨第八届中国—东盟博览会开幕晚会在广西体育中心隆重举行，拉开了第13届南宁国际民歌艺术节的序幕。出席晚会的嘉宾有：东盟各国代表团，中央、国家机关有关部门领导，各省（区、市）代表团，参加第八届中国—东盟博览会、第八届中国—东盟商务与投资峰会、第13届南宁国际民歌艺术节的部分代表、重要客商、参展商，广西壮族自治区和南宁市有关领导。

2011年10月21日，“大地飞歌·2011”第13届南宁国际民歌艺术节暨第八届中国—东盟博览会开幕晚会在广西南宁隆重举行

The 13th Nanning International Arts Festival of Folk Songs & Gala Show for the Inauguration of the 8th CAEXPO held in Nanning, Guangxi on October 21, 2011

广西壮族自治区党委常委、自治区副主席、南宁市委书记陈武通过视频宣布第13届南宁国际民歌艺术节暨第八届中国—东盟博览会开幕晚会开幕。南宁市市长周红波代表全体南宁市人民，通过视频欢迎中外嘉宾和各界朋友来到绿城南宁。

晚会以水为主题，分为《序：水从天上来》、《上篇：水之美》、《中篇：水之情》、《下篇：水之梦》和《尾声：奔流向大海》等五个部分。晚会由中央电视台主持人周涛、张泽群及广西电视台主持人高枫、邓璐联袂主持，1800平方米LED屏幕将广西、南宁的奇山秀水与晚会动态画面结合，争奇斗艳的冷焰火与荡漾在南宁夜空的经典民歌一起演绎了绿城南宁——天下民歌眷恋的地方。11位来自东盟10国与中国的小朋友表演的《共汇一江水》拉开了晚会的序幕；吴彤和宁可的一曲《天下黄河九十九道弯》配合LED显示屏里播放梦幻的水面场景，把现场观众带入了一个水的世界；李宇春、萨顶顶、王丽达、胡夏与金城女子合唱团分别倾情演唱《康定情歌》、《自由行走的花》、《山歌好比春江水》、《我唱刘三姐的歌》等歌曲，让观众再次领略了中华民歌的不朽魅力；著名跳水运动员田亮演唱的《亮出精彩》和香港著名歌手陈奕迅演唱的《好久不见》、《爱情转移》不断激起观众热情；本地优秀歌手廖鸿飞、方妮携“大地飞歌·2011”民歌大赛获奖歌手郭珍妮和搭档潘龙海、杨光春、娋妮组合精彩演绎本地民歌《站在这坡望那坡》；法语系歌剧天王、《巴黎圣母院》首席男主角Garou演绎经典歌剧《巴黎圣母院》的选段《艾斯美拉达》及情歌《seul》，并携手中国歌手曹芙嘉、金培达共同演唱本次晚会的主打曲目《左爱右爱》掀起晚会高潮；马来西亚著名歌手光良、内地人气组合凤凰传奇、台湾人气歌手信、内地偶像歌手韩庚也分别盛情演唱。晚会尾声，孙维良、五洲唱响乐团、哈嘹组合演唱新版《大地飞歌》，将晚会推向最高潮。

（二）外国艺术家专场演出

2011年10月22日晚，第13届南宁国际民歌艺术节外国艺术家专场晚会在南宁人民会堂举行，来自14个国家的艺术家们同台献艺，马来西亚手集团表演的《鼓典》、俄罗斯集市艺术团演唱的歌曲《喀秋莎》、泰国蓝莓乡村音乐组合演唱的《天堂般的泰国》、奥地利克拉根福民族音乐队演唱的《农夫之乐》和《幸福的人们》、保加利亚弦乐四重奏组合带来的《自由探戈》和《阿斯图里亚斯》、美国纽约芭蕾舞团表演的《壮乡梦缘》、美国女高音歌手考特尼·霍夫曼演唱的《青藏高原》异域风情博得观众阵阵喝彩声，为现场观众献上了一台艺术盛宴。

2011年10月22日，第13届南宁国际民歌艺术节外国艺术家专场晚会在广西南宁举行

The Foreign Artists Show of the 13th Nanning International Arts Festival of Folk Songs held in Nanning,Guangxi on October 22, 2011

（三）绿城歌台

2011年10月22—24日，由南宁国际民歌艺术节组委会主办的第13届南宁国际民歌艺术节绿城歌台分别在南宁六县六城区的广场、社区、旅游景点的14个歌台同时举行。主要有南宁市青秀区、兴宁区、西乡塘区、江南区、良庆区、邕宁区、南宁—东盟经济开发区、横县、宾阳、武鸣、马山、隆安县、上林等歌台，来自美国、俄罗斯、印度、丹麦等10多个国家和地区的近百名艺术家和中国演员同台献艺。

绿城歌台

Mini-shows in downtown Nanning

（四）“大地飞歌·2011”民歌大赛

2011南宁国际民歌艺术节隆重推出了“大地飞歌·2011”民歌大赛，大赛由南宁国际民歌艺术节组委会、广西电视台主办，中共南宁市委宣传部、南宁市文化新闻出版局、大地飞歌公司、广西电视台综艺频道等单位共同承

办。民歌大赛历时5个月，以本土选手唱民歌的方式，在全区14个地市举行海选，为广大民歌爱好者搭建展示平台，为民歌节开幕式晚会挑选优秀选手。通过民歌大赛选拔出来的民间优秀民歌选手潘龙海、郭珍妮、杨光春、娟妮组合、金城女子合唱团也首次走上大地飞歌的舞台，草根歌手与明星大腕同台引吭高歌，备受各方瞩目。民歌大赛作为南宁国际民歌艺术节的创新之举，提高了民歌艺术节的知名度和美誉度，引爆了民众积极参与的热情。

“大地飞歌·2011”民歌大赛
2011 Folk Songs Competition

二 2011南宁·东南亚国际旅游美食节

由广西南宁市人民政府主办，南宁市商务局、南宁市旅游局、江南区政府、南宁市礼之本广告策划有限公司承办的2011南宁·东南亚国际旅游美食节（以下简称“旅游美食节”）于2011年10月22—30日在南宁市江南区邕州老街举行。开幕式由南宁市人民政府副秘书长黄菊如主持，南宁市委政法委书记朱育兆、广西壮族自治区商务厅纪检组长张留现、广西烹饪协会会长黄桂辛先后致辞。随后，各领导一起为备受瞩目的美食节之最——“南宁美食小吃花盘”剪彩，鼓乐齐鸣，礼花齐放，彩烟腾空，2011南宁·东南亚国际旅游美食节拉开了精彩的序幕。

本届南宁·东南亚国际旅游美食节具有以下特点：

一是主题鲜明，成效显著。本届旅游美食节以服务中国—东盟博览会、中国—东盟商务与投资峰会、南宁国际民歌艺术节（“两会一节”）为指导，以品美食、观美景、赏文化为内容，集旅游、本土文化、美食为一体的

2011 年 10 月 22 日，2011 南宁·东南亚国际旅游美食节开幕式在广西南宁举行

The opening ceremony of 2011 Nanning-Southeast Asia International Tourism & Food Festival held in Nanning, Guangxi, China on October 22, 2011

极具刺激、别开生面的美食娱乐休闲盛会。据统计，美食节举办的9天时间，共接待参观人数37万人次，总销售额超过1850万元。特别是“两会一节”期间，吸引了众多的东盟各国客商现场参观，为“两会一节”增添了节日气氛，同时也大大提升了邕州老街商业街区的知名度，进一步促进南宁饮食、旅游、文化、经济的发展。

二是汇聚美食精品，开启美食盛会。在邕江老街的主会场内共设有5个展区：中华民族特色美展区、东南亚美食精品展区、现代餐饮原料（农副产品）展区、南宁市12县（区）绿色天然食品特色展区、餐饮品牌企业展区，共210个标准展位。本届美食节除吸引泰国、澳门的专业展团和餐厅前来展示系列东南亚美食外，还主推国际各地美食风味，同时还集中呈现最新发展变化中的广西各地美食精品，积极推动本土美食发展，推进南宁与国内、国际餐饮企业界的交流和合作，生动展现“绿城南宁、美食天堂”的品牌形象。

三是发扬壮乡文化，见证本土人文。与开幕式同时进行的是美食之最——“南宁美食小吃”品尝会，现场特别制作了一块长12米、宽4米的“南宁美食小吃”鲜花拼盘，将历届美食节创下美食“吉尼斯纪录”的小吃全部融汇其中，包括具有南宁美食特色的大粽子、卷肠粉、糍粑、马蹄糕、五色饭等，然后用南宁市花——朱槿花与本地青草点缀装饰，制作成独一无二的“南宁美食小吃拼盘”，寓示着本届美食节将承前启后，揭开一幅全新的美食篇章。

四是主题活动多，群众参与广。旅游美食节期间，各类主题活动多达几十场，现场主题展示、舞台展示活动和节庆时尚趣味活动形成紧密联动，是活动最丰富、形式最多样的一届旅游美食节。期间，主舞台每天都有各类精彩文化节目上演，除了开幕式的东南亚风情演出，美食节活动期间，“绿色天然食品选拔大赛”、“美食才艺达人秀”大赛、“趣味大胃王”竞技争霸赛、江南区百姓小舞台文艺演出、街舞大赛等精彩活动陆续闪亮登场，使得本届美食节有更多老百姓参与和互动，促进了现代饮食文化与百姓生活情趣的有机结合。精彩活动的成功开展，吸引了大量游客前来，并参与到活动和游戏中，极大地促进了旅游美食节节庆文化、旅游文化和本土民俗文化的传播。

三　中国老挝建交50周年“北部湾之声”节目落地老挝万象系列活动

2011年10月21日，为纪念中国与老挝建交50周年和中国—东盟友好交流年，由中国国际广播电台、老挝驻南宁总领事馆、广西广播电影电视局主办，广西人民广播电台、中国东盟经济文化研究中心承办的“北部湾之声”节目落地老挝万象启动仪式、老挝音乐广西展播周开幕式和中国国际广播电台《见证友谊》老挝文版首发仪式等系列活动在南宁举行。

老挝副总理宋沙瓦·凌沙瓦，老挝工贸部部长南·维亚吉，老挝计划投资部副部长通米·蓬维塞，老挝工贸部副部长肯玛妮·奔舍那，老挝公共工程与运输部副部长拉塔那玛尼·宽尼翁，老挝驻华大使宋迪·本库，老挝国家旅游局副局长苏卡申·普提山，广西壮族自治区党委常委、统战部部长黄道伟出席系列活动。

2011年10月21日，“北部湾之声”节目落地老挝万象启动仪式在广西南宁举行

Launching Ceremony of “Voice of Beibu Gulf” in Vientiane, Laos held in Nanning, Guangxi, China on October 21, 2011

“北部湾之声”节目落地老挝万象启动仪式上，老挝副总理宋沙瓦·凌沙瓦，广西壮族自治区党委常委、统战部部长黄道伟分别致辞。

宋沙瓦·凌沙瓦在致辞中说，老中两国是山水相连的友好邻邦，在泛北部湾和大湄公河次区域的合作中，广西发挥了重要的作用。2011年是老中建交50周年，在中国—东盟建立对话伙伴关系20周年、中国—东盟自由贸易区全面建成1周年、第八届中国—东盟博览会在南宁举行之际，广西人民广播电台为庆祝老中建交而举办的“传播真情，见证友谊”系列活动非常有意义。

黄道伟在致辞中说，中老两国友谊源远流长。中国—东盟博览会永久落户南宁，广西作为中国对东盟开放合作的“桥头堡”，在与东盟国家的交流合作上具有明显的区位优势。广西与老挝在大湄公河次区域合作、泛北部湾经济合作等多区域合作广泛，双方合作的基础深厚、互补性强、前景广阔。近年来，广西与老挝的友好交往日益频繁、日渐深化。双方高层实现定期互访，在教育领域的合作发展迅速，在农业领域的合作不断深入，在经贸合作方面非常成功。“北部湾之声”节目落地老挝万象等系列活动有利于促进广西和老挝之间增进了解、加强往来、深化交流，有利于“北部湾之声”更好地发挥中老合作的桥梁作用。

仪式上，中老两国留学生共同为大家献上一组中老两国歌舞。青山常在，绿水长流，中老友谊共长存；壮乡绣球，随歌起舞，各方宾客同欢乐。优雅的歌声传递着美好的祝福，吉祥的绣球寄托着永恒的友谊！

随后，宋沙瓦·凌沙瓦和黄道伟走上主席台，共同推动 “北部湾之声节目落地老挝万象”手柄，大屏幕上出现如水漾声波，向远方传递。接着老挝工贸部副部长肯玛妮·奔舍那和广西壮族自治区广播电影电视局局长彭钢共同推动调音台播出键，现场响起动听的老挝音乐，老挝音乐正式在“北部湾之声”节目中播出。在悠扬动听的音乐声中，宋沙瓦·凌沙瓦和黄道伟走到台前，为中国国际广播电台《见证友谊》一书揭幕并开启此书的首页。老挝国家主席朱马里·赛雅贡特意为此书题词，老挝新闻文化旅游部长宝散坎·冯达拉也为此书作序。

随后，出席仪式的领导和嘉宾还参观了“北部湾之声”直播室。

“北部湾之声”节目落地老挝万象、老挝音乐广西展播周的启动以及《见证友谊》老挝文版首发仪式这三场活动，见证了中老两国人民的友谊，凝聚了中老两国领导和人民的心血，为两国的经济文化交流作出了贡献，为加深中老两国人民的友谊发挥了桥梁和纽带的作用。

四 第八届中国—东盟高尔夫国际名人邀请赛、第八届中国—东盟博览会高尔夫国际精英邀请赛及"网球之友"联谊活动

2011年10月19日，第八届中国—东盟高尔夫国际名人邀请赛在南宁青秀山国际高尔夫俱乐部举行。

老挝工贸部部长南·维亚吉、老挝投资计划部副部长通米·蓬维赛、老挝工贸部副部长肯玛妮·奔舍那、老挝公共工程与运输部副部长拉塔那玛尼·宽尼翁、老挝国家旅游局副局长苏卡申·普提山等参加本次邀请赛。开杆仪式由中国—东盟博览会秘书处副秘书长、广西国际博览事务局副局长李文杰主持。

中国—东盟高尔夫国际名人邀请赛至今成功举办八届，共有柬埔寨首相洪森、老挝国家副主席本扬、缅甸总统吴登盛、菲律宾众议长诺格拉雷斯等

第八届中国—东盟高尔夫国际名人邀请赛
The 8th China-ASEAN Golf Masters' Invitational

20多名中国和东盟的国家政要参与赛事。中国—东盟高尔夫国际名人邀请赛已成为每届博览会期间的重要接待活动，成为友谊的纽带，交流的桥梁。

2011年10月23日，第八届中国—东盟博览会高尔夫国际精英邀请赛在南宁青秀山国际高尔夫俱乐部正式开赛。中国—东盟中心秘书长马明强出席开赛仪式。中国—东盟博览会秘书处副秘书长、广西国际博览局副局长李文杰，广西投资集团副总裁李少民，中国银行股份有限公司广西壮族自治区分行副行长陈秋高，中国—东盟博览会合作伙伴代表以及部分业余、半职业高尔夫球选手等80人参加此次邀请赛。

2011年10月22日下午，第八届中国—东盟博览会“网球之友”联谊活动在广西体育局江南训练基地新网球馆举行开球仪式。本届博览会“网球之友”联谊活动由广西体育局、广西国际博览事务局共同举办。广西壮族自治区人大常委会副主任文明出席开球仪式并宣布开球，中国—东盟博览会秘书处副秘书长、广西国际博览局副局长李文杰在仪式上致辞。

每届博览会期间举办的“网球之友”健身联谊活动，以球为媒，以球会友，为各国参展参会人员提供了良好的健身、休闲、会友方式和场所，成为博览会期间的重要体育交流活动。

五　第五届中国—东盟青年艺术品创作大赛获奖作品暨五周年成果展

2011年10月22—29日，第五届中国—东盟青年艺术品创作大赛获奖作品暨五周年成果展在广西壮族自治区博物馆隆重举行，并于10月22日上午举行了开展仪式。广西壮族自治区政协副主席蒋培兰出席开展仪式并讲话，广西壮族自治区高级人民法院院长罗殿龙，自治区人民检察院检察长张少康，自治区文化厅厅长余益中，自治区工业和信息化委员会党组书记唐成良，中国—东盟青年艺术品创作大赛组委会主任、共青团广西区委书记李泽，柬埔寨旅游部旅游工业司副司长孙光文，缅甸巩发党克伦邦帕安区党委书记文泰等出席了开展仪式，东盟青年代表及中国青年艺术家、企业家代表、高校艺术专业学生共300多人参加了开展仪式，并参观了展馆。本次活动进一步扩大中国—东盟青年艺术品创作大赛的影响力，充分展示五年来大赛的成果。

自治区政协副主席蒋培兰在讲话中指出，青年创造文化，文化锻造青年，中国—东盟青年艺术品创作大赛作为中国—东盟博览会的一项重要文化

2011年10月22日，第五届中国—东盟青年艺术品创作大赛获奖作品暨五周年成果展开展仪式在广西南宁举行

The opening ceremony of the Fifth China-ASEAN Youth Artwork Creativity Contest Award-winning Works and Fifth Anniversary Achievement Exhibition held in Nanning, Guangxi, China on October 22, 2011

艺术活动项目，已经成功举办了五届，搭建了中国与东盟文化艺术交流的桥梁，有效地促进了中国与东盟各国之间民族文化的交融，对于进一步激发中国与东盟各国青年对人文艺术的创作热情，提高中国与东盟各国艺术家对人文艺术创作的关注，具有十分重要的意义。希望通过中国—东盟青年艺术品创作大赛，使青年文化艺术交流能够超越国度，成为中国与东盟各国相互联系、相互了解的桥梁，使青年文化艺术交流在促进中国与东盟各国青年交流与合作、推动南新经济通道建设中发挥更加重要的作用，为推进中国—东盟自由贸易区建设、推动中国与东盟各国经济社会发展作出新的贡献。

中国—东盟青年艺术品创作大赛组委会主任、共青团广西区委书记李泽表示，中国—东盟青年艺术品创作大赛已经成为中国与东盟文化艺术合作交流的一个品牌活动，为中国与东盟各国青年艺术家的交流与合作提供了良好的平台。今后，我们将继续举办中国—东盟青年艺术创作大赛，不断创新大赛内容和形式，以作品展现风貌，以艺术搭建桥梁，以文化促进友谊，为促进中国与东盟各国青年文化艺术的繁荣发展作出积极贡献，努力打造以南宁为中心的中国—东盟青年文化艺术交流基地。

第五届中国—东盟青年艺术品创作大赛由共青团广西区委、广西国际博览事务局、广西壮族自治区文化厅、广西青年联合会共同主办，以“辉煌五年，艺术与我”为主题，大赛以人物油画为主要形式，共收到来自中国、越南、新加坡、菲律宾、泰国、马来西亚、印尼、文莱、老挝等国家和地区的1351件油画参赛作品。经过中国与东盟知名艺术大师组成的大赛评审委员会评审，从400多件入围决赛作品中，评出油画优秀作品20幅，入选作品70幅。这些参赛作品主题鲜明、构思新颖、寓意深刻、积极向上，具有较高的质量和艺术水准，代表了中国和东盟青年油画创作水平，体现了中国与东盟各国青年艺术创作的文化内涵和时代精神，展示了中国—东盟青年艺术整体实力和形象。

第五届中国—东盟青年艺术品创作大赛获奖作品暨五周年成果展主要展出了五届大赛来自中国、东盟各国的获奖艺术作品以及齐白石、张大千、阳太阳等中国大师级名家的艺术作品共150多件。这些作品集中展现了中国与东盟各国文化艺术创作与交流的精华，充分展现中国与东盟各国政治、经济、文化、社会蓬勃发展和欣欣向荣的风貌。展览期间，共有中外青年12000多人次前来参观成果展。同时，依托本次大赛还举办了中国—东盟艺术品竞拍会暨青年就业创业教育基金义拍活动，共拍卖齐白石、张大千、黄格胜、郑军里等艺术大师艺术精品及大赛获奖作品70多件，成交价达1200多万元。

小结　文化奇葩　相互交融　璀璨绽放

中国与东盟山水相连、文化相近。双方建立对话关系20周年来，不仅政治互信不断增强，经贸合作不断深入，而且文化交流不断丰富。中国—东盟博览会是中国与东盟各国文化交流的舞台。第八届中国—东盟博览会举办的文化交流活动，紧扣中国—东盟建立对话关系20周年，展示了中国和东盟各国的特色文化，各国文化在博览会相互交融、璀璨绽放。 本届中国—东盟博览会文化交流活动具有以下特点：

一是规格高。中国和东盟各国高度重视博览会期间的文化交流活动。各国政要和商界人士亲自出席多场交流活动。东盟各国代表团，中央和国家机关有关部门领导，各省（区、市）代表团出席了南宁国际民歌艺术节暨第八届中国—东盟博览会开幕晚会。老挝副总理宋沙瓦·凌沙瓦率老挝贸工部、投资计划部、公共工程与运输部、国家旅游局多位部长级官员及老挝驻华大使出席了中国老挝建交50周年“北部湾之声”节目落地老挝万象活动。第八届中国—东盟高尔夫国际名人邀请赛有5位部长级贵宾参赛。

二是区域文化特色鲜明。本届博览会系列文化交流活动展示了中国和东盟各国独特的文化。南宁国际民歌艺术节暨第八届中国—东盟博览会开幕晚会展示了中国—东盟以水相连、广西壮乡以水为家以及南宁打造“中国水城”的丰富内涵，全面展示广西风情、民族特色，展示东盟情怀、国际潮流。中国老挝建交50周年“北部湾之声”节目落地老挝万象启动仪式突出“传播真情，见证友谊”， 同时举办老挝音乐广西展播周开幕式和中国国际广播电台《见证友谊》老挝文版首发仪式。仪式上，中老两国留学生共同献上中老两国歌舞，传递着美好的祝福和友谊。第五届中国—东盟青年艺术品创作大赛获奖作品暨五周年成果展展示了具有区域特色的油画作品，体现了中国与东盟各国青年艺术创作的文化内涵和时代精神。

三是增进了中国与东盟各国之间的相互了解和友谊。第八届中国—东盟博览会文化交流活动吸引了双方政府层面及民间层面的广泛参与，丰富了博览会的内容，增进了相互了解和文化交流。南宁国际民歌艺术节暨第八届博览会开幕晚会吸引了数万名观众参加，外国艺术家专场演出和遍及南宁各城区（县）的绿城歌台，使广大民众欣赏到更多的东盟和其他国家的民歌艺术。中国老挝建交50周年“北部湾之声”节目落地老挝万象系列活动，以广播为媒介，以电波传友谊，使中老友谊迈上新台阶。高尔夫和网球比赛以球为友，增进了中国和东盟的友谊。艺术品创作大赛成果展通过油画创作和展览，使广大观众对中国与东盟各国政治、经济、文化、社会蓬勃发展和欣欣向荣的风貌有了更多的了解。

四是以文化交流促进了全面合作。第八届中国—东盟博览会的文化交流活动，除了上述活动外，还包括本书第五章和第六章提及的6个社会人文领域的会议论坛和交流活动和中国—东盟建立对话关系20周年系列纪念活动，这些丰富多彩的文化交流活动，与经贸促进活动结合在一起，形成了把经贸和人文结合在一起的复合型合作模式，推动了全方位、多层次、宽领域合作，促进了中国与东盟全面稳定持久的友好关系向前发展。

第八章

8 全心服务 安全便利
——第八届中国—东盟博览会服务支撑体系

中国—东盟博览会是非同一般的国际交流合作平台。

它规格非同一般，既有各国领导人、部长级贵宾、各国政府官员出席，又有企业家、专家学者和社会各界人士参会。

它内容非同一般，既有经贸活动，又有政要之间会见、政要与企业家的对话交流以及多领域交流活动。

它作用非同一般，务实推进中国—东盟友好合作和中国—东盟自由贸易区建设和发展。

每届中国—东盟博览会期间，高层聚首、商贾云集、媒体聚焦。开幕式、政要巡馆、政要会见、政商对话、各国推介会、商品展示、投资洽谈、签约仪式等一系列交流活动密集进行。要实现整个展会的圆满、安全、顺畅，统筹协调及各项服务保障是关键。

第八届中国—东盟博览会各项服务体系更加完善。统筹协调指挥效率和应变能力进一步提高；基础设施建设更加完善；展览现场管理更加专业；人员和展品通关和检验检疫更加便利；宾客接待服务更加贴心；证件申领制作和发放更加快捷；直航包机和交通服务更加周到；食品卫生、医生服务和志愿者等各项服务保障能力进一步增强；新闻宣传更有声势，安全保卫更加周密。

各方共同努力，密切协作，实现了第八届中国—东盟博览会圆满、热烈、安全、精彩、务实的预期目标。

Considerate, Safe and Convenient Services

— Supporting Services of the 8th CAEXPO

CAEXPO has proved itself as an extraordinary platform for international exchanges and cooperation.

Extraordinary participants: heads of state/government, ministers, government officials, entrepreneurs, experts, scholars and people from all walks of life.

Extraordinary contents: economic & trade programs, meetings of political leaders, dialogues and exchanges between political and business leaders, plus with exchange programs in other fields.

Extraordinary effects: pragmatically push forward China-ASEAN friendly cooperation and the construction and development of CAFTA.

Each CAEXPO is a grand gathering of political leaders, business professionals and media friends. A batch of programs and events are staged during the fair period, including the opening ceremony, pavilion tours of political leaders, meetings of heads of state/government, political- business dialogues, promotion conferences of the ASEAN countries, exhibitions, project talks and signing ceremonies, etc. To ensure the smooth running of all these programs, efficient coordination and supporting services really matter.

The 8th CAEXPO has perfected its supporting system, including more efficient coordination & commanding center, better infrastructure facilities, more professional on-site management in the exhibition halls, streamlined entry procedure customs clearance, and inspection & quarantine procedure for exhibitors and goods, better reception services for participants, more efficient pass issuing procedures, more convenient direct chartered flights and local transportation, and more professional food safety, medical and volunteer services, stronger promotion campaign and more effective security work, etc.

Thanks to the joint efforts and close work of all parties concerned, the 8th CAEXPO has been concluded successfully as a secure, wonderful and pragmatic grand trade event.

CHAPTER EIGHT

一 统筹协调

第八届中国—东盟博览会、中国—东盟商务与投资峰会在中国—东盟建立对话关系20周年、中国—东盟友好交流年和中国—东盟自贸区建成1周年的背景下举办，统筹协调工作面临更高要求。国务院办公厅、商务部、外交部、中国贸促会等有关部委对统筹协调工作高度重视，加强领导，派出工作组赴广西南宁指导工作。中国—东盟博览会、中国—东盟商务与投资峰会广西指挥中心（以下简称“两会”指挥中心）精心部署，各部门团结协作，高质量、高标准地完成领导人邀请、活动安排、任务统筹等各项工作，确保了展会有序、顺畅、圆满。

（一）精心统筹部署，创新工作模式

第八届中国—东盟博览会、中国—东盟商务与投资峰会的统筹协调工作在总结历年工作经验基础上，创新工作模式，活动安排更有针对性。“两会”指挥中心根据本届各阶段活动统筹的不同要点，将活动总表进行动态调整，便于指挥中心各部门按各场活动的时间、地点、出席人员等要素统筹工作安排，确保活动安排更加精确、细致。据不完全统计，第八届中国—东盟博览会、中国—东盟商务与投资峰会活动总表共修改32版66次。与此同时，提前做好应对各种情况的活动安排方案预案。整个活动统筹工作强度大，协调面广，工作效率高，统筹协调工作应对得法，处置得当，应急反应快，起到了“神经中枢”的作用。

（二）加强任务统筹，推进工作落实

“两会”指挥中心共收集、整理各工作部和执行小组的工作方案和应急预案253份，特别加强了向基础保障单位督收应急工作预案，督促各部门抓紧落实人员和任务，有效推进了各项筹备工作的落实。会期前后共组织17场工作协调会、1次综合演练和1次现场检查，集中、高效地研究解决各部门间

需协调事项，在综合演练及现场检查中及时发现问题并立即整改，有效应对了活动安排的临时调整，提高了指挥中心的工作效率和应变能力。

（三）健全贵宾信息统筹工作机制，贵宾信息管理更科学

"两会"指挥中心进一步健全贵宾信息统筹工作机制，完善贵宾信息管理系统，提高贵宾信息统筹工作效率，为领导会见、欢迎宴会、博览会开幕式等重大活动安排以及贵宾接待、住房安排、证件办理等方面工作提供了更加周到、全面、准确的信息服务。

（四）文秘工作运转更加成熟，联合值班职责明晰

第八届"两会"指挥中心集中办公时间短、文件会议密集，期间共办理文件2280份，流转文件13680份次，印发公文14554份，准备会议88场，最高峰时每天7场。文秘工作在人员配备、工作方法、工作流程等方面已运转成熟，业务过硬、反应迅速，实现文件收到即办即送，流转实时记录，去向清晰；文件印发基本实现当日签发当日印送，失误率低；会期各类会议情况复杂多变，会议通知延续各部门联络员机制，得到指令即以短信和电话形式发通知，快速、不误事，会议纪要做到当日会议最迟第二日出纪要，确保及时、准确；机要保密严格按规定要求执行；《工作手册》、《贵宾手册》不断完善，工作效率进一步提高。

此外，联合值班室保障了会期的上传下达随时畅通；改进会期集体参观模式，改善了会场秩序。会期间通讯保障、人力资源调配等工作比上届进一步提高。

展馆现场咨询服务
Information Services

第八届中国一东盟博览会、中国一东盟商务与投资峰会广西指挥中心

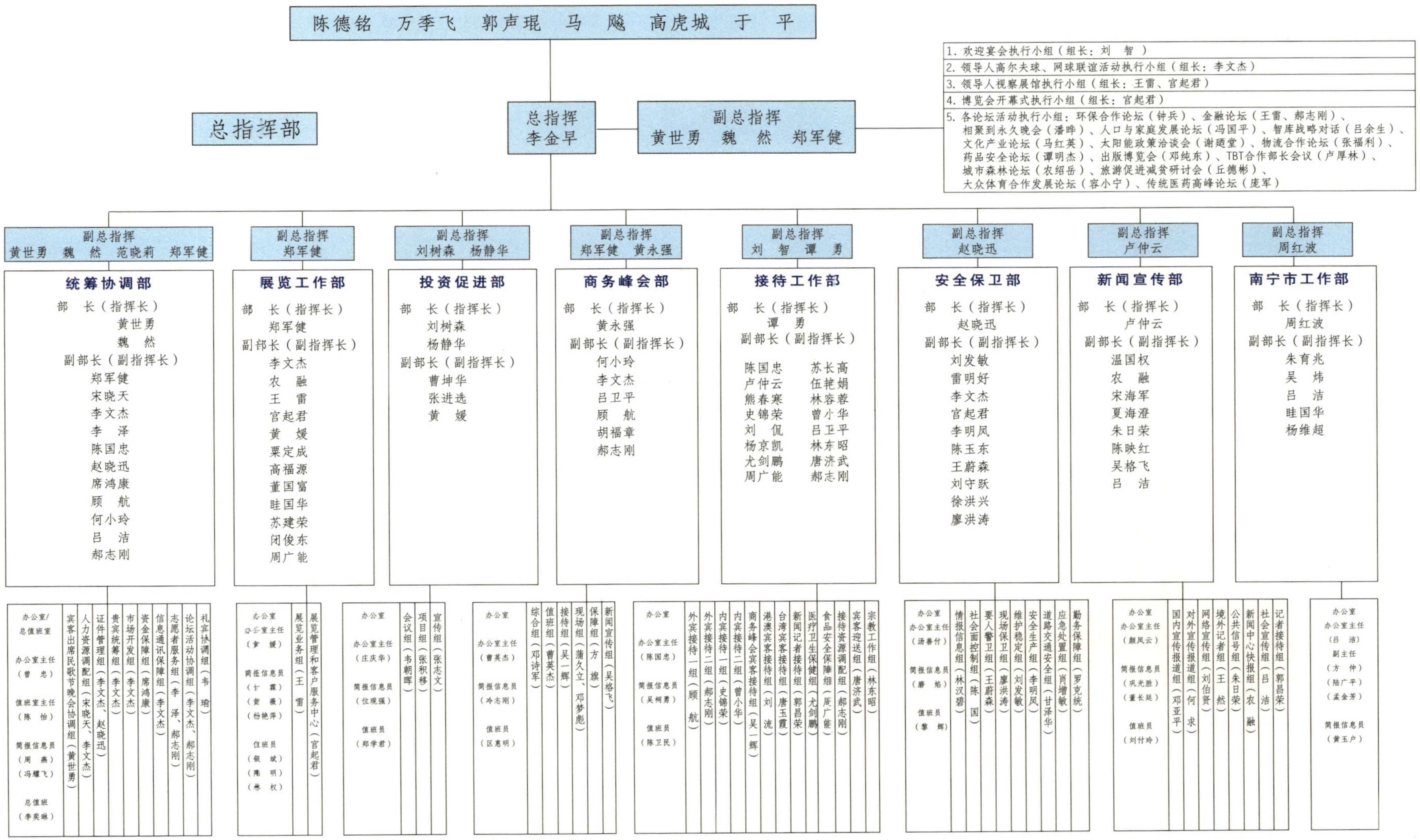

二 基础设施

2011年，为加快构建区域性国际城市，提升绿城南宁的城市形象，更好地为第八届中国—东盟博览会的顺利举行做好服务，南宁市不断加大城建投入，大力推进道路桥梁、宾馆设施、生态环境等基础设施建设，进一步完善城市功能，为博览会营造了环境优美、交通便利、设施完备的举办环境。2011年，南宁市全社会固定资产投资达到2003.68亿元，首次突破2000亿元大关，跃上新的台阶，实现历史性跨越。其中城建计划项目完成投资250.04亿元；百个重点项目建设项目完成投资250.13亿元，同比增长18.49%；统筹推进自治区层面建设项目72个，完成投资207.6亿元，同比增长36.76%，完成年度计划的107.27%。

（一）交通基础设施

南宁机场扩建工程项目进入实质性施工建设阶段；轨道交通1号线工程全线开工；五象新区路网框架基本拉开，初步形成“三横三纵”的路网格局，广西体育中心二期项目全面推进、进展顺利，金融街、文化街、民族风情街、五象大桥等一批五象新区开发建设重大项目开工建设；南湖隧道、五象大道西延长线、青山路南湖连接线项目建成通车；南宁至武鸣城市大道项目建设进入收尾阶段。

（二）水城建设

完善中国—东盟博览会周边水系建设，南湖—竹排江—民歌湖景观基本完整展现，初步展示了民族感与现代感相互交融的南宁都市魅力，“一江两湖”水上旅游航线的开通，呈现了美丽怡人的水系景观，成为首府城市建设的新亮点。完成了《南宁“中国水城”建设规划（2010—2020）》、《南宁市城市内河水系整治控制规划（2010—2020）》、《南宁市城市污水专项规划（2010—2020）》的报批工作。相思湖、青秀湖公园初步建成开园，可心

民歌湖风光
Folk Songs Lake

江河道主体工程及桥梁工程顺利完成，城市景观和谐与美化进一步提升。水城建设全年完成建设投资34.04亿元，同比增长27.06%。

（三）生态环境建设

城市建成区新增绿地面积6573亩，绿地率、绿化覆盖率和人均公园绿地面积分别达到35.20%、40.5%和12.96平方米，基本建成开放青秀湖公园；基本完成相思湖、明月湖、邕江滨水公园二期绿化建设，城市园林绿化发展水平再上新台阶，充分展现了绿城南宁的魅力。

（四）城乡基础配套设施建设

加快推进五象新区“七大板块”、总部基地、“三馆三街”等设施建设，广西规划馆建成启用。加强中国—东盟国际商务区配套设施建设，商务区道路、园林绿化、人行道等基础设施不断完善；完成了各国联络部基地园区中心主体建筑广场建设，广场园林景观建设基本完成。建设完成6座人行过街设施；完成了30条小街小巷的改造。建成运营8个污水处理项目和4个生活垃圾处理项目。加强供水、污水及燃气管网建设，全年累计完成售水量28127万立方米，销售液化气89305吨，销售管道气5325.58万立方米，完成了中国—东盟博览会供水供气保障。

三　展览现场管理和配套服务

（一）展览现场服务

第八届中国—东盟博览会以“保安全、优品质、促便利”为重心，进一步建立健全现场管理和服务保障体系，逐步优化各项规范、标准，为展商、客商提供了全方位便捷、优质、高效、顺畅的一站式服务。

1. 展馆安保力度增加，现场管控范围扩大。继续采用大型活动现场安保工作机制，通过现场安全检查和“全球眼”网络视频监控，形成多重安全防护网，实现了展会现场“零刑事案件”。会展中心闭馆警戒线首次扩大至会展中心行政综合北楼以外。人员和展品进出馆通畅，闭馆后夜间加班秩序井然，展会安全和便捷度提高。

安保力度加强
Security

2. 执法力度增强，案件查处范围拓宽。联合执法组采取集中打击和分散治理相结合的方式，对乱摆乱卖、兜售假冒伪劣商品、侵犯知识产权等现象进行了综合整治，会同有关部门对不符合国家规定的展品进行了查处。

3. 展品运输通关便捷，监管到位。现场物流继续采用竞争机制，由中国外运广西分公司和广西区邮政速递物流有限公司作为物流代理商，共同负责展品运输与通关工作，降低了运输成本，博览会运输服务和口岸通关服务满意度均比上届有所提高。

4. 现场服务模式优化，服务质量不断提升。一是成功打造了“客服中心—服务团队—先锋岗”三位一体的客商服务模式，馆长作用得到充分发挥，“现场服务联络人”和“馆长信息公示”两个制度得到贯彻执行。客商对会展服务组织水平的满意度达到历届最高水平。二是对博览会垃圾进行了分类管理，对搭建展位的板材、铁架，参展商留下的纸箱、木制品等进行了循环使用，对塑料制品、生活垃圾等进行了无污染处理，绿色展览理念得到贯彻。三是确定了5家餐饮企业提供中式快餐、清真餐、方便面和咖啡饮品服务，每日供餐数量不少于1万份。其中，捷佳咖啡全天供应糕点和饮品。

（二）通关服务

1. 海关。南宁海关认真贯彻海关总署“把好国门、做好服务、防好风险、带好队伍”的总体要求，以“通关高效、监管到位、服务优质、形象良好”为原则，创新思路，优化监管，热情服务，圆满完成第八届中国—东盟博览会监管服务工作。期间，共监管展品398票，总重181. 7吨、货值134. 8万美元，比上届分别增长36. 4%、10%和31. 3%；监管进出境航班155架次、进出境人员1. 46万人次，给予马来西亚总理纳吉布、柬埔寨首相洪森等东盟国家领导人及随行人员通关礼遇416人次，得到社会各界好评，实现了服务博览会“年年有进步、届届有提高”的目标。

海关服务
Customs

主要做法如下：

一是加强组织推动，完善工作机制。围绕本届博览会特点，南宁海关制定和完善工作方案，进一步健全应急预案，科学统筹、周密部署各项工作：成立以关长为组长、分管关领导和职能部门负责人参与的监管服务博览会领导小组；各隶属海关相应成立“一把手”为组长的现场工作组，在南宁、桂林空港和凭祥、东兴等展会通关重点口岸设立现场监管组；关区内抽调一批业务骨干组成驻会监管组，并首次将驻会监管组细分为通关小组、监管小组和后勤服务小组，各负其责，相互配合。通过上述做法，形成总关、基层单位、展会现场“三位一体”的完备工作体系，为做细工作、做实服务奠定了坚实基础。

二是落实便利措施，实现快速通关。南宁海关突出监管和服务效能，对会展中心海关监管区实行科学、规范管理；对进境展览品实施一次性行政许可审批制度；对展品实行口岸转关、展出地集中验放的快速通关模式；在各口岸设置专用通道，实行24小时预约通关制度；实行驻南宁会展中心监管，展品免收保证金，对进境展览品实行清单式申报进境的监管制度；实行海关、检验检疫局“一站式”通关作业模式；实行展览品布展时查验制度；对留购展品实行展前具保、展后结算制；实行陆路边境口岸“直通车”式监管制度。南宁海关与深圳、广州、昆明等6个区外直属海关建立了展品监管联系配合机制和应急处置机制，快速办理展品通关手续，规范展品入库监管，加强展品入馆管理，强化展会巡馆，形成封闭管理链条，确保展品快速通关。

三是加强执法检查，严防违禁展品。展会期间，南宁海关加大侵犯知识产权展品的查处力度，加强濒危野生动植物保护，邀请自治区濒管办的专家到现场协助对濒危野生动植物进行监管；对大米等重点进境展品进行价格调研，强化进境展品税收征管；理顺职责分工，将日常巡馆中发现涉及违禁展品的情况进行通报，及时协调有关部门妥善处置，防止不符合国家规定的展品参展；充分利用查验设施和查验手段，提高查验效率，防止燕窝等敏感商品走私入境；主动走访自治区政府和博览会有关部门，密切与口岸联检部门协作沟通，建立信息共享、协作联动、便捷通关的合作机制，有效查发和解决监管服务博览会工作过程中的各类问题，创造良好顺畅的执法环境。

四是提升服务品质，创立品牌形象。南宁海关提前10天进驻展会现场，向参展商宣传海关政策法规，发放《通关指南》和《申报单》，开通通关咨询电话，为参展人员提供政策和业务咨询；根据各国进境展品情况的不同，及时调整监管通关方式，做到展品“即到、即验、即放”；建立专人、专岗的服务模式，对参展商实施“贴身式、跟进式”服务，及时处理展品通关过程中的疑难问题和紧急情况，实现海关执法零投诉、业务操作零差错、服务展商零距离、廉政建设零事故；结合“创先争优”活动，设立“微笑服务”窗口和党员先锋模范岗，展现了海关良好的精神面貌。

2. 检验检疫。广西出入境检验检疫局高度重视中国—东盟博览会服务工作，举全局之力，做好筹备工作，在为前七届博览会提供优质服务的基础上，制定和完善服务博览会总体实施方案、工作指南、各类管理办法和应急预案，积极探索国际会展入境货物、人员检验检疫监管模式改革，提升服务博览会工作的有效性，圆满完成了各项任务。

在工作中，广西出入境检验检疫局积极向广西壮族自治区党委、政府汇报并争取支持，加强与地方政府有关部门沟通联系、研讨服务措施，确保服务第八届中国—东盟博览会工作有效开展。2011年7月19日，广西壮族自治区党委常委、自治区副主席陈武听取广西出入境检验检疫局局长卢厚林的工作汇报，指示要细化检验检疫服务工作措施，在服务好博览会的同时，承办好中国—东盟TBT合作部长会议，为全面推动中国—东盟合作平台作出新的贡献；8月8日，自治区政府组织召开第八届中国—东盟博览会中方组委会议题研讨会，表示将积极协调有关部门解决工作遇到的问题；10月15日，自治区政府举行广西出入境检验检疫局、南宁海关、自治区质监局服务第八届中国—东盟博览会、商务与投资峰会工作汇报会。广西壮族自治区党委常委、自治区常务副主席李金早对广西出入境检验检疫局会展现场入境参展物的检验检疫和宾客出入境查验工作的做法给予充分肯定，希望检验检疫部门继续一如既往地支持服务好本届博览会的各项工作。

检验检疫
Inspection & Quarantine

广西出入境检验检疫局重点做好以下工作：

（1）加强组织领导，提升服务水平。一是组织编制了《广西出入境检验检疫局服务中国—东盟博览会工作手册》和工作实施方案，完善相关措施和应急预案，建立检验检疫服务国际会展工作的管理文件和体系文件，成立服务博览会工作领导小组。通过加强组织领导，完善工作机构，确保各项工作环环紧扣、井井有条，提升检验检疫服务博览会的工作水平。

二是按照工作部署和要求，明确各部门职能，细化各部门工作职责、人员分工、工作进度，确保各项服务工作有序进行。如统筹协调部负责各现场各岗位人员协计、业务指导、技术保障、外联宣传、出入境参展物品和人员通检通关协调、各部门工作之间的业务协调；综合接待部负责与质检总局及广西政府各部门的联系，沟通工作；后勤保障部负责服务“两会”期间现场检验检疫工作用车的安排、有关会展现场办公和检验检疫设备设施的准备工作；广西出入境检验检疫局驻南宁国际会展中心现场办主要负责参展物的报检、检疫审批、备案及发证，对参展品进行抽样检验，对参展物及其包装材料、运输工具等进行检疫及消毒处理，对危险品及放射性物品进行检测及监控，对展馆内的境外参展物进行巡查，监督展后遗弃物的销毁处理；南宁机场办主要对出入境参会人员及其携带物进行检疫查验、对航空器进行检疫、对来自疫区的航空器进行卫生处理等。另外，凭祥、防城港、东兴、桂林、北海局等五个口岸局为第八届中国—东盟博览会指定的人员和货物出入境口岸，主要负责对出入境参会人员及其携带物进行检疫查验、对参展物的外包装进行初步查验及必要的检疫及消毒处理、对运输工具进行消毒处理等工作。

（2）创新监管举措，优化通关环境。2011年，第八届中国—东盟博览会的展品数量、品种比往年增多，参展货物和出入境人员通检的便利措施、把关服务备受各国参展商的关注，广西出入境检验检疫局结合服务历届中国—东盟博览会经验和广西各出入境口岸实际情况，采取多项便利措施，创新服务举措，助推博览会政治、经贸、文化的健康、和谐、可持续发展。

一是保持总局优惠政策的连续性。本届博览会上，国家质检总局继续向国家有关部门争取，一律免收参展物检验、检疫、除害处理和监管费用的政策；同时为部分进境参展动植物及其产品的检疫审批提供便利，审批周期由原规定的20个工作日，缩短为7个工作日以内。

二是在各主要出入境口岸开通参展物品和参会人员检验检疫专用通道，对入境参展物品实行“口岸查验，展出地集中检验检疫监管”的方式，提供提前预报检，实行优先检验检疫，优先出证，优先通关。

三是在南宁、凭祥、东兴、桂林、防城港和北海等主要出入境口岸应用电子检验检疫，提高参会人员和参展物的检验检疫通关速度。

四是开通广西检验检疫服务博览会专用网站，并与中国—东盟博览会官方网站、广西出入境检验检疫局门户网站链接。公布我国有关检验检疫政策、实用办事指南、重要信息等，并做成中英文双语版本，方便境内外客商及有关人士查询，为境内外参展商提供信息便利化服务。

（3）严格把关服务，确保展会安全。为做好2011年博览会各国入境参展商品的检验检疫工作，广西出入境检验检疫局按照“安全监管、便利通关”的要求，既做到严防疫情疫病和有害生物传入，又做到提前介入，全力为博览会保驾护航。

一是为进一步方便参展客商，强化对展会现场的质量安全监管，推出了现场报检、现场检测、现场监管、现场咨询的“一站式服务”。

二是实行24小时值班制度，随到随检，确保展品第一时间到达展会现场。

三是加强对食品等敏感商品的检验监管工作。广西出入境检验检疫局安排食品检验专家、经验丰富的检验员及时进驻会展中心开展检验工作，对食品微生物、添加剂、重金属等项目，确保能在48小时内得出检验结果。

据统计，截至2011年10月18日，广西出入境检验检疫局驻会展中心现场办共受理来自东盟10国、日本、韩国、中国台湾等国家和地区的展品报检共239批、总值46. 9万美元，涉及食品、化妆品、植物产品、机电设备、家具、陶瓷、日用品等1000多项展品。按有关规定对申报展品实施了检验检疫监管，对装载展品入境的20多个货柜实施了消毒处理；从100多批次参展植物及其产品涉及木制工艺品、木制家居用具、竹制品、大米、水果等500多项展品中检出有害生物16种、130多头（只），其中从进口大米中检出竹蠹、赤拟谷盗、食粮虱啮，从进口兰香子中检出野老鹳草、牛膝等杂草籽；从进口的白胡椒、木菠萝、柚子、海参、鱼鳔检出烟草甲、蚂蚁、壳虫、白带圆皮蠹……现场快速检测实验室和技术中心实验室共对68批次入境参展的食品、化妆品实施213项次的检测，检出不合格展品8个。对上述发现有害生物的货物已按有关规定妥善处理，对检验检疫合格参展物品准予放行参展。

3. 人员通关服务。2011年，广西公安边防总队以“最大限度地提供通关便利，最大限度地改善通关环境，最大限度地服务中国—东盟博览会”为目标，全面贯彻落实公安部《关于进一步提高边检服务水平工作的意见》精神，积极创新工作机制和方法，为博览会的成功举办营造了“安全、高效、便捷、顺畅”的外部环境。

（1）强化业务培训，打牢基础素质。广西公安边防总队以迎接中国—东盟博览会为切入点，围绕安全顺畅通关需要，不断强化检查员的业务培训。一是广泛开展边检业务岗位技能练兵竞赛活动，进一步提高检查员业务技能，积极营造比、学、赶、帮、超的良好氛围。二是根据东盟国家信仰宗教的特点，邀请专家开展东盟民俗礼仪和宗教信仰等方面的专题讲座，使检查员进一步熟悉掌握东盟10国的基本情况和风俗民情。三是设立东盟各国证照信息资料库，编印《出入境证件研究（中国—东盟博览会专刊）》，加强对东盟各国护照签证的研究，不断提高检查员证件鉴别能力。

（2）创新勤务模式，提高通关效率。广西总队围绕提高通关效率、查验手续办理等出入境人员最为关注的问题，创新工作机制，不断提高口岸通关效率。一是结合中国—东盟博览会期间专（包）机多、要客多、代表团规格高等实际，总结连续服务七届博览会的实践经验，建立完善重大专项勤务服务定式。二是针对当前警力紧张的实际困难，在分析口岸客流规律的基础上，选择试点单位，积极探索打破以科为单位整建制上下勤限制、缩小执勤单元的弹性化勤务组织模式，最大限度使用发挥警力资源效能，做到科学高效应对口岸边防检查任务。三是在全区海港口岸研究开发集快速通关、移动监管、流动办公和便民服务等功能为一体的“边检移动警务室”，实现“问题在一线解决、手续在一线办理、效率在一线体现”，最大限度地便利北部湾海港经济贸易往来，积极构建面向东盟的海上高效口岸。

（3）优化通关环境，展示边检形象。广西公安边防总队不断细化各个岗位和环节的通关服务工作，实现“安全通关零差错、顺畅通关零阻碍、快捷通关零等待、便利服务零距离”的“四零”工作目标。一是设立专职联络员，负责与主办和接待单位联系，提前掌握重要宾客入出境动态，随时准备应对通关中出现的各种问题。二是认真分析研究与会嘉宾的通关需求，在旅检口岸推出“温馨、VIP、救助、专勤、延时、预检”等六种服务，建立“移动、便利、优先、临时”四种查验模式，为与会嘉宾提供方便、舒适、安全的通关服务。三是开通 “24小时边检服务热线”，专门组成由英、越、泰语会话能力强的检查员成立现场服务小组，发放《边防检查通关服务指南》、“两会一节”通关指引等宣传册，为与会嘉宾提供咨询引导服务。

第八届中国—东盟博览会筹备和举办期间，广西公安边防总队圆满完成了与会柬埔寨首相洪森、副首相费南洪，缅甸副总统吴丁昂敏乌，马来西亚总理纳吉布，越南副总理阮春福，泰国副总理吉滴叻・纳拉农，老挝副总理宋沙瓦・凌沙瓦等东盟各国政要9个专机、67个包机、79个代表团、6000多名与会客商、3万多人次的入出境边防检查任务。

（三）接待服务

第八届中国—东盟博览会本着“重商、服务、透明、有序、实效”的服务理念，为广大参展参会宾客提供便捷、规范、安全、高效的接待服务。

一是优化宾馆资源配置，提高服务质量。南宁市可用于接待的宾馆总数已超过200家，基本满足博览会接待需求。在此基础上，“两会”指挥中心进一步规范“中国—东盟博览会指定接待宾馆”称号的使用，依据国家标准，并结合博览会具体情况，制定了相关接待标准和规范，启动指定接待宾馆评审工作，向荔园山庄、沃顿国际大酒店、明园新都酒店等15家酒店授予第八届中国—东盟博览会指定接待宾馆荣誉称号。博览会期间，优先让东盟团组客商选择下榻酒店，尤其是靠近会展中心的宾馆，满足各国客商的选择和要求；通过博览会官网的酒店信息平台、指定中国移动12580酒店预订咨询服务等多渠道为客商预订宾馆提供协助；继续出台和实施第八届博览会南宁市宾馆客房限价的临时干预措施，确保会期宾馆房价的稳定。

二是坚持和完善对口接待机制，提高服务水平。历年来，博览会对于宾客接待均采取对口接待制，即指定相关部门和机构对应接待博览会宾客。第八届博览会进一步完善对口接待机制。同时，为了逐步推进客商接待服务市场化，除中国国旅（广西）旅行社外，引入广西北部湾国际旅行社参与东盟国家客商团组接待工作。两家旅行社负责收集东盟各国客商参展参会信息，销售包机机票，为参展参会客商在南宁期间订房、订车、办理博览会证件、会后旅游安排等方面提供专业和优质服务。

三是提供“点对点”巴士及租车服务，为客商参加博览会各项活动提供便利。继续为乘坐包机的东盟客商开通机场至酒店的免费巴士服务，同时在东盟客商集中入住的宾馆设立至会展中心，以及博览会各主要展馆之间免费巴士服务。此外，“两会”指挥中心征调各种车辆，满足接待用车需求。

（四）证件服务

第八届中国—东盟博览会证件管理工作汲取往届成功经验，围绕实现“人到证到”的工作目标，提供优质服务，安全、便利、快捷、环保地完成工作任务，得到业内的各方好评。会期共制作发放人员证件117353张，发放车辆证件11901张。

本届博览会证件工作采取以下措施，取得良好成果：

1. 精心准备，实现“人到证到”。证件组在精心准备工作方案、细案、应急预案的同时，提前倒排时间，确定各项任务的关键时间控制点和责任人，全方位监控，保证证件申办、受理、发放工作有条不紊进行。会前预制证阶段所有资料合格并通过审核的人员证件全部制作完毕，发放到位；未能提前办证的境外客商在宾馆办证点顺畅办证，立等可取；现场办证，资料符合要求的客商，在受理后5分钟内均可领到证件，实现“人到证到”。

2. 加强制度管理，办证节奏平稳过渡。证件组按照ISO9000质量体系的要求优化工作流程，邀请中国移动的专家对工作人员以现场服务、接待礼仪为重点进行综合培训，在工作中贯彻“首问责任制”、“限时办结制”、“责任追究制”，提前通报办证要求和办证进度，实行预约发证及一对一的全程跟踪式服务，保证服务到位。

3. 技术保障，确保安全。网上办证系统进一步完善功能，通过技术设置，证件系统严格限制重复申办信息，并加以IP提示和追踪功能，从系统层面杜绝了证件信息多头报送、多头申办的情况，降低了“1个账号多人使用”导致证件管理员密码遗失的情况。同时，通过采取技术手段，设置证件系统黑名单数据，禁止其再次申办或领取证件，确保“两会”的安全。

同时按照安全保卫部门的要求，做到门禁不漏刷一张证件、一张门票，并专门安排巡逻小组对每个门禁口进行监督，确保门禁验证工作的顺利开展。根据博览会活动会议多、地点分散的特点，启用多种形式的门禁验证系统，确保“两会”各专场重要活动的顺利召开。

4. 服务人性化，确保重点。证件组专门成立贵宾小组，专人负责广西壮族自治区四家班子领导及参会贵宾证件，确保领导及参会贵宾能及时凭证参加活动。针对车证工作“车证少，需求大”的特点，车证小组与安保部门提前充分沟通联系，结合接待工作部及相关部门提供的接待和参会要求，提前部署，简化流程，抓住环节，采取定人、定车号的措施，确保满足重要领导

办证服务
Pass Center

和贵宾的参会用证需求。

5. 现场高效办证，服务质量提高。现场办证大厅通过区分业务方式设置合理的办证通道，更合理有效地提高了现场办证能力和办证速度，保证资料符合要求的客商在受理后5分钟内（平均）可拿到证件，并且完善现场办证咨询、查询、证件遗失补办等服务。为方便境外客商办证，在东盟各国客商集中的11家宾馆设立办证点，提供“一站式”办证服务。同时，根据部分境外客商及联络官的要求，将宾馆办证点服务时间延迟至深夜，得到境外客商的赞赏和肯定，受到广泛好评。

（五）直航包机

第八届中国—东盟博览会期间，继续开通南宁往返文莱斯里巴加湾、柬埔寨金边、印尼雅加达、老挝万象、马来西亚吉隆坡、缅甸仰光、菲律宾马尼拉、泰国曼谷、新加坡新加坡城、越南胡志明等东盟10国首都或主要城市20个班次的临时直航包机，共运送博览会参会参展商1763人次，平均上座率达62. 52%，与第七届博览会基本持平。

本届博览会包机工作采取以下措施，取得了良好成果：

1. 政府采购公开透明。第八届中国—东盟博览会包机采购工作，一方面严格按照政府采购规定，完成各项政府采购工作要求，并委托专业的招标公司公开招标，确保采购规范化、透明化；另一方面，又考虑到包机供应商体系较为脆弱的实际情况，优化采购模式，采取竞争性谈判的采购方式，既完成采购任务，又达到减低成本的预期目的。

2. 积极争取各方支持，确保包机顺利开通。一是联络各大航空公司，确保各公司积极应标，10条航线包机均有航空公司承运；二是要主动联系民航总局、广州军区空军司令部等空管部门，争取包机航线航权获得批复；三是保持信息通报渠道顺畅，及时向联络官、包机机票销售代理及各部门发布工作进展情况、解释涉及临时直航包机的专业性事项，获得各方面的理解和支持，避免因临时性变更需求导致的不必要成本支出。

3. 明确接待服务分工，保持销售渠道畅通。引入了广西北部湾国际旅行社，参与本届博览会东盟客商团组接待的相关工作，包括包机机票代理等。新的机票销售代理的加入有效地推进了市场运作，带动良性竞争，完善销售渠道，扩大了包机的影响力和辐射力。

4. 完善服务，保障乘客顺利成行。考虑到展品运输的特殊性，包机小组积极与航空公司协调，在安全许可的前提下，尽可能允许乘客按照飞机最大载重量托运行李。并按包机服务保障要求，统一印制发放通关标贴，配贴在护照及行李上，便于乘客行李辨认及快速通关。此外，为做好乘客抵达及登机的引导工作，派出多名地面服务员进入机场监管区提前准备，负责乘客的接待引导任务。

（六）食品安全

第八届中国—东盟博览会、中国—东盟商务与投资峰会举办期间，国家食品药品监管局对“两会”食品安全保障工作十分重视，全力支持并督促广西食品药品监管部门做好餐饮服务食品安全保障。承担食品安全保障任务的广西壮族自治区食品药品监管局，通过制定科学周密的工作方案、开展实施前风险评估及督导检查，组织力量实施，有力保障了食品安全，期间没有发生一起食品安全事故，确保了参会中外来宾及社会公众饮食安全万无一失，为“两会”的成功举办营造了安全、祥和、便利的环境。

食品安全保障
Food Security

1. 制订工作方案，明确责任目标。第八届“两会”重大活动多，出席的国家领导人级别高。“两会”指挥中心单独设置食品安全保障组，作为组长单位的自治区食品药品监管局积极协调有关部门共同开展食品安全保障工作，全力实施食品安全保障，确保参会的中外来宾饮食安全。2011年9月20日，印发《第八届中国—东盟博览会、商务与投资峰会食品安全保障总体方案》，对做好食品安全保障工作提出了工作要求和安排，明确了食品安全保障工作的目标。10月9日，组织召开全区食品药品监管系统食品安全保障工作视频会议，对“两会”期间食品安全保障工作进行动员部署，要求“点线面”相结合，全面实施食品安全保障工作。

2. 加强培训教育，严格监督检查。为确保“两会”的顺利进行，自治区食品药品监管局在全系统抽调了100多名专业人员和一批检验检测装备参与食品安全保障工作。2011年10月13日，举办了食品安全保障监督检验人员培训班，60多名食品安全保障监督员和检验人员参加了培训。重点讲解了如何预防食物中毒，原料采购、运输、储存、加工以及备餐上菜、餐具回收等各个环节的食品安全风险预防措施，重大活动期间应急事件的处置，宗教饮食习惯、禁忌、饮食礼仪。同时进行了食品快速检验项目的检验培训。

10月14—15日，自治区食品药品监管局派出3个督查组，分别对“两会”重点城市南宁市、桂林市、北海市食安办食品安全保障工作进行了督查。督查组对各市重点接待宾馆饭店等服务场所食品安全保障的落实情况、供应食品源头监管和突发食物中毒事件应急处置准备情况等方面的工作文件和相关资料进行了查阅，对重点接待宾馆饭店及部分旅游景区餐馆、食品超市共15个单位进行了现场检查，重点检查食品进货查验记录及索票索证管理、蔬菜水果农药残留监测、食品从业人员培训及健康证明等。

10月12—19日，自治区、南宁市两级食品药品监管部门组织人员，对接待单位的资格进行了风险评估，从食品加工场所、条件、设施和人员情况等方面严格审定，明确接待宾馆的职责，了解接待宾馆食品及原料的来源和供应方式，组织开展对接待宾馆进行全面的食品安全执法检查、巡查，督促其进一步完善餐饮服务食品安全保障的工作方案，督促接待宾馆制定并实施原料采购控制要求，确保所购原料符合食品安全标准。对不能满足接待任务要求的或不能确保食品安全的，提出减少其供应量或者取消其接待（供应）资格的意见。

3. 突出保障重点，防范安全事故。在食品安全保障工作中，自治区食品药品监管局坚持突出抓好重点城市、重点品种、重点区域、重点环节等保障重点，强化工作措施，扎实开展食品安全保障工作，防范食品安全事故的发生。

10月10日，组织突发食品安全事件应急处置演练，此次演练模拟突发细菌性食物中毒事件后，食品安全保障组启动重大食品安全事件应急预案，按照事件发生、指挥协调、事件处置、响应结束、后期处置等过程而进行的演习演练。通过演练，目的是规范食品安全事故处置流程，提高食品安全事故应急处置能力和应急队伍实战水平，确保“两会”期间中外来宾及公众食品安全。

10月16—26日，组织食品安全监管员、卫生专业人员、农残检测员进驻重要接待宾馆饭店，执行保障任务。主要加强原料使用前检测，对进入重点接待宾馆饭店的蔬菜、水果实行对每个品种、每批次全部进行农药残留快速检测；加强对菜单及加工、供应方式等进行审查，对加工现场进行全程监督，确保食品、原料的质量，预防污染、变质。

“两会”期间，累计为25870人次实施食品安全保障，对食品及餐具开展了11种检验项目、2360个批次的检验，保障供应中国—东盟博览会主会场快餐24743份，就地销毁1886份超过保质期限的快餐。整个会议期间，无食物中毒事件发生，食品安全保障任务圆满完成。

（七）医疗卫生

按照第八届中国—东盟博览会、中国—东盟商务与投资峰会指挥中心的要求，自治区卫生厅承担了“两会”的医疗卫生保健工作。2011年8月“两会”医疗卫生保健工作领导小组成立，由广西卫生厅副厅长、“两会”接待工作部副部长尤剑鹏任组长并成立了综合办公室，下设医疗保健组、卫生监督组、医疗救治组、疾病控制组、后勤保障组与维护稳定组等6个工作组。按照《2011年第八届中国—东盟博览会和中国—东盟商务与投资峰会医疗卫生保健工作实施方案》，通过广大医疗卫生人员不懈的努力，圆满完成了“两会”期间与会领导、嘉宾及广大群众的健康，确保生活饮用水安全和公共场所安全与医疗保健工作。

在工作规范和要求方面，领导小组先后下发了《关于印发2011年国庆及东盟“两会”期间突发公共卫生事件应急预案的通知》、《2011年中国—东盟博览会重点接待场所消杀工作实施方案》、《应对化学恐怖袭击事件应急工作预案》、《广西壮族自治区处置生物恐怖袭击事件应急预案》、《南宁市卫生局服务2011年“两会一节”医疗卫生保障方案》等方案和通知，保证了医疗卫生保健工作的规范、高效与科学。

在人员培训和演练方面，通过培训及考核，受训人员初步掌握了突发公共卫生事件应对的基础知识及基本技能，提高了服务人群应对突发公共卫生事件的整体水平。在西园饭店，急救医疗专家对“两会”期间参与重点接待宾馆共223名服务员进行了徒手心肺复苏培训，对直接参与“两会”医疗保健工作的7家区直保健基地的95名医务人员和救护车司机进行培训并模拟考核。对服务医疗单位负责人、医务人员、部分服务行业人员及“两会一节”青年志愿者共8500多人进行了11个相关专题的业务培训班，累计培训专业人员400多人，服务行业人员6000多人。南宁市卫生局模拟“两会一节”可能发生的突发事件，组织医疗救护、卫生监督、疾病控制等专业技术人员开展了2011年南宁市重大事故应急演练、重大食品安全事故演练等。通过培训与演练，使各类工作人员熟练掌握各种急救应对措施，为顺利完成医疗保健工作提供了有力保障。

在完善医疗站点建设方面，经过3个月的筹备和建设，位于金象大道99号的南宁急救医疗中心大沙田急救站在第八届中国—东盟博览会开幕前夕正式投入使用。以广西体育中心医务室为医疗保障中心，通过在周边各活动场馆内分置8个医疗保障点，在外围增派巡逻救护组等方式，打造了“两会一节”医疗卫生应急救援圈。

在落实医疗保障措施方面，“两会”期间医疗卫生保健组共派出驻点医疗保健组14组、大型活动医疗组6组。累计派出139个现场应急医疗保障组、331名医护人员和128辆（次）救护车。各类现场累计应急处置上呼吸道感染、胃肠疾病、软组织挫伤、中暑和外伤等各种伤病演员、嘉宾、工作人员和群众1800多人次，全面展示了广西医疗卫生的形象和作风。

在卫生监管工作方面，通过对荔园山庄、西园饭店、明园新都酒店、南宁饭店、凤凰宾馆、锦华大酒店等6家重点接待宾馆现场调查了解其环境卫生，监测“四害”密度，确定消杀对象及其范围，并对以上6家宾馆开展消杀灭的效果评估等工作。同时，疾控专业人员还对主要16家各类公共场所内的环境空气质量、公共用品、集中空调通风系统、二次供水水质和游泳池水质等进行监测。南宁市卫生局也对市管重点接待宾馆、饭店的环境、饮用水、高危食品及餐具进行采样监测，做好公共场所卫生监管等方面的保障。据不完全统计，在公共场所卫生监管等方面，根据《公共场所卫生管理条例》、公共场所有关卫生标准要求，广西卫生厅派出疾病预防控制专业技术人员，对重点宾馆的会场、元首楼等外内环境、会议室、厨房、餐厅、职工食堂、员工宿舍、地下室、走道、公共区域、花园绿地、下水道、垃圾场所等近11万平方米面积进行消杀，所有相应指标均符合中国—东盟博览会接待要求。“两会”期间，各重点宾馆和大型活动场所均未报告传染病疫情，全区未出现重大突发公共卫生事件，医疗卫生保健工作得到各方的肯定和好评。

（八）志愿者服务

第八届中国—东盟博览会、中国—东盟商务与投资峰会共招募1340名志愿者，服务于礼仪接待、文秘翻译、咨询接待、会场布置、现场办证、后勤保障、应急支援等120余个岗位。共青团广西区委、共青团南宁市委还以“爱心满绿城，志愿促和谐”为主题，组织了近1200人次的城市志愿者，主要开展活动介绍、交通指路、应急医疗处理、市民文明宣传、免费为群众提供饮用水等特色服务活动。在城市主要街道设立服务站点，发放宣传材料、志愿者徽章等共计万余份，服务市民近29010人次。

本届志愿者服务工作呈现以下亮点：

1. 首次根据志愿者的工作性质、内容、地点加以分类。为更好完成对志愿者的人力资源整合，2011年将志愿者分为以下三类：一是馆内（“会展中心”、“广西展览馆”、“南宁华南城”）专业志愿者，主要服务于在语言能力、计算机水平、财务知识、统计学原理等方面有较高要求的岗位。二是服务保障志愿者，即无特定专业技术要求，提供服务保障类工作的岗位。三是机动志愿者，临时调配任务的岗位。服务工作时间、内容不定。

2. 首次为馆内志愿者进行前期单独培训。在本届“两会”志愿者服务工作中，首次对馆内专业志愿者进行业务知识培训及服务技术指导，旨在提升馆内专业志愿者服务工作专业水平，进一步优化服务技能、改善服务质量。首次培训让馆内专业志愿者对本届博览会背景、意义等概况有更为深入的认识；并对馆内各项工作（主要涉及招商招展、展览管理、对外联络、宣传推介等处室）有全面了解。在培训过程中将工作任务明确至个人，使之掌握所服务岗位一定的专业知识。

3. 首次颁布《中国—东盟博览会、中国—东盟商务与投资峰会志愿者管理办法（试行）》。该《办法》就志愿者选拔工作、权利与义务、行为与规范、组织与管理、奖惩及表彰等方面做出了明确规定，并细化用人单位（部门）的用人责任及义务，加大对志愿者合理有效的保护力度，成为今后“两会”志愿者及志愿者管理人员工作的行为准则。

4. 首次推出“两会”志愿者卡通形象。该形象设计上是一男一女两个卡通人物，分别身着黄白两色志愿者服装，他们向大家挥手致意，笑容可掬，神态可爱，充满活力。通过志愿者卡通形象的打造，加大宣传广西青年志愿者蓬勃向上、奋勇争先的精神风貌，提升广西青年自豪感，倡导广大青年朋

志愿者服务
Volunteers

友们投入志愿服务队伍中以及激发志愿者们对志愿服务工作的热情。

5. 加大对城市志愿者宣传力度。一是制作了志愿者形象宣传片，该片在“两会一节”期间在主要媒体和场合播放，以展示南宁青年志愿者形象，号召更多青年加入志愿者服务队伍；二是设计了志愿者服务主题口号“志愿南宁，心在、爱在、我们在”；三是推行志愿者在从事志愿服务时使用的志愿者心手礼；四是通过社会征集，以突出青春时尚特色为重点，制作了志愿服务纪念徽章。这些志愿者公益宣传活动通过志愿者文化宣传来带动志愿者服务体系的建设，进一步激发志愿者服务的潜能，更加高效、圆满地完成志愿者服务。向国内外嘉宾展示南宁市作为全国文明城市的开放、包容、文明、和谐新形象，向中外友人诠释“能帮就帮，敢做善成”的南宁精神。

四 新闻宣传

2011年10月21—26日，第八届中国—东盟博览会、第八届中国—东盟商务与投资峰会、2011南宁国际民歌艺术节（以下简称“两会一节”）在南宁隆重举行。广西壮族自治区领导高度重视“两会一节”新闻宣传工作，自治区党委书记、自治区人大常委会主任郭声琨，自治区主席马飚在会前就做好相关工作作了重要指示；自治区党委常委、自治区常务副主席、“两会”指挥中心总指挥李金早，自治区党委常委、宣传部部长沈北海对“两会”宣传工作作了重要指示，提出明确要求。新闻宣传工作按照领导的指示、指挥中心的部署，紧紧围绕“二十年合作拓展，自贸区成果显著，博览会常办常新”的主题，精心策划专题专栏宣传，积极统筹协调各重要活动的现场直播，扎实有序推进新闻宣传各项工作，使“两会一节”的宣传报道形成强大声势，取得显著效果。据不完全统计，截至2011年10月27日，境内外各媒体发稿14000多篇（条、幅），百度搜索涉及“两会一节”页面记录达380多万条，组织“两会”宣传专版专题16个。其中，中央新闻媒体发稿1500多篇，广西区直媒体及新闻网站发稿5400多篇，中央涉外媒体和港澳台媒体发稿550多篇（幅），国外媒体发稿500多篇（幅），网络媒体刊发原创稿件、视频、图片共计6730篇（个、幅）。

（一）宣传策划“早”字当先，牢牢把握工作主动权

2011年的“两会一节”新闻宣传工作策划早，启动早，各项工作跟进及时。2011年6月，新闻宣传部就根据自治区党委书记、自治区人大常委会主任郭声琨重要指示精神，及时制定下发了“两会一节”新闻宣传工作方案，对宣传工作进行部署安排。9月，根据自治区党委、政府领导的重要指示精神和“两会”指挥中心确定的主题，及时制定下发“两会一节”宣传报道重点选题方案，下发各媒体贯彻执行。9月底，新闻宣传部有关执行小组就主动与《人民日报》、新华社《瞭望》新闻周刊、《光明日报》、《经济日

报》、《中国日报》和香港《文汇报》、《大公报》、《商报》等中央及港澳媒体对接，围绕宣传专版的内容、版式等问题，充分交换意见，提出具体要求，确保万无一失，确保所有专版宣传如期见报及在开幕式当天送到嘉宾和读者手中，有效地扩大了“两会一节”的影响，提升了广西的形象。

（二）媒体邀请“广”字当先，强化媒体采访报道阵容

2011年，“两会一节”新闻宣传工作着力加大媒体的邀请力度，并通过广泛邀请、重点引导、强化联络以及全面把握东盟国家媒体资源等措施，切实做好媒体邀请工作，从而吸引大批中外记者云集广西参会报道。据统计，前来采访报道“两会一节”的中外媒体和记者共275家1738名，分别比上届增加38.19%和19.23%。其中，国外媒体77家记者138名，港澳台媒体17家记者56名，中央媒体和国内行业媒体91家记者378名，外省媒体15家记者23名，广西区内媒体58家记者1022名。参会记者中的外国媒体、中央涉外媒体和港澳台媒体、网络媒体记者所占比重较往届呈普遍增多的趋势。尤其是参会东盟媒体69家95人，比上届增长20%，在中国境内举行的同类活动中，参会东盟媒体和记者是最多的。

（三）宣传手段“新”字当先，彰显工作特色亮点

2011年的“两会一节”的新闻宣传注重手段创新，主要表现在：

一是中央媒体全媒体报道。《人民日报》、新华社、《光明日报》、《经济日报》、中央人民广播电台、中央电视台、中国国际广播电台、中国新闻社，都派出强大的报道团队参加2011年“两会一节”的宣传报道工作，并成为宣传报道的主力军。中央电视台、人民网等还采取现场直播、连线互动、专访专题等方式，进行电视和网络直播。新华社实现包括微博在内的全媒体报道，截至2011年10月27日，新华社共发文字、图片、音视频等传统稿件1016条，新华网广西频道、手机短信、微博等新兴媒体共发稿2795条，总体发稿量较2010年大幅上升；除重点抓好内参和英文新华视点等精品报道及网络直播、手机短信外，还首次利用新华微博、新浪微博、腾讯微博，对博览会和峰会进行重点报道，以及组织博览会和峰会等微博话题，播发微博稿件300余条，覆盖粉丝3万余个。

二是电视媒体现场直播多面呈现。中央电视台、香港凤凰卫视和广西电视台联手现场直播“两会”开幕式。其中，中央电视台的新闻频道、第四频道向全世界观众现场直播了“两会”开幕式的盛况，香港凤凰卫视直播“两会”开幕式的时间长约80分钟。广西电视台的“两会”报道开创了五个“第一次”：10月21日在“两会”开幕当天，第一次在卫星频道、国际频道、资

新闻媒体聚焦“两会”
Media Focus

讯频道并机直播10小时的《盛会进行时》特别报道，开创了广西电视台卫星频道连续直播时间的新纪录；第一次于同一天在四个不同场地进行大型政治外交活动现场直播；第一次在超大型活动中用3G新闻直播系统承接直播连线；第一次使用该台高清演播室进行高频次连线直播；第一次实现了境外电视台的演播室级别的直接合作。据不完全统计，截至10月26日，广西电视台各栏目共播出相关报道400多条，直播时间超过1000分钟。

三是网络媒体多种手段立体传播。各大网络媒体紧紧围绕盛会要闻、论坛动态、广西北部湾经济区建设、中国—东盟建立对话关系20周年、中国—东盟友好交流年、自贸区建成1周年、博览会举办8周年、经贸合作、文化交流、媒体聚焦、嘉宾观点、南宁国际民歌艺术节等网民关注的重点展开，综合运用文字、图片、直播、音视频、FLASH、幻灯、调查、访谈、论坛、博客、微博、手机报、电子杂志等十余种网络手段和形式，对“两会一节”的盛况展开全方位、立体式、全覆盖、多角度的报道。人民网、新华网、中国网、中国网络电视台、国际在线、中国广播网、中国新闻网、广西新闻网及新浪网、腾讯网、第一财经、中国—东盟博览会官方网站等网站对“两会一节”等重大活动进行了网络现场直播。人民网、新华网、中国网络电视台、中国经济网、中国网、国际在线、中国广播网、广西新闻网、南宁新闻网等网站制作了专题页面，人民网、新华网、搜狐网、新浪网、腾讯网等网站还推出微博直播，实时更新新闻和相关资讯，满足网民对“两会一节”的信息需求。广西手机报向高端手机用户推送“两会一节”、“微杂志”等。广西新闻网首次深度联合网络图文新闻、网络电视、报刊、广西手机报、官方微博、红豆社区等平台，利用各种不同媒介的功能优势，实施各种媒介的优化组合策略，采用视频、图片、文字、微博、帖文等形式，以及首次采用演播室播报、嘉宾访谈、前方记者报道、现场活动视频直播等方式，实现52小时对中国—东盟博览会进行全媒体直播；首次推出微观“两会一节”大型直播互动平台系列活动，在“两会一节”的报道上形成合力，取得良好的效果。

四是广播电台多频率多语种全方位宣传报道。广西人民广播电台通过6套频率、5个语种全方位宣传报道“两会一节”，并联合中央人民广播电台、中国国际广播电台现场直播“两会”4场重要活动。其中，中国国际广播电台与广西人民广播电台“北部湾之声”，采用越南语、泰国语、英语、粤语、华语等多种语言对“两会”开幕式进行现场直播；该台的北部湾之声开设了《中国—东盟联播》节目，联合越南、泰国、新加坡、柬埔寨、老挝、印尼等国家电台共同连线直播“两会一节”盛况，“两会”新闻、专题节目共计约200分钟。从10月1日到26日，广西电台各频率共发稿1750篇。

（四）宣传效果“佳”字当先，社会各界反响热烈

人民日报（包括海外版）：共刊发相关稿件及照片43篇（幅），较2010年增长16%。其中，于2011年10月22日在头版用近一半版面对第八届“两会”进行报道，并在头版头条刊发了广西分社记者采写的《开放壮乡踏歌来》。在10月21日出版的博览会特刊，刊发了自治区党委书记、自治区人大常委会主任郭声琨和自治区主席马飚联合署名文章《携手办盛会 共创新辉煌》、《二十年合作拓展　自贸区成果显著　博览会常办常新——写在第八届中国—东盟博览会开幕之际》等多篇重点稿件。

新华社：据不完全统计，从2011年10月15日开始，文字通稿、对外中英文、图片中英文、音视频、内参、社办报刊、信息等线路共发稿1211条，较2010年增长17%。其中，重点栏目稿件47条，部分稿件采用超百家；《新华每日电讯》、《经济参考报》、《瞭望》等社办报刊进行了连续重点报道；新华网进行了直播、专题、微博报道；手机媒体滚动发稿300余条；会场新闻中心专门设置了新华社CNC电视访谈室，对重点人物、热点话题进行现场访谈。

光明日报：积极参与“两会”报道，共刊发报道130多篇。2011年10月19日、20日，刊发关于中国—东盟博览会的专刊，整个博览会期间主要以深度报道为主。10月22日，在3版要闻版全文刊发了温家宝总理在中国—东盟博览会的主旨讲话。光明网则第一时间于首页位置推出该网站的传统专题——“中国—东盟博览会专题”，设置了《最新动态》、《图片报道》、

《成就展》等多个栏目，推出了120多篇关于中国—东盟博览会的报道。

经济日报：2011年10月21日，刊发了专版宣传稿《二十年合作拓展 自贸区成果显著 博览会常办常新》。10月22日，分别刊发温家宝总理参加博览会和峰会的消息，全文刊登温总理在峰会的讲话，并刊发了记者采写的开幕式侧记《共享硕果 共创未来》。10月25日至27日，集中刊发报道博览会和峰会的文字共6篇，并报道了博览会闭幕消息。此外，经济日报报业集团所属中国经济网刊发相关稿件共11篇。

中央人民广播电台：博览会期间发稿达80多篇。会前，对第八届中国—东盟博览会进行预热报道，采写《第八届中国—东盟博览会展览规模扩大，参展企业回头率高》等10余篇稿件。2011年10月21日，中国之声对第八届中国—东盟博览会开幕式进行现场直播，经济之声对第八届中国—东盟商务与投资峰会进行了现场直播，并配以著名时事评论员曹景行等人的精彩点评，总时长达2小时。期间，还采写了《永不落幕的中国—东盟博览会 悄然改变民众生活》等多篇高质量、视角独特、贴近百姓的稿件。

中央电视台：派出50人的报道团队参加本届博览会和峰会的宣传报道工作，中央电视台第一频道、第二频道、第四频道和第九频道的各新闻栏目共计发稿30篇，其中《新闻联播》发稿3篇，单篇播出《第八届中国—东盟博览会、中国—东盟商务与投资峰会在广西南宁隆重开幕》和《温家宝会见出席第八届中国—东盟博览会的东盟国家领导人》的消息，以及《中国—东盟博览会参展商超过往届》、《第八届中国—东盟博览会闭幕》等消息，社会反响良好；新闻频道、第四频道向全世界观众现场直播了第八届中国—东

媒体云集“两会”
Media at the CAEXPO & CABIS

盟博览会、第八届中国—东盟商务与投资峰会的开幕式；二套财经频道派出两组记者来广西报道，在《经济信息联播》等栏目发稿20篇；九套《英语新闻》也派记者宣传本届博览会，制作10篇新闻向全世界介绍“两会”盛况。

中国国际广播电台：派出10个语种的记者参加报道，播发稿件200多篇，并用泰语、越南语、英语对第八届中国—东盟博览会、第八届中国—东盟商务与投资峰会开幕式进行了现场直播。国际在线报道20多篇。

中国新闻社：累计发出对外文字和图片通稿100余篇（幅）。对外通稿被东盟各国、美国、澳大利亚以及港澳台地区的媒体广泛采用，采用率达到100%。其中，《“南宁渠道”推动中国—东盟自贸区建设》等重点稿件同时被多家外报头版头篇或内版头篇全文采用，在海外产生了重大影响。此外，还发挥外宣优势，通过相关渠道，与菲律宾、泰国、越南、印尼、柬埔寨、马来西亚等东盟国家的媒体合作，先后制作并提供了10个包括华文、英文、越文、泰文等语种的外报专版，全面报道第八届中国—东盟博览会和第八届中国—东盟商务与投资峰会的盛况。

中央涉外媒体港澳台媒体：据初步统计，截至10月26日，中央涉外媒体和港澳台媒体共发稿290篇、图片225幅，直播时长共计约350分钟。其中，《中国日报》发稿115篇（包括网站发稿）、图片62幅，还专设了“两会一节”专题网站；港澳媒体发稿68篇、图片130幅；台湾媒体共发稿50篇。香港凤凰卫视直播“两会”开幕式，约80分钟，中国国际广播电台（华语）连线直播约80分钟。中央涉外媒体和港澳媒体共组织宣传专版6个，其中《中国日报》连版、香港《文汇报》头版、《大公报》头版、《商报》1个专版、《澳门日报》1个专版，共2万多字30多幅图片。香港亚洲电视制作时长约25分钟的“两会一节”专题节目。这些报道内容丰富、图文并茂、信息量大，及时对“两会一节”进行全方位、立体式的宣传报道，取得很好的外宣效果。

国外媒体：国外媒体有77家138名记者参会报道。越南之声、胡志明之声、柬埔寨国家电台、泰国国家电台、新加坡新传媒广播等多家外国媒体对本届博览会进行了直播。据不完全统计，文莱《婆罗洲纪事报》、柬埔寨国家电视台、印尼安塔拉通讯社、老挝《人民报》、马来西亚《新海峡时报》、《缅甸时报》、菲律宾《星报》、泰国国家广播电台、新加坡亚洲新闻台、越南之声广播电台、朝日新闻等国内外媒体刊发有关新闻稿件500多篇。

行业媒体：第八届中国—东盟博览会国内行业媒体到会总数为60多家，共140多人，报道总篇数在400篇以上，比上届100篇增加将近3倍。

本届中国—东盟“两会”在中外媒体记者的高度关注下圆满落下帷幕。

中外与会记者积极参加了各类采访活动，宣传报道对象涵盖中国和东盟国家领导、商务代表、地方领导、专家学者、企业家、参展商、观众等不同人群。中外媒体分别通过平面媒体新闻宣传浓墨重彩、电视媒体现场直播丰富多彩、网络媒体多种手段立体传播、广播媒体多频率多语种全方位宣传报道等不同的方式，给广大受众提供了直观、迅疾、丰富的信息，宣传中国与东盟国家在建立对话关系20年来各方面的发展，宣传广西在中国—东盟自贸区建成后发展的优势、潜力和广西经济社会发展取得的成就，宣传广西对外开放的良好形象，进一步扩大了“两会一节”的影响力，取得良好的实际效果，在社会上引起强烈反响。

（五）媒体服务针对性强，宣传推介亮点多

第八届“两会”新闻信息实现快速共享，促进媒体报道。博览会开幕式、巡馆等重要活动结束后30分钟内，在新闻中心即提供文字和图片供媒体共享；其他活动在活动结束后两个小时内，在博览会网站提供文字、图片。当天的活动，当天晚上全部上传博览会网站共享。对马来西亚总理纳吉布与中国企业CEO圆桌对话会、泰国副总理吉滴叻与中泰企业家见面会进行了网络直播。图文收集迅速，“两会一节十四论坛”新闻收集及图文收集整理等工作迅速完成。

中国—东盟博览会秘书处与强势媒体建立战略合作关系，完善与媒体的合作机制。电视方面，央视财经频道在博览会秘书处设立全国展会中独一无二的演播点，广西电视台在博览会秘书处设立了记者站；财经媒体方面，与“第一财经”签订了1500万元合作内容的协议；网络方面，与腾讯网、新浪网、央视网等建立了合作关系，对博览会进行了深入和全面的报道宣传，以极低的投入换来了强势媒体对博览会大量宣传。与东盟媒体、行业媒体合作方面，进一步向深度广度发展。经过多年的合作，博览会已经建立了国内机构在东南亚最大、最有效的宣传推介网络，与博览会共办方、支持商协会的行业媒体进行资源互换工作也取得了新进展。柬埔寨中国商会网站及其旗下媒体《金边晚报》、马中经贸会刊、文莱中华总商会网站都和博览会秘书处签署了媒体互换协议，为今后进一步扩大宣传、同时降低宣传成本打下良好基础。

第八届中国—东盟博览会新闻中心服务周到高效。中心的设计和布置兼顾服务功能和文化色彩，营造古典优雅的艺术氛围，为媒体记者提供温馨服务。会期出版《中国—东盟博览会》杂志特刊，编印《快报》，内容更丰富，更鲜活，图文并茂，时效性强，得到与会贵宾和客商的赞赏。此外，博

览会秘书处在全国商务、海关、检验检疫系统的对外服务窗口摆放中国—东盟自由贸易区政策宣传台卡、资料和中国—东盟博览会宣传品，在全区三星级以上宾馆摆放博览会宣传名片，扩大了面向企业和公众的宣传。

在博览会举办地的氛围营造方面，会前各媒体通过系列报道的形式，迅速营造起浓厚的舆论氛围。博览会秘书处提前制作宣传片，从2011年8月开始在广西和南宁市的电视台播出，提前营造氛围。首次采用网上渠道征集博览会口号，极大地扩大了征集范围，营造了全社会关注博览会的氛围，扩大了博览会的影响。设计标准宣传POP和主题国等相关重要元素，在南宁市营造氛围中使用。主题国马来西亚的媒体记者到南宁后说，一下飞机，就感受到了20周年的氛围，感受到了对主题国的重视，觉得很骄傲。

五　安全保卫

中央、公安部和广西壮族自治区党委、政府领导对第八届中国—东盟博览会的安全保卫工作高度重视，精心组织、周密部署。在全区公安机关、武警部队和社会各界力量的共同努力下，团结协作、全力以赴，狠抓各项安保措施落实，确保了参会的中国和东盟国家领导人等警卫对象的绝对安全、参会参展来宾和群众的生命财产安全及“两会一节”各项重要活动的安全顺利进行，达到自治区党委、政府和公安部提出的“绝对安全、万无一失”的工作要求，实现了“五个不发生”的工作总目标，圆满地完成了各项安全保卫任务。

安全保卫工作
Security Team

（一）强化组织领导和协调指挥

广西壮族自治区成立了“两会”安全保卫工作领导小组，在“两会”广西指挥中心组建了公安、武警、维稳、综治、安监、国安等部门为主的“两会”指挥中心安全保卫部，自治区“两会”安全保卫工作领导小组组长温卡华、副组长梁胜利以及自治区公安厅副厅长、“两会”指挥中心安保部部长赵晓迅等多次组织有关部门协调落实水、陆、空安保工作，靠前指挥，现场督导。公安部部长助理、警卫局局长刘彦平也率队亲临安保一线，检查指导，统筹协调。依靠各级党委政府，发动全区特别是南宁市共同参与，南宁市发动党政机关、企事业单位、社会团体、社区群防群治力量、治安志愿者近5万人参与安保工作，形成齐抓共管、共保平安的氛围。积极协调驻桂部队官兵、武警官兵和柳州、钦州、崇左、防城港、来宾市以及公安厅机关、广西警官高等专科学校、广西警官学校、广西政法管理干部学院等4490多名警力投入，支援南宁开展场所住地安保、社会面防控、排爆搜爆和低慢小目标防范处置、安检等工作。大力推进区域协作。积极部署“环桂”、“环邕”安保圈防控，在全区设立82个治安检查站，实行联防联控，把各类危险因素堵截在南宁之外。

（二）健全安保机制和督导落实

“两会一节”安全保卫部下设情报信息组、社会面控制组、要人警卫组、现场保卫组、维护稳定组、安全生产组、道路交通安全组、应急处置组、勤务保障组和办公室。全区各市、县公安机关成立由“一把手”挂帅的安保机构，构建了党委政府领导、公安机关主导、各部门分工负责、社会力量共同参与的大安保格局。根据安保工作需要，及时制定实施了包括总体方案、专项方案及实施方案在内近200多个安保方案，涉及包括情报信息、交通安全、社会治安整治、消防安全、网络安全、打击预防恐怖袭击、防爆炸事件等安保工作内容。在实际指导上，紧贴实际提出安保防控需求，就机动车总量控制、特殊群体管控、危险物品管理、涉外管理等方面研究提出了安保防控需求，制定有关预案和措施，有效解决了多个安保工作的防控难题，为安保执法提供了有力的法律保障和政策支持。

（三）创新安保模式和严密社会面管控

推行科技安保、人文安保、规范安保。协调警用直升机、“动中通”卫星传输车、排爆机器人以及远距离探测仪等一批先进设备应用到安保工作中，极大提高了安保工作效率和安全系数。重点加强信息收集、情报研判、风险评估、反恐处突、重点人群管控、“网上”安防、应急力量和装备部署。实行记者安检前移，对记者及所携器材采取事先安检后派警员专车送入场，在确保安全的同时方便记者入场报道。规范培训和演练，确保参战人员按规范要求上岗执勤，实现了安保执法“零差错、零失误、零投诉”的工作目标。同时协调南宁海事部门对邕江水域实行管制，南宁市公安局派出警用巡逻艇加强巡逻。启动环桂环邕治安检查卡点，在进邕的各个交通要道、路口设立卡点，24小时对进城的车辆进行安全检查，对可疑人员依法盘查，防止违禁物品和犯罪分子流入南宁。全区各地公安机关增派警力加强了面上治安巡逻防范，维护社会面上治安秩序，确保各重点要害部门、要害部位的安全。在“两会一节”期间，组织开展万人大巡防，组织开展对重点人员、不确定群体的监控和各类矛盾纠纷的调处排查，全面加强街面、繁华场所的巡逻防范和单位、住宅小区的看家护院工作，确保社会面治安得以有效控制。

小结　统筹和服务能力增强　展会安全便利

第八届中国—东盟博览会、中国—东盟商务与投资峰会服务体系进一步完善，统筹协调、基础设施建设、展览现场服务、新闻宣传、安全保卫等各项工作都比上届进一步提高，形成新的亮点。

一是统筹协调工作创新，活动安排更有针对性。“两会”指挥中心根据本届各阶段活动统筹的不同要点，将活动总表进行动态调整，提前做好应对各种情况的活动安排方案预案，加强综合演练，确保了领导人会见、开幕式、巡馆、宴会等重要活动的安全、有序、顺畅。任务统筹、贵宾统筹、文秘、联合值班、通讯保障、人力资源配调等工作较往届有了新的提高。整个统筹协调工作应对得法，处置得当，应急反应快，起到了“神经中枢”的作用。

二是基础设施投入大，保障能力提高。南宁市大力推进道路桥梁、宾馆设施、生态环境等基础设施建设，进一步完善城市功能，完成了南宁机场扩建工程项目、中国—东盟博览会周边水系建设、青秀湖公园建设、相思湖、明月湖、邕江滨水公园二期绿化建设、中国—东盟国际商务区配套设施建设等一批项目，为博览会营造了环境优美、交通便利、设施完备的举办环境。

三是展览现场管理机制更加完善，服务更加高效。“两会”指挥中心进一步健全现场管理和服务保障体系，逐步优化各项规范、标准，为展商、客商提供了全方位便捷、优质、高效、顺畅的一站式服务，在展览管理中体现了“以人为本”和绿色环保的理念。南宁海关、广西出入境检验检疫局和广西边防总队落实各项便利化措施，实现快速通关，优化服务，展示了国门形象。接待工作贯彻“重商、服务、透明、有序、实效”的服务理念，宾馆接待更加规范，对口接待机制更加细致完善，引进更多旅行社参与客商接待，提供更加便捷、规范、安全、高效的接待服务。证件工作高效快捷，加强个性化服务，实现“人到证到”目标。直航包机实行政府采购，优选航空公司，为东盟宾客提供服务水平进一步提升。食品安全保障有力，医疗卫生服务细致入微。志愿者管理和培训更加规范，服务更有针对性。

四是新闻宣传声势大，品牌影响力进一步提升。本届“两会”宣传策划早，媒体邀请更加广泛，东盟媒体数量是国内同类活动中最多。新闻宣传渠道多，涵盖平面媒体、广播电视以及网络、手机、微博等新媒体，实现了全媒体、多语种、全方位传播。媒体服务更加快捷，新闻信息实现快速共享。博览会秘书处与央视、第一财经等建立了战略合作关系。社会宣传营造良好氛围。总之，第八届博览会的新闻宣传工作，宣传中国与东盟国家在建立对话关系20年来各方面的发展，宣传中国—东盟博览会在促进中国—东盟合作中的作用，宣传广西在中国—东盟自贸区建成后发展的优势、潜力和广西经济社会发展取得的成就，宣传广西对外开放的良好形象，进一步扩大了“两会一节”的影响力，取得良好的实际效果，在社会上引起强烈反响。

五是安全保卫组织周密，确保了“两会”安全顺利。各级领导高度重视，“两会”指挥中心安全保卫部周密部署，各有关单位全力以赴，形成“环桂”、“环邕”安保圈防控；构建了党委政府领导、公安机关主导、各部门分工负责、社会力量共同参与的大安保格局；制定实施了包括总体方案、专项方案及实施方案在内近200多个安保方案，涉及包括情报信息、交通安全、社会治安整治、消防安全、网络安全、打击预防恐怖袭击、防爆炸事件等安保工作内容；创新安保模式，严密社会面管控。推行科技安保、人文安保、规范安保。协调警用直升机、“动中通”卫星传输车、排爆机器人以及远距离探测仪等一批先进设备应用到安保工作中，极大提高了安保工作效率和安全系数。全区各地公安机关增派警力加强了面上治安巡逻防范，维护社会面上治安秩序，确保各重点要害部门、要害部位的安全；组织开展万人大巡防，组织开展对重点人员、不确定群体的监控和各类矛盾纠纷的调处排查，确保社会面治安得以有效控制。

第九章

9 舞台广阔　企业受益

——第八届中国—东盟博览会企业案例

在经济全球化和区域经济一体化迅猛发展的形势下，中国和东盟10国政府达成了建设中国—东盟自由贸易区的共识。政府的共识如何转变为企业的共赢，需要一个务实的平台。

中国—东盟博览会就是把中国—东盟自由贸易区从政府层面推进到企业层面的务实平台。博览会所肩负的任务，决定了它把服务企业放在整个展会的重要位置。

如何服务企业？博览会由11国共办，有11国政府的强力坚持，有11国商协会和企业界的积极参与。博览会经过八年积累，已建立起跨国家、跨部门、跨省区的共办机制，能够把11国政府部门、地方政府、各国企业等各种资源进行有效集合，使企业得到一个无限广阔、资源丰富、渠道独特的平台，在中国—东盟自由贸易区大市场中大显身手，尽享商机。

2011年，中国有色集团成为第八届中国—东盟博览会首席战略合作伙伴；广西投资集团、广西农垦集团、广西柳州钢铁（集团）公司、广西有色金属集团、中国移动广西公司成为第八届中国—东盟博览会战略合作伙伴；广西三环集团、广西运德集团等一批企业成为第八届中国—东盟博览会合作伙伴。众多企业借助中国—东盟博览会开拓市场，分享商机，获得了实实在在的好处。

Broad Platform Brings Great Benefits to Businesses

—Trade Deal Cases of the 8th CAEXPO

With the increasing economic globalization and regional economic integration, China and the 10 ASEAN member states have decided to join hands to build the China-ASEAN FTA. We now need a pragmatic platform to materialize the government paperwork into the actual benefits and business opportunities for business circles.

The CAEXPO is just the right platform we desire, which can actually make the CAFTA facilitations accessible to business people, and it has always put the needs and demands of businesses at the top of its priorities.

But how can the CAEXPO better serve the enterprises? CAEXPO is a grand trade event co-sponsored by China and the 10 ASEAN member countries that has gained full support from the governments, and the active participation of major chambers of commerce and trade associations as well as the enterprises of both sides. Therefore, by establishing a co-sponsoring mechanism involving competent departments of China and the 10 ASEAN member states and different provincial/municipal governments of China, it has effectively pooled together the diverse resources of government departments, local governments and enterprises of both sides, to build a vast platform with rich resources and diverse channels for enterprises, thus to facilitate their efforts in exploring the huge CAFTA market.

In 2011, China Nonferrous was named the 8th CAEXPO Chief Strategic Partner, and Guangxi Investment Group, Guangxi State Farm, Guangxi Liuzhou Steel, Guangxi Nonferrous, China Mobile (Guangxi) were the strategic partners of the event. A batch of local enterprises became the 8th CAEXPO partners, including Guangxi Sanhuan Group and Guangxi Yunde Group. Quite a few of companies took the CAEXPO as a good passage for market exploring and a pool of business opportunities, gaining pragmatic results.

CHAPTER NINE

一 彰显殊荣 掌握先机

中国—东盟博览会经过八年发展，品牌影响力不断扩大，服务企业的能力不断增强，越来越多的企业通过与博览会合作，利用博览会独特的平台和资源优势及品牌影响力，塑造企业良好形象，占据市场“制高点”，分享中国—东盟自由贸易区商机。

（一）中国有色矿业集团有限公司牵手中国—东盟博览会

2011年，中国有色矿业集团有限公司（简称“中国有色集团”）成为第八届中国—东盟博览会首席战略合作伙伴。这是中央直属企业首次成为博览会合作伙伴，也是中国有色集团继2009年连续第三次牵手中国—东盟博览会。在2011年10月10日举行的第八届中国—东盟博览会首席战略合作伙伴签约暨揭牌仪式上，广西壮族自治区政府副主席林念修出席仪式，向中国有色集团颁发“中国—东盟博览会首席战略合作伙伴”证书并见证签约。

中国有色集团连续三年选择中国—东盟博览会，而且在2011年首次荣膺博览会首席战略合作伙伴。为什么中国有色集团如此青睐中国—东盟博览

中国有色矿业集团有限公司展位
China Non-ferrous Metal Mining (Group) Co.,Ltd. at the 8th CAEXPO

会？从该公司近年来通过博览会开拓东盟市场的成效中可以找到答案。

中国有色集团是国务院国资委直接监管的大型中央企业，是我国有色金属工业“走出去”的排头兵，也是开展国际投资合作最成功的中央企业之一。已与东盟10国中的8个国家建立了良好的业务往来，在这些国家投资开发了众多具有重大影响的优质资源项目。在成功实施海外投资开发的同时，中国有色集团在广西、宁夏、湖北、辽宁、内蒙古、江西、广东等省（区）也拥有一批骨干企业，并与这些省（区）建立了良好的合作关系，形成了国内外整体联动、协同发展的格局。

近年来，广西已成为国内最具增长潜力的省份之一，成为中央企业投资的热土。中国有色集团积极响应广西“希望中央企业抓住机遇，进一步加大在广西投资的力度，实现合作互利共赢”的号召，积极落实广西“以时间换空间、以存量换增量、以资源换产业”的总体要求，充分发挥资源、资金、管理、技术和政策优势，加快推进与广西在有色金属资源开发和整合等方面的友好合作，为广西的经济发展和社会进步作出了贡献。

依托中国—东盟博览会的良好平台，中国有色集团在广西壮族自治区党委、政府的关心下，在柳州、桂林、贺州先后重组了柳州中色锌品有限公司、中国有色（桂林）矿产地质研究院有限公司、中国有色集团（广西）平桂飞碟股份有限公司等三家企业，以这三家企业为平台积极拓展与广西的友好合作。2010年7月8日，中国有色集团与广西壮族自治区人民政府签订了战略合作框架协议，双方进一步明确将在经济建设、资源共享、拓展国内外市场等方面密切联系、加强合作、共同发展，致力于打造中央企业与地方政府的合作典范。

2011年是中国—东盟建立对话关系20周年、中国—东盟友好交流年、中国—东盟自由贸易区建成1周年，中国有色集团抓住这一机遇，充分利用中国—东盟博览会平台，强强联手，进一步加强与东盟合作，促进互利共赢。

中国有色集团总经理罗涛在第八届中国—东盟博览会首席战略合作伙伴签约暨揭牌仪式上说，中国—东盟博览会是中国与东盟国家互通有无、共享成长的重要平台，已成为我国对外交流合作的盛会。中国有色集团依托博览会的桥梁作用，进一步扩大与东盟国家的合作力度，已与东盟10国中的8个国家建立了良好的业务往来，在这些国家投资开发了众多具有重大影响的优质资源项目，形成了一定规模的有色金属矿产资源开发布局，产生了一定的国际影响力。

目前，中国有色集团正在稳步实施“12345”发展战略，全力向世界500强企业挺进、加快建设具有国际竞争力的世界一流矿业集团。东盟商圈是中国有色集团的重要投资区域，中国有色集团将继续依托东盟博览会的巨大辐射和带动作用，与广西和东盟国家加大合作力度，共创美好未来。

（二）独享尊荣，掌握先机

中国有色集团作为第八届中国—东盟博览会首席战略合作伙伴，在博览会各项活动中获得特别礼遇，独享尊荣，掌握市场先机。

本次展览，中国有色集团在近110平方米的展区内，用图文并茂的展板、内容丰富的产品、效果震撼的宣传片播放、精致写实的模型演示，立体地诠释了公司与东盟国家和广西开展的合作情况，全景展示了“走出去”的光荣与梦想。

2011年10月21日，中共中央政治局常委、国务院总理温家宝巡视第八届中国—东盟博览会展馆期间，兴致勃勃地前往中国有色集团展区参观，亲切关怀中国有色集团在境内外的投资发展，勉励中国有色集团再接再厉，实现更好更快的发展。在展馆门口，温家宝与迎候在那里的中国有色集团总经理罗涛亲切握手，在罗涛的陪同下健步走向中国有色集团展区。在缅甸达贡山镍矿沙盘模型前，温家宝驻足观看，认真听取罗涛的情况汇报。达贡山镍矿是中缅矿业领域最大的合作项目，也是中国有色集团在海外投资最大的单体项目。2004年7月12日，温家宝总理在人民大会堂见证了该项目的签约，此后又对项目作出重要批示，充分体现了党和政府对“走出去”企业的亲切关怀。

2011年10月21日，国务院总理温家宝巡视中国有色集团展区

On October 21, 2011, H.E. Wen Jiabao, primier of the State Council of China at the pavilion of China Non-ferrous Metal Mining (Group) Co.,Ltd.

展区上方，“建设具有国际竞争力的世界一流矿业集团”、“立足东盟、面向世界、共同发展”、“辐射东盟商圈、服务广西发展”等巨幅电子标语滚动播放，折射出中国有色集团的发展愿景和责任意识，温家宝看到后微笑着点点头，中国有色集团展区内流动着关怀与希望。

参观结束前，温家宝勉励中国有色集团实现更好更快的发展。罗涛表示，一定按照党和国家的要求，按照温家宝总理的重要指示，稳步实施“走出去”战略，为中外经贸友好往来作出更加积极的贡献。

2011年10月11日，广西壮族自治区党委书记、自治区人大常委会主任郭声琨在南宁会见了中国有色集团总经理罗涛。

郭声琨代表广西壮族自治区党委、政府对罗涛一行来桂出席第八届中国—东盟博览会首席战略合作伙伴签约暨揭牌仪式表示热烈欢迎。他说，中国有色集团是2009年、2010年中国—东盟博览会的战略合作伙伴，双方合作十分愉快，成效显著，2011年又成为博览会首席战略合作伙伴，充分体现了央企利用“两个市场”、“两种资源”的战略眼光和对广西经济社会发展的大力支持。

郭声琨说，中国有色集团是大型央企，实力雄厚、技术先进，近年来公司发展迅速，企业管理、经营水平、产品资源等方面均在有色金属行业名列前茅。广西有色金属资源十分丰富，是中国十大有色金属产区之一。双方优势互补，一起合作如虎添翼，是地方与央企合作的成功范例之一。希望中国有色集团在双方富有成效的合作基础上，充分利用中国—东盟博览会这个良好的发展平台，发挥资金、管理、技术等方面优势，加强与东盟国家的投资合作，进一步推动广西有色金属支柱产业发展。广西将继续本着对企业“力求所在，不求所有”的原则，坚持“以空间换时间，以资源换产业，以存量换增量”的战略思维，创造条件，做好服务，全力支持中国有色集团“走出去”战略和在广西的发展，双方互惠互利，共同发展，实现共赢。

罗涛说，近年来广西经济社会保持着快速发展的良好势头，取得了巨大成就，我们备受鼓舞。成功举办了七届的中国—东盟博览会已成为一个具有很强国际影响力的盛会和开展广泛务实合作的平台。集团将充分借助这个交流合作平台，配合广西加强和东盟国家合作，进一步开拓东盟市场。广西是一块投资热土，有色金属资源丰富，我们合作潜力巨大，前景广阔美好。集团将全面落实双方2010年签署的战略合作框架协议，在共同进行广西有色金属资源开发和整合、有色金属冶炼及深加工项目建设等的基础上展开全面合作，全力支持广西经济社会又好又快发展。

广西壮族自治区领导余远辉、林念修，中国有色集团党委书记张克利、副总经理严弟勇参加会见。

（三）媒体聚焦，塑造企业品牌

中国有色集团担任第八届中国—东盟博览会首席战略合作伙伴，引起了中外媒体的高度关注和聚焦，纷纷予以报道，让更多的公众了解中国有色集团与东盟开展合作、带动东盟国家经济发展的情况，树立企业良好形象。

在第八届中国—东盟博览会首席战略合作伙伴签约暨揭牌仪式上，《人民日报》、新华社、中央电视台、中新社、《广西日报》等媒体及东盟国家媒体到会采访，对中国有色集团连续三年担任博览会战略合作伙伴、特别是首次担任首席战略合作伙伴给予充分报道，对公司通过中国—东盟博览会平台“走出去”到东盟投资，并在广西开展项目合作所取得的成效给予积极评价。

2011年10月22日上午，中国有色集团总经理罗涛在第八届中国—东盟博览会新闻中心贵宾室接受各国媒体的集体采访。

在谈到中国有色集团在东盟国家的合作项目时，罗涛说，在缅甸投资的缅甸镍矿项目，是中缅历史最大合作项目，这个项目是温家宝总理在参加北京签约仪式开幕式当天唯一参观的展览。这个项目的总投资是8.3亿美元，公司今后不仅把这个项目经营好管理好，推动当地经济发展，同时还在跟缅甸方面商量开展其他合作项目。

在采访中，罗涛针对本届博览会重点主题“环保合作”，着重介绍了公司在实施合作项目中如何坚持环保和减少污染。他说，目前广西正在做城市矿山，就是八成是可回收的有色金属进行再回收利用。他说：“中国—东盟博览会办得非常成功，第六、七、八届我都参加了，我对各个论坛和各个峰会都感兴趣，特别是像科技进步、环保理念这样的内容。我认为环保这个主题开得非常好，这是全世界经济发展中很重要的一部分。”

罗涛介绍，中国有色集团在泰国的投资，就是生产再生铅、金铅，其原料完全来自于废旧，有助于解决二次污染城市的问题。他还举例，在缅甸投资8.3亿美元的镍矿项目，现在已经在做深入的研究，要把尾矿全部再利用起来。不能把山挖掘了，山挖了要回填，要复垦，要长草和树。尾矿要做阻拦的，建筑房子的隔板，还要变成造纸的原料，要做到没有一吨的废弃物的排放。

罗涛说，每一个国家的发展都需要符合环保的要求，全球都重视环保，中国企业更重视环保，我们这几年增长速度很快，但是我们节能环保也在提高，我们排放量不断下限，我们不会把污染带到东盟国家，我们要把最好的技术和管理带到东盟国家去，在这个方面要理念更新，舍得资金投入。

二 助企业开拓大市场 树立好形象

第八届中国—东盟博览会为企业搭建更加广阔的平台，为众多企业展示形象，开拓市场提供更好服务。

（一）广西投资集团：通过博览会走向东盟

2011年10月21日，第八届中国—东盟博览会战略合作伙伴广西投资集团有限公司董事长管跃庆作为博览会合作伙伴主要代表迎接国务院总理温家宝巡视展馆。管跃庆还应邀出席了马来西亚总理纳吉布会见中国企业家CEO圆桌对话会。公司多位高官出席了泰国副总理吉滴叻与中泰国企业家座谈会。博览会期间，管跃庆接受中央电视台财经频道专访，并在《经济信息新闻联播》栏目中播出，获得了良好的社会效应。

广西投资集团已连续八年担任博览会战略合作伙伴。八年来，广西投资集团通过博览会积极与东盟各国开展合作，取得多方面的成效。“十一五”期间，集团资产总额连续跨越100亿元、200亿元、300亿元、400亿元；营业收入连续跨越50亿元、100亿元、150亿元、200亿元四个台阶。2008年开始

广西投资集团展位
Guangxi Investment Group at the 8th CAEXPO

连续四年进入中国企业500强。

八年来，广西投资集团精心布置展台，频频精彩亮相，广泛接触东盟国家政商各界人士，积极进行品牌推广，寻找发展机遇，成功找到了合作伙伴，签署了一系列合作协议。公司多次荣获博览会组委会授予的“投资促进活动组织奖”。

通过博览会，广西投资集团加深了对东盟国家的了解，迅速掌握多种投资信息与机会，先后在泰国、老挝、柬埔寨、越南、印尼、马来西亚等国开展了系列投资考察调研工作。为加快“走出去”步伐，广西投资集团与越南大型国有企业——越南安圆集团开展战略合作，开展的项目主要有高平铝土矿资源开发项目、高平铅锌矿项目、宁顺省安风风力发电项目。在印度尼西亚，广西投资集团与实力雄厚的印尼华泰能源有限公司进行战略合作，开展的合作项目包括印尼东加佳丁2号2×10万千瓦火力发电项目、印尼玛丽瑙煤矿项目、印尼巴厘岛地产项目等。同时，公司还在印尼积极开展煤炭贸易工作，公司驻印尼代表处已正常运营。

（二）广西农垦集团：投资贸易并举

广西农垦集团是第八届中国—东盟博览会战略合作伙伴，也是连续第八年担任博览会战略合作伙伴。第八届博览会期间，广西农垦集团有限责任公司董事长刘刚出席了马来西亚总理纳吉布会见中国企业家CEO圆桌对话会。广西农垦集团精心布置了专门展区，展示企业形象和商机，签署了一系列合作协议，与东盟国家开展了务实的合作。

广西农垦充分利用博览会平台，按照“引进来、走出去”和“立足东盟、走向世界、投资贸易并举”的发展思路，充分利用国内外两个市场、两种资源，发挥农垦企业产业发展优势和技术优势，支持农垦管区企业在研

广西农垦集团展位
Guangxi State Farms at the 8th CAEXPO

发、生产、销售等方面开展国际化经营，加快全方位、多元化发展步伐，推进再造一个海外农垦战略，实现新时期广西农垦跨越式发展。

在历届博览会上，广西农垦多次独立主办了农垦东盟合作发展论坛暨合作项目签约仪式，集中向外界展示了农垦对外合作的新成就，开展了一系列的经贸活动，取得了巨大成功。目前，广西农垦与新加坡国际企业发展局、新加坡中华总商会、新加坡制造商联合会、新加坡裕廊顾问公司分别建立了战略合作伙伴关系，马来西亚麒麟阁有限公司已经在农垦产业园区落户投资。新加坡裕廊顾问公司规划设计了广西农垦新兴、北部湾和中国—印尼三个产业园区的规划，广西农垦已成为东盟国家投资的热点。广西农垦还与东盟国家积极开展农业技术交流活动。

目前，广西农垦与东盟国家已签订一批国际经济合作项目。其中，广西农垦承建的中国·印尼经贸合作区是中国在印尼设立的唯一的国家合作区，是目前国家批准在境外设立的19个国家合作区之一，也是广西在国家争取到的在境外设立的第一个合作区。目前项目实施进展顺利。广西农垦在越南、泰国、印尼、柬埔寨、缅甸的农业合作项目也积极推进。

（三）广西柳州钢铁集团公司：展示企业形象

广西柳州钢铁集团公司（简称“广西柳钢”）是第八届中国—东盟博览会战略合作伙伴。这也是广西柳钢第三次出任中国—东盟博览会战略合作伙伴。在第四届、第六届、第八届中国—东盟博览会期间，广西柳钢通过博览会平台，利用现场互动展示、户外广告、LED视频广告、平面广告、会刊内页广告、新闻快报等多元媒体形式，对公司品牌形象进行了广泛宣传；公司参加了博览会期间相关主题会议与论坛，使公司对中国与东盟各领域交流合作的新商机与新政策有了深入了解。公司高层领导参加了博览会高尔夫国际精英邀请赛等高层次交流活动，与东盟各国政商人士进行了深入交流，取得了良好的合作成果。

（四）广西有色金属集团有限公司：合作设立产业基金

2011年10月23日，第八届中国—东盟博览会战略合作伙伴广西有色金属集团有限公司与广东粤财投资控股有限公司签署战略合作框架协议，双方将共同建立100亿元的产业基金，推动广西有色金属工业快速健康发展。博览会期间，公司董事长李阳通出席了马来西亚总理纳吉布会见中国企业家CEO圆桌对话会。

广西有色金属集团此次是第五次作为中国—东盟博览会合作伙伴。几年来，集团充分利用博览会平台，按照“立足广西、辐射周边、面向东盟”

2011年10月23日，广西有色金属集团有限公司与广东粤财投资控股有限公司签署战略合作框架协议

On October 23, 2011, Guangxi Non-Ferrous Metals Group Co.,Ltd. and Guangdong Financial Investment Holding Co.,Ltd. signed a framework agreement on strategic cooperation

的资源发展战略，积极对东盟、南非、澳大利亚等国家和地区的矿产资源状况、资源勘查及矿业开发投资条件、投资政策环境等进行考察和论证。先后与柬埔寨、老挝、澳大利亚、印尼等国家的合作伙伴达成了矿产资源开发合作意向，其中部分项目进展顺利，已经进入开工生产阶段。

广西有色金属集团柬埔寨有限公司的“柬埔寨柏威夏省罗文铁矿普查”项目，2010年投入勘查经费3300万元，初步探获高品位铁矿石资源量近2400万吨，项目获得了国家专项资金500万元。该集团的南非北开普省一大型锰矿，经专业中介公司评估，资源储量近5000万吨，锰的平均品位达38%，预计远景储量达1亿吨以上。2011年一季度，所属桂林矿产地质研究院在澳大利亚设立了桂林矿产地质研究院资源公司，并获得两个探矿权证，面积近300平方公里。

有了博览会这一平台作为依托，广西有色金属集团对下一步“走出去”发展信心十足，正着手建立海外风险勘查公司，实行市场化运作，不断扩大海外市场份额。通过成熟项目的股权流转，募集资金投入新的项目，以实现海外投资项目的良性滚动发展，在海外资源竞争中站稳脚跟。

此次博览会上，广东粤财投资控股有限公司发挥在信托理财、信用担保、资产管理、股权投资、产业基金等方面的综合优势和协同效应，为广西有色金属集团调整和优化资本结构、增强融资和防范财务风险能力提供综合类金融服务；广西有色金属集团以自身在矿业领域的人才优势和优质项目储备，为对方拓展资产管理规模提供产业领域的技术支持和优质项目来源。双方通过共同设立基金管理公司并发起设立矿业产业投资基金的模式，初步目标在未来5年募集资金约100亿元，共同打造国内一流的矿业资本运作平台。

（五）中国移动广西公司：展现了区域信息服务行业领先者风采

中国移动广西公司是第八届中国—东盟博览会战略合作伙伴。这是中国移动广西公司从2005年起连续7年出任中国—东盟博览会战略合作伙伴。其中，4年是首席战略合作伙伴。

作为第八届博览会的战略合作伙伴，中国移动广西公司再次派出网络保障和服务精英团队，圆满完成了中国—东盟博览会、中国—东盟商务与投资峰会、南宁国际民歌艺术节（简称“两会一节”）服务和通信保障工作，向中外嘉宾展现了区域信息服务行业领先者的风采和“无线城市”的魅力。

为做好“两会一节”服务工作，广西移动成立了以总经理为组长的专项服务及保障领导小组，着手对机场、会展中心、广西体育中心、荔园山庄、华南城等主要活动场所和四星级以上酒店进行地毯式的网络强化测试，并对各活动场馆周边24个基站进行优化扩容。

广西移动还专门为盛会通信保障工作配置了目前最轻便的便携式卫星传输系统。该设备为单兵操作，可轻易地进入车辆、大型机械无法达到的区域，在5分钟内实现电话、视频、数据传输等功能。同时，公司还为全区的应急通信保障车辆更换了一套新的视频会议系统，使通信保障的领导小组能第一时间清晰、全面地了解保障现场情况，准确进行应急通信调度，更好地指导应急通信保障工作的开展。

第八届中国—东盟博览会期间，广西移动精心编织了通信大网，共出动应急通信车12车次，出动服务及保障人员403人次，确保了本次盛会通信服务及保障任务的圆满完成。中国移动的WLAN网络作为“无线城市”的支撑网络之一，在南宁国际会展中心和吴圩机场实现全覆盖。本届博览会服务水平更趋国际化，不仅专门开发东盟10国话务表，细化分析东盟话务数据，细心为3000多位客商推出WLAN东盟周体验包，并通过12580为9000多位客户提供了展会路况、天气、酒店、机票等咨询服务。

中国移动广西公司还针对“两会”推出无线城市技术之一的“二维码电子门票”，连续5年为东盟博览会提供电子入场券服务，五届博览会共销售了25000余张电子门票，为参会人员提供了方便。

8年来，中国移动广西公司为各届中国—东盟博览会全力提供物质支持、通信保障和信息服务，合作朝深度和广度发展。

当前，广西正在建设中国—东盟区域性信息交流中心，中国移动广西公司借助博览会这个广阔的舞台，将在区域信息服务业中迈向更高台阶，同时进一步向世界展示一个迈向信息化、现代化的广西新形象。

三　中国—东盟博览会提供舞台　企业大显身手

第八届中国—东盟博览会发挥平台优势，为更多的企业提供了展示形象及合作发展的广阔舞台。

广西三环企业集团股份有限公司是全国最大的日用陶瓷龙头兼广西100强企业。从2004年开始，三环集团与中国—东盟博览会秘书处建立了密切合作关系，成为中国—东盟博览会的国礼及贵宾礼品供应商，通过中国—东盟博览会平台，三环集团获得长足发展，知名度显著提高，品牌影响力显著增强。

三环集团的产品有品位，质量好，艺术价值高。目前，三环集团以中国红玉红瓷、帝王黄瓷、釉下五彩、珐琅彩、青花瓷等极具典藏价值的500多款花瓶和100多款艺术挂盘已投放市场。中国陶瓷美术大师、国家级美术大师等30多位名家大师进入了三环集团名家工作室挥毫泼墨，提升了产品的艺术价值。2011年，三环集团艺术陶瓷又被选定为中国—东盟博览会国礼及贵宾礼品供应商。通过与中国—东盟博览会合作，社会各界更加了解三环品

广西三环企业集团股份有限公司展位
Guangxi Sanhuan Porcelain at the 8th CAEXPO

牌，在公众中树立了好口碑。

通过中国—东盟博览会，三环集团认识世界的视野进一步拓宽，看到了广阔的市场生机，尤其看到了三环集团艺术陶瓷的发展潜力。为此，三环集团全面建设广西艺术瓷自主创新体系和广西艺术瓷生产基地。为填补广西工艺陶瓷行业的空白，三环集团把“名瓷、名家、名画、名山、名水”融为一体，使产品在设计、科技含量、艺术价值和产品附加值方面有了新的提高，向世界水平迈进。

目前，三环产品销往80多个国家和地区，国内市场销售额由2008年的5%提高到2010年的30%以上，2001年至2010年，日用陶瓷产量、销售收入连续10年位居全国同行业首位。这些成绩的取得，与中国—东盟博览会提供大舞台是分不开的。

广西运德集团是多届中国—东盟博览会的合作伙伴，第八届博览会继续作为博览会合作伙伴。运德集团不仅为博览会提供优质的物流服务，而且利用博览会平台，与东盟国家物流企业合作，在跨国运输、跨国旅游和跨国物流中不断发展壮大，成效显著。

如今，广西运德公司的陆地旅游班线已深入越南，开通了南宁到越南的河内、下龙、海防、顺化、宁平、清化、岘港等省市的客运班线，旅游线路已经达到越南的中部。通过中国—东盟博览会，运德集团还与柬埔寨商家签订合作协议，在柬埔寨首都金边组建柬埔寨运德国际旅游有限公司，这标志着运德集团开拓东盟运输市场又迈进了一大步。目前，运德集团每天前往越南的跨国客运旅游专线加上山德公司在越南国内运行的旅游班线，已经发展到了22条线路共53辆班车。

运德集团副总经理陈中平说，为了充分利用中国—东盟自贸区巨大的商机，运德集团在越南旅游、客运市场站稳脚跟之后，正将目光投向中国与东盟物流市场，借助强大的运输管理优势和跨国运输经验，运德集团在中国—东盟自贸区这个巨大的商机面前，大显身手，前景广阔。

三环集团和运德集团的案例，只是众多企业通过博览会受益的其中代表。随着中国—东盟自贸区深入发展，中国—东盟博览会这个大舞台上，将为广大企业提供更好的服务，让企业获得更多商机。

小结　中国—东盟博览会品牌影响力助企业拓市场

对于经贸展会来说，为企业搭好平台，为企业创造商机，是最终目的。因此，一般的商业性展会主要是通过经贸活动的策划、组织和实施，实现对企业的服务。

中国—东盟博览会与众不同，它由11国共同主办，每届博览会都有中国和东盟各国领导人、部长、各国地方政府负责人、商协会负责人、知名企业家、专家学者等重量级人物出席。会期不仅安排经贸活动，而且有多场领导人和企业家的政商高端对接活动。因此，博览会可以发挥政治外交影响力，利用11国共办机制，整合11国的政府部门和企业资源，让参展参会企业在更高层面、更宽视野、更广空间开展务实合作，得到更好的经贸成效。第八届博览会就有众多企业受益于此。

中国有色集团作为本届博览会首席战略合作伙伴，得到了领导人的亲切关怀。中共中央政治局常委、国务院总理温家宝在巡视展馆时，专门到中国有色集团展区参观，与中国有色集团总经理罗涛亲切握手，勉励中国有色集团再接再厉，实现更好更快的发展。广西壮族自治区党委书记、自治区人大常委会主任郭声琨会见了罗涛，表示广西将全力支持中国有色集团“走出去”战略和在广西的发展。罗涛在博览会新闻中心还接受了中外媒体的集体采访，宣传了企业在开展资源开发的同时注重环保的良好社会形象。

依托博览会平台，中国有色集团已与东盟10国中的8个国家建立了良好的业务往来，在这些国家投资开发了众多具有重大影响的优质资源项目，形成了一定规模的有色金属矿产资源开发布局，产生了一定的国际影响力。在广西通过重组3家企业，获得更大的发展空间。

广西投资集团、广西农垦集团、广西柳州钢铁集团公司、广西有色金属集团、中国移动广西公司都是多年来与博览会合作的企业，2011年继续作为博览会战略合作伙伴。这些企业负责人出席了马来西亚总理纳吉布与中国企业CEO圆桌对话会、泰国副总理吉滴叻与中泰企业家座谈会及其他重要活动，精心布置展区，并为博览会提供专业服务，全方位与东盟和其他国家地区企业开展合作，展示了企业风采，获得实实在在的成效。

目前，广西投资集团已连续四年进入中国企业500强，在越南、印尼都开展了项目合作。广西农垦承建的中国·印尼经贸合作区进展顺利，在越南、泰国、印尼、柬埔寨、缅甸的农业合作项目也积极推进。广西柳钢集团通过博览会增进了与东盟各国政商人士的深入交流。广西有色金属集团在本届博览会与广东企业签约，共同建立100亿元的产业基金，推动广西有色金属工业快速健康发展。中国移动广西公司通过博览会向中外嘉宾展现了区域信息服务行业领先者的风采和“无线城市”的魅力。

此外，广西三环企业集团股份有限公司作为中国—东盟博览会的“国礼”及贵宾礼品供应商，通过博览会平台，知名度显著提高，品牌影响力显著增强。广西运德集团是博览会多年的合作伙伴，不仅为博览会提供优质的物流服务，而且利用博览会平台，与越南物流企业合作，在跨国运输、跨国旅游和跨国物流中不断发展壮大。越来越多的企业通过博览会平台走向东盟、走向国际市场。

第十章

10 合作结硕果 共赢创辉煌
——第八届中国—东盟博览会的重要成果

10+1>11，这不是一个简单的不等式，而是中国—东盟博览会精神的体现。它反映了中国—东盟博览会的集聚、辐射、带动、增值作用，创造了跨越11国的广阔市场和巨大商机。

中国—东盟博览会的巨大作用，最根本的体现是经贸实效。博览会举办了八届，贸易成交额、国际国内投资合作签约项目数量、投资额每年都上一个台阶。各国企业商家带来了商品，拿走了订单；带来了项目，引进了资本；合作交流的意愿变成了现实的商机，互利共赢的目标得到了全面实现。

第八届中国—东盟博览会首次举办闭幕式。闭幕式形式新颖，意义深刻，体现了博览会共办水平和成果，彰显了博览会在新形势下实现了新发展、新跨越。

第八届中国—东盟博览会受到了中国和东盟10国政要、各界嘉宾和世界各国客商的一致好评，充分肯定了博览会在推动中国与东盟友好合作、服务中国—东盟自由贸易区、为企业搭建平台等方面作出的杰出贡献。博览会展示了快速发展的广西，团结和谐的广西，开放包容的广西。

中国—东盟博览会再次获得国内会展业界评选的2011年中国十大政府主导型展会等多个奖项，体现了博览会的品牌影响力进一步得到肯定和提升。

Fruitful Cooperation and Win–Win Partnership

—Rich Outcomes of the 8th CAEXPO

10+1>11, an inequality with rich connotations, is a good showcase of the CAEXPO spirit. It reflects the role of CAEXPO in promoting bilateral cooperation and enhancing exchanges in all fields, and in creating a huge market, with abundant business opportunities, reaching far beyond the China–ASEAN region.

The profound influence of the CAEXPO is easily seen in the economic and trade outcomes it has achieved. During the past 8 years, CAEXPO's total trade volume, quantity of investment cooperation projects, both international and domestic ones, as well as their investment volume, all enjoy year–on–year increase. Exhibitors bring in commodities and take back home orders; project–owners bring in projects and bring back capital. The good will of cooperation and exchanges has been materialized into actual business opportunities, thus achieving the goal of reciprocal and win–win cooperation.

It is the first time for the CAEXPO to stage a closing ceremony this year, which features ingenious ideas and rich connotations, well reflecting the rich outcomes of the CAEXPO as a grand trade event co–sponsored by both sides, and its new growth in the new context.

The CAEXPO has gained high credits from the political leaders, VIPs and visitors from China–ASEAN region and beyond, who all sing highly of its proactive role played in promoting China–ASEAN friendly cooperation, CAFTA development and the exchanges and cooperation of business circles. What's more, the event has well showcased Guangxi which is now enjoying fast economic growth, an unite and harmonious atmosphere and ready to open arms to friends from home and abroad.

Once again the CAEXPO is awarded with quite a few of prizes in the country including China's Top 10 Government–Guided Conventions & Exhibitions, marking that its influence has been widely acknowledged.

CHAPTER TEN

一　经贸合作结硕果

随着中国—东盟经贸合作不断扩大，以及中国—东盟博览会平台优势日益突出和市场认可度逐年提高，国内外企业利用中国—东盟博览会平台开展和扩大经贸合作的热情高涨，成效不断提高。

第八届中国—东盟博览会突出了中国—东盟建立对话关系20年合作领域不断拓展的成果，博览会常办常新推动自贸区建设快速发展的成效，国内外企业在商品贸易、投资合作等方面收获了丰硕成果，累计商品贸易成交额、签订国际国内经济合作项目总投资额创历史新高，进一步深化了中国—东盟的经贸合作。

（一）商品贸易成交额再创新高

第八届中国—东盟博览会商品贸易成交额达到18.07亿美元，比上届增长5.6%，成交总额为历届最高。商品出口额继续保持增长势头，进口额增长迅猛。

1. 中国各省（区、市）与东盟经贸合作硕果累累。

第八届中国—东盟博览会上，中国各省（区、市）积极根据东盟市场的需求和当地优势，有针对性地组织优势行业企业参展参会，取得实实在在的成效。

各省（区、市）企业参加了博览会期间的贸易对接会、东盟采购商对接会、越南专场采购对接会、农产品食品采购对接会、轻工工艺品专场采购对接会等商贸促进活动，部分省（区、市）积极开展特色产品推介会，收获良好成效。如中国企业专门为东盟市场推出的低速汽车、小型工程机械、小型农用机械，受到东盟采购商的青睐，达成了一批采购意向。中国农业部举办的“四西”（广西、江西、山西、陕西）优质水果推介活动，对这些省份的多种优质水果进行专门推介，多家中国果品企业与东盟国家采购商现场签约，合同总金额达4.2亿元。广西神达新能源公司在本届博览会已经与泰国

2011年10月22日，中国—东盟博览会举行优质水果推介活动

On October 22, 2011, a promotion campaign for quality fruits was held during the CAEXPO

国际贸易有限公司签署了400套太阳能风光互补路灯产品的供货协议，还有不少客商留下联系方式，表达合作意向。神达新能源公司销售部冯玉婷经理说：“展出效果还是蛮好的，泰国客商看上我们的太阳能风能互补路灯，订了400套。”

2. 东盟各国企业以特色赢得市场。

第八届中国—东盟博览会期间，东盟国家踊跃参展参会，共办特色更加鲜明，各国参展参会水平进一步提高，贸易配对和推介活动实效明显。

东盟各国在参展方面形成更多亮点和特色：

一是参展展品进一步集中，突出东盟特色。主要集中到食品农产品、家具家居、特色工艺品及珠宝饰品、日用消费品、服务业产品等具有市场竞争优势的主要行业。

二是参展企业质量进一步提高。第八届中国—东盟博览会上，东盟10国继续在本国展区推出品牌展，优选本国有代表性的知名企业参展。马来西亚森那美集团、新加坡星展银行、越南威拿咖啡等41家东盟知名品牌企业参加了品牌展，行业涵盖环保、金融、教育、医疗、旅游、食品等行业，成为专业买家及媒体关注的焦点。

三是针对双方大宗商品交易活跃的特点，在商品展区首设大宗商品展。马来西亚橡胶出口促进局、棕油局、森那美集团，泰国泰华橡胶、越南橡胶贸易与旅游服务有限公司等17家橡胶、棕油、木材、矿产品、大米等大宗商品企业集中展示了东盟国家的优势大宗商品，备受中国和区域外采购商的关注。

四是将优势商品按行业布展，专业化水平进一步提高。第八届中国—东盟博览会期间，东盟各国在各自展区内设置品牌展区、食品农产品展区、工艺品及珠宝展区、木制品及家具展区、大宗商品展区。各大展区集中布展、统一标识、重点宣传，形成一定规模和宣传效果。其他行业展品也都按行业布展，展馆布置更为专业化。在搭建效果上，东盟展区整体特装率超过90%，凸显了各国风情。

东盟采购商踊跃参与贸易配对活动，成效好。第八届中国—东盟博览会上共有近600家东盟采购商报名参加专场贸易配对会，共有10个东盟采购团组的214家企业和机构举行了4场专场配对会。8个东盟国家参与了22场次与中国各省市领导、商协会、大型企业等机构的高端对接。东盟国家食品农产品商协会、林木产品商协会及相关行业企业代表参加了行业协会联谊会。此外，东盟国家采购商团组还到国内商品展区进行巡馆，与国内商家直接进行交流。

东盟国家举办了多场贸易研讨会和配对会，受到中外客商的普遍欢迎。如越南举办了越南采购商专场配对会，马来西亚出口促进局与广东益华百货公司举行了进口食品论坛（马来西亚展商专场采购会）。泰国、马来西亚等东盟国家配合大宗商品展示区的设置，举办了首届中泰橡胶研讨会、大宗商品采购配对会（橡胶）、中马大宗商品贸易对接会。活动受到参会采购商的踊跃参加，组织中马大宗商品贸易对接会的马来西亚沙巴棕油局负责人说：“参会的企业家是预期的两倍多，让我们感到很荣幸。”活动务实推动了各

第八届中国—东盟博览会上举行的中马大宗商品贸易对接会
The 8th China-ASEAN Expo Sourcing Seminar on Commodities during the 8th CAEXPO

方的供需对接，其中，越南、老挝等东盟国家的轻工、家具等产品受到中国采购商的青睐，达成了一批采购意向。

（二）投资合作项目多质量高

本届博览会投资合作签约项目数量多、金额大、质量高，是历届投资促进活动中成果最丰硕的一次。据统计，本届博览会共签订投资合作项目207个，其中国际经济合作项目105个，总投资74.2亿美元，较上届增长10.86%；签订国内经济合作项目102个，总投资731.1亿元人民币，较上届增长8.39%。本届博览会投资合作有以下特点：

1. 国际合作持续升温。

随着中国—东盟自贸区如期建成，《货物贸易协议》、《服务贸易协议》和《投资协议》等一系列文件的签署和实施，中国—东盟博览会不仅极大地推动了中国与东盟的经贸合作，而且唤起了区域外其他国家和地区投资者的投资热情，博览会投资促进签约项目的国际性大大提高。本届博览会签订的国际经济合作项目中，对外投资合作项目52个，合同金额26.5亿美元，比上届增长37.8%；利用外资项目53个，合同金额47.36亿美元，与上届基本持平。从国别看，中国与东盟的合作项目58个，合同金额35.7亿美元，分别占国际经济合作项目总数和合同金额的55.2%和48.1%，中国与东盟的投资合作项目继续唱主角。此外，作为经济合作国际大舞台，博览会投资促进活动还吸引了大批区域外国家的项目进行签约。国际经济合作签约项目中除了中国和东盟10国外，还有美国、加拿大、德国、荷兰、日本等其他国家和地区共21个。

2. 政商高端对接促成项目更多。

第八届中国—东盟博览会上，东盟国家的系列政商高端对接活动，实实

泰国投资机遇推介会
Promotion conference on Thailand investment opportunities

在在推动了双方投资合作。如，马来西亚举办了马来西亚总理纳吉布与中国企业CEO圆桌对话会，纳吉布总理与中国企业家围绕中马双边经贸合作展开了热烈的建设性对话，就中马两国在能源、水电开发及污水处理、通信、林业等领域的合作展望进行了交流。泰国副总理吉滴叻在与中泰企业家见面会上，与中泰企业家共商合作，共谋发展。两场见面会上还分别举行了中马合作项目签约仪式和中泰合作项目签约仪式，签约了一批项目。两个东盟国家领导人亲自出席会议并与企业家对话，增强了中国企业"走出去"投资东盟的信心。在中国—缅甸企业家座谈会上，缅甸商务部部长吴温敏与30多位中缅企业家就增强中缅在通信电子、农业技术开发、能源开发及基础设施建设等领域的交流与合作进行了座谈，中缅签约了一批合作项目。

3. "走出去"特色更加凸显。

本届博览会明确提出了打造中国企业"走出去"投资东盟最好平台，"走出去"成为本届投资促进活动的一大亮点。据统计，本届博览会投资合作签约项目中，中国对东盟国家的投资合作项目48个，投资总额25.9亿美元，比上届增长72.4%。其中广西对东盟"走出去"项目21个，合同金额6.05亿美元，比上届增长348%。此外，对东盟国家有直接投资项目的还包括：央企9个、浙江7个、福建5个、江西4个、天津、江苏、湖南、云南、四川各1个。"走出去"合作的项目涵盖领域广泛，涉及基础设施建设、能源化工、有色金属、装备制造、商贸物流和农产品领域，其中基础设施建设和金融合

中国境外（东盟）经贸合作区推介会
Promotion Seminar on Chinese Overseas (ASEAN) Economic and Trade Cooperation Zone

作是本届博览会签约项目的新亮点。重大基础设施合作项目有中国技术进出口总公司、天津电力建设公司联合体投资的越南海阳1200MW发电厂项目，合同投资额14.88亿美元，中国水利电力对外公司投资的老挝“南椰2”水电站项目，合同投资额3.45亿美元。金融合作项目包括国家开发银行内蒙、广西、广东分行，以及中国建筑股份有限公司、中国技术进出口总公司，中国—东盟投资合作基金凯富投资顾问有限公司等分别与越南、柬埔寨、老挝、菲律宾签订了“金融合作”融资安排合作协议或合作备忘录，这些合作协议或合作备忘录的签署和实施，将为上述东盟国家在基础设施、交通能源、矿产开发和中国企业集群式“走出去”提供强大的金融支持。

4. 重大项目多，规模和质量明显提升。

本届博览会签约的重大项目多，规模和质量明显提高，成为一大特点。据统计，签约的国际合作项目，合同金额达1亿美元以上有21个，国内合作项目，投资额5亿元人民币以上的有44个，其中超10亿元人民币以上的重大项目多达29个。国际合作项目投资额较大的包括：美国联邦航太控股集团投资2.35亿美元建设的桂林飞虎通用航空产业基地项目，菲律宾各界联合会、美国电器产品公司、厦门瀚盛游艇有限公司等投资2亿美元建设的广西北部湾国际游艇度假城项目。国内合作项目投资额较大的有：山东青岛九联集团股份有限公司投资建设的九联肉食鸡养殖善宰加工项目，总投资额70亿元；广州美索集团有限公司投资建设的桂林国际医药、化妆品物流产业园项目，总投资额25亿元；上海黑石投资有限公司投资建设40万吨/年碳四综合利用项目，总投资额17.5亿元；河北省凌云工业股份有限公司在柳州投资建设的凌云

第八届中国—东盟博览会上举行的中国采购商采购对接会

Procurement matchmaking for Chinese buyers during the 8th CAEXPO

工业汽车零部件生产项目，总投资额16亿元。这些重大项目的落地开工建设，将产生“引进一个，带来一批”的效应，促进当地经济社会的快速发展。

5. 产业结构更趋优化。

本届博览会签约的国内合作项目，一、二、三产业比例为15：48：37，产业结构继续呈现优化势头，其中第二产业的项目数和合同金额仍占第一位，制造业继续唱主角，合同金额达到185亿元，占全行业合同金额的25.3%；第三产业比例持续升高，比2010年提高23个点，商贸物流行业合同金额157亿元，占全行业合同金额的21.5%，现代服务业加速发展特色明显。投资合作签约项目中，新技术、新能源、新材料等技术含量高、发展潜力大的战略性新兴产业项目明显增多。其中有华电南宁新能源有限公司在南宁高新区投资8亿元建设的华电集团分布式能源项目，北京五洲百尚科技发展有限公司在柳城县投资11亿元建设的工业超细（纳米）轻质碳酸钙、CHF系列离子型土壤固化剂项目，成都新星成明生物科技股份有限公司在防城港港口区投资5亿元建设的年产5万吨天然绿色生物胶体的产业园项目，深圳市逢时能源科技有限公司在北海工业园投资2亿元建设的逢时太阳能电池生产等项目。这些项目既符合世界经济发展趋势，也符合本届博览会“低碳环保”的主题。

6. 科技合作成果显著。

第八届中国—东盟博览会先进技术展展出期间，集中举行了中外项目签约，科技合作项目成果显著。主要的科技领域签约项目有：一是中国科学院自动化研究所与南宁市平方软件新技术有限责任公司，就联合开展东盟多语言信息处理技术研究和开发进行合作签约；二是广西柳州市柳城县鹏鑫源茧丝绸有限公司与陕西安康干燥设备研究所，就建造节能环保180座烘炉技改项目进行签约，签约合同金额为5600万元；三是广西科技信息网络中心与越南岘港科技信息中心签署合作备忘录，双方就开展技术信息交流、组织科技展览、举办培训、市场考察等合作事项进行合作；四是中国广西农业科学院园艺研究所与越南谅山省科技厅科技进步应用中心，就《中越合作在越南谅山省推广种植中国葡萄》项目进行签约。这些项目签约进一步体现了博览会高新科技展平台的作用，拓展了与东盟国家的科技合作与交流。

合作项目精彩看点

●越南海阳发电厂项目——中国工程承包企业“走出去”一大亮点

东盟国家能源资源丰富，市场开发潜力巨大，如何把资源优势转化为经济优势是东盟国家经济发展的重要任务，东盟国家在互联互通、电力、电信等基础设施领域加强与中国企业互利合作，日益成为中国—东盟投资合作的一大亮点。近年来，中国工程承包企业结合东盟市场需求，对东盟“走出去”步伐不断加快。在本届博览会上，中国技术进出口总公司、天津电力建设公司签订了由马来西亚捷硕集团投资兴建的越南海阳1200MW发电厂项目EPC总承包合同，合同总额14.88亿美元，这是近年来我国工程承包企业对东盟国家投资合作的一个大项目。该项目地处越南海阳省京门县,占地面积300公顷，投资总额达22.5亿美元，一号机组预计将于2016年第四季度投产。项目全部投产后将有效缓解该地区电力供应紧张的局面，对保障该地区加工制造业快速发展和人民生活水平的提高将起到积极推动作用。

●桂林创意产业园项目——发挥秀美山水优势，推动创意产业发展

文化创意产业是服务业的一个重要领域，加快文化创意产业发展是丰富文化产品、满足国民文化需求、提高文化消费水平的重要举措。文化创意产业作为技术密集型产业，具有占地少、附加值高、投资回报快等特点，成为越来越多城市产业发展的首选。桂林市是世界著名的旅游胜地和历史文化名城。在产业发展上对环境保护、节能减排等方面要求较高，不仅要发展经济，更要保护秀美山川。因此，大力发展旅游、文化创意等第三产业成为桂林市产业发展的首选。近年来，桂林市不断加大对文化创意产业发展的支持力度，出台了专门扶持政策，搭建了诸如动漫测试平台和培训基地，工业设计和软件外包培训基地等服务平台，培养了一大批文化创意、软件设计、服务外包、动漫设计企业，成为广西文化产业发展的重要基地。在本届博览会上，由灵川县人民政府和广州市希力电子科技有限公司签订的桂林创意产业园项目，协议总额达到21亿元。该园区将主要发展动漫设计、软件开发、服务外包等，吸引一大批文化创意产业聚集发展，积极打造具有广西文化特色的文化产业基地。

●宁明东亚蔗渣发电项目——开发生物质能源，推动可持续发展

我国“十二五”规划纲要明确提出积极发展太阳能、生物质能、地热能等其他新能源，大力发展循环经济，提高资源利用率。广西拥有丰富的可再生生物质资源，生物质能发电行业有着广阔的发展前景。作为我国蔗糖生产的主要基地，充分利用蔗渣发电成为提高产业附加值，是缓解能源供应紧张的重要举措。在本届博览会上，泰国两仪糖业有限公司在广西宁明县投资建设30MW生物质能（蔗渣）发电项目。该项目总投资4600万美元，预计2011年底开工、2012年11月完成。经初步计算，项目建成后，每年可向公共电网输送清洁能源电量约1.5亿度，新增110多个就业机会，并可为广西东亚宁明糖业有限公司创造新增利润3200多万元，为社会新增税金800多万元。

●缅甸腊戍水泥生产项目——发挥互补优势，实现互利共赢

缅甸是我国传统友好国家，也是资源丰富、开发潜力巨大的东盟国家。广西与缅甸经贸合作历史悠久，特别是广西参与大湄公河次区域合作以后，与缅甸的合作领域不断拓宽，合作水平不断提高，在资源开发、农业替代种植等领域开展了一系列互利合作项目，带动了当地经济发展，取得了良好的经济和社会效益。本届博览会上，广西水电工程局和缅甸大勐宜昌达公司签订了缅甸腊戍水泥2500T/D水泥熟料的新型干法水泥生产线项目。该项目位于缅甸掸邦省的腊戍地区，协议金额达8599万美元，其中中方投资8169万美元，将建造一座日产量2500吨的水泥厂，预计年产高标号水泥熟料77.5万吨，年产高品质水泥87.5万吨。该项目的实施既能够发挥广西水泥产业的技术优势，加大"走出去"步伐，又能够满足缅甸经济发展对水泥供应日益增加的需求，发挥市场与产业的互补优势，实现互利共赢。

二　第八届中国—东盟博览会、中国—东盟商务与投资峰会闭幕式暨新闻发布会

2012年10月26日下午，中国—东盟博览会、中国—东盟商务与投资峰会组委会举行闭幕式暨新闻发布会，对外通报第八届中国—东盟博览会和商务与投资峰会成效，宣布第八届中国—东盟博览会和商务与投资峰会胜利闭幕。广西壮族自治区党委常委、自治区常务副主席李金早，中国和东盟10国共办方代表，东盟秘书处代表，“两会”广西指挥中心领导，以及参加本届“两会”的中外记者共200多人出席。博览会闭幕式形式新颖，意义深刻，体现了博览会共办水平和成果，彰显了博览会在新形势下实现了新发展、新跨越。

（一）彰显共办　反映成果

中国—东盟博览会自首届举办以来，一直得到东盟各国共办方以及中国国内各省、市、自治区的大力支持。为表彰各方的努力和成就，根据往届惯

2011年10月26日，中国—东盟博览会、中国—东盟商务与投资峰会组委会举行闭幕式暨新闻发布会

On October 26, 2011, closing ceremony & press conference on the 8th CAEXPO and 8th CABIS was held

广西壮族自治区党委常委、自治区常务副主席李金早向获奖机构颁奖

H.E. Li Jinzao, first vice-governor of Guangxi presented awards to the CAEXPO co-organizers at the closing ceremong

例，中国—东盟博览会组委会评出了本届博览会的各个奖项，并在闭幕仪式上对中方和东盟方参会组织机构进行了表彰。中国—东盟博览会组委会分别向东盟10国共办方、东盟秘书处和海南、福建、青岛等省市颁发了最佳参展商组织奖、最佳采购商组织奖、最佳行业组织奖、最佳品牌展示奖、最佳投资合作推介奖、最佳魅力之城展示奖、主题国纪念奖、重大贡献及支持奖。这些奖项体现了各方为办好本届博览会而作出的不懈努力，以及在博览会平台取得的显著成就。

第八届中国—东盟博览会颁奖情况表

奖项	获奖方	奖项	获奖方	奖项	获奖方
最佳品牌展示奖	文莱	最佳参展商组织奖	柬埔寨	最佳采购商组织奖	马来西亚
	缅甸		印度尼西亚		泰国
	越南		马来西亚		越南
最佳“魅力之城”展示奖	文莱		福建对外贸易经济合作厅		青岛外商投资服务中心
	柬埔寨	最佳行业组织奖	老挝	重大贡献及支持奖	东盟秘书处
	印度尼西亚		新加坡		
	老挝		泰国	主题国纪念奖	马来西亚
	菲律宾	最佳投资合作推介奖	缅甸		
	新加坡		菲律宾		
	海南省商务厅		泰国		

在闭幕仪式后举行的新闻发布会上，“两会”广西指挥中心副总指挥、中国—东盟秘书处秘书长郑军健代表“两会”组委会发布了本届盛会的成果和下届工作的考虑。他表示，本届博览会突出了中国—东盟建立对话关系20年合作领域不断拓展的成果，博览会常办常新推动了自贸区建设快速发展的成效，影响深远。

东盟秘书处代表蓬猜主持闭幕仪式，中国商务部外贸发展局副局长贾国勇主持闭幕新闻发布会，体现了中国和东盟共办盛会，共享成果。

（二）牵手传承　共展风采

本届博览会闭幕式上，本届主题国马来西亚向下届主题国缅甸移交了主题国标志，海南省代表本届“魅力之城”向下届“魅力之城”代表广州市交接“魅力之城”印章，以及公布第九届中国—东盟博览会各国“魅力之城”展区位置顺序。

主题国移交仪式
CAEXPO Country of Honor handover ceremony

中国—东盟博览会主题国

届次	魅力之城	届次	魅力之城
第二届	北京	第六届	深圳
第三届	上海	第七届	钦州
第四届	天津	第八届	海南
第五届	苏州	第九届	广州

"魅力之城"展区的位置由东盟10国和中国通过抽签的形式确定。每届博览会主题国"魅力之城"展位位置安排在展馆中央的6号位。从第二届开始，每届博览会均由中国与东盟10国选择本国有代表性的城市参加"魅力之城"展示；从第四届博览会开始，每届博览会确定一个东盟国家为主题国。

"魅力之城"印章和主题国标志交接的环节反映了博览会不断传承、持续发展的内涵，寓意深远。

中国—东盟博览会中国"魅力之城"

	第四届	第五届	第六届	第七届	第八届	第九届
主题国	文莱	柬埔寨	老挝	印度尼西亚	马来西亚	缅甸

三 各界评价

作为中国—东盟建立对话关系20周年系列纪念活动的重要组成部分，第八届中国—东盟博览会圆满、热烈、安全、精彩、务实，受到了中外嘉宾和客商的一致好评，充分肯定了博览会在推动中国与东盟友好合作、服务中国—东盟自由贸易区、为企业搭建平台等方面作出的杰出贡献。

（一）中国—东盟博览会在中国—东盟友好合作中发挥重要作用

中国和东盟国家领导人和部长级贵宾对本届博览会给予高度评价，认可博览会在促进中国—东盟传统友谊和交流合作等方面发挥的重要作用，并对博览会继续发挥作用寄予了殷切希望。

中国国务院总理温家宝：在双方政府和工商界的共同努力下，20年来双边贸易额年均增长20%以上，目前已接近3000亿美元。中国成为东盟第一大贸易伙伴，东盟也成为中国的第三大贸易伙伴。我们创建了中国—东盟博览会、商务与投资峰会等经贸交流平台，设立了中国—东盟合作基金、中国—东盟公共卫生合作基金和中国—东盟投资合作基金，为东盟国家进行了数万人的能力建设培训。中国—东盟经贸合作正处于历史上最活跃、最富有成效的时期。

马来西亚总理纳吉布：中国—东盟博览会已日益壮大，汇聚来自中国、东盟和世界其他地区的商家，促进区域合作及全球融合。

柬埔寨首相洪森：中国—东盟博览会在促进中国与东盟合作交流中发挥了积极的作用，为促进中柬之间的传统友谊作出了新的贡献。

缅甸副总统吴丁昂敏乌：缅方高度重视缅中全面战略合作伙伴关系，将与中方保持密切沟通，积极寻求解决问题的办法，维护共同利益。

泰国副总理吉滴叻：希望借助此次见面会，促进泰中两国企业家携手迈进，促进商业投资各领域的成功合作。泰国政府将继续支持两国企业家合作。

越南副总理阮春福：中国—东盟博览会组织工作非常好，紧张有序。越南在中国—东盟博览会上的展位搭建漂亮，展品丰富，观众及顾客很多。

东盟秘书长素林：本届开幕式上能邀请到这么多国家的领导人共同出席，显示了中国—东盟博览会政治外交规格之高和意义之重。中国—东盟博览会是一个开放包容的合作平台。

中国商务部国际贸易谈判代表兼副部长高虎城：中国和东盟建立对话关系20年来，各领域友好互利合作不断推进，经贸合作成效尤其显著。中国和东盟携手合作，实现了全面建成中国—东盟自由贸易区的目标。双方共同搭建了中国—东盟博览会平台，增进企业间的交流与合作，促进了双边贸易和投资，为双方企业和人民带来了实实在在的利益。

印尼贸易部部长助理穆赫达塔尔：中国和印尼的经济发展模式互补，中国作为一个巨大的新兴市场能给印尼带来很多机会。两国间在许多领域都有广阔的投资前景，包括能源、自然资源、基础设施建设、制造业和科技等。

菲律宾贸工部投资署司长奥利佛：中国—东盟博览会是很好的平台，我们应该支持它，这里有很多合作机会。

（二）中外嘉宾盛赞中国—东盟博览会开幕式

本届博览会开幕式继承了一贯的隆重、热烈、大气与精彩，给中外嘉宾留下了深刻的印象。

主题国马来西亚贸工部部长穆斯塔法作为开幕式主持人，在开幕式结束后说："我本人非常荣幸主持博览会开幕式。开幕式办得很好，每个细节都做得很到位，非常完美，非常精彩！"

越南工商会中国关系部部长阮秋煌在评价开幕式时表示，本届开幕式注重细节，亦把握整体效果，本开幕式规格高，庄重大体，充满创新精神和文化内涵。

新加坡贸工部长林勋强说，中国—东盟博览会和商务与投资峰会举办得非常好，每年都有创新，开幕式非常成功，令人振奋。

中国商务部办公厅副主任陈国凯参加完博览会开幕式后说，博览会的开幕式规模宏大、组织水平很高，各环节衔接紧密，例如主持人上场的卡点、主持词即将说完，发言嘉宾就已在场边候场等，衔接非常紧密。从这些细节可以看出，博览会开幕式已经达到高规格国际性水平，组织工作非常成熟，在国内属于一流水平。

文莱中国友好协会副会长洪汝铭说，本届开幕式进行得隆重而顺畅，非常难得，堪称一场视觉盛宴。

参加剪彩仪式的柬埔寨青少年迟送那说，能够代表自己的国家在博览会开幕式说出祝福，感到非常荣幸。我们青少年是传递中国—东盟友谊的接力者，祝愿中国东盟友好代代相传。

来自文莱的青少年罗思蓝说，博览会拓展和深化了中国与东盟国家青少年间的友好交流和合作，为中国与东盟各国青年学习交流、传播友谊提供优质平台。

（三）务实平台汇聚大商机

本届博览会的贸易投资促进活动务实有效，为企业了解行业信息、发掘合作机遇、寻找合作伙伴提供了绝佳场所。

泰国贸易院副主席陈树铭：我是第一次来参加博览会，感觉组织得非常好，整个场馆的布置、设计，包括很多亮点的安排都非常好，商贸、旅游、教育、电子等方面的展示都不错，内容非常精彩。这也是我第一次同时看到11个国家的文化，我看了各个国家不同特色的展馆，非常兴奋。

泰国孔敬府商会主席Mr.Chatchai Kosavisutte：魅力之城的展现，让更多的泰国绿色酒店、绿色食品，包括保健等方面都能够推广出去，促进双方旅游的合作。

柬埔寨联合商业银行董事长兼首席执行官任瑞生：自从2004年举办第一届中国—东盟博览会以来，博览会已经成为中国—东盟自由贸易区内一项重要活动，它的活动以及取得的成果在全球广为传播，备受瞩目。

中国—东盟商务理事会中方常务副秘书长许宁宁：2011年是一个具有特殊意义的节点，博览会的主题就是很好的体现。今天我们聚在一起，共享20年合作的成果、自贸区的繁荣和博览会带来的商机，表达我们对未来的坚定信心。

文莱中国友好协会副会长洪汝铭：中国与东盟合作拓展20年，双方从对话关系上升为战略伙伴关系，从政治、外交的友好交流，拓展到经贸、交通、文化、教育、旅游、金融等领域的全方位合作。博览会的举办让远古的“海上丝绸之路”，成为更为广阔的、多领域的合作通道，彰显了10+1 > 11的巨大合力。这是11国共同努力取得的成果。

加拿大中华总商会副会长张木绪：每年来这里都有一定的收获，我们利用博览会这个平台实行了很好的交流，往后每年我们都会来。

（四）细致周到服务享盛誉

中外嘉宾和客商对博览会的组织和服务工作给予了积极评价。

中国有色矿业集团有限公司总经理罗涛：本次盛会，中国有色集团近距离地感受到广西国际博览事务局从会议议程、领导参观、宣传采访、住宿安排等方面给予的细致周到的关照，体现出来的敬业精神与专业素养，使我们深受感动、倍感敬佩！

越南科技部区域发展研究中心副主任陈玉鄰：这里服务热情周到，我们都很满意。来南宁的这些天，无论食宿还是交通出行，都安排得很妥当，还有翻译全程陪同，服务可谓无微不至。

欧美马达加有限责任公司总经理罗善德：博览会的规模非常大，整个建筑很漂亮，人员素质方面也觉得很好，服务也非常到位。

北京四季沐歌太阳能技术集团有限公司总裁李骏：博览会我是第一次来参加，整个平台的起点非常高，规格非常高，级别非常高，规模也很大。中国—东盟博览会在代表的接待、会议的安排以及各方面的细节都很好。

集成创投高级投资经理黄红云：第一次参加中国—东盟博览会活动，感觉组委会工作人员热情，工作细致，会议期间的短信通知能为参会机构提供更便捷的会议动态信息，为参会人员提供了便利。

雷遁控股集团执行董事李计良：这次博览会开得非常成功，我已经连续多年参加中国—东盟博览会了。一个优秀的展会，展现了一个城市的面貌，会议安排井然有序，开幕式气势恢宏。工作人员细致认真，热情体贴，拥有很高的素养，赢得了大家赞赏。

（五）八桂大地传承友谊

由于地缘相近、人文相通，广西与东盟的友好交往源远流长。近年来，特别是中国—东盟博览会的永久落户广西，广西与东盟国家的友好往来和交流合作不断深入。博览会的举办，八方宾客纷至沓来，团结和谐、开放包容的广西给他们留下了深刻的印象。

老挝副总理宋沙瓦·凌沙瓦为再次率团到广西参加本届博览会感到高兴，对广西为老挝参展参会给予的便利表示感谢，对广西经济社会发展取得的成绩给予赞赏。他说，老挝与中国的友谊源远流长，广西与老挝地缘相近，通过中国—东盟博览会平台，双方的交流合作日益深化。当前，中国已进入“十二五”发展的新时期，老挝也在实行开放政策，双方应继续落实两党两国领导人达成的共识，将老中全面战略伙伴关系提高到新的水平。他希望广西与老挝在经贸、文化等方面进一步加强交流合作。

缅甸副总统吴丁昂敏乌表示很高兴能率团参加本届博览会，来到南宁就像回到了自己的家一样。他对广西为缅甸代表团参展参会及参观考察所作的精心安排和热情接待表示感谢。缅甸政府一定精心组织、精心安排，当好2012年博览会的主题国。他对广西为缅甸驻南宁总领事馆开馆及日常工作给予的支持表示感谢，强调缅方高度重视缅中全面战略合作伙伴关系，将一如既往地与广西加强合作交流，增进传统友谊，取得共同发展。

东盟秘书长素林说，凭借中国—东盟博览会这一平台，加上中国—东盟自由贸易区的建成和投入使用，广西作为中国—东盟“桥头堡”的作用日益凸显，在对东盟国家投资和商贸往来中可以发挥更积极的作用，并带动中国更多省市和地区与东盟开展合作。

中国商务部商务参赞张克宁对广西在中国—东盟自贸区建设进程中作出的贡献和取得的成就赞赏有加。他表示，多年来，广西在中国—东盟自贸区建设中发挥了积极的作用，充分展示了作为中国与东盟接壤省区所具有的区位优势并体现了出色作为。

雷氏国际投资集团经理韦志评价说，他到世界各地参加过不少展会，但是少有像中国—东盟博览会给他留下如此深刻印象的，广西人民热情好客，并且结合民歌节是一大亮点，如果说博览会是一场经济交流的盛会，那么民歌节就是精神食粮的盛宴了。

四　2011年中国—东盟博览会再获殊荣

2011年，中国—东盟博览会续写辉煌，斩获5项业内大奖，博览会秘书处秘书长郑军健也获得两项殊荣，分别是：

2011年5月5—7日，世界园艺博览会城市与会展高峰论坛暨第九届中国会展节事财富论坛在西安举办，5月6日，在2010—2011年中国会展业“金手指”颁奖典礼上，中国—东盟博览会被评为“2010—2011年度中国会展业金手指奖·中国十大影响力展会”；中国—东盟博览秘书处秘书长、广西国际博览事务局局长郑军健被评为“2010—2011年度中国会展产业金手指奖·十大新闻人物”。

2011年8月25日，在上海举办的2011中国国际会展创新与发展论坛暨第八届“中国会展之星”颁奖典礼上，中国—东盟博览会被评为“2011年度‘中国会展之星’品牌展会”和“2011年度中国十大政府主导型展会”；中国—东盟博览秘书处秘书长、广西国际博览事务局局长郑军健被评为“2011年度中国会展之星·新闻人物”；南宁国际会展中心荣膺“2011年度最佳展览场馆奖”。

2011年11月12日，在成都举行的第七届中国节庆产业年会暨2011中国节庆产业金手指奖颁奖盛典上，中国—东盟博览会被评为“2011中国节庆产业金手指十大经贸博览类节庆奖”。

2011年12月12—14日，2011年广州（海珠·琶州）会展经济论坛中及2011中国会展经济年度研讨会召开，12月13日，在2011年度中国会展业十佳品牌颁奖晚会上，中国—东盟博览会被评为“2011年中国十佳品牌展会”。

2011年中国—东盟博览会获奖情况

获奖时间	狀奖内容	获该奖项次数	获奖论坛	主办机构
5月6日	2010—2011年度中国会展业金手指奖·中国十大影响力展会	2	西安世界园艺博览会城市与会展高峰论坛暨第九届中国会展节事财富论坛2010—2011年中国会展业“金手指”颁奖典礼	亚洲财富论坛、国际商报、新华网
	2010—2011年度中国会展产业金手指奖·十大新闻人物	3		
8月25日	2011年度“中国会展之星”品牌展会	3	2011中国国际会展创新与发展论坛暨第八届“中国会展之星”颁奖盛典	全国城市会展办公室、全国会展联盟、中国会展经济研究会、《第一会展》杂志联合
	2011年度中国十大政府主导型展会	3		
	2011年度“中国会展之星·新闻人物”	2		
11月12日	2011中国节庆产业金手指十大经贸博览类节庆奖	2	第七届中国节庆产业年会暨2011中国节庆产业金手指奖颁奖盛典	亚洲财富论坛、成都市人民政府、中国节庆产业年会组委会
12月13日	2011年中国十佳品牌展会	2	2011年广州（海珠·琶州）会展经济论坛及2011中国会展经济年度研讨会2011年度中国会展业十佳品牌颁奖晚会	商务部国际贸易经济合作研究院、中国会展经济研究会、广州经济贸易委员会、广州对外贸易经济合作局、广州海珠区人民政府

小结　务实合作享成果　盛会盛典赢盛誉

随着中国—东盟自由贸易区《货物贸易协议》、《投资协议》和《服务贸易协议》的实施，中国—东盟进一步加强贸易与投资合作的愿望更加强烈，双方更注重充分利用中国—东盟博览会平台共享商机。第八届中国—东盟博览会在新形势下举办，突出中国—东盟建立对话关系20周年合作成果和中国—东盟自贸区显著成果，更受中外企业客商的关注并积极参与。从本届博览会的成效来看，呈现以下特点：

一是经贸成效务实，再上新台阶。第八届中国—东盟博览会有更多的中国和东盟各国名优企业参展，更多各国采购商参会，商品贸易成交额再创新高。同时，本届博览会着眼于打造中国企业“走出去”投资东盟的最好平台，在推动“走出去”等方面举办了务实的投资促进活动，收到了实实在在的效果。本届博览会签约投资合作项目数量多、金额大、质量高，是历届投资促进活动中成果最丰硕的一次。尤其是“走出去”项目涵盖领域更加广泛，涉及基础设施建设、能源化工、有色金属、装备制造、商贸物流和农产品领域等。“走出去”大项目包括：越南海阳1200MW发电厂项目、老挝“南椰2”水电站项目等。

二是首次举办闭幕式，展示共办共赢。本届博览会不仅在经贸方面收获了硕果，也在合作共办上获得了喜人的成绩。首次举办的闭幕仪式格外隆重，凸显中国—东盟共办的特点。中国—东盟博览会组委会在闭幕仪式上对中方和东盟方参会组织机构进行了表彰。东盟10国共办方、东盟秘书处和海南、福建、青岛等省市分别获得了最佳参展商组织奖、最佳采购商组织奖、最佳行业组织奖、最佳品牌展示奖、最佳投资合作推介奖、最佳魅力之城展示奖、主题国纪念奖、重大贡献及支持奖等多个奖项。这些奖项的颁发，说明了东盟各国共办方和国内各省高度重视博览会，在博览会招商招展、组织服务及展示方面的工作中发挥越来越重要的作用。此外，闭幕式上还举行了本届中国“魅力之城”向下届中国“魅力之城”交接“魅力之城”印章、本届主题国向下届主题国移交主题国标志的仪式。交接仪式的举行，是博览会的精神与风采不断传承的实际行动，在促进合作共赢方面具有深远的意义。

三是中外嘉宾盛赞博览会，博览会再获多项行业大奖。中国和东盟国家领导人、部长级贵宾对本届博览会给予高度评价，充分肯定博览会在促进中国—东盟传统友谊和交流合作等方面发挥的重要作用，并对博览会继续发挥平台作用寄予了殷切希望。各国商协会会长、企业家等各界人士盛赞博览会在搭建平台、传导中国—东盟自贸区商机等方面的重要作用。各界嘉宾对博览会不断提升的服务水平给予肯定。博览会在广西举办，团结和谐、开放包容的广西给中外嘉宾留下了深刻的印象。各界嘉宾认为，随着中国—东盟博览会每年举办和中国—东盟自贸区建成和发展，广西作为中国—东盟“桥头堡”的作用日益凸显，将发挥更积极的作用，并带动中国更多省、市和地区与东盟开展合作。

中国—东盟博览会受到了国内会展业内的好评。2011年中国—东盟博览会再获殊荣，共获得业内5项顶级大奖。至此，博览会举办8年共获得21个（次）业内顶级大奖。

在世界政治、经济形势不断变化的环境中，中国—东盟自由贸易区的发展也不断出现新的形势，产生新的需求。中国—东盟博览会作为在该区域内唯一以中国—东盟自由贸易区为主题的国际盛会，将紧扣中国—东盟自贸区发展形势，进一步发挥平台作用，为中国与东盟友好合作服务，中国—东盟自贸区服务，为各国企业服务。

第十一章

11 非凡成就　影响深远
——第八届中国—东盟博览会的深远影响

记录历史是为了展望未来，总结经验是为了开创未来。

第八届中国—东盟博览会的成功举办，反映了中国—东盟建立对话关系20周年的成果，服务了中国—东盟自由贸易区建设和发展，为促进中国—东盟战略伙伴关系作出了重要贡献。

第八届中国—东盟博览会对双方友好合作的作用是全面、深入、务实的。

本届博览会进一步促进了中国与东盟的政治互信和政商互动。多边和双边会晤及各层次交流活动密集，政商互动踊跃，中国—东盟建立对话关系20周年系列纪念活动丰富多彩。本届博览会为今后双方合作指明了方向。

本届博览会进一步服务中国—东盟自由贸易区，展览内容更加适应中国—东盟自由贸易区建成和发展的需要。展会从更高层次促进了经贸务实合作，取得一批新成果。重大项目引人注目，贸易投资合作成效进一步提升。

本届博览会为中国各省（市）与东盟国家的合作提供更大的平台，为更多经济体加强合作提供了更加广阔的平台，进一步服务了举办地广西的发展。

第八届中国—东盟博览会成就非凡，影响深远。

Significant Achievements, Far–reaching Impact

—The 8th CAEXPO's Profound Influence

To look back at the history is for a better look into the future, and to summarize experiences is for a brighter tomorrow of the CAEXPO.

The successful 8th CAEXPO is an outcome of ASEAN–China dialogue relations which were established 20 years ago, which not only serve the CAFTA construction and development, but greatly contribute to the ASEAN– China strategic relations as well.

It is commonly agreed that the 8th CAEXPO has effectively promoted the bilateral friendly cooperation in an all–round and pragmatic way.

It has served as a sound meeting place for both sides to enhance political mutual trust and political–business interactions. Diverse multilateral and bilateral meetings and exchanges were held during the fair period, and splendid celebrations were arranged for the 20th anniversary of ASEAN–China dialogue relations. It actually shows a direction for the bilateral cooperation in the future.

It has provided better services for the CAFTA for its contents are designed to cater to the needs of CAFTA development. Its exhibitions has effectively promoted the bilateral economic and trade cooperation at a higher level, gaining new and pragmatic outcomes. It well displays a batch of major projects, thus increasing its own trade and investment cooperation outcomes.

It has built up a vast platform for the exchanges and cooperation between Chinese provinces/cities and the ASEAN nations, which is also a platform for enhancing cooperation among different economies, thus further promoting the development of Guangxi itself.

The 8th CAEXPO has thus gained tremendous achievement and exerted profound influence in all areas.

CHAPTER ELEVEN

一　进一步密切中国与东盟战略伙伴关系

2011年是中国—东盟建立对话关系20周年、中国—东盟友好交流年、中国—东盟自由贸易区建成1周年。这是一个总结历史、开拓未来的重要年份，第八届中国—东盟博览会作为双方建立对话关系20周年系列纪念活动的重要组成部分，对进一步密切中国与东盟战略伙伴关系，作出了重大贡献。

（一）第八届中国—东盟博览会进一步促进了中国与东盟的政治互信和政商互动

作为中国—东盟建立对话关系20周年系列纪念活动的重要组成部分，本届博览会得到中国东盟领导人高度重视，中国总理温家宝、马来西亚总理纳吉布、柬埔寨首相洪森、缅甸副总统吴丁昂敏乌、老挝副总理宋沙瓦、泰国副总理吉滴叻、越南副总理阮春福出席了本届博览会、商务与投资峰会。东盟秘书长素林以及中国和东盟各国商务、环保、质检、金融、电信等多个领域的部长出席本届盛会。出席本次博览会、商务与投资峰会的部长级贵宾有240人，其中中方141人，东盟和其他国家部长级贵宾99人。中国和东盟10国商协会会长、知名企业家、社会各界知名人士出席盛会。

中国和东盟各国领导人率团高规格出席本次盛会，表明了在中国—东盟建立对话关系20周年的特殊历史背景下，面对复杂的世界经济形势，中国和东盟更加重视博览会和商务与投资峰会的平台作用，显现出进一步加强互利合作，继续共同推进自贸区建设，实现共同发展、共同繁荣的信心和决心。会期所进行的一系列友好交流活动有力证明了这点。

1. 多边和双边会晤和交流活动密集，政治互信进一步增强。

本届博览会期间，举行了6场国家领导人会见，中国和东盟国家领导人、各国代表团团长巡视了展馆，共同出席了博览会开幕式、商务与投资峰会开幕式和欢迎宴会。主题国马来西亚举行了丰富多彩的主题国活动，中国总理温家宝和马来西亚总理纳吉布共同出席了早餐会、见证了中马钦州产业

第八届中国—东盟博览会盛况
The splendid 8th CAEXPO

园区签约仪式并为该园区揭牌。中马钦州产业园区是中马两国政府合作的第一个国家级产业园区，是博览会推动中马经贸合作的重要成果，将按照打造中国—东盟合作典范区的目标，着力建设先进制造基地、信息智慧走廊、文化生态新城、合作交流窗口。博览会期间，温家宝总理与纳吉布总理还共同出席了主题国“魅力之城”开馆仪式。老挝副总理宋沙瓦出席了庆祝中老建交50周年“北部湾之声”节目落地老挝万象活动。会期还举行了中国—东盟经贸部长晚餐会，促进了友好交流。这些活动对增进中国与东盟的政治互信非常及时而有效。

第八届中国—东盟博览会开幕前，缅甸单方面宣布搁置中缅两国密松电站合作项目。随后，缅甸副总统吴丁昂敏乌通过媒体表达了在第八届博览会与中方就此事进行沟通的意愿。10月20日下午，中国国务院总理温家宝在南宁会见缅甸副总统吴丁昂敏乌。温总理表示，实施好中缅重大合作项目符合双方的共同利益，双方要认真落实两国领导人达成的各项共识，切实履行承诺，加强协调沟通，妥善解决出现的问题，确保中缅经贸合作健康顺利发展。吴丁昂敏乌表示，缅方高度重视缅中全面战略合作伙伴关系，将与中方保持密切沟通，积极寻求解决问题的办法，维护共同利益。这次会见对维护中国与缅甸之间的政治互信具有重要的作用。

2011年10月9日，中国商船“华平号”和“玉兴8号”两艘商船在湄公河金三角水域遭遇袭击，13名船员全部遇难，这起发生在第八届中国—东盟博览会召开之际的恶性事情，引起了国际社会的广泛关注。10月20日下午，中国国务院总理温家宝在南宁会见泰国副总理吉滴叻，温家宝希望有关国家政府切实做好在湄公河遇难中国船员的善后事宜，加快案件调查处理工作，共同采取行动，加强在湄公河的执法合作，确保人民生命和财产安全。泰国等有关国家领导人对中方人员遇害深表哀悼，表示愿与中方密切合作，做好案情调查及善后工作，共同维护湄公河航运安全。此次中泰两国领导人的高层会见，对于稳妥处理湄公河遇难中国船员的善后事宜，维护中泰友好合作关系具有重要的影响。

在第八届中国—东盟博览会期间进行了各场会晤中，温家宝总理积极评价中国同东盟各国的双边关系，表示中国愿同各国一道，落实好达成的各项共识，推动双边关系取得新进展。东盟国家领导人均认为，发展同中国的友好关系至关重要，前景广阔，愿与中方一道，推动双边框架下的互利合作深入发展。这些会晤与表态，大大增进了中国与东盟的政治互信。

2. 政商互动踊跃，合作更加深入。

第八届中国—东盟博览会是在国际金融市场出现急剧动荡、世界经济复苏的不确定性和不稳定性增强、中国—东盟自贸区实施效果不断显现的背景下举办。第八届中国—东盟博览会针对这一新形势，举办更多的政商高端对接活动，共22场，解决了经贸合作中的实际问题，让企业及时掌握经济发展的风向标，促进经贸合作。第八届中国—东盟博览会政商高端对接活动既有东盟国家领导人与中国地方政府领导、企业家的会见、对话，也有中国有关部委领导、各省市领导与中外企业家的会见、交流。这些高端对接活动取得了显著成效，促进了政商互动，为企业创造更多的商机。

马来西亚领导人与中国企业家的互动最为典型。博览会期间，马来西亚总理纳吉布与中国企业CEO举行了圆桌对话会。会上，纳吉布总理提出，

马来西亚总理纳吉布与中国企业 CEO 圆桌对话会
Round-table Dialogue between H.E. Dato' Sri Mohd Najib Tun Abdul Razak, prime minister of Malaysia and CEOs from China

希望中国企业更多地进入高科技领域，包括电信、水利、污水处理、绿色技术、生物医药等领域，这些都是马来西亚关注的重点领域，希望吸引更多的外商投资。马来西亚政府将全力支持中马共建的钦州产业园区的发展。本次对话会签约100亿美元的合作项目，务实推动了商界的合作。博览会期间，纳吉布总理不仅出席马来西亚“魅力之城”开馆仪式，而且出席了本国商品馆开馆仪式，巡视了本国商品馆，与企业进行了互动。巡馆时，纳吉布总理饶有兴致地参观了教育、医疗护理服务、餐饮、保健等各个展位，鼓励马来西亚参展商利用中国—东盟博览会这个平台，大力开拓中国市场，与中国客商共拓商机。巡馆之后，纳吉布总理还见证了马来西亚隆基马中国际集团公司与中国永州市政府的合作项目协议书交换仪式。

中国与泰国的政商活动也取得良好成效。10月21日，出席第八届中国—东盟博览会、中国—东盟商务与投资峰会的泰国副总理兼商业部部长吉滴叻，在南宁与中泰企业家见面，共叙友谊，共商合作，共谋发展。吉滴叻说，泰国政府非常支持泰国经济均衡发展，特别在开发产品、进出口贸易和投资出口等领域发展。2011年前8个月，泰中双边贸易额接近400亿美元。泰中政府计划在2015年双边贸易额达到1000亿美元。在旅游业方面，目前，泰国到中国旅游的游客以及中国到泰国旅游的游客约为110万人。他希望借助此次见面会，促进泰中两国企业家携手迈进，促进商业投资各领域的成功合作。见面会结束后，进行中泰合作项目签约仪式。

其他政商活动也丰富多彩。例如中国与缅甸的缅甸企业家座谈会上，缅甸商务部部长吴温敏与企业家进行了座谈，来自中国以及缅甸的30余位企业家代表出席座谈会。座谈会上，中缅企业家代表从深化中缅传统友谊、促进贸易交流、增进企业投资合作等领域展开务实、坦诚的对话与交流。

3. 建立对话关系20周年系列活动多姿多彩，主题更为鲜明。

第八届中国—东盟博览会从开幕式、布展，到闭幕式都突出了中国东盟建立对话关系20周年的元素。会前，广西作为博览会的承办地，参与主办和承办了20周年系列纪念活动，如中国—东盟建立对话关系20周年纪念招待会文艺演出、友谊知识竞赛、互联互通战略研讨会等，为博览会的召开营造了浓郁的氛围，突出了本届博览会鲜明的主题。

博览会开幕式隆重热烈，形象地表达出博览会11国共办、领导人亲自推动的特点，反映中国—东盟建立对话关系20周年的辉煌成就，展示博览会促进中国—东盟友好交流、推动自贸区建设取得的成果和作出的贡献。开幕式上举行了有11国青少年参加的中国—东盟青少年交流活动中心揭牌仪式，展示了中国与东盟友谊代代相传的深刻寓意，博览会取得的成果得到更具体的展现。博览会开幕式受到了中国和东盟国家领导人、政府官员、商协会会长、企业家的普遍赞誉。

马来西亚贸工部部长穆斯塔法说：“我本人非常荣幸主持博览会开幕式。开幕式办得很好，每个细节都做得很到位，非常完美，非常精彩！”东盟秘书长素林说：“本届开幕式上能邀请到这么多国家的领导人共同出席，显示了中国—东盟博览会政治外交规格之高和意义之重”，“11国少年的互动，充分体现了中国—东盟博览会是一个开放、包容的合作平台。”

第八届中国—东盟商务与投资峰会开幕式在场地安排、会场布置、内容设计等方面创新，更加隆重、大气、务实，给贵宾留下深刻印象。中国和东盟国家领导人分别在开幕式上阐述了促进双方合作的政策主张，为进一步深化和拓展合作、实现共同繁荣指明了方向。

第八届中国—东盟博览会开幕晚会暨南宁国际民歌艺术节开幕式紧扣中国—东盟建立对话关系20周年，节目内容更加丰富，更具特色。

本届博览会和商务与投资峰会闭幕式形式新颖，意义深刻，体现了博览会共办水平和成果。在闭幕式上，本届博览会主题国马来西亚与下届博览会主题国缅甸、本届博览会中国“魅力之城”海南省与下届中国“魅力之城”广州分别举行了交接仪式。组委会向中国和东盟各国组展机构颁发了“主题国纪念奖”、“重大贡献及支持奖”、“最佳参展商组织奖”、“最佳采购商组织奖”、“最佳魅力之城展示奖”等8类奖项，体现了本届博览会在共办机制、展会组织等方面取得了新的成效。

第八届中国—东盟博览会和商务与投资峰会闭幕式
Closing ceremony of the 8th CAEXPO and 8th CABIS

（二）第八届中国—东盟博览会从更高层次促进了经贸务实合作，取得一批新成果

第八届中国—东盟博览会秉承其一贯的经贸合作传统，紧紧围绕自由贸易区发展的主题，以形式多样的展览、圆桌会、推介会、说明会、研讨会、对接会等为载体，开展了一系列卓有成效的经贸促进活动，收获了丰硕成果，赢得了各方赞誉，取得了圆满成功。

1. 重大项目引人注目。

本届博览会签约的重大项目多，规模和质量明显提高，成为一大特点。据统计，签约的国际合作项目，合同金额达1亿美元以上有21个，国内合作项目，投资额5亿元人民币以上的有44个，其中超10亿元人民币以上的重大项目多达29个。国际合作项目投资额较大的包括：美国联邦航太控股集团投资2.35亿美元建设的桂林飞虎通用航空产业基地项目，菲律宾各界联合会、美国电器产品公司、厦门瀚盛游艇有限公司等投资2亿美元建设的广西北部湾国际游艇度假城项目。国内合作项目投资额较大的有：山东青岛九联集团股份有限公司投资建设的九联肉食鸡养殖善宰加工项目，总投资额70亿元；广州美索集团有限公司投资建设的桂林国际医药、化妆品物流产业园项目，总投资额25亿元；上海黑石投资有限公司投资建设40万吨/年碳四综合利用项目，总投资额17.5亿元；河北省凌云工业股份有限公司在柳州投资建设的凌云工业汽车零部件生产项目，总投资额16亿元。这些重大项目的落地开工建设，将产生“引进一个，带来一批”的效应，促进当地经济社会的快速发展。

本届博览会重大项目的最大亮点无疑是中国和马来西亚围绕钦州产业园区而开展的一系列卓有成效的工作。马来西亚是东盟10国经济发展较快的国家，也是一个新兴的工业化国家。近年来，中马双边贸易额大幅增长，2011年达到900多亿美元的历史新高，中国同时已成为马来西亚第一大贸易伙伴和第二大出口国和进口国，也是马来西亚棕榈油出口的最大市场。快速增长的双边贸易，带动了双方投资的加速，马来西亚企业在中国大陆投资的项目和投资额逐年增加，两国企业对双边扩大投资的期望很高。2011年4月，中国—马来西亚经贸投资合作论坛在马来西亚首都吉隆坡举行。4月28日，出席论坛的中国国务院总理温家宝发表演讲，提议设立中马钦州产业园区，并指出“广西钦州中马产业园区是双方在中国西部地区合作的第一个工业园区，具有示范意义，中国政府欢迎马方有实力的企业积极参与园区的规划和开发建设”。同日，温家宝与马来西亚总理纳吉布进行会谈时，再次提议双方合作共建中马钦州产业园区，纳吉布十分赞同。期间，两国总理多次关注

中马钦州产业园区，认为该园区是中马合作的新平台、新动力和新亮点，双双表示支持该园区的建设，鼓励两国有实力的企业家以该园区为平台，扩大双向投资，进一步深化中国与马来西亚的战略伙伴关系。

2011年10月21日上午，在第八届中国—东盟博览会举办期间，温家宝与纳吉布共同见证了中马钦州产业园区的签字仪式，并一同揭开“中马钦州产业园区”的牌扁，这是一个历史性的时刻，是中国与马来西亚这两个亚洲经济快速增长国家扩大合作的重要里程碑。中马钦州产业园区是中马两国政府合作的第一个产业园区，是继中新苏州工业园区、中新天津生态城后我国第三个中外两国政府合作的产业园区，是中国—东盟自由贸易区建成后中马两国合作的新平台、新动力、新亮点，是中国—东盟博览会作为推动中国与东盟交流合作重要平台取得的重要成果，是广西北部湾经济区产业园区建设的重大突破，是广西和钦州经济社会发展的重大机遇，必将进一步深化中国与东盟的合作、全面提升广西开放合作水平、推动广西和钦州经济社会发展。2011年10月21日下午，纳吉布在与中国企业CEO圆桌对话会上明确表示，他本人不久将再次来广西出席园区的启动仪式。

2012年4月1日，中马两国总理温家宝和纳吉布如约来到广西钦州，共同转动金色钥匙，为中马钦州产业园区开园揭幕。中马钦州产业园区规划总面积55平方公里，规划人口50万人。首期开发建设15平方公里，其中启动区7.87平方公里。产业园区将按照打造中国—东盟合作典范区的目标，着力建设先进制造基地、信息智慧走廊、文化生态新城、合作交流窗口。至此，第八届博览会催生的重要经贸合作深深落地、开花结果。

2012年4月1日，中国国务院总理温家宝和马来西亚总理纳吉布共同为中马钦州产业园区揭幕

On April 1, 2012, H.E. Wen Jiabao, premier of the State Council of China and H.E. Dato' Sri Mohd Najib Tun Abdul Razak, prime minister of Malaysia jointly unveiled the China-Malaysia Qinzhou Industrial Park

2. 贸易投资合作成效进一步提升。

本届博览会经贸成效进一步提升，突出了中国—东盟自由贸易区显著成果。主要表现为以下几个方面：

一是本届博览会展览规模扩大，参展参会企业更多。总展位数4700个。参展企业总数2300家，同比增长4.6%。参展参会客商50600人，比上届增长3.26%。

二是东盟及区域外国家参展更加踊跃，共办特色更加鲜明。东盟及区域外国家使用展位数达到历史最高水平。印尼、老挝、马来西亚、缅甸、泰国、越南等6个东盟国家包馆， 40多家东盟知名品牌企业参展，马来西亚、泰国等组织橡胶、棕榈油、矿产品等大宗商品企业积极参展。东盟国家优势行业集中参展，展会专业化进一步提高。

三是国内企业参展空前高涨，博览会在区域内外的市场吸引力进一步增强。国内企业申请展位数超过计划数的30.2%，名优企业多，参展产品更加契合东盟市场的需求。台湾企业在每届博览会参展的基础上，2011年由台北世界贸易中心组织企业首次整体参展。日本也首次组织企业整体参展。国内企业在国际经济合作展区和工程机械、运输车辆展区重复参展率高达90%，东盟国家企业重复参展率较高，缅甸达71.9%，新加坡、柬埔寨均达55%。表明博览会在区域内外的市场认知度和吸引力进一步增强。采购商数量和质量进一步提高。本届采购团组有70多个，多于往届。东盟采购商团组数比上届增加20%以上。

第八届中国—东盟博览会上的台湾展位

Exhibitors from Chinese Taipei at the 8th CAEXPO

四是经贸成效取得新突破。本届博览会商品贸易成交额达到18.07亿美元，比上届增长5.6%。本届博览会签订国际经济合作项目105个，总投资额74.2亿美元，同比增长10.86%。

国际合作项目不乏诸多亮点。如，开发生物质能源、推动可持续发展的宁明东亚蔗渣发电项目。在本届博览会上，泰国两仪糖业有限公司在广西宁明县投资建设30MW生物质能（蔗渣）发电项目。该项目总投资4600万美元，预计2011年底开工、2012年11月完成。经初步计算，项目建成后，每年可向公共电网输送清洁能源电量约1.5亿度，新增110多个就业机会，并可为广西东亚宁明糖业有限公司创造新增利润3200多万元，为社会新增税金800多万元。在国际经济合作项目中，中国企业“走出去”项目52个，总投资额26.5亿美元，同比增长37.8%。中国工程承包企业“走出去”一大亮点就是越南海阳发电厂项目。在本届博览会上，中国技术进出口总公司、天津电力建设公司签订了由马来西亚捷硕集团投资兴建的越南海阳1200MW发电厂项目EPC总承包合同，合同总额达14.88亿美元，这是近年来我国工程承包企业对东盟国家投资合作的一个大项目。该项目地处越南海阳省京门县，占地面积300公顷，投资总额达22.5亿美元，一号机组预计将于2016年第四季度投产。项目全部投产后将有效缓解该地区电力供应紧张的局面，对保障该地区加工制造业快速发展和人民生活水平的提高将起到积极推动作用。

本届博览会签订国内经济合作项目102个，总投资731.1亿元，比上届增长8.39%。这方面比较典型的项目是桂林创意产业园项目。文化创意产业是服务业的一个重要领域，加快文化创意产业发展是丰富文化产品、满足国民文化需求、提高文化消费水平的重要举措。文化创意产业作为技术密集型产业，具有占地少、附加值高、投资回报快等特点，成为越来越多城市产业发展的首选。桂林市是世界著名的旅游胜地和历史文化名城。在产业发展上对环境保护、节能减排等方面要求较高，不仅要发展经济，更要保护秀美山川。因此，大力发展旅游、文化创意等第三产业成为桂林市产业发展的首选。近年来，桂林市不断加大对文化创意产业发展的支持力度，出台了专门扶持政策，搭建了诸如动漫测试平台和培训基地，工业设计和软件外包培训基地等服务平台，培养了一大批文化创意、软件设计、服务外包、动漫设计企业，成为广西文化产业发展的重要基地。在本届博览会上，由灵川县人民政府和广州市希力电子科技有限公司签订的桂林创意产业园项目，协议总额达到21亿元。该园区将主要发展动漫设计、软件开发、服务外包等，吸引一大批文化创意产业聚集发展，积极打造具有广西文化特色的文化产业基地。

举办地广西在本届博览会上共签订国际合作项目69个，总投资46.9亿美元，占国际合作项目合同金额的63.2%。这方面比较典型的项目是缅甸腊戌水泥生产项目。缅甸是我国传统友好国家，也是资源丰富、开发潜力巨大的东盟国家。广西与缅甸经贸合作历史悠久，特别是广西参与大湄公河次区域合作以后，与缅甸的合作领域不断拓宽，合作水平不断提高，在资源开发、农业替代种植等领域开展了一系列互利合作项目，带动了当地经济发展，取得了良好的经济和社会效益。本届博览会上，广西水电工程局和缅甸大勐宜昌达公司签订了缅甸腊戌水2500T/D水泥熟料的新型干法水泥生产线项目。该项目位于缅甸掸邦省的腊戌地区，协议金额达8599万美元，其中中方投资8169万美元，将建造一座日产量2500吨的水泥厂，预计年产高标号水泥熟料77.5万吨，年产高品质水泥87.5万吨。该项目的实施既能够发挥广西水泥产业的技术优势，加大“走出去”步伐，又能够满足缅甸经济发展对水泥供应日益增加的需求，发挥市场与产业的互补优势，实现互利共赢。

中国—缅甸企业家座谈会
China-Myanmar Business Seminar

五是商务与投资峰会取得丰硕成果。本届商务与投资峰会以“深化区域合作，实现共同繁荣”为主题，中国国务院总理温家宝发表了主旨演讲，柬埔寨首相洪森发表了讲话，广西壮族自治区党委书记、自治区人大常委会主任郭声琨主持开幕式。中国、东盟以及世界10多个国家和地区的政府高官、商界领袖、企业精英、区域组织代表、知名专家学者和媒体记者1100多人参会，各方就进一步深化区域行业之间的务实合作、实现共同发展和繁荣进行讨论和展望。

六是系列会议和交流活动富有成效。本届博览会保持“展会结合”特色，举办会议和交流活动14个，其中，环保部围绕博览会重点主题“环保合作”，主办了中国—东盟环保合作论坛；其他有关部委围绕质检、金融、太阳能、药品安全、智库、人口与家庭发展、文化产业论坛、出版、森林、物流等领域，举办了相关会议和交流活动。中国和东盟国家部长级官员、企业家、银行家、专家学者等出席了系列会议和活动，围绕各领域的热点议题，展开了深入研讨和对话，促进了全方位、多层次、宽领域合作，形成了一批务实成果，例如，环保论坛启动了中国—东盟绿色使者计划。质检论坛通过了关于加强中国—东盟产品质量安全合作的《南宁联合声明》。出版论坛达成《南宁共识》。金融论坛围绕金融及财政合作，在区域内货币结算、金融机构支持企业“走出去”、金融合作发展机制研究等方面，取得了新成果。

本届博览会在会议与系列交流活动上增加了更多的社会人文领域的会议和交流活动，社会人文交流活动丰富多彩。中国—东盟文化产业论坛在博物馆运营管理及其文化产品创意开发方面，中国—东盟出版博览会在图书展销、论坛及版权贸易等方面，全面展示了中国与东盟国家历史文化和人文魅力。中国—东盟人口与家庭发展论坛在人口与家庭发展方面，开展了研讨和交流。会期还举办了南宁国际民歌艺术节、高尔夫球精英赛、“网球之友”联谊活动、中国—东盟媒体汽车拉力赛、国际商务书画展等一系列文化交流活动，增进了友谊。

（三）第八届中国—东盟博览会为今后的合作指明了方向

2011年是中国—东盟建立对话关系20周年、中国—东盟友好交流年、中国—东盟自由贸易区建成1周年。与会贵宾云集，规格高，中国和东盟各国领导人在会期活动中分别发表了讲话，充分肯定了双方20年合作成果，深入分析了当前形势，指明了下一步合作的方向。这对于充分发挥博览会、商务与投资峰会平台作用，进一步深化双方友好合作，具有指导意义。

中国政府总理温家宝在本届商务与投资峰会主旨演讲中提出重点办好几件大事：

一是共同建设好自贸区。中方愿意继续扩大东盟国家优势产品的进口，妥善解决自贸区建设中出现的各种问题。将在南宁建设中国—东盟商品交易中心，作为双方产品的展示交易平台和商贸物流基地。

二是大力推进互联互通。中方将与东盟方面密切合作，加强对中国与东盟有关国家互联互通的投入，为促进本地区商品、资本、信息的自由流通、人员往来和经济社会发展创造更好条件。中方愿意继续利用好中国—东盟投资合作基金、中国—东盟银联体及对东盟国家建立的信贷渠道，支持中国—

东盟互联互通合作项目的落实。

三是扩大双方投资合作。中方已经承诺在东盟国家各建一个经贸合作区，通过集群式投资提高双方经贸合作水平。中马钦州产业园是双方在中国西部地区合作建设的第一个工业园，具有示范意义，欢迎马方有实力的企业积极参与园区的规划和开发建设。

四是深化区域经济合作。中方将鼓励企业参与东盟东部增长区、大湄公河、泛北部湾等次区域合作，给予金融、技术、市场等方面的有力支持，推动形成若干经济增长极。中方愿与东盟密切合作，进一步深化现有各项区域财金合作，扩大货币互换规模和参与范围，完善“清迈倡议”多边化危机救助机制，加强区域经济监测能力建设，推进亚洲债券市场发展，逐步建立稳定、成熟的地区资本市场，进一步增强本地区应对国际金融风险的能力。

五是拓展人文领域交流。以办好“中国—东盟友好交流年”为契机，继续加强文化、教育、旅游、青年等领域的交流与合作，努力实现2015年双方人员往来达到1500万人次的目标。

温家宝总理的建议，高屋建瓴，内涵深刻，方向明确，保障措施有力，为未来通过博览会、商务与投资峰会这个平台发挥更大的作用奠定了基础。

马来西亚总理纳吉布在本届博览会开幕式致辞中说，今后数年里，随着《中国—东盟环保合作战略（2009—2015年）》的实施，中国—东盟环保中心有望在中国成立。纳吉布总理在与中国企业CEO圆桌对话会上提出，希望中国企业更多地进入高科技，包括电信、水利、污水处理、绿色技术、生物医药等领域。这些都是马来西亚关注的重点领域，希望吸引更多的外商投资。马来西亚政府将全力支持中马共建的钦州产业园区的发展。

柬埔寨首相洪森在本届商务与投资峰会讲话中说，希望中国可以向东盟欠发达的成员国转让绿色科技，以增加农业产量。

泰国副总理吉滴叻在与中泰企业家见面会上说，希望借助此次见面会，促进泰中两国企业家携手迈进，促进商业投资各领域的成功合作。泰国政府将继续支持两国企业家合作。

中国和东盟国家领导人的讲话，对双方开展进一步的合作具有很强的指导意义。尽管，未来的发展存在许多不确定的因素，但只要中国和东盟各国充分利用博览会、商务与投资峰会平台作用，认真加以研究和落实，博览会、商务与投资峰会的未来图景会越来越好。

二 进一步服务中国—东盟自由贸易区

促进中国—东盟自由贸易区建设，共享合作与发展机遇，是中国—东盟博览会一以贯之的宗旨。第八届中国—东盟博览会紧扣中国—东盟自由贸易区发展，在展览内容上创新，举行了一系列经贸促进活动，进一步彰显了博览会为中国—东盟自由贸易区服务的特色。本届博览会上，这一特色在两个方面得到了很好的体现。

（一）展览内容更加紧扣中国—东盟自由贸易区建成后发展的新需求

1. 商品展示。

各国展示了零关税条件下互补性更强的品类。本届博览会的7号展厅是机械设备（食品加工和包装机械）展区，这是中国—东盟合作潜力巨大的行业。中国建材产品与东盟国家互补性强，合作潜力大，本届博览会在8号和9号展厅集中展示。电子电器是中国与东盟贸易中的重要门类，本届博览会在10、11号展厅集中展示。作为中国与东盟重点合作领域之一的能源领域，被

电子电器展区
Electronics & Electrical Appliances Exhibition

集中安排于12号展厅，展示了发电设备、输/配/变电设备、电线电缆风能、太阳能、核能等新能源发电设备。

这些互补性很强的专业、专题展览，主题明确，一目了然，深受客商的欢迎。美国佛罗里达州朱庇特市政项目中国区营运副总裁泰龙说，博览会为来自全世界各国国家的人提供一个交流合作的平台，不同国家的人们把他们各自的产品都带在这里，然后大家相互分享和交流，为以后的长远发展提供更多的选择。

英国华商协会会长许快乐说，博览会的平台可以让我们看到哪些商品有商机，我们可以进一步确定哪一种商品是可以进行合作和投资。

华泰汽车市场部长高红军说，博览会就是中国的舞台、世界的看台，向10个东盟国家及世界各国展示商机。

滨海国际控权交易所总裁陆纬雄说，博览会整个活动的组织和各项活动和议题的设计，很贴近当前的国际国内形势的平台，还紧扣中国和东盟相互合作、共同面向未来的主题。博览会所设计的议题都是非常务实，我们也从中获取了很多信息。现场还很热闹，各方企业齐聚这里，在一个很好的气氛里面，有一些实际的收获。

本届博览会有印尼、老挝、马来西亚、缅甸、泰国、越南等6个东盟国家包馆， 40多家东盟知名品牌企业参展。这些包馆国家，充分利用博览会的平台作用，展示了这些国际特色、优质的商品。其中马来西亚、越南是连续第六次包用独立展厅参展。马来西亚集中展示了食品饮料、大宗商品、保健产品 环保产品、生活时尚、教育经营连锁等特色商品。越南集中展示了咖啡、手工艺品、木制家具等特色商品。泰国与印度尼西亚是连续第五次包用独立展厅参展。泰国展示了食品农产品、工艺品及珠宝饰品、日用消费品等商品。印度尼西亚集中展示了汽车配件、橡胶、农产品、木材家具、传统手工艺品等印度尼西亚特色商品。

各包馆的东盟商品展区，均集中到其市场竞争优势的主要行业上，突出了东盟国家的商品特色，也体现了浓郁的东盟国家文化与风情。因而获得各方的高度评价。泰国贸易院副主席陈树铭说，我是第一次来参加博览会，我感觉组织得非常好，无论是在整个场馆的布置、设计，包括很多亮点的安排都安排得非常好，包括商贸、旅游、教育、电子等方面的展示都不错，内容非常精彩。这也是我第一次同时看到11个东盟国家的文化，我看了各个国家不同特色的展馆，非常兴奋。越南馆德诚食品中国区市场总经理阮明泰说，我们充分相信博览会的影响力，连续三年参展，我们的食品更为人们所熟知，代理商已遍布中国多个省市。老挝参展商贝利说，我感觉这次博览会是最好的，它给我们提供了很好的交流与合作平台，除了带来不错的经济效益外，还可以展示老挝的文化。

会期商贸配对活动针对性强，深受客商欢迎，会期举办了越南、马来西亚等专场配对会，橡胶、棕榈油等大宗商品采购配对会，中泰橡胶产业发展合作研讨会，农产品、轻工产品行业贸易对接活动，以及参展商讲坛、联合国采购说明会、商务早餐会等一系列对接活动，企业获得了更多的商机和实效。例如，越南、老挝等东盟国家轻工、家具产品受到中国采购商的欢迎，达成了一批采购意向。中国企业专门为东盟市场推出的低速汽车、小型工程机械、小型农用机械，也受到东盟采购商的青睐。会前举行的中国—东盟矿业合作论坛签署了31.6亿美元的合作项目和产品贸易协议。

首届中泰橡胶产业发展合作研讨会
First Sino-Thai Symposium of Rubber Industry

越南安江省副省长在10月23日的越南专场贸易配对会上就高度评价说：配对会为中越两国企业提供了一个很好的平台，这个想法很好，能直接促成并提高经贸成效。现场到会的企业众多，场面热闹。

南宁华南城副总经理张利阳说，中国—东盟博览会的成功举办为双方开展轻工行业合作搭建了务实平台。2011年的博览会从展会组织到内容以及整个展示的产品品质，都有极大的提升，而且整个形象包括宣传各方面非常到位。

2. 投资合作。

本届博览会在做好商品贸易的基础上，突出投资合作特别是“走出去”的特色，投资合作更加务实，“走出去”的未来走向更加鲜明。

（1）首次举办有中国和东盟10国投资促进部门代表参加的中国—东盟博览会投资合作圆桌会，发布中国和东盟各国最新的投资合作政策和项目信息，介绍各国投资环境，为企业提供与各国投促机构直接交流互动的机会，推动企业“走出去”。

（2）举办了“走出去”企业与金融机构对接活动。包括：中国—东盟基础设施投融资合作论坛、金融支持企业“走出去”洽谈会、企业股权（债券）投融资交易会等，邀请了出席金融论坛的金融机构和中央企业负责人进行洽谈对接，为企业投资东盟提供务实的金融支持。

（3）本届博览会将1号展厅作为国际经济合作展区，充分表达了对国际经济合作的高度重视。该展区以促进中国企业“走出去”到东盟国家开展投资和国际经济合作为特色，参展企业70家，其中中央直属企业8家，各省市外经企业62家，使用展位166个，涉及机械、电子、冶金工程、路桥建设、水电等行业。吸引了中国电子信息产业集团、中国铝业、中国有色金属集团、中国通用技术公司、中国水利电力对外公司等知名企业参展。整体上看，国际经济合作展区参展结构更优，形成了“以中直企业为重点，各省市外经企业为新生力量”的格局；经济技术开发区整体特装展示，成为推动园区招商及园区企业“走出去”的新亮点。

（4）会期还举办了东盟各国投资推介会、海外投资论坛及项目推介会等一系列投资促进活动，在推动企业“走出去”方面取得了一批务实的成果。

本届博览会推动中国企业“走出去”收到了很实在的成效，据统计，本届博览会投资合作签约项目中，中国对东盟国家的投资合作项目48个，投资总额25.9亿美元，比上届增长72.4%。“走出去”合作的项目涵盖领域广泛，涉及基础设施建设、能源化工、有色金属、装备制造、商贸物流和农产品领域。

“走出去”的策略也获得了各方人士的高度评价。钦州市委书记、市人大常委会主任张晓钦说，我觉得博览会作为东盟合作的一个平台，在中国—东盟合作当中发挥越来越重要的作用，首先在友好合作方面发挥越来越重要的作用。2011年还举办中国和东盟11国投资促进局的局长会议，这也是第一次把11个投资促进机构聚集在一起，在贸易合作发展到一定阶段的时候，贸易必然带动投资。

广西投资集团有限公司董事长管跃庆说，我们连续8年成为博览会的战略合作伙伴，首先是博览会给我们一个很好的展示平台，同时通过博览会更多地结识了朋友，我们对东盟国家的一些业务合作，已经从过去的单纯的贸易合作，上升到了投资合作。如果没有博览会这个平台来开展这项工作，我们是不可能在这么短短的几年里，迅速地把我们企业在“走出去”这一方面迈出大步伐。

广西投资项目建设管理协会副会长汪廷强说，博览会比往年办得大气场一些，办得要好。从会展的情况来看，参加的企业比以往多，参加的人数也比以往多。特别是现在我们国家很多企业家想通过博览会这个平台“走出去”，也借这个机会到广西来找一些项目。博览会给中国和东盟各国企业家们都创造了很好的机会。

3. 服务贸易。

服务贸易专题内容更丰富，文化特色得到进一步展示。

本届博览会服务贸易专题重点展示金融服务、教育服务和旅游服务三个方面的内容。服务贸易专题展设在2号展厅，展示中国和东盟金融服务和旅游服务，参展机构11家。金融服务展区集中展示各类金融管理机构的金融政策、主要职能服务理念、信息资讯等。

本届博览会“魅力之城”突出环保理念，并与旅游合作展示相结合，综合展示11国代表性城市在贸易、投资、科技文化、旅游等方面的发展和商机，举办了中国“魅力之城”海南国际旅游岛推介会等一系列活动，促进了旅游合作,使中国与东盟合作从国家层面延伸至地方层面，特色更为鲜明，受到广泛关注。旅游服务展区还集中展示了广西旅游资源、旅游城市、旅游合作项目以及东盟国家的旅游资源。泰国孔敬府商会主席Mr.Chatchai Kosavisutte说，“魅力之城”的展现，让更多的泰国绿色酒店、绿色食品，包括保健等方面都能够推广出去，促进双方旅游的合作。

此外，会期举行了中国—东盟电信高峰论坛，签约项目金额8亿美元，推动双方在电信服务领域的合作。

（二）加强了对中国—东盟自由贸易区投资贸易便利化政策的宣讲和解读

本届中国—东盟博览会加强了对中国—东盟自由贸易区投资贸易便利化政策的宣讲、解读，进一步呈现了博览会为自由贸易区服务的服务意识与服务能力。

为提高东盟基础设施建设水平，推动东盟内部以及中国—东盟的互联互通，中国政府2009年宣布设立100亿中国—东盟投资合作基金，并向东盟国家提供150亿美元的信贷。“两金”设立后在东盟国家中产生强烈反响。2011年10月21日，由中国进出口银行、广西壮族自治区人民政府联合主办的“善用金融杠杆，共创美好未来——中国进出口银行全面支持中国—东盟经济合作情况介绍会”，对中国—东盟投资合作基金的募集和项目报批情况，

中国—东盟基础设施投融资合作论坛
China-ASEAN Infrastructure Investment and Financing Cooperation Forum

以及基金的使用方向、申报程序等作了详细说明，对中国向东盟国家提供的150亿美元信贷资金情况进行了介绍。四川开元集团、国际通信控股等有关企业介绍了资金申报及使用经验。目前，中国—东盟投资合作基金已经完成菲律宾最大的国内船运公司、泰国的集装箱港口项目、柬埔寨通信基础设施项目以及入股亚洲钾肥集团投资老挝钾肥矿项目等4项投资，投资金额约4亿美元，有力地推动了项目所在国经济社会协调发展。

现代产业分工的飞速发展为服务外包产业发展提供了巨大的市场需求，成为区域经贸合作的重要推动力量。2011年10月21日，由中国商务部服务贸易和商贸服务业司举办的“服务外包政策宣讲及企业交流会”上，来自商务部服务贸易和商贸服务业司、中国国际投资贸易促进会、香港贸易发展局的领导和专家对当前世界服务外包业发展的新趋势以及中国服务外包发展面临的新机遇进行了详细分析。会议介绍了中国商务部促进服务外包发展的“千百十”工程，讲解了中国政府扶持服务外包发展的重要政策，介绍了印度、菲律宾、马来西亚、香港等国家和地区发展服务外包业的成功经验，增进了公众对中国服务外包政策动态以及国际服务外包市场状况的了解，提高了公众对发展服务外包产业重要意义的认识，对深化中国与东盟乃至世界的国际服务外包合作起到了很好的促进作用。

本届博览会围绕泛北部湾经济合作、中越跨境经济合作区等区域合作热点问题，举办了一系列会议，同样对中国—东盟自由贸易区发展起到了积极促进作用，收到了良好的效果。

例如，2011年10月21日举行的中越跨境经济合作区中国凭祥综合保税区、越南同登口岸经济区非关税区建设情况交流会上，双方通报了推进中越凭祥—同登跨境经济合作区建设工作进展情况，并就进一步加快合作区建设进程深入交换意见，签署了会议纪要。在“加快合作区建设进度”、“加快跨境通道建设”、“推动一站式通关”、“加强园区招商引资”、“加强人力资源交流合作”、“建立定期会晤机制”等九个方面达成广泛共识，为下一步务实推动跨境经济合作区建设探明了方向。

又如，2011年10月22日，由商务部国际贸易经济合作研究院与广西商务厅联合主办的泛北部湾经济合作发展研讨会，呼应第10次中国—东盟经贸部长会议欢迎将《泛北部湾经济合作可行性研究报告》提交2011年的中国—东盟领导人会议的决定，对由商务部贸研院和广西商务厅联合起草编制的泛北部湾经济合作发展规划和系列专项规划进行了闭门讨论和交流。来自商务部、中国驻东盟各国经济商务参赞、商务部贸研院、国务院发展研究中心、中国国际问题研究所、广东省外经贸厅、海南师范大学等有关单位的领导与学者出席了会议，并对规划进行了热烈讨论。与会专家认为，泛北部湾经济合作发展规划与系列专项规划，对深化各领域务实合作具有重要战略意义，具有开创性和探索性，是促进次区域合作的重要亮点。规划提出的战略思路、合作目标、重点项目和保障措施，具有针对性和操作性，将对务实开展

中越跨境经济合作区中国凭祥综合保税区、越南同登口岸经济区非关税区建设情况交流会
Exchange Meeting on the Construction of China-Vietnam Cross-border Economic Cooperation Zones: China Pingxiang Comprehensive Bonded Zone & Vietnam Dong Dang Port Economic Zone Non-tariff Area

泛北合作产生积极推动作用。与会专家还对规划存在的不足提出了具体修改完善建议。再如，境外经贸合作区日益成为中国企业集群式“走出去”的重要平台，也成为本届博览会参会客商关注的热点。

此外，由中国商务部合作司主办的“中国境外（东盟）经贸合作区推介会”，对中国境外经贸合作区、境外农业示范区的规划建设情况、相关优惠政策等进行了详细介绍，吸引了参会客商的高度关注，中国有实力“走出去”企业参与境外经贸合作区建设的意愿不断高涨。这些会议都促进了区域经济合作和中国—东盟自由贸易区发展。

三　为中国各省市与东盟国家的合作提供更大的平台 为更多经济体加强合作提供更加广阔的平台

第八届中国—东盟博览会为中国国内各省（区、市)分别举办了面向东盟的多种交流活动，为中国各省（区、市)与东盟国家的合作搭建了更加务实的平台。

本届博览会，中国共有41个省（区、市)代表团参会。广东、福建、浙江、江苏、上海等经济发达大省保持较大参展规模，此外，湖南、江西等中部省份的参展规模也较往届有大幅提高。广东、上海、福建、山东、安徽、北京、江西等省市组织采购团组和投引资项目参会。各省市参展参会积极性普遍增强，证明国内各省（区、市)更加认可和重视利用博览会平台开展与东盟国家的贸易和投资合作。

本届博览会将海南作为本届“魅力之城”，为其举办了开馆仪式、领导人特别参观、专场旅游产业推介会、海南省与老挝计划投资部、马来西亚旅游局官员分别举行了会谈；海南省领导与老挝计划投资部副部长会谈等活动，充分展示了海南形象。广州积极参与“魅力之城”活动，在本届博览会闭幕式、新

海南国际旅游岛专场推介会
Promotion Conference on Hainan International Tourist Island

闻发布会上被宣布确定为第九届中国—东盟博览会中国“魅力之城”。

本届博览会为各省举办多场专场推介活动。湖南省举行了中国永州—东盟商务投资推介会、宁夏举行了投融资说明会、桂赣陕晋四省联合举办了中国—东盟优质水果推介会、甘肃投资环境说明暨葡萄酒品鉴会、宁夏回族自治区投融资说明会、安徽企业与中国印尼经贸合作区项目对接会、山西运城市代表团项目签约仪式等，这些专场推介活动均取得很好的宣传推介效果。

第八届中国—东盟博览会除了为中国与东盟、中国国内各省区搭建合作平台外，也为更多经济体加强合作提供了更加广阔的平台。本届博览会吸引了更多区域外组织和机构参展参会。日本、韩国、加拿大、芬兰等6个区域外国家企业参展，意大利、法国、德国、瑞士、西班牙、瑞典、卢森堡、埃及、日本、韩国、乌兹别克斯坦等国家和地区企业踊跃参展参会，会期举办了投资加拿大说明会等一系列活动。本届博览会为其他经济体加强合作提供了更大平台、更多商机。

四 服务了举办地广西的发展

通过本届博览会、商务与投资峰会，广西与东盟及国内省（区、市)的合作得到了进一步加强。会期，广西壮族自治区党委书记、自治区人大常委会主任郭声琨，自治区主席马飚及其他自治区领导分别与东盟国家领导人、各国代表团、友好城市代表团等举行了12场会见，就共建广西北部湾经济区，共同推进泛北部湾经济合作、大湄公河次区域合作、南宁—新加坡经济走廊、跨境经济合作区，促进中国—东盟自贸区发展等问题，达成了广泛共识。缅甸副总统吴丁昂敏乌顺访了玉林，并出席了中国（玉林）中小企业商机博览会（玉博会）。会期还举办了广西重点产业招商项目推介会、广西钦州保税港区产值超百亿元情况通报会暨项目签约仪式、广西壮族自治区政府与上海交大战略合作座谈会暨战略伙伴签字仪式、广西有色集团与广东粤财投资控股公司签署战略合作框架协议、2011南宁投资贸易洽谈会暨重大项目签约仪式等活动，促进了广西与东盟国家及国内省（区、市)的交流合作。

博览会对广西和南宁经济社会发展的带动作用显著，主要表现为以下几个方面：

一是促进了南宁市服务业的发展。据广西统计局统计，10月20—26日，南宁市酒店平均入住率达51.03%，累计接待宾客8.62万人，其中境外宾客1.19万人，比上届增长6.47%。南宁市12家大型商场共实现商品销售总额1.54亿元，日平均销售额2205万元。南宁市五大公路客运站累计出发和到站车次50632次；铁路旅客到达17.15万人次，发送16.81万人次；南宁吴圩国际机场累计起、降航班1286次，经由航空抵达和发送的旅客人数分别达到6.8万人次和7.1万人次。以上数据均比日常大幅增加。

会后广西统计局对南宁市民进行了第八届博览会的满意度调查，83.84%的被访者感到满意。其中认为非常满意的为33.22%。

二是服务了广西各地市。在博览会期间，展示了中国—马来西亚钦州产业园的形象和钦州对外合作成果，举办了中马钦州产业园项目签约仪式，推进钦州重点项目签订实施。组织南宁市高新区企业参加博览会企业股权交易会、投融资项目对接会等投资促进活动，帮助企业获取更多信息和商机。马来西亚玻璃市政府代表团参观考察南宁高新区企业，进行了深入交流对接。广西国际博览事务局还支持柳州市举办中国—东盟（柳州）汽车、工程机械及零部件博览会、中国—东盟（百色）现代农业展示交易会、中国（玉林）中小企业商机博览会、梧州宝石节等活动，带动区内会展业发展。

2011 南宁投资贸易洽谈会暨重大项目签约仪式

2011 Nanning Investment and Trade Fair & Key Projects Signing Ceremony

三是服务了广西各厅局。博览会继续支持广西科技厅举办先进技术展，举办太阳能政策对话与技术洽谈会，巩固和深化博览会先进技术专题内容，既配合了本届博览会环保合作的主题，也为第九届中国—东盟博览会科技合作主题做好准备。广西旅游局在二号馆整体展示广西的旅游资源、旅游城市、旅游合作项目，及东盟国家的旅游资源，设置“旅游信息咨询中心”展位，还举办专场与东盟国家旅游部门洽谈会。旅游服务成为本届博览会服务贸易专题的创新点。与商务厅、投促局保持密切合作，举办博览会投资促进活动。支持农业厅举办优质水果推介会、支持出版局举办出版博览会、与林业厅共同举办林业展等，加强与各厅局的互利合作。

四是服务了企业。本届博览会举办联合国采购说明会，联合国采购机构发布产品采购信息，国内外参展企业尤其是广西企业积极参与对接，效果明显。博览会举行的企业股权交易会，为企业提供融资推介、项目撮合等专项服务，通过企业推介、投资商点评和现场洽谈的方式，进行面对面的投融资对接与交流，探索创新企业股债权投融资的新机制，促进企业发掘新的投资机遇。博览会举办的项目对接会，以“走出去”为特色，组织多个高端商务领域的投引资方参加了对接会，现场氛围热烈，企业反映对接效果好。

五　第九届中国—东盟博览会展望

（一）第九届中国—东盟博览会面临新形势

第八届中国—东盟博览会作为中国—东盟建立对话关系20周年系列纪念活动的重要组成部分，为深化双方战略伙伴关系、服务中国—东盟自由贸易区作出了新贡献，成就非凡，影响深远。

2012年举办的第九届中国—东盟博览会面临以下新形势：

一是中国—东盟友好关系深入发展。2011年11月18日，第十四次中国—东盟“10+1”领导人会议暨中国—东盟建立对话关系20周年纪念峰会在印度尼西亚巴厘岛举行。中国国务院总理温家宝在会上发表了重要讲话，高度评价中国—东盟关系发展成就和重要意义，表示当前双方作为致力于和平与繁荣的战略伙伴，在前所未有的广泛领域和高水平上开展交流与合作，成为休戚相关、荣辱与共的命运共同体。中国与东盟共同取得的辉煌成就，为增进本地区人民福祉，促进和平与发展的崇高事业作出了突出贡献，对亚洲乃至世界的进步产生了深远的积极影响。

温家宝总理就深化中国—东盟务实合作提出以下六点倡议：完善中国—东盟自贸区建设，扩大贸易投资合作；成立中国—东盟互联互通合作委员会，加快推进互联互通等基础设施建设；深化金融领域合作；开拓海上务实合作，中方将设立中国—东盟海上合作基金；深化科技和可持续发展领域合作，将2012年作为“中国—东盟科技合作年”；进一步加强社会和民生领域的合作。他还表示，中国—东盟关系基础牢固，潜力巨大，前景广阔。中国愿与东盟永做好邻居、好朋友、好伙伴，密切协调与配合，努力推动落实达成的各项共识，更多造福人民，为地区和平与繁荣作出更大贡献。

温家宝总理的讲话和倡议坦诚、真挚、务实，受到东盟国家领导人普遍欢迎和高度认同。他们赞赏中国长期以来奉行睦邻友好政策，以实际行动支持东盟国家发展和东盟一体化建设，支持东盟在区域合作中的主导地位，表示愿与中国继续相互支持，密切配合，深化战略互信，抓住机遇，全面提升合作水平。

会议发表《纪念峰会联合声明》，全面规划中国—东盟各领域合作，有利于进一步推进双方面向和平与繁荣的战略伙伴关系。

中国—东盟友好关系深入发展，为第九届中国—东盟博览会的举办注入了强大动力。

二是中国—东盟自由贸易区深入实施，成效不断显现。随着中国与东盟各国的经济快速发展，中国—东盟自由贸易区建成，使双方经济互补性得到进一步释放，双方良好的政治关系和完善的各层级、多领域合作，为双方经贸合作提供了可靠的政治和机制性保障，经贸合作发展迅速。2011年中国与东盟双边贸易总额3628.5亿美元，同比增长23.9%。东盟超过日本成为中国第三大贸易伙伴。中国是东盟第一大贸易伙伴。截至2011年底，中国—东盟双向投资累计已超过850亿美元。其中，中国对东盟的投资存量达151.2亿美元。东盟已成为中国企业海外投资的重要目的地。

综上所述，第九届中国—东盟博览会面临诸多有利因素，也面临新的挑战。表现在：世界正处于深刻复杂的变化之中。国际金融危机进入第四个年头，全球经济金融形势依然不容乐观。一些发达国家经济复苏乏力，出现严重的金融和债务危机。新兴国家和发展中国家的地位在上升，但整体实力仍不够强大。西亚北非地区发生社会动荡。全球性粮食、能源、环境问题日益威胁着人类的可持续发展。世界经济前景的不确定性、不稳定性有可能长期存在。这对第九届中国—东盟博览会筹备工作提出了更高要求。

（二）第九届中国—东盟博览会思路

2012年是中国—东盟友好关系全面深入发展的一年，也是《中国—东盟全面经济合作框架协议》签署10周年、中国—东盟科技合作年。第九届中国—东盟博览会将紧扣新形势，继续塑造品牌，坚持创新，提高成效，要实现四个目标：

1. 友好交流有新成果。

突出11国共办特色，邀请中国和东盟国家领导人、部长出席博览会，办好主题国系列活动，安排更多的政界商界高端对话，增进政治互信，以此带动商家的务实合作和人文等多领域交流，取得更多成果。

2. 经贸实效有新收获。

紧扣自贸区已实施的《货物贸易协议》、《服务贸易协议》、《投资协议》内容，创新和优化展会内容，加大采购商邀请力度，深化贸易配对，让企业获得更好的经贸实效。

3. 多领域合作有新进展。

继续围绕中国—东盟十一大重点合作领域举办一系列高层次会议论坛和交流活动，开展部长级磋商对话，邀请各国各个领域的企业家、专家学者参会交流，推动形成相关领域更多合作机制，为经贸、人文等领域的交流合作提供更好的机制保障。

4. 品牌影响力有新提高。

加强策划，在博览会的宣传推介、开幕式、布展上创新，突出本年度中国—东盟合作的主题，也是博览会的重点主题——“科技合作”，扩大博览会的品牌影响力。

为实现上述目标，突出以下工作重点：

一是继续邀请中国和东盟国家领导人出席博览会，加强政商互动。中国和东盟国家领导人共同出席博览会，对增进政治互信、带动企业合作和多领域交流，具有重要意义。第九届博览会将继续邀请中国和东盟国家领导人出席。缅甸将担任第九届博览会的主题国，举办主题国系列活动。会期将继续安排更多的政商高端对接活动，带动双方在经贸人文等多领域合作。

二是优化展览内容，让企业更好地享受中国—东盟自由贸易区商机。第九届博览会继续设商品贸易、投资合作、先进技术、服务贸易、“魅力之城”五大专题，在展览内容上优化，首次举办东盟咖啡展，更加突出展示东盟国家的品牌企业、大宗商品企业及农产品食品、家具家居、工艺品及珠宝饰品、日用消费品等特色商品。中国展品更加契合东盟市场。继续举办农业展、轻工展等专业展，满足专业客商需求。

三是优化投资合作内容，突出中国企业投资东盟的特色。加强与中国和东盟各国投资促进部门的合作继续举办博览会投资合作圆桌会议，首次举办东盟产业园区招商大会，首次设立东盟产业园区形象展示区。这将是博览会的第一个东盟产业园区招商大会，也是东盟10国产业园第一次在中国集中招商。继续把博览会的投资合作专题与会期金融论坛等相关活动紧密结合，为中国企业投资东盟提供金融支持。继续举办投融资项目对接会、东盟10国和中国重点省（区、市)推介会等一系列投资促进活动，发布投资合作信息，促进项目对接。

三是优化服务贸易内容，突出针对性。第九届博览会服务贸易专题重点展示金融服务、旅游服务和技术外包服务三个方面内容。金融服务方面，将结合金融论坛及博览会投资促进活动，为参展参会企业提供更具实效的金融服务。旅游服务将与“魅力之城”相结合，突出展示东盟国家的优势和特色，继续举办“魅力之城”系列交流活动。技术外包服务方面，将通过多样化的展示形式和对接活动，充分展现中国与东盟在服务贸易领域互利合作的广阔前景。

四是加大采购商邀请与组织力度，强化商贸配对服务。第九届博览会邀请更多的中国和区域外采购商。包括：中国央企及各省（区、市)的专业采购商以及欧美、澳大利亚、日本、韩国等区域外采购团体参会。会期将继续举办参展商讲坛、采购说明会、商贸对接会等各种形式的商贸配对活动。充分利用中国—东盟中心服务平台、博览会官方网站、中国—东盟商务数据库等，为东盟各国企业做好日常贸易投资咨询和配对服务。

五是提升展览服务水平，营造良好的洽谈交易环境。第九届博览会各项服务进一步机制化、体系化、常态化，继续引进竞争机制，在客户服务、物流代理、现场餐饮、展馆保洁和现场管理等方面，努力为参会宾客提供全方位便捷、规范、安全、高效的服务。

六是继续举办高层次会议、论坛和活动，扩大多领域合作。随着中国—东盟经贸合作的快速发展，双边对海关、检验检疫、金融、港口、物流等相关领域的服务配套提出了新需求，对经贸合作如何与人文交流相结合、促进全面合作，也提出了更高要求。第九届博览会根据这一形势需要，继续举办了多领域的系列交流活动，邀请各国各个领域的政府官员、企业家、专家学者参会进行对话交流，研究解决上述领域相关问题的办法和机制，为双方全面持久稳定友好合作提供保障。其中，围绕“科技合作” 主题，举办第一届中国—东盟科技部长会议，以及技术转移、金融、物流合作等系列会议论坛和交流活动。

七是加强宣传推介、开幕式、展会形象设计等方面的创新，提升品牌影响力。展会影响大小看宣传。做好博览会的宣传推介，不仅有利于提高博览会的知名度，塑造政治外交品牌，为东盟国家、城市和企业的形象展示做好服务，而且有利于让双方企业通过媒体加深对博览会的了解，更好地把握自贸区的商机。第九届中国—东盟博览会继续发挥博览会媒体资源的优势，完善与媒体的合作机制，做好社会宣传和市场推介。除了邀请中国与东盟各国主流媒体参与博览会的宣传报道，还增强专业和行业媒体的报道，扩大博览会的品牌影响力，也为参展国家、城市和企业的品牌塑造作出贡献。

小结 大平台促进大合作大发展

中国—东盟建立对话关系、携手合作发展，已有20年。在这期间，中国—东盟博览会走过了8年的历程，既是中国—东盟友好合作的成果，也是促进中国—东盟自由贸易区建设的“助推器”。简而言之，就是大平台促进了大合作、大发展。

首先，中国—东盟博览会肩负着为中国—东盟自由贸易建设服务的重大使命，承载着11个国家共同发展、19亿人口共享福祉的重大责任。这种历史的重大责任，时代的重大使命，决定了中国—东盟博览会不是一般的展会，它是非同一般的合作大平台。第八届中国—东盟博览会作为中国—东盟建立对话关系20周年系列纪念活动的重要组成部分，取得了一系列新成果，推动双方战略伙伴关系迈上新台阶，这就是大平台促进大合作大发展的最好例证。

其次，中国—东盟博览会的舞台巨大。博览会的平台，实际上是中国—东盟自由贸易区的大舞台。中国—东盟自由贸易区建成后，东盟和中国的双边贸易额占世界贸易总值的13%，成为一个涵盖11个国家、19亿人口、GDP达6万亿美元的经济体，是目前世界人口最多的自由贸易区，也是发展中国家间最大的自由贸易区。

从中国—东盟博览会8年发展的历程可以看到，博览会不仅搭建了中国与东盟合作的平台，而且为区域外更多的经济体加强合作提供了更加广阔的平台。例如，本届博览会吸引了更多区域外组织和机构参展参会。日本、韩国、加拿大、芬兰等6个区域外国家企业参展，意大利、法国、德国、瑞士、西班牙、瑞典、卢森堡、埃及、日本、韩国、乌兹别克斯坦等国家和地区企业踊跃参展参会，博览会的舞台实际已经超越出了中国—东盟自由贸易区区域，成为面向全球开放的大平台。

其三，中国—东盟博览会内涵丰富。中国—东盟博览会动议于经贸，但其发展的实践证明，经贸只是博览会的主线，不是博览会的全部内容。中国—东盟博览会是一个涵盖政治外交、经贸、人文活动于一体的综合性专业展会，如此巨大的内涵，是诸多展会所不能比拟的。本届博览会的内容不仅有多场领导人之间的会见、政要与商界对话，以及展览洽谈活动，而且有更多的社会人文内容，例如，会期举办了中国—东盟文化产业论坛、中国—东盟出版博览会等多场社会人文交流活动。

其四，博览会自身的发展能力与潜力巨大。中国—东盟博览会形成了集政治外交、经贸、人文为一体与东盟合作的新模式。建立了集合中央各部委和东盟10国资源、协调全区对东盟开放合作的工作机制。实现了服务国家战略，服务中国—东盟自贸区建设，服务各部委、各省（区、市）与东盟交流合作，服务广西发展“四个服务”的目标。这一切都表现出了中国—东盟博览会在自身发展能力建设上的大视野、大气魄、大手笔。

中国—东盟自由贸易区建设的大需要，促成了中国—东盟博览会这个中国—东盟友好交流、经贸促进和多领域合作的大平台的产生，而大平台的直接成果就是中国—东盟自由贸易区的大合作、大发展。八届中国—东盟博览会共有42位中国和东盟国家领导人、1500多位部长级贵宾出席，参展参会客商31.6万人，贸易成交额116.9亿美元，签约国际合作项目投资额491.72亿美元，签约国内合作项目投资额4759.02亿元，围绕贸易、投资、海关、质检、金融、港口、电信、环保及社会人文等多领域举办了200多个高层次会议论坛和活动，成效显著。透过这些貌似简单实际沉甸甸的数据，我们看到了中国与东盟世界政治互信的不断增加，经济交往的日益密切，文化沟通的显著加强。这既是中国与东盟国家在面临日益复杂的世界政治格局、起伏不定的世界经济形势、冲突与融合相济的世界文化态势时，所作出的共同努力，也是彼此分享中国—东盟自由贸易区建设给大家带来的工作成果。

中国与东盟国家面临的共同话题都是发展，发展需要合作，合作需要制度安排与落地的平台，中国—东盟博览会用8年时间形成的合作大平台，证明合作能够促进更大的发展，证明中国—东盟博览会在中国—东盟自由贸易区建设与发展中，具有不可替代的地位与作用。

历史必将证明，中国—东盟博览会将越办越好，为中国—东盟自由贸易区的美好明天作出贡献！

附 录

第八届中国—东盟博览会组委会中方成员名单

Chinese Members of the 8th CAEXPO Organizing Committee

名誉主任 Honorary Chair	王岐山 Wang Qishan	国务院副总理 Vice Premier of the State Council of China
主　任 Co-chair	陈德铭 Chen Deming	商务部部长 Minister of Commerce of China
副主任 Vice Co-chairs	马　飚 Ma Biao	广西壮族自治区主席 Governor of Guangxi Zhuang Autonomous Region
	毕井泉 Bi Jingquan	国务院副秘书长 Vice Secretary General of the State Council of China
	高虎城 Gao Hucheng	商务部国际贸易谈判代表兼副部长 China International Trade Representative and Vice Minister of Commerce of China
	李金早 Li Jinzao	广西壮族自治区党委常委、自治区常务副主席 First Vice Governor of Guangxi Zhuang Autonomous Region
	陈　武 Chen Wu	广西壮族自治区党委常委、自治区副主席 Vice Governor of Guangxi Zhuang Autonomous Region
秘书长 Secretary General	李金早（兼） Li Jinzao （and）	广西壮族自治区党委常委、自治区常务副主席 First Vice Governor of Guangxi Zhuang Autonomous Region

	陈　武（兼） Chen Wu （and）	广西壮族自治区党委常委、自治区副主席 Vice Governor of Guangxi Zhuang Autonomous Region
委　员 Members	蔡名照 Cai Mingzhao	中宣部副部长 Vice Minister of the Publicity Department of Chinese Communist Party Central Committee
	刘振民 Liu Zhenmin	外交部部长助理 Assistant Minister of Foreign Affairs of China
	张晓强 Zhang Xiaoqiang	国家发展和改革委员会副主任 Vice Commissioner of the National Development and Reform Commission of China
	曹健林 Cao Jianlin	科技部副部长 Vice Minister of Science & Technology of China
	毕根敬 Bi Genjing	公安部警卫局副局长 Vice Director General of Ministry of Public Security of China
	李　勇 Li Yong	财政部副部长 Vice Minister of Finance of China
	翁孟勇 Weng Mengyong	交通运输部副部长 Vice Minister of Transport of China
	鲁培军 Lu Peijun	海关总署副署长 Vice Commissioner of China Customs
	魏传忠 Wei Chuanzhong	国家质量监督检验检疫总局副局长 Vice Minister of the General Administration of Quality Supervision, Inspection and Quarantine of China
	祝善忠 Zhu Shanzhong	国家旅游局副局长 Vice Commissioner of China National Tourism Administration
	边振甲 Bian Zhenjia	国家食品药品监督管理局副局长 Vice Minister of State Food and Drug Administration
	王国庆 Wang Guoqing	国务院新闻办副主任 Vice Director General of the State Council Information Office of China
	于　平 Yu Ping	中国国际贸易促进委员会副会长 Vice Chairman of China Council for the Promotion of International Trade （CCPIT）

第八届中国—东盟商务与投资峰会组委会中方成员名单

Chinese Members of the 8th CABIS Organizing Committee

主　任 Chair	万季飞 Wan Jifei	中国国际贸易促进委员会会长 Chairman of China Council for the Promotion of International Trade （CCPIT）
副主任 Vice Co–chairs	李金早 Li Jinzao	广西壮族自治区党委常委、自治区常务副主席 First Vice Governor of Guangxi Zhuang Autonomous Region
	于　平 Yu Ping	中国国际贸易促进委员会副会长 Vice Chairman of China Council for the Promotion of International Trade （CCPIT）
秘书长 Secretary General	李金早 Li Jinzao	广西壮族自治区党委常委、自治区常务副主席 First Vice Governor of Guangxi Zhuang Autonomous Region
常务副秘书长 First Vice Secretaries General	黄永强 Huang Yongqiang	广西国际贸易促进委员会会长 Chairman of CCPIT Guangxi Sub–council
副秘书长 Vice Secretaries General	王　俐 Wang Li	中国国际贸易促进委员会国际联络部副部长 Vice Director General of the Department of International Affairs of CCPIT
	何小玲 He Xiaoling	广西国际贸易促进委员会副会长 Vice Chairman of CCPIT Guangxi Sub–council
	吕卫平 Lv Weiping	广西国际贸易促进委员会副会长 Vice Chairman of CCPIT Guangxi Sub–council
	胡福章 Hu Fuzhang	广西国际贸易促进委员会副巡视员 Vice Director General of CCPIT Guangxi Sub–council
	李文杰 Li Wenjie	广西国际博览事务局副局长 Vice Secretary General of CAEXPO Secretariat
	顾　航 Gu Hang	广西壮族自治区外事办公室副主任 Vice Director General of Foreign Affairs Office of Guangxi

第八届中国—东盟博览会主办单位
The 8th CAEXPO Co-sponsors

中华人民共和国商务部
Ministry of Commerce of the People's Republic of China
文莱工业和初级资源部
Ministry of Industry and Primary Resources of Brunei Darussalam
柬埔寨商业部
Ministry of Commerce of the Kingdom of Cambodia
印度尼西亚贸易部
Ministry of Trade of the Republic of Indonesia
老挝工业贸易部
Ministry of Trade and Industry of the Lao People's Democratic Republic
马来西亚国际贸易和工业部
Ministry of International Trade and Industry of Malaysia
缅甸商务部
Ministry of Commerce of the Union of the Republic of Myanmar
菲律宾贸易和工业部
Department of Trade and Industry of the Republic of Philippines
新加坡贸易和工业部
Ministry of Trade and Industry of the Republic of Singapore
泰国商业部
Ministry of Commerce of the Kingdom of Thailand
越南工业贸易部
Ministry of Industry and Trade of the Socialist Republic of Vietnam
东盟秘书处
The ASEAN Secretariat

第八届中国—东盟博览会支持商协会

The 8th CAEXPO Supporting Chambers of Commerce

国家	商协会名称
中国	中国机电产品进出口商会
	中国轻工工艺进出口商会
	中国医药保健品进出口商会
	中国纺织品进出口商会
	中国食品土畜进出口商会
	中国五矿化工进出口商会
	中国对外承包工程商会
	中国食品和包装机械工业协会
	中国电力企业联合会
文莱	文莱中华商会 Chinese Chamber of Commerce of Brunei Darussalam
	文中友协 Brunei-China Friendship Association
柬埔寨	柬埔寨总商会 Cambodia Chamber of Commerce
	柬埔寨成衣厂商协会 Garment Manufacturers Association in Cambodia
	柬埔寨中国商会 Chinese Chamber of Commerce in Cambodia
	柬埔寨中国港澳侨商总会 China Hong Kong & Macao Expatriate & Business Association of Cambodia
印尼	印尼工商会馆中国委员会 Indonesian Chamber of Commerce and Industry-China Committee
	印尼中华总商会 Indonesian Chinese Entrepreneur Association
	印尼—中国经济社会与文化合作协会 Association of Indonesia-China Economic, Social and Cultural Cooperation

老挝	老挝国家工商会 Lao National Chamber of Commerce and Industry
马来西亚	马来西亚制造商联合会 Federation of Malaysian Manufacturers
	马来西亚中国经济贸易总商会 Malaysia-China Chamber of Commerce
	马中友好协会 Malaysia-China Friendship Association
	马来西亚中华工商联合会 The Associated Chinese Chamber of Commerce and Industry of Malaysia
缅甸	缅甸联邦工商会 The Republic of the Union of Myanmar Federation of Chambers of Commerce & Industry （RUMFCCI）
	缅甸农产品与食品加工及出口协会 Myanmar Agro Based Food Processors & Exporters Association
	缅甸林木产品商协会 Myanmar Forest Products & Timber Merchants Association
	缅甸工业联合会 Myanmar Industries Association
	缅甸豆类商协会 Myanmar Pulses, Beans & Sesame Seeds Merchants Association
	缅甸渔业协会 Myanmar Fisheries Federation
菲律宾	菲华商联总会 Federation of Filipino-Chinese Chambers of Commerce and Industry, INC
新加坡	新加坡工商联合总会 Singapore Business Federation
	新加坡制造商联合会 Singapore Manufacturers' Federation
	新加坡中小型企业商会 Association of Small & Medium Enterprises
	新加坡中华总商会 Singapore Chinese Chamber of Commerce & Industry
	新加坡中国商会 Singapore-China Business Association
泰国	泰国中华总商会 Thai-Chinese Chamber of Commerce
	泰国工业院 Federation of Thai Industries
	泰中商务委员会 Thailand-China Business Council
	泰国工商总会 All-Thai Traders Association
越南	越南工商会 Vietnam Chamber of Commerce & Industry

第八届中国—东盟博览会、第八届中国—东盟商务与投资峰会活动日程表

专场活动		
时间	地点	活动名称
10月17日（星期一）		
全天	明园饭店5号楼2楼多功能厅	第四届中国—东盟智库战略对话论坛
10月19日（星期三）		
全天	广西民族博物馆	2011中国—东盟文化产业论坛
下午	青秀山国际高尔夫俱乐部	第八届中国—东盟高尔夫国际名人邀请赛
10月20日（星期四）		
16:30-17:30	湄公河大酒店A栋6楼会议室	新闻吹风会
10月21日（星期五）		
08:30-12:00	明园饭店5号楼2楼多功能厅	中国—东盟太阳能政策对话与技术洽谈会
上午	荔园山庄国际会议中心	中马钦州产业园区签约及揭牌仪式
09:00-09:40	南宁国际会展中心	第八届中国—东盟博览会开幕式
上午	南宁国际会展中心	马来西亚“魅力之城”开馆仪式
上午	南宁国际会展中心	中外贵宾巡视展馆
上午	荔园山庄	泰国领导人与中泰企业家见面会
10:00-12:00	红林大酒店19楼福林厅	中国—东盟药品安全论坛暨药品监督管理局局长会议
11:00-11:45	荔园山庄	第八届中国—东盟商务与投资峰会开幕式

12:10-13:10	荔园山庄	第八届中国—东盟博览会、商务与投资峰会欢迎宴会
下午	广西人民会堂	马来西亚领导人与中国企业CEO圆桌对话会
20:30-22:30	广西体育中心	“大地飞歌·2011”第13届南宁国际民歌艺术节暨第八届中国—东盟博览会开幕晚会
10月22日（星期六）		
待定	广西体育局江南训练基地新网球馆	第八届中国—东盟博览会“网球之友”开幕式
08:30-12:00	广西沃顿国际大酒店3楼北京厅	第三届中国—东盟金融合作与发展领袖论坛
08:30-12:00	邕江宾馆多功能厅	中国—东盟物流合作论坛
08:30-18:00	红林大酒店2楼红林厅	中国—东盟城市森林论坛
09:00-18:00	荔园山庄国际会议中心2楼大会议厅	2011中国—东盟环保合作论坛
09:00-12:00	广西沃顿国际大酒店南湖国宴厅1-3号厅	第一届中国—东盟TBT合作部长会议
09:00-18:00	广西民族博物馆	2011中国—东盟出版博览会
09:30-17:00	南宁国际会展中心106会议室	中国—东盟博览会投资合作圆桌会
10:00-10:30	广西展览馆	中国—东盟博览会农业展开展仪式
10:00-10:30	华南城会展中心A、B馆	中国—东盟博览会轻工展开展仪式
10:30-11:30 11:30-12:00	鑫伟万豪酒店1楼大宴会厅	第八届中国—东盟博览会签约仪式（国际、国内）
10月23日（星期日）		
10:00	南宁嘉和城温泉高尔夫俱乐部	第八届中国—东盟高尔夫国际精英邀请赛
10月24—25日		
全天	南宁国际会展中心、广西展览馆、华南城等	展览及各类经贸活动
10月26日（星期三）		
09:00-17:00	南宁国际会展中心	博览会公众开放日
14:00-15:30	荔园山庄国际会议中心1层小会议厅	博览会高官会暨第九届中国—东盟博览会国家专题展区位置抽签仪式
16:00-17:30	荔园山庄国际会议中心2楼宴会厅	第八届中国—东盟博览会、商务与投资峰会闭幕式暨新闻发布会
会期相关重要活动		
10月20日（星期四）		
09:00-11:30	鑫伟万豪酒店会议厅	广西重点产业招商项目推介暨合作项目签约仪式
09:00-12:00	南宁沃顿国际大酒店3楼北京厅	中国—东盟民间资本投资论坛

10:00-11:00	南宁饭店锦绣楼红棉厅	《新越汉辞典》出版首发式
10:00-11:00	广西科技馆	中国（南宁）国际商务书画展开幕式
15:00-17:00	自治区党校多功能厅	上海广西两地企业家高峰论坛暨企业合作宣言签署仪式
16:00-17:30	南宁沃顿国际大酒店2楼南国国宴厅	2011年中国永州—东盟商务投资推介会暨项目签字仪式
10月21日（星期五）		
14:30-17:00	南宁国际会展中心106会议室	中越跨境经济合作区——中国凭祥综合保税区、越南同登口岸经济区非关税区建设情况交流会
15:00-16:40	南宁国际会展中心102会议室	中国—东盟合作基金和面向东盟的信贷资金说明会
15:00-16:00	南宁国际会展中心107会议室	安徽企业与中国印尼经贸合作区对接会
15:00-16:00	南宁国际会展中心110会议室	第八届中国—东盟博览会山西运城市代表团项目签约仪式
15:00-17:00	南宁国际会展中心103会议室	服务外包政策宣讲及企业交流会
15:00-17:00	南宁国际会展中心105会议室	境外经贸合作区、境外农业示范区说明会
15:00-17:00	凤凰宾馆6楼多功能厅	甘肃投资环境说明暨葡萄酒品鉴会
15:30-17:00	自治区党校多功能厅	广西壮族自治区人民政府与上海交大战略合作座谈暨战略合作协议签字仪式
16:00-16:40	广西人民广播电台演播大厅	纪念中老建交50周年“北部湾之声”节目落地老挝万象活动
10月22日（星期六）		
08:30-15:30	南宁锦华大酒店4楼芳华厅、海吉星农产品批发市场	中国—东盟博览会优质水果推介活动
09:00-16:30	明园饭店5号楼2楼多功能厅	泛北部湾经济合作发展规划研讨会
09:00-12:00	南宁国际会展中心105会议室	中国—东盟基础设施投融资合作论坛
09:00-12:00	广西博物馆	第五届中国—东盟青年艺术品创作大赛获奖作品暨五周年成果展开展仪式
09:30-11:30 11:30-12:40	南宁国际会展中心103、107会议室	联合国采购说明会（企业对接）
09:30-12:00	南宁国际会展中心102会议室	新加坡——您环球的商务枢纽
09:30-12:30	南宁国际会展中心101会议室	印尼国家推介会
10:00-12:00	南宁国际会展中心2号馆、111会议室	中国“魅力之城”海南开馆仪式及海南旅游产业推介会
10:40-12:30	华南城会展中心2楼1号会议室	中国—东盟商品交易中心启动仪式暨中国—东盟商会领袖论坛
12:45-14:00	南宁沃顿国际大酒店3楼北京厅	广西壮族自治区政府招待酒会暨金融支持企业“走出去”洽谈会

13:30-14:00	南宁国际会展中心109会议室	2011年中国（海南）——老挝经贸会谈
13:30-14:10	南宁国际会展中心107会议室	食品包装机械采购对接会
14:00-14:45	南宁国际会展中心110会议室	中国—缅甸企业家座谈会
14:00-17:00	南宁国际会展中心朱槿花厅	东盟采购商专场贸易配对会
14:00-17:00	南宁国际会展中心111会议室	中马大宗商品采购对接会
14:00-18:20	广西人民会堂5楼会议室	中国—东盟电信高峰论坛
14:30-17:00	南宁国际会展中心101会议室	柬埔寨投资潜力和商业前景
14:30-17:00	南宁国际会展中心102会议室	老挝国家推介会
14:30-17:00	南宁国际会展中心105会议室	菲律宾商机
15:00-16:00	凤凰宾馆6楼多功能厅	宁夏回族自治区投融资说明会
15:00-17:00	南宁国际会展中心107会议室	电力设备采购对接会
15:00-17:00	南宁国际会展中心103会议室	金色缅甸——缅甸国家推介会
15:30-17:00	华南城A号馆2楼会议室	中国—东盟国际茶文化节评选活动
18:00-20:00	沃顿国际大酒店	旅游合作洽谈会
10月23日（星期日）		
09:00-10:00	南宁国际会展中心108会议室	广西有色集团与广东粤财投资控股公司签署战略合作框架协议
09:00-12:00	南宁国际会展中心朱槿花厅	东盟采购商专场贸易配对会（越南专场）
09:00-11:00	南宁国际会展中心103会议室	文莱国家推介会
09:30-11:30	南宁国际会展中心107会议室	投资促进国际经验和最佳实践研讨会
09:30-11:30	南宁国际会展中心110会议室	轻工工艺品采购对接会
09:30-12:00	南宁国际会展中心105会议室	泰国投资机遇推介会
09:30-14:50	南宁国际会展中心102会议室	中国—东盟博览会企业股权（债权）投融资交易会
10:00-11:30	南宁国际会展中心106会议室	广西钦州保税港区产值超百亿情况通报会暨项目签约仪式
12:00-14:00	万豪酒店6楼中餐厅	中国—东盟行业协会联谊会
13:00-18:00	南宁国际会展中心103会议室	参展商讲坛——2011四季沐歌绿色财富峰会
15:00-17:00	南宁国际会展中心朱槿花厅	中国—东盟博览会投融资项目对接会

15:00-17:00	南宁国际会展中心106会议室	中国银行·维伯教育——2011海外投资论坛及项目推介会
15:00-17:00	南宁国际会展中心111会议室	农产品食品采购对接会
16:00-17:00	南宁国际会展中心107会议室	参展商讲坛——新型环保燃油机推介
10月24日（星期一）		
09:00-12:00	南宁国际会展中心102会议室	美在广西旅游联盟成立大会暨“广西旅游卡”发行仪式
09:15-12:00	鑫伟万豪酒店1楼3号宴会厅	投资加拿大说明会
09:30-12:10	南宁国际会展中心105会议室	首届中泰橡胶产业发展合作研讨会
10:00-11:30	南宁国际会展中心106会议室	江苏产品万里行南宁展销会新闻发布会
14:00-17:00	南宁国际会展中心105会议室	中国—东盟大宗商品（橡胶）配对会
10月25日（星期二）		
09:30-11:00	南宁国际会展中心103会议室	城市居住产品推介会
10:00-11:00	南宁国际会展中心107会议室	广东益华百货采购马来西亚产品说明会
09:00-17:00	南宁国际会展中心105会议室	泰国魅力之城推介会
会期相关活动		
10.13-10.16	华南城	2011中国—东盟国际汽车工业展览会
10.21-10.25 19:30-23:30	广西体育局江南训练基地新网球馆	第八届中国—东盟博览会“网球之友”联谊活动
10.22-10.26	广西展览馆	中国—东盟博览会农业展
10.22-10.26	华南城	中国—东盟博览会轻工展
10.22-10.24	广西民族博物馆	2011中国—东盟出版博览会
10.23-10.26	百色田阳	中国—东盟（百色）现代农业展示交易会
10.31-11.2 08:30-18:00	明园新都酒店	中国—东盟旅游促进减贫研讨会
11.3-11.4	南宁国际会展中心	第十三届全国肥料信息交流暨产品交易会
11.4-11.6	南宁国际会展中心	中国国际果蔬加工技术及物流展览会
11.18-11.21	南宁国际会展中心	2011年中国—东盟博览会林产品与木制品展
11.21-11.23	荔园山庄	亚洲及大洋洲地区大众体育合作发展论坛暨中国—东盟大众体育合作发展论坛
12.8-12.9	荔园山庄（医药展设在广西药用植物园）	2011中国—东盟传统医药高峰论坛暨传统医药展

第八届中国—东盟博览会大事记

3月

19日

第八届中国—东盟博览会政要及贵宾礼品创作会在广西北流举行。郑军里、柒万里等广西知名画家与广西三环集团联袂打造的具有东方艺术韵味的精美瓷瓶成为第八届中国—东盟博览会国礼。

4月

3—12日

广西壮族自治区党委书记、自治区人大常委会主任郭声琨率广西代表团访问马来西亚。期间，代表团拜会了马来西亚副总理丹斯里慕尤丁、房屋与地方政府部部长曹智雄、贸工部副部长耶谷·沙岸等马来西亚政要，会见了中国驻马来西亚大使柴玺和中国—东盟博览会共办单位的负责人。

8日

第八届中国—东盟博览会筹备工作会议在广西桂林召开。商务部国际贸易谈判代表兼副部长高虎城到会讲话并部署工作。广西壮族自治区党委常委、自治区副主席陈武出席会议并致辞。商务部相关司局和全国各省（自治区、直辖市）商务主管部门负责人参加了会议。

12日

广西壮族自治区主席马飚主持召开自治区政府常务会议，研究“走出去”等事项。会议要求各级各有关部门、企业进一步加快实施“走出去”战略，坚持以企业为主体、以东盟为重点，充分利用通过承办中国—东盟博览会所建立起来的重要合作资源，开展一批境外合作重大项目，积极参与东盟市场开发和利用，通过实施“走出去”来促进广西加快转变经济发展方式，推动产业转型升级。

20日

广西壮族自治区党委书记、自治区人大常委会主任郭声琨主持召开自治区党委常委会。会议强调，要着力深化改革开放，突出办好第八届中国—东盟博览会和商务与投资峰会等重大活动，充分发挥各类开放平台和载体的作用。

5月

5日

在陕西西安举办的第九届中国会展节事财富论坛（CEFF）上，中国—东盟博览会再获殊荣，被评为“2010—2011年度中国会展产业金手指奖·十大影响力展览会”。

6月

1日

第八届中国—东盟博览会高官会议在广西北海召开。商务部亚洲司副司长梁文洮和东盟秘书处经济一体化合作司司长苏柏什共同主持会议，商务部投资促进事务局副局长张迎新及东盟各国经贸主管部门和投资主管部门高官出席了会议。会议期间，广西壮族自治区党委常委、自治区副主席陈武会见了与会代表。

7月

8日

第八届中国—东盟博览会国际经济合作展区筹备工作会议在贵州贵阳召开。商务部对外投资和经济合作司副司长刘迎军、中国对外承包工程商会秘书长于晓虹以及相关省（区、市）商务主管部门、投资促进机构和中直企业代表参加了会议。

26日

中国—东盟建立对话关系20周年经贸关系成效暨第八届中国—东盟博览会、中国—东盟商务与投资峰会新闻发布会在国务院新闻办公室召开。商务部国际贸易谈判代表兼副部长高虎城，广西壮族自治区党委常委、自治区副主席陈武，中国国际贸易促进委员会副会长王锦珍出席会议并发布新闻、回答记者提问。新闻发布会由国务院新闻办新闻局副局长华清主持。

8月

23日

中国—东盟建立对话关系20周年纪念招待会在北京钓鱼台国宾馆举行。中国国务委员戴秉国出席招待会，并就中国—东盟关系发展作主题发言。东盟北京委员会轮值主席、柬埔寨驻华大使西索达在会上发表致辞。广西壮族自治区领导郭声琨、马飚、陈武、余远辉等应邀出席招待会。东盟各国驻华使节、中国和东盟国家有关部门官员、专家学者及工商界代表参加了招待会。

由外交部和广西壮族自治区人民政府主办，外交学院与中国—东盟博览会秘书处承办的中国—东盟互联互通战略研讨会在北京召开。来自中国和东盟10国政府、企业、银行、智库以及东盟秘书处的代表齐聚一堂，围绕中国—东盟互联互通与制度建设、产业对接、地方动议等议题，深入探讨中国—东盟互联互通合作和未来发展方向。外交部部长助理刘振民与广西壮族自治区党委常委、自治区副主席陈武在会上分别致辞。

24日

第八届中国—东盟博览会和中国—东盟商务与投资峰会组委会会议在北京召开。会议围绕在中国—东盟建立对话关系20周年、中国—东盟友好交流年、中国—东盟自由贸易区建成1周年以及当前国际新的形势下，进一步办好博览会、商务与投资峰会，为加强中国与东盟在多领域的合作搭好平台、做好服务进行了研究部署。博览会组委会主任、商务部部长陈德铭，广西壮族自治区党委书记、自治区人大常委会主任郭声琨，博览会组委会副主任、广西壮族自治区主席马飚出席会议并分别讲话。博览会组委会副主任、商务部国际贸易谈判代表兼副部长高虎城主持会议。博览会组委会副主任兼秘书长、广西壮族自治区党委常委、自治区副主席陈武，外交部部长助理刘振民，国家旅游局副局长祝善忠，国家食品药品监督管理局副局长边振甲，公安部警卫局副局长张智文少将，中国国际贸易促进委员会副会长于平，广西壮族自治区党委常委、秘书长余远辉，以及中宣部、国务院办公厅、发展改革委、科技部、财政部、环保部、交通运输部、海关总署、质检总局、国务院新闻办等组委会成员单位和自治区有关部门负责人等出席会议。

25日

在上海举行的第八届“中国会展之星”暨2010—2011年度中国会展业品牌大奖颁奖盛典上，中国—东盟博览会再获殊荣，被评为“中国十大政府主导型展会”。

26日

广西壮族自治区党委常委会召开会议，听取第八届中国—东盟博览会和中国—东盟商务与投资峰会筹备工作情况汇报，研究相关问题。自治区党委书记、自治区人大常委会主任郭声琨强调，深入贯彻落实胡锦涛总书记关于把博览会“长期办下去，办出特色，办出成效”的重要指示精神，紧紧依靠博览会组委会的力量，把准广西自身定位，创新工作，强化措施，举全区之力办好“两会一节”，进一步提升博览会的规格、规模和成效，要下大力气营造更加良好的环境氛围、文化氛围和社会氛围，为办好博览会打下更加坚实的基础。

9月

16日

第八届中国—东盟博览会、中国—东盟商务与投资峰会“携手共进35天”启动仪式在南宁国际会展中心举行。广西壮族自治区主席马飚宣布活动启动，自治区领导李金早、沈北海、车荣福、陈武、梁胜利，自治区政府秘书长王跃飞以及东盟国家驻南宁外交使节出席启动仪式。

第八届中国—东盟博览会、中国—东盟商务与投资峰会广西指挥中心第一次工作会议在广西南宁召开。广西壮族自治区党委常委、自治区副主席、“两会”指挥中心总指挥陈武出席会议并作重要讲话。会议由自治区党委副秘书长、“两会”指挥中心副总指挥黄世勇主持，各工作部汇报了本部门第八届“两会”筹备工作情况。

20日

2011中国—东盟国际汽车拉力赛暨中国—东盟媒体汽车拉力赛发车仪式在南宁市国际会展中心举行。拉力赛由中国国家体育总局、广西壮族自治区人民政府、东盟秘书处共同主办，中国汽车运动联合会、广西壮族自治区体育局联合承办。中国国家体育总局原副局长、中华全国体育总会顾问张发强，广西壮族自治区副主席李康分别在仪式上致辞。发车仪式由广西壮族自治区党委副秘书长、拉力赛组委会副主任王仕威主持。会议宣读了东盟秘书处秘书长发来的贺电。越南、老挝、缅甸、泰国等东盟各国驻南宁的外交使节参加了发车仪式。

22日

第八届中国—东盟博览会指定宾馆授匾仪式在广西南宁举行。南宁市15家宾馆酒店获得第八届中国—东盟博览会指定接待宾馆荣誉称号。

23日

中国—东盟中心和广西国际博览事务局举行中国—东盟中心网站签约仪式。广西壮族自治区副主席高雄、中国—东盟中心秘书长马明强出席签约仪式。

28日

中国—东盟友谊知识竞赛决赛之夜暨颁奖典礼在南宁举行。广西壮族自治区副主席李康、教育部国际司副司长黄颖、东盟各国驻南宁外交使节，以及区直有关部门负责人、广西大学生代表等参加活动。

广西壮族自治区党委常委、自治区常务副主席、“两会”指挥中心总指挥李金早，自治区党委常委、宣传部部长沈北海召开专题会议，研究部署“两会”宣传工作和第八届中国—东盟博览会开幕式工作。

29日

中国—东盟博览会、中国—东盟商务与投资峰会广西领导小组召开会议。会议由广西壮族自治区主席、“两会”领导小组组长马飚主持并作重要讲话。自治区党委常委、自治区常务副主席、“两会”指挥中心总指挥李金早，自治区党委常委、宣传部部长沈北海，自治区党委常委、秘书长余远辉，自治区副主席梁胜利，自治区人民政府秘书长王跃飞出席了会议。“两会”广西领导小组成员、“两会”指挥中心各工作部相关负责人以及南宁市有关单位负责人参加了会议。

10月

2日

广西壮族自治区党委常委、自治区常务副主席、“两会”指挥中心总指挥李金早召开“两会”指挥中心工作会议，研究部署相关工作。

4日

广西壮族自治区党委书记、自治区人大常委会主任、“两会”组委会副主任郭声琨代表自治区党委、自治区人民政府到“两会”指挥中心看望慰问国庆期间仍坚守在工作岗位上的工作人员，听取“两会一节”筹备工作进展情况汇报并作重要指示。自治区领导李金早、陈武、余远辉等陪同视察。

广西壮族自治区党委常委、自治区常务副主席、“两会”指挥中心总指挥李金早听取第八届中国—东盟商务与投资峰会开幕式、马来西亚领导人与中国企业CEO圆桌对话会、第八届中国—东盟博览会招商招展工作、投资促进工作、泰国副总理与中泰企业家恳谈会、新闻宣传工作和接待工作等情况汇报，研究部署相关工作。

5日

广西壮族自治区党委常委、自治区常务副主席、“两会”指挥中心总指挥李金早听取第八届中国—东盟博览会开幕式情况汇报，研究部署相关工作。自治区人民政府副秘书长、“两会”指挥中心副总指挥魏然参加会议。

7—9日

广西壮族自治区党委常委、自治区常务副主席、“两会”指挥中心总指挥李金早率工作组赴北京向国务院办公厅、外交部汇报第八届“两会”筹备工作进展，并走访了中国人民银行和中国邮储银行。

9日

南宁市2011年服务“两会一节”领导小组（组委会）召开会议。广西壮族自治区党委常委、自治区副主席、南宁市委书记陈武要求全市各级各部门各单位要提高认识，统筹推进，做好服务“两会一节”各项工作，确保“两会一节”圆满成功。

10日

第八届中国—东盟博览会首席战略合作伙伴签约暨揭牌仪式在南宁举行，宣布中国有色集团成为第八届中国—东盟博览会首席战略合作伙伴，并举行中国有色集团（广西）平桂飞碟股份有限公司、中国有色（桂林）矿产地质研究院有限公司两个项目的揭牌仪式。广西壮族自治区党委常委、自治区副主席林念修出席仪式，向中国有色集团颁发证书并见证签约。

11日

由中国国家人口和计划生育委员会与广西壮族自治区人民政府主办的中国—东盟人口与家庭发展论坛在广西南宁举行。国家人口计生委主任李斌，广西壮族自治区主席马飚，国家人口计生委副主任崔丽，广西壮族自治区党委常委、宣传部部长、广西计生协会会长沈北海，广西壮族自治区副主席李康出席开幕式。缅甸移民与人口部部长吴钦伊，印度尼西亚国家人口和计划生育委员会主任苏吉瑞·塞亚瑞夫，菲律宾人口委员会执行主任托马斯·欧塞斯，老挝卫生部副部长因拉文·凯博潘，柬埔寨卫生部副部长坦沃乘，国际计划生育联合会总干事特沃德斯·梅莱斯，人口与发展南南合作伙伴组织执行主任哈利·乔瑟里，联合国人口基金驻华代表处代理代表玛丽安等外宾参加开幕式。

广西壮族自治区党委常委、自治区常务副主席、“两会”指挥中心总指挥李金早主持召开“两会”工作会议，研究部署“两会”相关工作。

12日

广西壮族自治区党委常委、自治区常务副主席、“两会”指挥中心总指挥李金早主持召开专题会议，审议“两会”相关事项。“两会”指挥中心副总指挥黄世勇、魏然参加了会议。

第八届中国—东盟博览会战略合作伙伴签约仪式暨合作伙伴授牌仪式在广西南宁举行。广西壮族自治区党委常委车荣福出席仪式，为签约仪式见证并向各合作伙伴授牌。仪式由自治区党委副秘书长、“两会”指挥中心副总指挥黄世勇主持。

第八届中国—东盟博览会指定国礼交接仪式暨新闻发布会在广西南宁举行。由孔家钧窑中国工艺美术大师孔相卿设计的钧瓷珍品“坤元鼎”被选定为第八届中国—东盟博览会国礼，这是自2006年以来，孔家钧窑连续6年获此殊荣。

14日

广西壮族自治区党委、自治区人民政府召开第八届中国—东盟博览会和商务与投资峰会暨全区深化与东盟开放合作动员大会。自治区党委书记、自治区人大常委会主任郭声琨在自治区党委礼堂主会场出席会议并强调要继续举全区之力，奋力做好各项工作，确保2011年“两会”办得更加隆重、更加热烈、更有实效、更具影响力。会议由自治区主席马飚主持。车荣福、温卡华、陈武、石生龙、余远辉、周新建、刘新文、莫永清、陈章良、杨道喜、高雄、梁胜利、李达球、蒋培兰、苏道俨、张少康、李勇等自治区领导出席主会场会议。

15日

广西壮族自治区党委常委、自治区常务副主席、“两会”指挥中心总指挥李金早主持召开“两会”安保工作会议，研究部署相关工作。自治区党委常委、政法委书记温卡华，自治区副主席、自治区公安厅厅长梁胜利，“两会”指挥中心副总指挥黄世勇、魏然参加了会议。

17日

由中国社会科学院国际研究学部、广西社会科学院、广西国际博览事务局、广西北部湾发展研究院联合主办的第四届中国—东盟智库战略对话论坛在南宁明园新都酒店举行。广西壮族自治区人大常委会副主任刘新文，柬埔寨皇家科学院副院长宋春奔，老挝社会科学院副院长坎飞，菲律宾企业领导人研究所总裁兼首席执行官、亚洲团结学会主席（菲律宾前任财政部长）约瑟思·艾思塔尼斯劳，中国社会科学院国际研究学部主任张蕴岭等出席论坛。

为确保第八届中国—东盟博览会、中国—东盟商务与投资峰会等重要专场活动的顺利进行，“两会”指挥中心在南宁国际会展中心和荔园山庄进行了多场重要活动的实时综合演练。广西壮族自治区党委常委、自治区常务副主席、“两会”指挥中心总指挥李金早在现场观摩了演练，并提出了相关工作要求。

19日

由文化部、国家文物局、广西壮族自治区人民政府主办，广西壮族自治区文化厅承办，中国博物馆协会、中国文化传媒集团、广西日报传媒集团协办的2011中国—东盟文化产业论坛在广西南宁开幕。文化部党组成员、国家文物局局长单霁翔发表主旨演讲，广西壮族自治区副主席李康致辞。来自东盟10国和东盟秘书处、日本以及中国的专家、学者、官员出席会议。

第八届中国—东盟高尔夫国际名人邀请赛在南宁青秀山国际高尔夫俱乐部开杆。老挝工贸部部长南・维亚吉、老挝投资计划部副部长通米・蓬维赛、老挝工贸部副部长肯玛妮・奔舍那、老挝公共工程与运输部副部长拉塔那玛尼・宽尼翁、老挝国家旅游局副局长苏卡申・普提山等出席了开球仪式。

广西壮族自治区党委常委、自治区常务副主席、“两会”指挥中心总指挥李金早主持召开“两会一节”开幕前最后一次指挥中心工作会议，研究部署相关工作。“两会”指挥中心副总指挥黄世勇、魏然参加了会议。

20日

中共中央政治局常委、国务院总理温家宝在广西南宁分别会见了前来出席第八届中国—东盟博览会、中国—东盟商务与投资峰会的柬埔寨首相洪森、老挝副总理宋沙瓦、越南副总理阮春福、泰国副总理吉滴叻和缅甸副总统吴丁昂敏乌。广西壮族自治区党委书记郭声琨、自治区主席马飚、外交部副部长张志军、商务部国际贸易谈判代表兼副部长高虎城等会见时在座。

21日

第八届中国—东盟博览会在南宁国际会展中心隆重开幕。中共中央政治局常委、国务院总理温家宝宣布开幕。第八届中国—东盟博览会主题国马来西亚总理纳吉布、柬埔寨首相洪森、缅甸副总统吴丁昂敏乌、老挝副总理宋沙瓦、泰国副总理吉滴叻、越南副总理阮春福、文莱工业和初级资源部部长叶海亚、新加坡贸工部部长林勋强、菲律宾贸工部副部长马拉雅、印度尼西亚贸易部部长助理穆赫达塔尔、广西壮族自治区党委书记郭声琨、广西壮族自治区主席马飚、东盟秘书处秘书长素林出席开幕式。马来西亚总理纳吉布、广西壮族自治区主席马飚、中国商务部国际贸易谈判代表兼副部长高虎城先后致辞。马来西亚国际贸易和工业部部长穆斯塔法、东盟秘书处秘书长素林共同主持开幕式。温家宝与各国领导人、代表团团长、东盟秘书长素林、中国商务部部长陈德铭、广西壮族自治区党委书记郭声琨等嘉宾共同为第八届中国—东盟博览会开幕剪彩，共同为“中国—东盟青少年交流活动中心”揭牌。中国财政部部长谢旭人，人力资源和社会保障部部长尹蔚民，住房和城乡建设部部长姜伟新，卫生部部长陈竺，国务院研究室主任谢伏瞻，国务院副秘书长、总理办公室主任项兆伦，外交部副部长傅莹，国家发改委副主任穆虹，中国国际贸易促进委员会会长万季飞，民政部副部长姜力，国务院研究室副主任田学斌等中方组委会成员单位领导，国家其他有关部委领导，自治区领导马铁山、陈际瓦、李文潮、李金早、沈北海、车荣福、温卡华、陈武、石生龙、黄道伟、余远辉、周新建、吴恒、刘新文、莫永清、荣仕星、文明、陈章良、杨道喜、李康、梁胜利、林国强、蒋济雄、李达球、蒋培兰、彭钊、李彬，自治区高级人民法院院长罗殿龙，自治区人民检察院检察长张少康，以及世界知名企业家、商协会会长、区域经济研究专家与参展参会客商代表共1000多人参加开幕式。

出席第八届中国—东盟博览会的中共中央政治局常委、国务院总理温家宝，东盟各国政要、国际组织负责人、各代表团领导巡视了博览会展馆。期间，温家宝总理与马来西亚总理纳吉布共同出席了第八届中国—东盟博览会主题国马来西亚“魅力之城”开馆仪式。温家宝总理随行人员及自治区领导郭声琨、马飚、李金早等陪同温家宝总理巡视展馆并出席开馆仪式。

由中国和马来西亚两国政府支持建设的中马钦州产业园区签约暨揭牌仪式在广西南宁举行。中共中央政治局常委、国务院总理温家宝和马来西亚总理纳吉布见证签约并共同揭牌。中国商务部国际贸易谈判代表兼副部长高虎城，马来西亚国际贸易和工业部部长穆斯塔法分别代表中马两国在“中马钦州产业园区项目”文本上签字。广西壮族自治区党委书记、自治区人大常委会主任郭声琨，自治区主席马飚，自治区党委常委、自治区常务副主席李金早，中国驻马来西亚大使柴玺，国务院副秘书长、总理办公室主任项兆伦，外交部副部长傅莹，国家发改委副主任穆虹及钦州市主要领导参加仪式。

第八届中国—东盟商务与投资峰会在南宁荔园山庄国际会议中心隆重开幕。中共中央政治局常委、国务院总理温家宝，马来西亚总理纳吉布，柬埔寨首相洪森，缅甸副总统吴丁昂敏乌，老挝副总理宋沙瓦，泰国副总理吉滴叻，越南副总理阮春福，文莱工业和初级资源部部长叶海亚，新加坡贸工部部长林勋强，菲律宾贸工部副部长马拉雅，印度尼西亚贸易部部长助理穆赫达塔尔，东盟秘书处秘书长素林，中国国际贸易促进委员会会长万季飞，广西壮族自治区主席马飚，中国商务部国际贸易谈判代表兼副部长高虎城等出席开幕式。广西壮族自治区党委书记郭声琨主持开幕式并致欢迎辞。开幕式上，中国国务院总理温家宝、柬埔寨首相洪森分别发表演讲。中国国际贸易促进委员会会长万季飞发表致辞。中国财政部部长谢旭人、人力资源和社会保障部部长尹蔚民、住房和城乡建设部部长姜伟新、卫生部部长陈竺、国务院研究室主任谢伏瞻、国家质检总局局长支树平、中华全国供销总社理事会主任杨传堂，国务院副秘书长、总理办公室主任项兆伦，自治区领导马铁山、陈际瓦、李文潮、李金早、沈北海、车荣福、温卡华、陈武、石生龙、黄道伟、余远辉、周新建、吴恒、刘新文、莫永清、荣仕星、文明、杨道喜、梁胜利、林国强、蒋济雄、李达球、蒋培兰、彭钊、李彬，自治区高级人民法院院长罗殿龙，自治区人民检察院检察长张少康等，以及东盟各国代表团主要成员、外交使节、中国政府有关部门和各省、自治区、直辖市的领导，中国和东盟各国商协组织的负责人，中国和东盟企业界代表、专家学者和新闻界人士，区域外的贵宾共1000多人参会。

泰国副总理吉滴叻与中泰企业家见面会暨中泰合作项目签约仪式在南宁荔园山庄举行。广西壮族自治区党委副书记陈际瓦出席了见面会并致欢迎词，泰国副总理吉滴叻作主旨发言。

马来西亚总理纳吉布与中国企业CEO圆桌对话会在广西南宁举行。马来西亚总理纳吉布，中国国际贸易促进委员会会长万季飞，中国商务部国际贸易谈判代表兼副部长高虎城，广西壮族自治区党委常委、宣传部部长沈北海出席并致辞。会议由马来西亚贸工部部长穆斯塔法主持。

由国家食品药品监管局和广西壮族自治区人民政府共同主办的中国—东盟药品安全论坛暨药品监督管理局局长会议在广西南宁举行。国家食品药品监管局局长邵明立、广西壮族自治区人民政府副主席李康，以及中国和东盟10国的食品药品监管官员和专家参加了会议。会议由国家食品药品监管局副局长边振甲主持。

由中国科技部与东盟科学技术委员会共同主办、广西科技厅承办的中国—东盟太阳能政策对话与技术洽谈会在广西南宁举行。来自东盟国家和中国的100多位政府官员、专家学者和企业家参加了本次会议。

为纪念中老建交50周年和中国—东盟友好交流年，由中国国际广播电台、老挝驻南宁总领事馆和广西广播电影电视局主办的“北部湾之声”节目落地老挝万象启动仪式、老挝音乐广西展播周开幕式和中国国际广播电台《见证友谊》老挝文版首发仪式等系列活动在南宁举行。老挝副总理宋沙瓦，广西壮族自治区党委常委、统战部部长黄道伟出席。

“大地飞歌·2011”第十三届南宁国际民歌艺术节暨第八届中国—东盟博览会开幕晚会在广西体育中心举行。广西壮族自治区党委常委、自治区副主席、南宁市委书记陈武宣布晚会开幕。南宁市市长周红波发表致辞。

22日

中国—东盟博览会农业展开展仪式在广西展览馆举行。广西壮族自治区政协主席马铁山出席仪式并宣布农业展开幕。广西壮族自治区副主席陈章良、中国农业部纪检组长朱宝成分别致辞。

第八届中国—东盟博览会轻工展开展仪式在南宁华南城会展中心举行。广西壮族自治区主席马飚出席仪式，宣布第八届中国—东盟博览会轻工展开展。广西壮族自治区党委常委、自治区副主席、南宁市委书记陈武在仪式上致辞。自治区政府秘书长王跃飞参加了仪式。

由广西壮族自治区人民政府和环境保护部联合主办的2011中国—东盟环保合作论坛在广西南宁举行。环境保护部副部长李干杰，广西壮族自治区党委常委、自治区副主席林念修，广西壮族自治区政协副主席李彬，东盟秘书处副秘书长卡尔梅，亚洲开发银行副行长洛哈尼，以及东盟各国高级代表、联合国机构高级代表应邀出席。李干杰代表环境保护部部长周生贤作主旨发言。来自国内外专家、学者、政府官员和国际组织代表参加此次论坛。

由中国国家质检总局与东盟秘书处共同举办的第一届中国—东盟TBT合作部长会议在南宁召开。此次会议是中国—东盟在TBT合作领域的首次部长级会议。会议由中国国家质检总局局长支树平和马来西亚科技创新部部长翁凯里为会议联合主席共同主持。支树平、东盟秘书处秘书长素林、广西壮族自治区政协主席马铁山分别代表中国、东盟和广西壮族自治区人民政府在会议开幕式上致辞。中国国家质检总局副局长、国家认监委主任孙大伟代表中方介绍了中国TBT管理的基本情况。来自东盟成员国TBT工作主管部门部级领导和高官，中国国家发改委、科技部、工信部、商务部、国家质检总局、国家食药局、国家认监委、国家标准委等八个部门的代表和中国国家质检总局直属的泛珠江三角洲地区、与东盟贸易密切相关的各直属检验检疫局负责人参加了会议。

由国家新闻出版总署和广西壮族自治区人民政府共同主办的2011中国—东盟出版博览会在广西民族博物馆开幕。这是首次举办的中国—东盟出版博览会，为中国—东盟博览会注入了新的文化元素。2011中国—东盟出版博览会组委会主任、新闻出版总署副署长邬书林，2011中国—东盟出版博览会组委会主任、广西壮族自治区党委常委、宣传部部长沈北海，2011中国—东盟出版博览会组委会主任、广西壮族自治区副主席李康，全国政协委员、中国出版集团公司原总裁聂震宁，缅甸联邦共和国信息部副部长苏温，以及东盟10国文化官员出席了开幕式。

由中国国家林业局、广西壮族自治区人民政府主办，南宁市人民政府、广西壮族自治区林业厅承办的中国—东盟城市森林论坛在广西南宁开幕。缅甸环境保护及林业部部长温吞，国家林业局党组副书记、副局长赵树丛，国家林业局党组成员、中央纪委驻局纪检组组长陈述贤，广西壮族自治区党委常委车荣福，广西壮族自治区政府副主席陈章良以及东盟国家林业部门主管官员和中国国家林业局及其直属单位人员、各省（自治区、直辖市）林业部门负责人、国内林业专家参加论坛。

由中国—东盟商务理事会、广西壮族自治区人民政府、中国物流与采购联合会主办，广西发展与改革委员会、广西投资促进局、广西物流与采购联合会、广西物资集团有限责任公司共同承办的第二届中国—东盟物流合作论坛在广西南宁举行。广西壮族自治区政协副主席林国强出席论坛并致辞。中国物流与采购联合会副会长蔡进、中国—东盟商务理事会中方常务副秘书长许宁宁等分别出席论坛并作主题演讲。来自国内外物流专家、政府机构负责人、企业界代表及主办、协办单位400多人参加会议。

第五届中国—东盟青年艺术品创作大赛获奖作品暨五周年成果展在广西博物馆开幕。广西壮族自治区政协副主席蒋培兰出席开幕式并讲话，各主办单位领导和东盟各国嘉宾、留学生代表及中国艺术家、企业家代表、高校艺术专业学生共300多人参加了开幕仪式。

第八届中国—东盟博览会投资合作圆桌会在南宁国际会展中心举行。中国商务部国际贸易谈判代表兼副部长高虎城出席会议并致辞。会议由中国商务部投资促进事务局副局长张迎新女士、东盟秘书处经济一体化合作司司长苏柏什先生共同主持。与会代表就积极通过中国—东盟博览会这一平台进一步加大中国与东盟在投资领域的合作，落实中国—东盟自由贸易区投资协议，实现多（双）边投资便利化以及今后每年在博览会期间举办投资合作圆桌会等事宜达成共识。

第三届中国—东盟金融合作与发展领袖论坛在广西南宁召开。广西壮族自治区党委常委、自治区人民政府常务副主席李金早，中国人民银行行长助理金琦，中国银行业监督管理委员会副主席蔡鄂生，中国证券监督管理委员会主席助理姜洋，中国保险监督管理委员会纪委书记陈新权，马来西亚银行大中华及东北亚行政总裁、香港分行总经理张贵兴，文莱佰都利银行首席执行官彼尔英豪，柬埔寨国家银行行长谢占多，柬埔寨加华银行执行总裁方侨生，柬埔寨联合商业银行首席执行官任瑞生，老挝证券交易所副主席兼首席运营官朴正皓，泰华农民银行高级副总裁、中国业务总监邱楚南，泰国盘谷银行（中国）有限公司首席执行官洪钦雄，越南河内证券交易所董事会副主席兼总裁阮文俊等出席论坛。

中国—东盟商品交易中心在南宁华南城正式启动。广西壮族自治区党委常委、自治区副主席、南宁市委书记陈武、东盟秘书处秘书长素林、中国国际贸易促进委员会会长万季飞等为中心揭牌。

由中国—东盟博览会秘书处、广西体育局共同举办的第八届中国—东盟“网球之友”联谊活动在广西体育局江南训练基地综合馆网球场举行开球仪式。广西壮族自治区人大常委会副主任文明，自治区人大常委会副秘书长、办公厅副主任冯恒出席仪式。

23日

广西壮族自治区党委书记、自治区人大常委会主任郭声琨在自治区党委副书记陈际瓦，自治区党委常委、自治区常务副主席李金早和自治区党委常委、秘书长余远辉的陪同下，巡视南宁国际会展中心和广西展览馆等第八届中国—东盟博览会主要展馆。

广西壮族自治区主席马飚巡视南宁国际会展中心和广西展览馆等第八届中国—东盟博览会主要展馆。自治区党委常委、自治区常务副主席李金早，自治区政府秘书长王跃飞等陪同巡馆。

26日

第八届中国—东盟博览会、中国—东盟商务与投资峰会闭幕式暨新闻发布会在广西南宁举行，广西壮族自治区党委常委、自治区常务副主席李金早，中国和东盟10国共办方代表，东盟秘书处代表，第八届“两会”广西指挥中心领导，以及中外记者共200多人出席。闭幕式上，组委会对参展组织机构进行了表彰。举行了主题国和“魅力之城”交接仪式及“魅力之城”展位抽签仪式。“两会”广西指挥中心副总指挥、中国—东盟博览会秘书处秘书长郑军健向中外媒体介绍第八届中国—东盟博览会、商务与投资峰会的基本情况和主要成果，公布第九届中国—东盟博览会举办时间、地点、重点主题和重要活动安排。东盟秘书处代表蓬猜主持闭幕式。闭幕式新闻发布会由商务部外贸发展局副局长贾国勇主持。第八届中国—东盟博览会商品贸易额18.07亿美元，比上届增长5.6%。签订国际经济合作项目105个，总投资额74.2亿美元，同比增长10.86%；签订国内经济合作项目102个，总投资731.1亿元，比上届增长8.39%。

11月

18日

中国国务院总理温家宝在印度尼西亚巴厘岛召开的第十四次中国与东盟领导人会议上就深化中国东盟务实合作提出六点倡议，其中提到，中方将在广西南宁设立东盟产品展示中心。

中国—东盟中心在印度尼西亚巴厘岛举行成立仪式。

2011年中国—东盟博览会林产品及木制品展在南宁国际会展中心开幕。国家林业局党组副书记、副局长赵树丛，广西壮族自治区副主席陈章良出席了开幕式。

21日

亚洲及大洋洲地区大众体育合作发展论坛暨中国—东盟大众体育合作发展论坛在广西南宁开幕。中国国家体育总局副局长、亚洲及大洋洲地区大众体育协会主席冯建中，广西壮族自治区人民政府副主席李康分别致辞。来自中国和东盟国家以及港澳台地区的体育官员、专家和学者就亚太地区尤其是中国—东盟地区的大众体育合作与发展进行了广泛深入的探讨。

12月

8日

由中国国家中医药管理局、国家民族事务委员会、广西壮族自治区人民政府共同主办的2011中国—东盟传统医药高峰论坛在广西南宁举行。中国卫生部副部长、国家中医药管理局局长王国强，国家民族事务委员会副主任丹珠昂奔，广西壮族自治区副主席李康，东盟秘书处副秘书长米斯然·卡梅，柬埔寨卫生部国务秘书欧库摩娜，中国工程院院士姚新生等出席了开幕式。世界卫生组织同期发来贺电。来自中国、东盟以及俄罗斯、澳大利亚等18个国家、地区和组织的官员、专家学者参加了论坛系列活动。

17—22日

广西壮族自治区主席马飚率广西代表团到缅甸参加大湄公河次区域经济合作第四次领导人会议并顺访缅甸。在缅期间，代表团拜会了缅甸副总统吴丁昂敏乌，会见了缅甸计划发展部部长吴丁乃登、商务部部长吴温敏、工商联主席吴温昂和仰光省行政长官吴敏瑞，就配合缅方做好第九届中国—东盟博览会主题国工作，进一步深化广西与缅甸、仰光省的交流合作等，深入交换了意见，达成了重要共识，为双方进一步开展务实合作打下了良好的基础。缅方确认吴登盛总统2012年将率团出席第九届中国—东盟博览会和商务与投资峰会。

第八届中国—东盟博览会重要文件汇编（一）
会议文件

在第八届中国—东盟博览会开幕式上的致辞

马来西亚总理　纳吉布

（2011年10月21日）

尊敬的中国总理温家宝阁下，
尊敬的东盟国家领导人，
各位嘉宾，
女士们、先生们：

我很高兴今天能与各位相聚于中国—东盟博览会，此项盛会已日益壮大，汇聚来自中国、东盟和世界其他地区的商家，促进区域合作及全球融合。

今年我感到特别自豪，因为马来西亚是本届博览会的主题国。我谨此代表我个人及参加博览会的超过100家马来西亚企业对主办方特别致谢，因为我们深感荣幸。

今年的博览会尤为重要，因为今年恰逢东盟与中国正式建立对话关系20周年。在此期间，在共同发展理念的支撑下，双边关系蓬勃发展。通过密切合作，我们努力推进了公共卫生的发展，包括在马来西亚建立风险通报资源中心来管理传染性疾病的暴发。通过控制和打击药品滥用的行为，我们努力织就社会安全网。并且我们努力加快经济一体化进程，通过实施中国—东盟自贸区协议来促进资源增长，这一协议使来自中国与东盟的商家，不管他们是来自吉隆坡、北京，还是曼谷、上海，均可从贸易中获得更大收益并扩展投资机会，从而在本地区和世界其他地方产生更大影响。

然而，经济持续一体化和发展，并不能以无视自然世界、牺牲下一代利益为代价。我们可以轻而易举地建设一个溜冰场或者给足球场加个顶盖，可我们对冰川或者臭氧层却无能为力。

我们所能做的就是，改变自己的行为方式，发展更清洁环保的技术，降低排放，试图改善已经造成的损害。我们必须从现在做起，而不是仅仅流于空谈。本届博览会将环保和可持续发展作为重点主题，意义也在于此。

这一进步当然与2007年第11届“10+1”峰会密不可分。会上，与会国达成一致意见，环保应当成为新的优先合作领域。今后数年里，随着《中国—东盟环保合作战略（2009—2015年）》的实施，中国—东盟环保中心有望在中国成立。

该中心的职能范畴显而易见，包括为环保项目和策略做规划，促进中国和整个东盟的环保事业。我期待该中心能成为极其重要的机构。该中心已公布的项目之一就是中国—东盟绿色特使计划，其旨在推广使用对环境无害的技术、环境标志产品以及低能耗生产。

然而，此项工作责任重大，非单一机构所能承担。因此全世界国家的政府都应加大工作力度，唤醒公众对环保的意识，推进环境教育，发展环保技术。

只有这样，我们才能阻洪水猛兽于家园之外，确保我们的子孙能从我们手里继承一个清洁、安全和健康的星球。在这个星球上，物产富饶，水源清洁安全，人民衣食无忧。

当然，我们的经济和环境发展密不可分，今天我们相聚一堂，应该关注当前欧美面临的经济挑战，及其对我们亚洲的可能影响，因为对欧美地区的出口增长有可能在未来一段时间内停滞不前，我们有必要寻找维持发展的其他动力。

即便我们无法与西方国家进行更多的贸易，我们仍可以加大内部贸易。中国—东盟间贸易额在过去20年内快速增长，从1991年的80亿美元增至2010年的2312亿美元。中国目前已成为东盟首要贸易伙伴，2010年对东盟贸易额占其贸易总额的11%。而东盟也成为中国的第四大贸易伙伴，对华贸易额为其贸易总额的10%。

这并非意味着双边贸易再无发展空间，恰恰相反，事实上，我对中国誓言将双边贸易额在2015年增至5000亿美元由衷赞赏。

要达成此目标并非易事。有效的合作意味着双方应更好地了解对方的需求和想法，在推进货物和服务市场准入的同时，更应加强双方的沟通和相互理解。

首届中国—东盟货物贸易技术壁垒部长级会议就是加强双方沟通和相互理解的重要一步，我希望双方能保持这个发展势头，加强合作，以达成多赢局面。

在此，我再次感谢主办方给我这次机会发言，我谨代表所有东盟国家，祝福大家博览会之行愉快。

谢谢！

在第八届中国—东盟商务与投资峰会开幕式上的讲话

柬埔寨王国首相　洪森

（2011年10月21日）

中华人民共和国总理温家宝阁下，
尊敬的东盟各国领导人阁下，
贵宾们，女士们、先生们：

首先，我谨代表柬埔寨王国政府和在座的东盟各国领导人对第八届中国—东盟商务与投资峰会和第八届中国—东盟博览会组委会致以最诚挚的谢意，感谢中国政府对所有代表团的周到安排和热情接待。

今天，我很荣幸就此次峰会的主题，也就是“深化区域合作，实现共同繁荣”谈谈我的几点看法。

在过去几年中，本地区在政治、经济和社会领域都经历了快速的变革。中国经济的强劲增长使得亚洲地区不仅成为世界经济增长的中心，同时也成为世界经济复苏的区域性引擎。我们深知，中国在全球金融危机之后，迅速地成为世界第二大经济体，使得中国在维持全球和区域稳定方面发挥着不可或缺的作用。我想再次强调，中国的财政刺激政策和持续的快速增长，不仅有利于区域经济复苏，同时也有助于东盟地区比世界其他地区更快走出经济危机。

然而，美国经济二次探底和欧洲主权债务危机引起的不确定性，以及中东、北非的政治动荡和冲突，加上食品和能源的价格攀升，成为东盟和中国共同面临的挑战。尽管如此，大多数观察家仍然乐观地认为亚洲经济将在中期引领世界增长。在这个意义上来说，近期世界金融的发展形势表明，亚洲必须通过增加内需以减少对美国和欧洲市场的过度依赖。

因此，在我们前进的道路上，深化东盟与中国的合作是非常必要的。同时，我们亦需加强包括10+1、10+3、东亚峰会和其他次区域的合作伙伴在内的所有东盟对话伙伴的合作。明确这一点后，东盟和中国确定了一个新的行动计划来落实《中国—东盟面向和平与繁荣的战略伙伴关系联合宣言》（2011—2015），携手合作，以求在2015年实现东盟经济共同体。

回顾过去10年，2002年东盟和中国签署了《全面经济合作框架协议》，这为我们在2010年实现东盟—中国自贸区打下了坚实的基础。近些年来，东盟与中国的关系不断地拓展和加深，体现了中国与东盟建立密切合作关系的战略必要性。让我们倍感鼓舞的是，东盟与中国的双边贸易以年均26%的增长速度，从2003年的596亿美元增加到2008年的1969亿美元。此外，由于全球金融危机的影响，东盟与中国的贸易在2009年曾一度下滑，但在2010年出现了强劲反弹，双方的合作也因此进一步深化。东盟对中国的出口从2009年的816亿美元增加到2010年的1135亿美元，增加了39.1%。中国上升为东盟第二大出口目的地。从中国的进口则增长了21.8%，从2009年的966亿美元，增加到2010年的1171亿美元。尽管中国对东盟的直接投资下降了32%，从2009年的39亿美元减少到2010年的27亿美元，但中国仍然上升为东盟的第三大贸易伙伴。虽然东盟—中国自贸区需到2015年才在柬埔寨、老挝、缅甸和越南实施，但我相信，《中国—东盟投资协议》的签订，东盟—中国中心以及东盟—中国自贸区商务门户网站的建立，将不仅有助于促进我们在贸易、投资、旅游和教育、文化等领域的合作，也将鼓励这些国家的私营经济积极参与到区域复苏中来。

为进一步深化区域合作，促进可持续发展，更好地应对未来的挑战，我认为中国与东盟应该加强在以下领域的合作，以促进私营经济的参与。

首先，我们要完成《东盟—中国全面经济伙伴框架协议》的所有必要的技术性工作，来确保中国—东盟自贸区的顺利实施，更加充分地利用优惠政策，吸引更多中国的投资，促进中国与每一个东盟成员国之间的贸易，充分体现各自的比较优势。此外，进一步放宽非关税壁垒，比如植物和非植物检疫标准，让更多的东盟的农产品，尤其是欠发达成员国的农产品能够进入中国市场。所有这些将有助于实现东盟—中国领导人会议提出的共同目标，即在2015年，双边的贸易额达到5000亿美元，中国对东盟的直接投资增长到100亿美元。

第二，我们要加强互联互通的合作，以缩小区域内的发展差距。我们应该完成新加坡至昆明的铁路的修建工作，它是《东盟互联互通总体规划》不可或缺的部分。柬埔寨感谢中国慷慨支持，特别是在我们从金边—越南边界，缺失路段的可行性调查和研究方面的支持，柬埔寨高度重视这个缺失路段，中国继续支持这条全长257公里、穿越柬全境的缺失路段的建设，符合东盟与中国人民的利益。我高度赞赏最近以来中方向东盟提供的援助，特别是100亿美元的东盟—中国投资合作基金、150亿美元贷款，包括67亿美元的优惠贷款，用以推进中国与东盟之间在基础设施、能源、资源、信息和通讯技术等领域的主要合作项目。总的来说，我认为，中国的资金和技术支持对东盟基础设施基金的继续运作十分重要，它可以使东盟基础设施基金继续运作，实现东盟的互联互通，这是实现我们缩小区域发展差距的基础，就长远方向而言，也是实现东亚一体化的重要步骤。同时，私营经济更加积极地参与，对东盟互联互通总体规划成功实施至关重要。在这一方面，私营实体和政府在项目层面上更加密切地合作，将有利于整个地区基础设施互联互通的最终实现。

第三，我们要继续支持和推动私营部门参与农业生产，增加现代技术、培育良种、提高农业生产力、增加产量、提高农产品加工水平方面的投资，以增加农民的收入，减少农村地区的贫困，确保国家和地区的粮食安全。中国正成为绿色科技的领先国家，我希望中国可以向东盟的欠发达的成员国转让绿色科技，以增加农业产量。柬埔寨在许多领域都有巨大的潜力，如农业、农用工业、基础设施、劳动力密集型产业、出口导向型产业、油气和矿业这些自然资源和旅游业。这些领域还有待于进一步开发，所以蕴涵着大量的投资商机，以实现可持续发展。通过加强经济贸易和投资的合作，我们就可以和中国真正实现共赢。

贵宾们，女士们、先生们，我们伟大邻居中国的稳定和经济发展对于整个区域的经济增长都至关重要，所以我要再次重申，我们会致力于加强柬埔寨与中国，以及东盟与中国的密切关系，使我们成为真正的经济、贸易、投资、政治、安全领域的战略伙伴。此外，我认为东盟的选择是正确的，也就是对像中国这样的重要的主要伙伴扩大开放、密切合作，我希望通过东盟—中国自贸区以及私营经济的积极参与，我们都可以从贸易和投资的增长中获益，分享经济合作带来的成果。

我再一次代表柬埔寨王国政府和人民，深深地感谢中国政府和人民，感谢你们的不断支持，通过提供无偿援助和优惠贷款以及鼓励更多的中国投资者和游客到柬埔寨投资或旅游。柬埔寨王国政府会大力确保每一个外国投资者获得良好的投资环境。

最后，我很高兴能够有这样一个难得的机会，在这个重要的论坛上与在座的各位分享我的想法。祝本届峰会圆满成功，祝愿会议的主办方和各位代表身体健康、万事如意、事业有成。谢谢大家！

柬埔寨王国首相洪森给郭声琨、马飚的感谢信

中共广西壮族自治区委员会书记、广西壮族自治区人大常委会主任郭声琨阁下，
中国广西壮族自治区主席马飚阁下：

很高兴有机会来到南宁这座美丽的城市，并与二位阁下见面。2011年10月20日至21日，我率柬埔寨代表团出席了第八届中国—东盟博览会、第八届中国—东盟商务与投资峰会开幕式，开幕式非常成功。感谢贵区给予我和代表团成员的热烈欢迎和盛情接待。

当前，柬埔寨遭遇了严重洪灾，几百人因此丧生，经济损失惨重。阁下代表广西5000万人民，对柬埔寨表示了深切同情，并承诺提供价值300万元的物资用于灾后重建，此举令我深受感动。我谨代表柬埔寨政府，衷心感谢阁下和广西人民对我国灾区重建的大力支持。

在二位阁下的卓越领导下，贵区尤其是南宁市取得了惊人的成绩和快速的发展，给我留下了深刻印象。阁下和贵区政府功不可没，谨致以衷心祝贺。同时也祝贺贵区精心筹备并成功举办了历届中国—东盟博览会、中国—东盟商务与投资峰会。借助博览会这一平台，东盟与中国、与本地区乃至全世界其他伙伴的经贸联系更为紧密，合作进一步深化。

谨致以最崇高的问候。

柬埔寨王国首相　洪森

第八届中国—东盟博览会重要文件汇编（二）
其他重要文件

在第八届中国—东盟博览会、第八届中国—东盟商务与投资峰会闭幕式暨新闻发布会上的讲话

中国—东盟博览会、中国—东盟商务与投资峰会
指挥中心副总指挥
中国—东盟博览会秘书处秘书长
郑军健
（2011年10月26日）

女士们，先生们，新闻界的朋友们：

在中国和东盟各国的共同努力下，第八届中国—东盟博览会、中国—东盟商务与投资峰会即将落下帷幕。本届博览会、商务与投资峰会在中国—东盟建立对话关系20周年、中国—东盟友好交流年之际举办，背景特殊。作为中国—东盟建立对话关系20周年系列纪念活动的重要组成部分，本次展会突出了中国—东盟建立对话关系20年合作领域不断拓展的成果，博览会和商务与投资峰会常办常新推动了自贸区建设快速发展的成效，总的来看隆重热烈、创新务实、安全便利。本届博览会、商务与投资峰会规格高，各国领导人高层会晤和政商互动交流活动更加丰富务实；开幕式、展馆布置和城市氛围营造更加盛大、恢宏、热烈；展会内容、活动安排等方面都根据2011年的特殊背景进行了

创新，更加科学，更有实效；参展参会企业规模和质量都有很大提高，各场活动安全、有序、顺畅，接待和服务在保障安全的基础上更加快捷便利。本届博览会、商务与投资峰会取得了显著成效，影响深远。受组委会委托，下面我介绍本次博览会、商务与投资峰会的有关情况。

一、本届博览会、商务与投资峰会成果显著，为中国—东盟友好交流和经贸合作作出了新的贡献

博览会、商务与投资峰会不同于一般的商业性展会。它不仅是经贸盛会，也是外交舞台。每届博览会、商务与投资峰会都有各国领导人和部长出席，会期举行多场双边和多边会晤、政商对话交流等一系列活动，增进了解与互信，促进友好合作，今年这一特色更为突出：

（一）中国和东盟国家领导人高规格出席，多层次活动内容丰富务实，突出了20年合作领域不断拓展

中国总理温家宝、马来西亚总理纳吉布、柬埔寨首相洪森、缅甸副总统吴丁昂敏乌、老挝副总理宋沙瓦、泰国副总理吉滴叻、越南副总理阮春福出席了本届博览会、商务与投资峰会。东盟秘书长素林以及中国和东盟各国商务、环保、质检、金融、电信等多个领域的部长出席本届盛会。出席本次博览会、商务与投资峰会的部长级贵宾有240人，其中中方141人，东盟和其他国家部长级贵宾99人。中国和东盟10国商协会会长、知名企业家、社会各界知名人士出席盛会。

中国和东盟各国领导人率团高规格出席本次盛会，表明了在中国—东盟建立对话关系20周年的特殊历史背景下，面对复杂的世界经济形势，中国和东盟更加重视博览会和商务与投资峰会的平台作用，显现出进一步加强互利合作，继续共同推进自贸区建设，实现共同发展、共同繁荣的信心和决心。

中国和东盟各国领导人在会期活动中分别发表了讲话，充分肯定了双方20年合作成果，深入分析了当前形势，指明了下一步合作的方向。这对于充分发挥博览会、商务与投资峰会平台作用，进一步深化双方友好合作，具有指导意义。

温家宝总理在本届商务与投资峰会主旨演讲中提出重点办好几件大事：

一是共同建设好自贸区。中方愿意继续扩大东盟国家优势产品的进口，妥善解决自贸区建设中出现的各种问题。将在南宁建设中国—东盟商品交易中心，作为双方产品的展示交易平台和商贸物流基地。

二是大力推进互联互通。中方将与东盟方面密切合作，加强对中国与东盟有关国家互联互通的投入，为促进本地区商品、资本、信息的自由流通、人员往来和经济社会发展创造更好条件。中方愿意继续利用好中国—东盟投资合作基金、中国—东盟银联体及对东盟国家建立的信贷渠道，支持中国—东盟互联互通合作项目的落实。

三是扩大双方投资合作。中方已经承诺在东盟国家各建一个经贸合作区，

通过集群式投资提高双方经贸合作水平。中马钦州产业园是双方在中国西部地区合作建设的第一个工业园，具有示范意义，欢迎马方有实力的企业积极参与园区的规划和开发建设。

四是深化区域经济合作。中方将鼓励企业参与东盟东部增长区、大湄公河、泛北部湾等次区域合作，给予金融、技术、市场等方面的有力支持，推动形成若干经济增长极。中方愿与东盟密切合作，进一步深化现有各项区域财金合作，扩大货币互换规模和参与范围，完善“清迈倡议”多边化危机救助机制，加强区域经济监测能力建设，推进亚洲债券市场发展，逐步建立稳定、成熟的地区资本市场，进一步增强本地区应对国际金融风险的能力。

五是拓展人文领域交流。以办好“中国—东盟友好交流年”为契机，继续加强文化、教育、旅游、青年等领域的交流与合作，努力实现2015年双方人员往来达到1500万人次的目标。

马来西亚总理纳吉布在本届博览会开幕式致辞中说，今后数年里，随着《中国—东盟环保合作战略（2009—2015年）》的实施，中国—东盟环保中心有望在中国成立。纳吉布总理在与中国企业CEO圆桌对话会上提出，希望中国企业更多地进入高科技，包括电信、水利、污水处理、绿色技术、生物医药等领域。这些都是马来西亚关注的重点领域，希望吸引更多的外商投资。马来西亚政府将全力支持中马共建的钦州产业园区的发展。

柬埔寨首相洪森在本届商务与投资峰会讲话中说，希望中国可以向东盟欠发达的成员国转让绿色科技，以增加农业产量。

泰国副总理吉滴叻在与中泰企业家见面会上说，希望借助此次见面会，促进泰中两国企业家携手迈进，促进商业投资各领域的成功合作。泰国政府将继续支持两国企业家合作。

中国和东盟国家领导人的讲话，对双方开展合作具有很强的指导意义。我们将充分利用博览会、商务与投资峰会平台，认真加以研究和落实。

本届博览会期间，举行了6场国家领导人会见，中国和东盟国家领导人、各国代表团团长巡视了展馆，共同出席了博览会开幕式、商务与投资峰会开幕式和欢迎宴会。主题国马来西亚举行了丰富多彩的主题国活动，中国和马来西亚领导人共同出席了早餐会、见证了中马钦州产业园区签约仪式并为该园区揭牌，共同出席了主题国“魅力之城”开馆仪式。马来西亚总理纳吉布还出席了马来西亚商品馆开馆仪式，并与中国企业家CEO举行了圆桌对话会，取得良好成效。泰国副总理吉滴叻与中泰企业家见面会圆满成功。老挝副总理宋沙瓦出席了“庆祝中老建交50周年‘北部湾之声’节目落地老挝万象”活动。会期还举行了中国—东盟经贸部长晚餐会，促进了友好交流。

会期政商高端对接和多层次交流活动比往届更多。既有东盟国家领导人与中国地方政府领导、企业家的会见、对话，也有中国有关部委领导、各省市领导与中外企业家的会见、交流。例如，中国—缅甸企业家座谈会上，缅甸商务部部长吴温敏与企业家进行了座谈等。这些高端对接活动促进了政商互动，为企业创造更多的商机。

本届博览会、商务与投资峰会反映了中国—东盟建立对话关系20周年来合作领域不断拓展的特点，促进了友好合作。

（二）开幕式和闭幕式隆重热烈，反映了中国—东盟合作和博览会的成果

博览会开幕式隆重热烈，形象地表达出博览会11国共办、领导人亲自推动的特点，反映中国—东盟建立对话关系20周年的辉煌成就，展示博览会促进中国—东盟友好交流、推动自贸区建设取得的成果和作出的贡献。开幕式上举行了有11国青少年参加的中国—东盟青少年交流活动中心揭牌仪式，展示了中国与东盟友谊代代相传的深刻寓意，博览会取得的成果得到更具体的展现。博览会开幕式受到了中国和东盟国家领导人、政府官员、商协会会长、企业家的普遍赞誉。

马来西亚贸工部部长穆斯塔法说："我本人非常荣幸主持博览会开幕式。开幕式办得很好，每个细节都做得很到位，非常完美，非常精彩！"

东盟秘书长素林说："本届开幕式上能邀请到这么多国家的领导人共同出席，显示了中国—东盟博览会政治外交规格之高和意义之重"，"11国少年的互动，充分体现了中国—东盟博览会是一个开放、包容的合作平台。"

商务与投资峰会开幕式在场地安排、会场布置、内容设计等方面创新，更加隆重、大气、务实，给贵宾留下深刻印象。中国和东盟国家领导人分别在开幕式上阐述了促进双方合作的政策主张，为进一步深化和拓展合作、实现共同繁荣指明了方向。

博览会开幕晚会暨南宁国际民歌艺术节开幕式紧扣中国—东盟建立对话关系20周年，不仅节目内容更加丰富，而且更具特色。

博览会与商务与投资峰会闭幕式形式新颖，意义深刻，体现了博览会共办水平和成果。在闭幕式上，本届博览会主题国马来西亚与下届博览会主题国缅甸、本届博览会中国"魅力之城"海南省与下届中国"魅力之城"广州分别举行了交接仪式。组委会向中国和东盟各国组展机构颁发了"主题国纪念奖"、"重大贡献及支持奖"、"最佳参展商组织奖"、"最佳采购商组织奖"、"最佳魅力之城展示奖"等8类奖项，体现了本届博览会在共办机制、展会组织等方面取得了新的成效。

（三）博览会经贸成效进一步提升，商务与投资峰会以"深化区域合作，实现共同繁荣"为主题，交流更加深入，系列会议和活动更有实效，突出了中国—东盟自由贸易区显著成果

——本届博览会展览规模扩大，参展参会企业更多。总展位数4700个。参展企业总数2300家，同比增长4.6%。参展参会客商5.06万人，比上届增长3.26%。

——东盟及区域外国家参展更加踊跃，共办特色更加鲜明。东盟及区域外国家使用展位数达到历史最好水平。印尼、老挝、马来西亚、缅甸、泰国、越南等6个东盟国家包馆，40多家东盟知名品牌企业参展，马来西亚、泰国等组织橡胶、棕榈油、矿产品等大宗商品企业积极参展。东盟国家优势行业集中参展，展会专业化进一步提高。

——国内企业参展空前高涨，博览会在区域内外的市场吸引力进一步增强。国内企业申请展位数超过计划数的30.2%，名优企业多，参展产品更加契合东盟市场的需求。台湾企业在每届博览会参展的基础上，2011年由台北世界贸易中心组织企业首次整体参展。日本也首次组织企业整体参展。国内企业在国际经济合作展区和工程机械、运输车辆展区重复参展率高达90%，东盟国家企业重复参展率较高，缅甸达71.9%，新加坡、柬埔寨均达55%。表明博览会在区域内外的市场认知度和吸引力进一步增强。

——采购商数量和质量进一步提高。2011年采购团组有70多个，多于往届。东盟采购商团组数比上届增加20%以上。

——经贸成效取得新突破。截至10月26日下午4时，累计交易总额达到18.07亿美元，比上届增长5.6%。签订国际经济合作项目105个，总投资额74.2亿美元，同比增长10.86%。其中，中国内地各省市及中央直属企业对外合作的“走出去”项目52个，总投资额26.5亿美元，同比增长37.8%。签订国内经济合作项目102个，总投资731.1亿元，比上届增长8.39%。举办地广西共签订国际合作项目69个，总投资46.9亿美元，占国际合作项目合同金额的63.2%。

——商务与投资峰会取得丰硕成果。本届商务与投资峰会以“深化区域合作，实现共同繁荣”为主题，温家宝总理发表了主旨演讲，柬埔寨首相洪森发表了讲话，广西壮族自治区党委书记、自治区人大常委会主任郭声琨主持开幕式。中国、东盟以及世界10多个国家和地区的政府高官、商界领袖、企业精英、区域组织代表、知名专家学者和媒体记者1100多人参会，各方就进一步深化区域行业之间的务实合作，实现共同发展和繁荣进行讨论和展望。

——系列会议和交流活动富有成效。随着中国—东盟经贸合作快速发展，双方对海关、检验检疫、金融等相关领域的服务配套提出了新的需求，对经贸合作与人文领域相结合也有新的要求。因此，每届博览会都围绕多个领域，举办系列会议和交流活动，研究解决这些领域合作中的问题，推动形成了多领域合作机制，促进全面合作。

本届博览会保持“展会结合”特色，举办会议和交流活动14个，特别是增加了更多的社会人文领域的会议和交流活动，促进了全方位、多层次、宽领域合作。其中，环保部围绕博览会重点主题“环保合作”，主办了中国—东盟环保合作论坛；其他有关部委围绕质检、金融、太阳能、药品安全、智库、人口与家庭发展、文化产业论坛、出版、森林、物流等领域，举办了相关会议和交流活动。

各场会议和交流活动规格高，成果务实。中国和东盟国家部长级官员、企业家、银行家、专家学者等出席了系列会议和活动，围绕各领域的热点议题，展开了深入研讨和对话，形成了一批务实成果。例如，环保论坛启动了中国—东盟绿色使者计划。质检论坛通过了关于加强中国—东盟产品质量安全合作的《南宁联合声明》。出版论坛达成《南宁共识》。金融论坛围绕金融及财政合作，在区域内货币结算、金融机构支持企业“走出去”、金融合作发展机制研究等方面，取得了新成果。

社会人文交流活动丰富多彩。中国—东盟文化产业论坛在博物馆运营管理及其文化产品创意开发方面，中国—东盟出版博览会在图书展销、论坛及版权贸易等方面，全面展示了中国与东盟国家历史文化和人文魅力。中国—东盟人口与家庭发展论坛在人口与家庭发展方面，开展了研讨和交流。会期还举办了南宁国际民歌艺术节、高尔夫球精英赛、“网球之友”联谊活动、中国—东盟媒体汽车拉力赛、国际商务书画展等一系列文化交流活动，增进了友谊。

二、展会创新务实、安全便利，突出了博览会和商务与投资峰会常办常新

本届博览会、商务与投资峰会紧扣中国—东盟合作的新形势，各项工作创新务实，安全便利，体现了博览会、商务与投资峰会承办工作水平不断提高，为企业创造了更多商机。

（一）展览内容创新，专业化水平有了新的提高

本届博览会根据自贸区建成后企业开拓市场的新需求，在展馆安排上采取新举措，除使用南宁国际会展中心、广西展览馆外，2011年新增华南城展区，形成“一会三馆”的格局。

——展品更加贴近市场需求。专设东盟品牌展区，吸引了新加坡星展银行、越南威拿咖啡等多家品牌企业参展。新增大宗原材料展示区，马来西亚橡胶出口促进局、棕油局，泰国泰华橡胶、越南橡胶贸易与旅游服务有限公司等大宗商品企业参展；东盟展品进一步集中到食品农产品、家具家居、特色工艺品及珠宝饰品、日用消费品等具有市场竞争优势的主要行业上。

——专业展特色更鲜明，商机更多。农业展不仅展示了中国各省区市特色农产品、名优食品、绿色果蔬、精品茗茶，也有马来西亚食品、越南咖啡、新西兰乳制品等国外特色产品，举办了葡萄酒品鉴会等一系列有特色的推介活动。轻工展展示了中国与东盟国家互补性强、需求量大的珠宝首饰及工艺品、数码电子产品、日用消费品、境外特色精品等。农业展、轻工展受到了专业客商和消费者的欢迎。

——总体形象设计和布展水平高。突出了中国—东盟建立对话关系20周年合作成果，体现11国共办的特点，东盟展位整体特装超过90%，保持国内一流

水平。

（二）商贸对接活动更有针对性，企业获得实惠更多

通过政商高端对接活动带动企业商家的合作，是博览会的一个特色。本届博览会期间，马来西亚总理纳吉布与中国企业CEO圆桌对话会签约了100亿美元的合作项目。泰国副总理与中泰企业家见面会、中国—缅甸企业家座谈会上也签约了一批合作项目。

商贸配对活动富有成效。会期举办了越南、马来西亚等专场配对会，橡胶、棕榈油等大宗商品采购配对会，中泰橡胶产业合作研讨会，农产品、轻工产品行业贸易对接活动，以及参展商讲坛、联合国采购说明会、商务早餐会等一系列对接活动，企业获得了更多的商机和实效。例如，越南、老挝等东盟国家轻工、家具产品受到中国采购商的欢迎，达成了一批采购意向。中国企业专门为东盟市场推出的低速汽车、小型工程机械、小型农用机械，也受到东盟采购商的青睐。会前举行的中国—东盟矿业合作论坛签署了31.6亿美元的合作项目和产品贸易协议。

（三）投资合作更加务实，“走出去”特色更加鲜明

本届博览会在做好商品贸易的基础上，突出投资合作特别是“走出去”的特色。

——首次举办了有中国和东盟10国投资促进部门代表参加的中国—东盟博览会投资合作圆桌会，发布中国和东盟各国最新的投资合作政策和项目信息，介绍各国投资环境，为企业提供与各国投促机构直接交流互动的机会，推动企业“走出去”。

——举办了“走出去”企业与金融机构对接活动。包括：中国—东盟基础设施投融资合作论坛、金融支持企业“走出去”洽谈会、企业股权（债券）投融资交易会等，邀请了出席金融论坛的金融机构和中央企业负责人进行洽谈对接，为企业投资东盟提供务实的金融支持。

——国际经济合作展区参展结构更优，形成了“以中直企业为重点，各省市外经企业为新生力量”的格局；经济技术开发区整体特装展示，成为推动园区招商及园区企业“走出去”的新亮点。

——会期还举办了东盟各国投资推介会、海外投资论坛及项目推介会等一系列投资促进活动，在推动企业“走出去”方面取得了一批务实的成果。

（四）服务贸易专题内容更丰富，“魅力之城”突出环保理念和旅游特色

本届博览会服务贸易专题重点展示金融服务、教育服务和旅游服务三个方面的内容。其中，“魅力之城”突出环保理念，并与旅游合作展示相结合，受到广泛关注。会期举办了中国“魅力之城”海南国际旅游岛推介会等一系列活动，促进了旅游合作。此外，会期举行了中国—东盟电信高峰论坛，签约项目金额8亿美元，推动双方在电信服务领域的合作。

（五）安保工作措施周密，在确保安全的同时为客商提供更多便利，营造良好的展览洽谈环境

本届博览会、商务与投资峰会在安全保卫方面周密部署，精心组织，确保了与会中外国家领导人、参会嘉宾和客商的安全。各场活动安全、有序、顺畅。在确保安全的同时，积极改进安保方式，在市区交通、场馆安检等方面，为参会客商市民群众提供了便利。

本届博览会、商务与投资峰会继续坚持以客户为中心，不断改善各项服务质量。会期继续开通了南宁往返东盟10国首都和重要城市的包机航线。展览管理更加机制化，展馆秩序比往年更好。海关、检验检疫部门采取便利化措施，展品通关快捷便利。证件工作全面实现“人到证到”目标。接待方面加强了对餐饮、住宿、用车等资源的统筹，在节俭的前提下提高了服务质量。对口接待机制进一步完善，宾馆服务更加规范。

（六）会期宣传报道形式有创新，报道持续时间长，深度广度进一步增强，展会影响力进一步扩大

本届博览会、商务与投资峰会继续受到国内外主流媒体和专业媒体的高度关注。到会采访的媒体共275家1738名记者，分别比上届增加38.19%和19.2%。其中，东盟媒体69家，比上届增长20%，在中国境内举行的同类活动中，参会东盟媒体和记者是最多的。

会期中央电视台、香港凤凰卫视、香港亚洲电视、广西电视台与东盟以及区域外的媒体采取连线互动、专访等多种形式报道本届博览会。其中，马来西亚总理纳吉布、东盟秘书长素林等政要接受了多家媒体的专访。据不完全统计，中外媒体累计发稿8300多篇；网络播发相关新闻（含转载）16万篇，图片3.178万幅，视频415个，网页记录达380多万条，还通过微博和手机报等新的传播方式，扩大宣传效果，提升了影响力。中外媒体对会期重要活动进行了大范围、深层次、聚焦式的宣传报道，给人留下深刻印象，营造了隆重热烈的氛围，引起强烈反响。

重大活动的现场直播场次多、规模大。中央电视台、新华网、人民网等众多媒体对博览会开幕式、商务与投资峰会开幕式等重大活动进行了现场直播。对马来西亚总理纳吉布与中国企业CEO圆桌对话会、泰国副总理吉滴叻与中泰企业家见面会进行了网络直播。

大会新闻服务更加快捷。开幕式、巡馆等重要活动结束后30分钟在新闻中心提供了图文共享资料，其他各场活动均于两小时内在博览会官方网站提供图文和视频资料。

本届博览会围绕2011年的特点，宣传报道声势大，持续时间长，亮点多。广西作为博览会承办方，今年积极参与主办或承办了一系列国家层面的纪念20周年系列活动，包括20周年纪念招待会、中国—东盟互联互通战略研讨会、东盟经贸记者研修班、中国—东盟友谊知识竞赛、外语比赛等，为博览会的举办营造了良好氛围。会前我们还制作了博览会歌曲集光碟，设计制作更多吉祥物等各种纪念品，提高博览会的品牌影响力。

三、本届博览会、商务与投资峰会进一步密切了中国与东盟战略伙伴关系，服务了中国—东盟自贸区

通过本届博览会、商务与投资峰会，中国与东盟各国加深了友谊，深化了合作，巩固和深化了友好合作，增强了继续共同推进自贸区建设的信心。

（一）进一步密切了中国与东盟战略伙伴关系

会期，领导人会见、巡馆、开幕式、东盟国家领导人与企业家对话会、宴会等一系列重大活动规格高，内容务实，经贸和人文等多领域交流活动精彩纷呈。这些活动增进了中国与东盟的了解与互信，为企业创造更多的商机，进一步深化了双方战略伙伴关系。

与会各方对本届博览会、商务与投资峰会给予高度评价：

马来西亚总理纳吉布说："中国—东盟博览会已日益壮大，汇聚来自中国、东盟和世界其他地区的商家，促进区域合作及全球融合。"

柬埔寨首相洪森说："中国—东盟博览会在促进中国与东盟合作交流发挥了积极的作用，为促进中柬之间的传统友谊作出了新的贡献。"

老挝副总理宋沙瓦说："老挝与中国的友谊源远流长，通过中国—东盟博览会平台，双方的交流合作日益深化。"

新加坡贸工部长林勋强说："中国—东盟博览会和商务与投资峰会举办得非常好，每年都有创新，开幕式非常成功，令人振奋。"

东盟秘书长素林说："中国—东盟博览会是中国与东盟友谊与合作的最好象征"，"博览会也办得越来越成功，越来越全面。"

中外客商对本届博览会、商务与投资峰会给予广泛赞誉，普遍认为中国—东盟博览会作为中国与东盟各国的经贸合作平台和自贸区建设与发展的"助推器"，发挥越来越重要的作用。据抽样调查，本届博览会、商务与投资峰会各国参展参会满意度进一步提高。

（二）进一步服务了中国—东盟自由贸易区

举行了中国—东盟商品交易中心揭牌仪式暨中国—东盟商会领袖论坛，近100家来自东盟10国的商家在现场签署了入驻中国—东盟商品交易中心协议。本届博览会、商务与投资峰会加强了对自贸区投资贸易便利化政策的宣讲、解读，举办了中国—东盟合作基金和面向东盟的信贷资金申报说明会、服务外包政策宣讲及企业交流会等会议，帮助企业了解自贸区政策。本届博览会围绕泛北部湾经济合作、中越跨境经济合作区等区域合作热点问题，举办了泛北经济合作发展规划研讨会、境外经贸合作区及境外农业示范区说明会、中越跨境经

济合作区建设情况交流会等会议，促进了区域经济合作和自贸区发展。

（三）为中国各省（市）与东盟国家的合作提供了更大的平台

本届博览会中国共有41个省（区、市）代表团参会。会期，海南省与老挝计划投资部、马来西亚旅游局官员分别举行了会谈；湖南省举行了中国永州—东盟商务投资推介会、宁夏举行了投融资说明会；桂赣陕晋四省联合举办了中国—东盟优质水果推介会。各省（区、市）分别举办了面向东盟的交流活动。博览会为中国各省（市）与东盟国家的合作搭建了更加务实的平台。

通过本届博览会、商务与投资峰会，广西与东盟及国内省（区、市）的合作得到了进一步加强。会期，广西壮族自治区党委书记、自治区人大常委会主任郭声琨，自治区主席马飚及其他自治区领导分别与东盟国家领导人、各国代表团、友好城市代表团等举行了12场会见，就共建广西北部湾经济区，共同推进泛北部湾经济合作、大湄公河次区域合作、南宁—新加坡经济走廊、跨境经济合作区，促进中国—东盟自贸区发展等问题，达成了广泛共识。缅甸副总统吴丁昂敏乌顺访了玉林，并出席了中国（玉林）中小企业商机博览会（玉博会）。会期还举办了广西重点产业招商项目推介会、广西钦州保税港区产值超百亿元情况通报会暨项目签约仪式、自治区政府与上海交大战略合作座谈会暨战略伙伴签字仪式、广西有色集团与广东粤财投资控股公司签署战略合作框架协议等活动，促进了广西与东盟国家及国内省区市的交流合作。

（四）为更多经济体加强合作提供了更加广阔的平台

本届博览会吸引了更多区域外组织和机构参展参会。日本、韩国、加拿大、芬兰等6个区域外国家企业参展，意大利、法国、德国、瑞士、西班牙、瑞典、卢森堡、埃及、日本、韩国、乌兹别克斯坦等国家和地区企业踊跃参展参会，会期举办了投资加拿大说明会等一系列活动。本届博览会为其他经济体加强合作提供了更大平台、更多商机。

四、第九届中国—东盟博览会、商务与投资峰会的初步考虑

在举行第八届中国—东盟博览会的同时，我们对第九届博览会和商务与投资峰会的有关问题进行了专题研究，在充分听取东盟和中国国内各组展单位、专业观众、商协会等各方面意见的基础上，经过反复讨论，形成了第九届博览会有关安排的初步意见，并在刚才举行的中国—东盟博览会高官会上获得一致通过。

1．关于第九届中国—东盟博览会举办时间。为了便于中外领导人活动安排及广大客商参展参会和洽谈业务，第九届中国—东盟博览会的举办时间是2012年9月21日至25日。

2．第九届中国—东盟博览会主题国是缅甸，届时将举办主题国系列活动。

3．第九届中国—东盟博览会的重点主题是“科技合作”，届时将围绕这一主题举办相关活动。

4．第九届中国中国—东盟东盟博览会继续同期举办第九届中国—东盟商务与投资峰会。

女士们，先生们，

博览会、商务与投资峰会举办八年来，中国和东盟10国政府、东盟各共办方、组委会各成员单位及社会各界给予了高度重视和大力支持。在此，我谨代表组委会和举办地广西向东盟10国共办部门和中国商务部、外交部、贸促会、公安部、中宣部、国务院新闻办等国家部委以及组展单位和参与博览会的安保、接待、宣传等有关部门表示衷心感谢！向所有支持博览会、商务与投资峰会的各界人士表示衷心感谢！向参与博览会和商务与投资峰会报道的新闻界朋友们表示衷心感谢!

我们相信，在大家的共同努力下，博览会和商务与投资峰会一定会越办越好，越办越有特色，越办越有实效，为促进中国—东盟友好合作、服务中国—东盟自贸区作出新的贡献!

现在，我代表中国—东盟博览会组委会宣布：第八届中国—东盟博览会胜利闭幕!

第八届中国—东盟博览会、第八届中国—东盟商务与投资峰会工作总结

第八届中国—东盟博览会、第八届中国—东盟商务与投资峰会（以下分别简称“博览会”、“商务与投资峰会”，总称“两会”）于2011年10月21—26日顺利举办并取得圆满成功。

2011年是中国—东盟建立对话关系20周年、中国—东盟友好交流年和中国—东盟自贸区建成1周年，第八届博览会作为20周年系列纪念活动的重要组成部分，是20年辉煌成就的体现，展示了双方合作的美好前景，意义重大。

本届博览会、商务与投资峰会面临南海问题等国际环境日益严峻的影响和出席“两会”的领导人活动安排不断变化的复杂情况。我们在自治区党委、自治区人民政府强有力的领导下，充分借鉴前七届展会积累的丰富经验，发扬团结协作、迎难而上的精神，灵活应变，借中国—东盟建立对话关系20周年之势扩大影响力，在领导人活动安排、开幕式、场馆布置、经贸活动设计、宣传报道、安全保卫、会议论坛等方面都根据今年的特殊背景进行了策划组织，确保了隆重热烈、创新务实、安全便利，再次充分显示出“两会”在服务国家战略，在与东盟的政治、外交、经贸、人文等全方位合作中具有的重要作用，实现了圆满、热烈、安全、精彩、务实，取得了成功。现将第八届博览会、商务与投资峰会有关情况总结如下：

一、基本情况

本届“两会”领导人高规格出席，政治外交影响力大，政商互动成效更显著。突出的特点是，实质性合作全面推开，实质性建议更多提出，经贸成效取得新突破，会期氛围隆重热烈，宣传报道形式新、效果好，安全保障和接待服务工作到位。

本届“两会”的成功举办再次证明，广西壮族自治区党委、自治区人民政府

高度重视，举全区之力举办“两会”，是确保圆满成功的重要保证。特别是在领导人邀请工作上，自治区主要领导郭声琨、马飚亲自抓，李金早、陈武、林念修等自治区领导出面做了许多工作，才确保了这样的高规格。会期在家的自治区四家班子领导都参与了各国领导人陪同工作和各场外事、内事等活动，确保了各项活动的规格，使各方面都感到满意。

本届“两会”取得以下成效：

（一）领导人高规格出席，政治外交影响力大，政商互动，成效更为显著

中国国务院总理温家宝、马来西亚总理纳吉布、柬埔寨首相洪森、缅甸副总统吴丁昂敏乌、老挝副总理宋沙瓦、泰国副总理吉滴叻、越南副总理阮春福共7位国家领导人出席了“两会”。特别是温总理两次出席，在“两会”和广西的历史上添上了浓重一笔。东盟秘书长素林等240位部长级贵宾出席，创历史新高。

中国和东盟各国领导人率团高规格出席本次盛会，表明了在中国—东盟建立对话关系20周年的特殊历史背景下，面对复杂的世界经济形势，中国和东盟更加重视博览会和商务与投资峰会的平台作用，显现出进一步加强互利合作，继续共同推进自贸区建设，实现共同发展、共同繁荣的信心和决心。

中国和东盟各国领导人在会期活动中分别发表了讲话，充分肯定了双方20年合作成果，深入分析了当前形势，指明了下一步合作的方向。这对于充分发挥博览会、商务与投资峰会平台作用，进一步深化双方友好合作，具有指导意义。

中国国务院总理温家宝在本届商务与投资峰会主旨演讲中提出重点办好几件大事：

一是共同建设好自贸区。中方愿意继续扩大东盟国家优势产品的进口，妥善解决自贸区建设中出现的各种问题。将在南宁建设中国—东盟商品交易中心，作为双方产品的展示交易平台和商贸物流基地。

二是大力推进互联互通。中方将与东盟方面密切合作，加强对中国与东盟有关国家互联互通的投入，为促进本地区商品、资本、信息的自由流通、人员往来和经济社会发展创造更好条件。中方愿意继续利用好中国—东盟投资合作基金、中国—东盟银联体及对东盟国家建立的信贷渠道，支持中国—东盟互联互通合作项目的落实。

三是扩大双方投资合作。中方已经承诺在东盟国家各建一个经贸合作区，通过集群式投资提高双方经贸合作水平。中马钦州产业园是双方在中国西部地区合作建设的第一个工业园，具有示范意义，欢迎马方有实力的企业积极参与园区的规划和开发建设。

四是深化区域经济合作。中方将鼓励企业参与东盟东部增长区、大湄公河、泛北部湾等次区域合作，给予金融、技术、市场等方面的有力支持，推动形成若干经济增长极。中方愿与东盟密切合作，进一步深化现有各项区域财金合作，扩大货币互换规模和参与范围，完善“清迈倡议”多边化危机救助机制，加强区域经济监测能力建设，推进亚洲债券市场发展，逐步建立稳定、成熟的地区资本市场，进一步增强本地区应对国际金融风险的能力。

五是拓展人文领域交流。以办好“中国—东盟友好交流年”为契机，继续加强文化、教育、旅游、青年等领域的交流与合作，努力实现2015年双方人员往来达到1500万人次的目标。

马来西亚总理纳吉布在本届博览会开幕式致辞中说，今后数年里，随着《中国—东盟环保合作战略（2009—2015年）》的实施，中国—东盟环保中心有望在中国成立。他还在与中国企业CEO圆桌对话会上提出，希望中国企业更多地进入高科技领域，包括电信、水利、污水处理、绿色技术、生物医药等领域，这些都是马来西亚关注的重点领域，希望吸引更多的外商投资。马来西亚政府将全力支持中马共建的钦州产业园区的发展。

柬埔寨首相洪森在本届商务与投资峰会讲话中说，希望中国可以向东盟欠发达的成员国转让绿色科技技术，以增加农业产量。

泰国副总理吉滴叻在与中泰企业家见面会上说，希望借助此次见面会，促进泰中两国企业家携手迈进，促进商业投资各领域的成功合作。泰国政府将继续支持两国企业家合作。

中国和东盟国家领导人的讲话，对双方开展合作具有很强的指导意义。我们将充分利用博览会、商务与投资峰会平台，认真加以研究和落实。

会期举行了6场国家领导人会见、12场自治区领导与东盟国家领导人和代表团团长、友好城市代表团的会见，举行了巡馆、博览会开幕式、商务与投资峰会开幕式、欢迎宴会、中马钦州产业园区签约及揭牌仪式、主题国“魅力之城”开馆仪式，马来西亚总理纳吉布与中国企业家CEO举行了圆桌对话会、泰国副总理吉滴叻与中泰企业家见面会等一系列活动，增进了政治互信，促进了经贸合作。

（二）开幕式和闭幕式隆重热烈，反映了中国—东盟合作和博览会的成果，凸显国际性和广西的创新和组织能力

博览会开幕式隆重热烈，反映中国—东盟建立对话关系20周年的辉煌成就，展示博览会促进中国—东盟友好交流、推动自贸区建设的成果和广西所作出的贡献。11国青少年参加中国—东盟青少年交流活动中心揭牌和剪彩仪式，具有中国—东盟友谊代代相传的深刻寓意，也展现博览会取得的成果，受到各国领导人和各界的高度评价。

马来西亚贸工部部长穆斯塔法说：“我本人非常荣幸主持博览会开幕式。开幕式办得很好，每个细节都做得很到位，非常完美，非常精彩！”

东盟秘书长素林说：“本届开幕式上能邀请到这么多国家的领导人共同出席，显示了中国—东盟博览会政治外交规格之高和意义之重”，“11国少年的互动，充分体现了中国—东盟博览会是一个开放、包容的合作平台。”

商务与投资峰会开幕式在场地安排、会场布置、内容设计等方面创新，更加隆重、大气、务实，给贵宾留下深刻印象。中国和东盟国家领导人分别在开幕式上阐述了促进双方合作的政策主张，为进一步深化和拓展合作、实现共同繁荣指明了方向。

南宁国际民歌艺术节暨博览会开幕晚会紧扣中国—东盟建立对话关系20周年，节目内容更加丰富，更具特色。

博览会和商务与投资峰会闭幕式形式新颖，意义深刻，体现了博览会的共办水平和成果。在闭幕式上，本届博览会主题国马来西亚与下届博览会主题国缅甸、本届博览会中国“魅力之城”海南省与下届中国“魅力之城”广州分别举行了交接仪式。组委会向中国和东盟各国组展机构颁发了“主题国纪念奖”、“重大贡献及支持奖”、“最佳参展商组织奖”、“最佳采购商组织奖”、“最佳魅力之城展示奖”等8类奖项，体现了本届博览会在共办机制、展会组织等方面取得了新的成效。

（三）经贸成效取得新突破

本届博览会展览规模扩大，参展参会企业更多。总展位数4700个。参展企业总数2300家，同比增长4.6%。参展参会客商5.06万人，比上届增长3.26%。

东盟及区域外国家参展更加踊跃，共办特色更加鲜明。东盟及区域外国家使用展位数达到历史最好水平。印尼、老挝、马来西亚、缅甸、泰国、越南等6个东盟国家包馆，40多家东盟知名品牌企业参展，马来西亚、泰国等组织橡胶、棕榈油、矿产品等大宗商品企业积极参展。东盟国家优势行业集中参展，展会专业化进一步提高。

国内企业参展空前高涨，博览会在区域内外的市场吸引力进一步增强。国内企业申请展位数超过计划数的30.2%，名优企业多，参展产品更加契合东盟市场的需求。台湾企业在以往各届博览会都参展的基础上，2011年由台北世界贸易中心组织企业首次整体参展。日本也首次组织企业整体参展。国内企业在国际经济合作展区和工程机械、运输车辆展区重复参展率高达90%，东盟国家企业重复参展率较高，缅甸达71.9%，新加坡、柬埔寨均达55%。表明博览会在区域内外的市场认知度和吸引力进一步增强。

采购商数量和质量进一步提高。2011年采购团组有70多个，多于往届。东盟采购商团组数比上届增加20%以上。

经贸成效取得新突破。本届博览会商品贸易额18.07亿美元，比上届增长5.6%。签订国际经济合作项目105个，总投资额74.2亿美元，同比增长10.86%。其中，中国企业“走出去”项目52个，总投资额26.5亿美元，同比增长37.8%。签订国内经济合作项目102个，总投资731.1亿元，比上届增长8.39%。广西共签订国际合作项目69个，总投资额46.9亿美元，占国际合作项目投资额的63.2%。

（四）商务与投资峰会取得丰硕成果

本届中国—东盟商务与投资峰会以“深化区域合作，实现共同繁荣”为主题，中国国务院总理温家宝发表了主旨演讲，柬埔寨首相洪森发表了讲话，自治区党委书记、人大常委会主任郭声琨主持开幕式。中国、东盟以及世界10多个国家和地区的政府高官、商界领袖、企业精英、区域组织代表、知名专家学者和媒体记者约1100多人参会，各方就进一步深化区域行业之间的务实合作，实现共同发展和繁荣进行讨论和展望。

（五）系列会议和交流活动富有成效

本届博览会根据中国—东盟经贸合作快速发展对海关、检验检疫、金融等相关领域的服务配套提出的新需求，以及经贸合作与人文领域相结合、推动双方全面持久合作的新要求，继续举办系列会议和交流活动，特别是增加了社会人文领域的会议和交流活动，取得了务实的成果。

本届博览会以“环保合作”为重点主题，环保部主办了2011中国—东盟环保合作论坛；其他有关部委在会期前后举办了第一届中国—东盟TBT合作部长会议、第三届中国—东盟金融合作与发展领袖论坛、中国—东盟太阳能政策对话与技术洽谈会、中国—东盟药品安全论坛暨药品监督管理局局长会议、第四届中国—东盟智库战略对话论坛、中国—东盟人口与家庭发展论坛、2011中国—东盟文化产业论坛、2011中国—东盟出版博览会、中国—东盟城市森林论坛、第二届中国—东盟物流合作论坛、中国—东盟旅游促进减贫研讨会、2011中国—东盟传统医药高峰论坛暨传统医药展、亚洲及大洋洲地区大众体育合作发展论坛暨中国—东盟大众体育合作发展论坛等领域共14个相关会议和交流活动。

各场会议和交流活动规格高，成果务实。中国和东盟国家部长级官员、企业家、银行家、专家学者等出席了系列会议和活动，围绕各领域的热点议题，展开了深入研讨和对话，形成了一批务实成果。例如，环保论坛启动了中国—东盟绿色使者计划。质检论坛通过了关于加强中国—东盟产品质量安全合作的《南宁联合声明》。出版博览会达成《南宁共识》。金融论坛围绕金融及财政合作，在区域内货币结算、金融机构支持企业“走出去”、金融合作发展机制研究等方面，取得了新成果。

社会人文交流活动丰富多彩。中国—东盟文化产业论坛在博物馆运营管理及其文化产品创意开发方面，中国—东盟出版博览会在图书展销、论坛及版权贸易等方面，全面展示了中国与东盟国家历史文化和人文魅力。中国—东盟人口与家庭发展论坛在人口与家庭发展方面，开展了研讨和交流。会期还举办了南宁国际民歌艺术节、高尔夫球精英赛、“网球之友”联谊活动、中国—东盟媒体汽车拉力赛、国际商务书画展等一系列文化交流活动，增进了友谊。

二、主要成效

本届博览会、商务与投资峰会，进一步巩固和深化了中国—东盟友好合作，服务了自贸区，为各省区市与东盟合作提供了更广阔的平台，为各经济体加强合作提供了更多商机。

（一）进一步密切了中国与东盟战略伙伴关系

会期，领导人会见、巡馆、开幕式、东盟国家领导人与企业家对话会、宴会等一系列重大活动规格高，内容务实，经贸和人文等多领域交流活动精彩纷呈。这些活动增进了中国与东盟的了解与互信，为企业创造更多的商机，进一步深化了双方战略伙伴关系。

与会各方对本届博览会、商务与投资峰会给予高度评价：

马来西亚总理纳吉布说："中国—东盟博览会已日益壮大，汇聚来自中国、东盟和世界其他地区的商家，促进区域合作及全球融合。"

柬埔寨首相洪森说："中国—东盟博览会在促进中国与东盟合作交流发挥了积极的作用，为促进中柬之间的传统友谊作出了新的贡献。"

老挝副总理宋沙瓦说："老挝与中国的友谊源远流长，通过中国—东盟博览会平台，双方的交流合作日益深化。"

新加坡贸工部长林勋强说："中国—东盟博览会和商务与投资峰会举办得非常好，每年都有创新，开幕式非常成功，令人振奋。"

东盟秘书长素林说："中国—东盟博览会是中国与东盟友谊与合作的最好象征"，"博览会也办得越来越成功，越来越全面。"

中外客商对本届博览会、商务与投资峰会给予广泛赞誉，普遍认为中国—东盟博览会作为中国与东盟各国的经贸合作平台和自贸区建设与发展的"助推器"，发挥越来越重要的作用。据抽样调查，本届博览会、商务与投资峰会各国参展参会满意度进一步提高。

（二）进一步服务了中国—东盟自由贸易区

会期举行了中国—东盟商品交易中心揭牌仪式暨中国—东盟商会领袖论坛，近100家来自东盟10国的商家在现场签署了入驻协议。会期加强了对自贸区投资贸易便利化政策的宣讲、解读，分别举办了中国—东盟合作基金、服务外包政策等方面的说明会，帮助企业了解自贸区政策。会期还围绕泛北部湾经济合作、中越跨境经济合作区等区域合作热点问题举办一系列会议，促进了区域经济合作和自贸区发展。

（三）为各省（市）与东盟国家的合作提供了更大的平台

本届博览会我国共有41个省（区、市）代表团参会。会期，海南省与老挝计划投资部、马来西亚旅游局官员分别举行了会谈；湖南、宁夏、江西、陕西、山西等省（区、市）分别举办了面向东盟的交流活动。博览会为国内各省（区、市）与东盟国家的合作搭建了更加务实的平台。

通过本届博览会、商务与投资峰会，广西与东盟及国内各省（区、市）的合作得到了进一步加强。会期，自治区党委书记、人大常委会主任郭声琨，自治区主席马飚及其他自治区领导分别与东盟国家领导人、各国代表团、友好城市代表团等举行了12场会见，就共建广西北部湾经济区，共同推进泛北部湾经济合作、大湄公河次区域合作、南宁—新加坡经济走廊、跨境经济合作区，促进中国—东盟自贸区发展等问题，达成了广泛共识。缅甸副总统吴丁昂敏乌顺访了玉林，并出席了中国（玉林）中小企业商机博览会（玉博会）。会期还举办了广西重点产业招商项目推介会、广西钦州保税港区产值超百亿元情况通报会暨项目签约仪式、广西政府与上海交大战略合作座谈会暨战略伙伴签字仪式、广西有色集团与广东粤财投资控股公司签署战略合作框架协议等活动，促进了广西与东盟国家及国内省（区、市）的交流合作。

（四）为更多经济体加强合作提供了更加广阔的平台

本届博览会吸引了欧洲、北美、日韩、北非、中亚等更多的区域外组织和机构参展参会。会期举办了投资加拿大说明会等一系列活动。本届博览会为其他经济体加强合作提供了更大平台、更多商机。

三、主要措施

本届博览会、商务与投资峰会各项工作创新务实，安全便利，体现了博览会承办工作水平不断提高。

（一）展览内容创新，专业化水平有了新的提高

本届博览会根据自贸区建成后企业开拓市场的新需求，在展馆安排上采取新举措，除使用南宁国际会展中心、广西展览馆外，2011年新增华南城展区，形成“一会三馆”的格局。

展品更加贴近市场需求。专设东盟品牌展区，吸引了新加坡星展银行、越南威拿咖啡等多家品牌企业参展。新增大宗原材料展示区，马来西亚橡胶出口促进局、棕油局，泰国泰华橡胶、越南橡胶贸易与旅游服务有限公司等大宗商品企业参展；东盟展品进一步集中到食品农产品、家具家居、特色工艺品及珠宝饰品、日用消费品等具有市场竞争优势的主要行业上。

专业展特色更鲜明，商机更多。农业展不仅展示了中国各省（区、市）特色农产品、名优食品、绿色果蔬、精品茗茶，也有马来西亚食品、越南咖啡、新西兰乳制品等国外特色产品，举办了葡萄酒品鉴会等一系列有特色的推介活动。轻工展展示了中国与东盟国家互补性强、需求量大的珠宝首饰及工艺品、数码电子产品、日用消费品、境外特色精品等。农业展、轻工展受到了专业客商和消费者的欢迎。

总体形象设计和布展水平高。突出了中国—东盟建立对话关系20周年合作成果，体现11国共办的特点，东盟展位整体特装超过90%，保持国内一流水平。

（二）商贸对接活动更有针对性，企业获得实惠更多

通过政商高端对接活动带动企业商家的合作，是博览会的一个特色。本届博览会期间，马来西亚总理纳吉布与中国企业CEO圆桌对话会签约100亿美元的合作项目。泰国副总理与中泰企业家见面会、中国—缅甸企业家座谈会上也签约了一批合作项目。

商贸配对活动富有成效。会期举办了越南、马来西亚等专场配对会，橡胶、棕榈油等大宗商品采购配对会，中泰橡胶产业合作研讨会，农产品、轻工产品行业贸易对接活动，以及参展商讲坛、联合国采购说明会、商务早餐会等一系列对接活动，企业获得了更多的商机和实效。例如，越南、老挝等东盟国家轻工、家具产品受到中国采购商的欢迎，达成了一批采购意向。中国企业专门为东盟市场推出的低速汽车、小型工程机械、小型农用机械，也受到东盟采购商的青睐。会前举行的中国—东盟矿业合作论坛签署了31.6亿美元的合作项目和产品贸易协议。

（三）投资合作更加务实，“走出去”特色更加鲜明

本届博览会在做好商品贸易的基础上，突出投资合作特别是“走出去”的特色。

首次举办了有中国和东盟10国投资促进部门代表参加的中国—东盟博览会投资合作圆桌会，发布中国和东盟各国最新的投资合作政策和项目信息，介绍各国投资环境，为企业提供与各国投促机构直接交流互动的机会，推动企业“走出去”。

举办了“走出去”企业与金融机构对接活动。包括：中国—东盟基础设施投融资合作论坛、金融支持企业“走出去”洽谈会、企业股权（债券）投融资交易会等，邀请了出席金融论坛的金融机构和中央企业负责人进行洽谈对接，为企业投资东盟提供务实的金融支持。

国际经济合作展区参展结构更优，形成了“以中直企业为重点，各省市外经企业为新生力量”的格局；经济技术开发区整体特装展示，成为推动园区招商及园区企业“走出去”的新亮点。

会期还举办了东盟各国投资推介会、海外投资论坛及项目推介会等一系列投资促进活动，在推动企业“走出去”方面取得了一批务实的成果。

（四）服务贸易专题内容更丰富，“魅力之城”突出环保理念和旅游特色

本届博览会服务贸易专题重点展示金融服务、教育服务和旅游服务三个方面的内容。其中，“魅力之城”突出环保理念，并与旅游合作展示相结合，受到广泛关注。会期举办了中国“魅力之城”海南国际旅游岛推介会等一系列活动，促进了旅游合作。此外，会期举行了中国—东盟电信高峰论坛，签约项目金额8亿美元，推动双方在电信服务领域的合作。

（五）安保工作措施周密，在确保安全的同时为客商提供更多便利，营造良好的展览洽谈环境

本届博览会、商务与投资峰会在安全保卫方面周密部署，精心组织，确保了与会中外国家领导人、参会嘉宾和客商的安全。各场活动安全、有序、顺畅。在确保安全的同时，积极改进安保方式，在市区交通、场馆安检等方面，为参会客商市民群众提供了便利。

本届博览会、商务与投资峰会继续坚持以客户为中心，不断改善各项服务质量。会期继续开通了南宁往返东盟10国首都和重要城市的包机航线。展览管理更加机制化，展馆秩序比往年更好。海关、检验检疫部门采取便利化措施，展品通关快捷便利。证件工作全面实现“人到证到”目标。接待方面加强了对餐饮、住宿、用车等资源的统筹，在节俭的前提下提高了服务质量。对口接待机制进一步完善，宾馆服务更加规范。

（六）会期宣传报道形式有创新，报道持续时间长，深度广度进一步增强，展会影响力进一步扩大

本届博览会、商务与投资峰会继续受到国内外主流媒体和专业媒体的高度关注。到会采访的媒体共275家1738名记者，分别比上届增加38.19%和19.2%。其中，东盟媒体69家，比上届增长20%，在中国境内举行的同类活动中，参会东盟媒体和记者是最多的。

会期中央电视台、香港凤凰卫视、香港亚洲电视、广西电视台与东盟以及区域外媒体采取连线互动、专访等多种形式报道本届博览会。其中，马来西亚总理纳吉布、东盟秘书长素林等政要接受了多家媒体的专访。据不完全统计，中外媒体累计发稿8300多篇；网络播发相关新闻（含转载）16万篇，图片31780幅，视频415个，网页记录达380多万条，还通过微博和手机报等新的传播方式，扩大宣传效果，提升了影响力。中外媒体对会期重要活动进行了大范围、深层次、聚焦式的宣传报道，给人留下深刻印象，营造了隆重热烈的氛围，引起强烈反响。

重大活动的现场直播场次多、规模大。中央电视台、新华网、人民网等众多媒体对博览会开幕式、商务与投资峰会开幕式等重大活动进行了现场直播。对马来西亚总理纳吉布与中国企业CEO圆桌对话会、泰国副总理吉滴叻与中泰企业家见面会进行了网络直播。

大会新闻服务更加快捷。开幕式、巡馆等重要活动结束后30分钟在新闻中心提供了图文共享资料，其他各场活动均于2小时内在博览会官方网站提供图文和视频资料。

本届博览会围绕2011年的特点，宣传报道声势大，持续时间长，亮点多。广西作为博览会承办方，2011年积极参与主办或承办了一系列国家层面的纪念20周年系列活动，包括20周年纪念招待会、中国—东盟互联互通战略研讨会、东盟经贸记者研修班、中国—东盟友谊知识竞赛、外语比赛等，为博览会的举办营造了良好氛围。会前我们还制作了博览会歌曲集光碟，设计制作更多吉祥物等各种纪念品，提高博览会的品牌影响力。

（七）统筹工作进一步系统化，指挥协调和应变能力增强

本届博览会、商务与投资峰会的重要贵宾、重要人员、重要活动及日程安排变化较频繁，统筹的难度加大，我们完善指挥系统，增强协调应变能力，对国家领导人和自治区领导活动安排、证件、宾馆、车辆调度、机场迎宾、宴会、交通、安保等环节进行了周密安排，不断完善和细化方案预案，多次演练，狠抓细节，做好各场活动的转场衔接，保证了整体工作和具体工作的推进，实现了各场活动有序、顺畅。

中国—东盟博览会、中国—东盟商务与投资峰会广西指挥中心

2011年11月

出席第八届中国—东盟博览会的部分贵宾

一、首长一行

温家宝　中共中央政治局常委、国务院总理
谢旭人　财政部部长
尹蔚民　人力资源社会保障部部长
姜伟新　住房城乡建设部部长
陈　竺　卫生部部长
谢伏瞻　国研室主任
项兆伦　国务院副秘书长、总理办公室主任
穆　虹　发展改革委副主任
姜　力　民政部副部长
田学斌　国研室副主任

二、博览会组委会成员单位领导及成员

高虎城　商务部国际贸易谈判代表兼副部长
张志军　外交部党委书记、副部长
傅　莹　外交部副部长
曹健林　科技部副部长
刘彦平　公安部部长助理，警卫局局长
毕根敬　公安部警卫局副局长
张智文　公安部警卫局副局长
陈　飞　公安部消防局副局长
李小刚　海关总署总工程师
戴东昌　交通运输部总规划师

祝善忠　国家旅游局副局长
支树平　国家质量监督检验检疫总局局长、党组书记
孙大伟　国家质量监督检验检疫总局副局长
邵明立　国家食品药品监督管理局局长、党组书记
边振甲　国家食品药品监督管理局副局长
王国庆　国务院新闻办副主任
万季飞　中国国际贸易促进委员会会长

三、其他中央国家机关部委领导及特邀省部级领导

杨传堂　中华全国供销总社理事会主任
尚　冰　工业和信息化部副部长
姜志刚　国资委副主任
卢中原　国务院发展研究中心副主任
吴　吟　国家能源局副局长
赵显人　中华全国供销合作总社理事会副主任
曲淑辉　国家民政部纪检组长
楼士礼　北京航空航天大学原校党委书记

四、广西籍及在广西工作过的现职领导

马庆生　全国政协民族和宗教委员会副主任
聂震宁　中国出版集团公司原总裁、全国政协委员
胡存智　国土资源部党组成员、总规划师
彭祖意　全国人大常委、广西法学会会长

五、中央企业领导

罗　涛　中国有色矿业集团总经理
罗建川　中国铝业股份有限公司总裁
徐福贵　中国石油天然气股份有限公司副总裁
王久玲　中国南方电网公司有限责任公司副总经理
蔡哲夫　中国大唐集团公司副总经理
米树华　中国国电集团公司副总经理
杨　军　中国电子信息产业集团公司副经理
胡望明　武汉钢铁（集团）公司党委常委、副总经理
张汝恩　中国通用技术（集团）控股有限责任公司副总经理、董事

六、中国—东盟博览会高级顾问及法律顾问

方嘉德　博览会高级顾问、中华全国总工会原副主席、书记处书记
张蕴岭　博览会高级顾问、中国社科院国际研究学部主任

七、国内各省（区、市）代表团

蒋定之　海南省代省长
王正福　贵州省政协主席
程　红　北京市政府副市长
布小林　内蒙古自治区政府副主席
薛　康　吉林省政协副主席
柏苏宁　江苏省人大常委会副主任、党组副书记
盛昌黎　浙江省政协副主席
叶双瑜　福建省副省长
叶继革　福建省政协副主席
朱秉发　江西省人大常委会副主任
阎启俊　山东省政府特邀咨询
田承忠　湖北省副省长
何报翔　湖南省副省长
李崇禧　四川省委副书记、人大常委会副主任、党组书记
蒙启良　贵州省副省长
曹洪兴　贵州省原省委副书记、原纪委书记
和段琪　云南省副省长
李金柱　陕西省副省长
刘永富　甘肃省副省长
陈资全　青海省政协副主席
马秀芬　宁夏回族自治区人大常委会副主任
史大刚　新疆维吾尔自治区副主席
成家竹　新疆生产建设兵团党委常委、兵团党委，兵团秘书长
李国梁　海南省副省长

八、东盟国家政府代表团

（一）文莱

叶海亚　工业与初级资源部部长
张慈祥　文莱驻华大使

（二）柬埔寨

洪 森 柬埔寨王国首相

贺南洪 副首相兼外交与国际合作大臣

占蒲拉西 国务兼商业大臣

凯·西索达 柬埔寨驻华大使

乌拉本 首相特别助理、财经部国务秘书

霍索提 首相特别助理、首相办公厅主任

布拉索昆 首相特别助理、内阁办公厅国务秘书

乌本穆尼列 首相特别助理、财经部国务秘书

苏庆达 首相特别助理、柬埔寨发展理事会秘书长

斯雷塔玛隆 首相特别助理

刘明勤 参议院议员

本桑波 内阁办公厅国务秘书

隆萨维罗 外交与国际合作部国务秘书

（三）印度尼西亚

穆赫达塔尔 印度尼西亚贸易部部长助理兼印度尼西亚贸易部反倾销委员会主席

易慕龙·卓丹 印度尼西亚驻华使馆大使

（四）老挝

宋沙瓦·凌沙瓦 老挝人民民主共和国副总理

南·维亚吉 工贸部部长

通米·蓬维赛 投资计划部副部长

肯玛妮·奔舍那 工贸部副部长

苏卡申·普提山 国家旅游局副局长

（五）马来西亚

达图·斯里·纳吉布·敦·拉扎克 马来西亚总理

穆斯塔法·穆罕默德 国际贸易与工业部部长

达图·斯里纳·彼得·陈华贵 能源部部长

穆罕默德·卡玛雅·亚哈亚 总理国际关系特别顾问

西提·阿兹扎·谢赫·亚博 总理特别事务官员

胡斯里查·亚克博 外交部副秘书长

伊斯甘达·萨鲁汀 马来西亚驻华大使

（六）缅甸

吴丁昂敏乌 缅甸联邦共和国副总统

吴丁乃登 国家计划与经济发展部部长

吴埃敏　科技部部长
吴温敏　商务部部长
吴貌敏　外交部副部长
吴当伦　铁道部副部长
吴翁丹　农业灌溉部副部长
吴丁吴　缅甸驻华使馆大使

（七）菲律宾

珍艾达·马拉雅　贸工部副部长

（八）新加坡

林勋强　贸工部部长
张思乐　贸工部贸工部政务部长
陈振泉　外交部高级政务次长

（九）泰国

吉滴叻·纳拉农　泰王国副总理兼商业部部长
沙里·安阿皮南　商业部部长助理
练猜·奇帕　商业部部长助理

（十）越南

阮春福　越南社会主义共和国副总理
阮友万　老街省委书记
范明政　广宁省委书记
阮文诗　驻华使馆大使
胡春山　外交部副部长
阮友宇　政府办公厅副主任
阮成边　工贸部副部长
阮文忠　计划投资部副部长
胡英俊　文化体育旅游部副部长
韦文成　谅山省人委主席
阮玉林　中央组织部副部长
丁文疆　西北指导委员会副主任

九、东盟秘书处代表团

素　林　东盟秘书处秘书长

十、博览会组委会东盟方副秘书长和联络官

孙·索塔　柬埔寨商务部顾问、贸促局局长

十一、第八届中国—东盟博览会魅力之城

Nataniel Mandacan　印尼西巴布亚经济、建设及社会福利事务局省长助理

鲍韩方　柬埔寨拉达那基里省省长

唐萨翁　柬埔寨拉达那基里省副省长

布阿森·翁宋坎　老挝占巴塞省副省长

丁文秋　越南广南省副省长

陈山海　越南庆华省副省长

十二、国外友好城市和友好交流地区团组

兵谷芳康　熊本县政府副知事

井手顺雄　熊本县议会副议长

KIM KYUNG YONG　韩国忠清北道Director General

十三、东盟10国投资促进机构

Chea Vuthy　柬埔寨发展理事会副秘书长

诺哈努丁　马来西亚工业发展局局长

十四、国内支持商协会

刁春和　中国对外承包工程商会会长

谢振华　中国电力企业联合会专职顾问、中国电力企业联合会原常务副理事长

十五、东盟10国国家工商协会

何鸣杰　新加坡工商联合总会总裁（前外交部副常任秘书）

十六、对博览会有重要贡献的东盟10国知名人士

黄家定　马中商务理事会主席、前马华公会会长、前马来西亚房屋及地方政府部部长

YBhg.Dato'Mah Siew Keong　MATRADE主席、马来西亚前工贸部副部长

YB Mulia Dato' Seri DiRaJa Syed Razlan Ibni Syed Putra　马来西亚国家高级议会成员（皇族成员）

十七、出席各论坛活动的部分贵宾

（一）2011中国—东盟环保合作论坛

李干杰　国家环保部副部长

米斯然·卡尔梅　东盟秘书处副秘书长

宾度·罗哈尼　亚洲开发银行副行长

尹金西恩　柬埔寨环保部国务秘书

（二）第三届中国—东盟金融合作与发展领袖论坛

李礼辉　中国银行行长

金　琦　中国人民银行行长助理

蔡鄂生　中国银监会副主席

姜　洋　中国证监会主席助理

陈新权　中国保监会纪委书记

周清玉　国家开发银行纪委书记

张　云　农业银行行长

唐双宁　中国光大银行董事长

孙　平　中国进出口银行副行长

刘永信　中国出口信用保险公司副总经理

张红力　工商银行副行长

谢占多　柬埔寨国家银行行长

方侨生　柬埔寨加华银行执行总裁

任瑞生　联合商业银行首席执行官

闫冰竹　北京银行董事长

（三）中国—东盟人口与家庭发展论坛

李　斌　国家人口计生委主任

崔　丽　国家人口计生委副主任

吴钦伊　缅甸移民和人口部部长

苏吉瑞·塞亚瑞夫　印尼家庭计划和人口委员会主席

因拉文·凯博潘　老挝卫生部副部长

托马斯·欧塞斯　菲律宾人口委员会执行主任

坦沃乘　柬埔寨卫生部副部长

沃斯德·梅莱斯　国际计生联执行总干事

哈利·乔瑟里　人口与发展南南合作伙伴组织执行主任

（四）第四届中国—东盟智库战略对话论坛

约瑟思·艾思塔尼斯劳　菲律宾企业领导人研究所总裁兼首席执行官、亚洲团结学会主席、前菲律宾财政部长

宋春奔　柬埔寨皇家科学院副院长

Khamphay RASMY　老挝社会科学院副院长

（五）2011中国—东盟文化产业论坛

单霁翔　文化部副部长、国家文物局局长

（六）2011中国—东盟出版博览会

邬书林　新闻出版总署副署长

苏　温　缅甸信息部副部长

（七）第一届中国—东盟TBT合作部长会议

马西姆斯·佐尼迪·翁凯里　马来西亚科技创新部部长

陈越青　越南科技部副部长

梅顿·琛田纳辛　老挝科技部副部长

（八）中国—东盟城市森林论坛

赵树丛　国家林业局常务副局长

陈述贤　中央纪委驻国家林业局纪检组组长

唐守正　中国科学院院士

温　吞　缅甸环境保护及林业部联邦部长

CHHENG KIMSUN　缅甸环境保护及林业部林业司总司长

Regidor M.DB Leon　菲律宾环境与资源部部长助理

十八、区直、各市邀请贵宾

朱保成　中央纪委驻农业部纪检组组长、农业部党组成员

袁隆平　中国工程院院士

王赛芝　马来西亚妇女、家庭和社会发展部议员副部长

德利玛·哈利斯·妮尔玛婉　印度尼西亚农业部秘书长兼副部长

Vilayvanh HOMKHE　老挝农业与林业部部长

十九、其他重要特邀贵宾

马德秀　上海交通大学党委书记

第八届中国—东盟博览会合作伙伴

首席战略合作伙伴

中国有色矿业集团有限公司

战略合作伙伴

广西投资集团有限公司
中国移动通信集团广西有限公司
广西有色金属集团有限公司
广西农垦集团有限责任公司
广西柳州钢铁（集团）公司

媒体战略合作伙伴

上海第一财经传媒有限公司

行业合作伙伴

中国银行股份有限公司广西壮族自治区分行
安徽古井贡酒股份有限公司
广西三环企业集团股份有限公司
广西北部湾银行
中国电信股份有限公司广西分公司
上海通用汽车有限公司
南宁市伊洛奇亚酒业有限公司
广西区农村信用社联合社
广西运德汽车运输集团有限公司

合作伙伴

孔家钧窑有限公司
广西永明珍珠宫珠宝有限公司（永明珍珠宫）

北海国发南珠宫珍珠首饰制造有限公司（南珠宫）
广西北部湾国际旅行社
贵州省茅台镇淳源酒业有限公司（君宴酒）
兴东恒业（北京）投资管理有限公司（东君白露酒）
广西保利置业集团有限公司
广西区邮政公司
广西益强投资管理有限公司（莲泉）
广西综路传媒有限公司
广西中源山泉有限公司（九千万水）
青岛红领服饰股份有限公司
广州统一企业有限公司
广西凌云浪伏茶业有限公司
广西通天香茶叶有限责任公司
南宁昱科汽车销售有限公司（广汽传祺）
广西洁宝纸业投资股份有限公司
广西高手商贸有限责任公司（岩磐浴）
梧州中茶茶业有限公司（六堡茶）
南宁市威进达商贸有限责任公司（舒达源）
广西壮牛水牛乳业有限责任公司
北海市恒兴珠宝有限责任公司
意大利达芬奇红酒（三环代理红酒）
广西元之源健康产业有限责任公司
太阳黑子企业策划有限公司（绅浪）
广西上龙旅游发展有限责任公司（姑辽红茶）
广西小海豚职装干洗中心有限公司
广西惠康生物科技有限公司（百泓罗汉果）
广西八桂蚕坊丝绸有限公司（八桂蚕坊）
广西柳州市柳韵春晓茶业有限公司
广西绝特投资有限公司
广西俊德人力资源服务有限公司

媒体合作伙伴

深圳市腾讯计算机系统有限公司
新浪网
中国网络电视台

图书在版编目（CIP）数据

中国—东盟博览会发展报告. 2011第八卷 / 蓝天立编委会主任；郑军健主编.
—桂林：广西师范大学出版社，2012.7
ISBN 978-7-5495-2369-6

I. 中… Ⅱ.①蓝…②郑…Ⅲ.展览会—研究报告—中国、东南亚—2011 Ⅷ.①G245
中国版本图书馆CIP数据核字（2012）第167704号

图片摄影者及提供单位（排名不分先后）

刘 宇 何运斌 黎克平 莫 云 黄大年 甘伟良 彭 寰
夏文宁 袁存昭 王 宾 梁广宁 唐安军 陈治安 龙 江
陈宇翔 陶誉源 邓海波 区 阳 龚晓军 梁 春 李建城
黄 辉 古里平 周 华 廖 菲 黄 愿 张小宁 王龙飞
新华社 自治区党委宣传部 广西国际博览事务局 广西国际贸易促进委员会
自治区公安厅 武警广西边防总队 自治区对外事务办公室
自治区食品药品监督管理局 广西出入境检验检疫局 自治区卫生厅
自治区环保厅 自治区文化厅 自治区科技厅 自治区计生委
自治区新闻出版局 自治区工商联 自治区体育局 共青团广西区委
广西社会科学院 广西物流与采购联合会 广西人民广播电台 南宁市政府
南宁海关 中国—东盟国际汽车拉力赛办公室等

策划编辑 李庭华
责任编辑 韦兰琴 黄佳梦 黄 毓
英文编辑 陈俊泉
艺术顾问 张 明 刘 凛
设计总监 梁雪芬 黄小纯
责任技编 沈 明 石玉珏

广西师范大学出版社出版发行
（广西桂林市中华路22号 邮政编码：541001
网址：http://www.bbtpress.com）
出版人：何林夏
服务热线：0771-2092977
全国新华书店经销
广西民族印刷厂印刷
（广西南宁市高新三路1号 邮政编码：530007）
开本：889mm × 1 194mm 1/16
印张：28.5 字数：375千字 图片：199幅
2012年9月第1版 2012年9月第1次印刷
定价：236.00元